Refounding
Public
Administration

Refounding Public Administration

Gary L. Wamsley
Robert N. Bacher
Charles T. Goodsell
Philip S. Kronenberg
John A. Rohr
Camilla M. Stivers
Orion F. White
James F. Wolf

SAGE PUBLICATIONS
The International Professional Publishers
Newbury Park   London   New Delhi

For information address:

SAGE Publications, Inc.
2111 West Hillcrest Drive
Newbury Park, California 91320

SAGE Publications Ltd.
28 Banner Street
London EC1Y 8QE
England

SAGE Publications India Pvt. Ltd.
M-32 Market
Greater Kailash I
New Delhi 110 048 India

Printed in the United States of America

Library of Congress Cataloging-in-Publication Data

Refounding public administration / by Gary L. Wamsley . . . [et al.].
    p. cm.
   Includes bibliographical references.
   ISBN 0-8039-3723-7
   1. Public administration.   2. Bureaucracy--United States.
  3. United States--Politics and government.   I. Wamsley, Gary L.
  JF1351.R43   1989
  350--dc20   89-24241
                                                     CIP

FIRST PRINTING, 1990

Sage Production Editor: Mary Beth DeHainaut

Contents

Preface

It does not seem possible that nearly seven years have passed since the ideas that led to this volume first began to take shape. Events, people, and years have flashed by like the whirling images created when a train passenger glances out the window at the same moment a speeding train passes in the opposite direction. In this preface I would like to speak in a personal "voice" and to reflect briefly upon those kaleidoscopic events in an effort to explain why and how we came to write the paper entitled, "The Public Administration and the Governance Process: Shifting the American Political Dialogue," and this volume that is derived from it. That paper, which quickly came to be labeled the Blacksburg Manifesto by both sympathizers and critics, appears as Chapter 2 of this book.

One of the most frequent questions asked of any of us involved in the original Manifesto is, "What motivated you to write such an unusual paper?" It had virtually no footnotes nor bibliography, was written in a style that was decidedly not typical of social science, and, depending on one's sympathies, was either polemical or "preachy" but, in any case, decidedly normative.

With equal frequency academicians wonder how five colleagues could reach agreement on such a statement. (They know how rare such agreement is in our profession.) Those familiar with the considerable differences in backgrounds and intellectual stances of the Manifesto's co-authors have had even more reason to wonder how we reached sufficient agreement to produce something so normative in character—something so central to our professional identities. I recall asking Dwight Waldo if he had any further criticisms that we might wish to consider in doing a second draft of the Manifesto. His only suggestion was that we not try a redraft because we would probably never be able to sustain agreement.

Normally this would have been good advice, but we have found our accord surprisingly strong and durable. Though we have been as surprised as anyone, we not only continue to be in basic agreement but that agreement continues to deepen as we expand and elaborate the ideas in the Manifesto and explore dimensions heretofore only implied. When more than one of us have been present in dialogue with critics, we have been somewhat startled to find ourselves staking out a common but completely unplanned defense and supporting it with arguments that are spontaneously synchronous. In a world in which it is difficult to be understood, it is a rare experience to find ourselves in such fundamental agreement that we anticipate one another's thoughts or to find that our arguments, though offered from different perspectives, are congruent. It has been an astonishing and thrilling intellectual experience.

When I first sent a prospectus for this book to a university press for assessment, I received what seemed a rather querulous and ambivalent letter from the editor. He allowed that we were all fairly well known in the field and the subject was of interest, but he also demanded to know the philosophical foundations for the stand we were taking. That was not at all an unreasonable demand; it was simply one with which we were not prepared to spend a lot of time wrestling. For unlike many academic enterprises, the Manifesto did not begin in philosophy and end in practical application. (At least that is the conventional assumption made about how theory and action are related; some of us have serious doubts that the assumption is correct.) In any event, the Blacksburg Manifesto was only partially an outgrowth of our academic roles.

Certainly in my case it was in my role as practitioner or "pracademic" that I first began to puzzle over the issues and concepts that emerged in the Manifesto. This was also true to a large degree for the others, for all of us were, and are, involved to various degrees in consulting and other work outside academe. All of us had a longstanding concern for the public service, and whatever our differing ideological inclinations, we had been concerned about the tone that American political dialogue had been taking for several years. Whether that tone was best labeled antibureaucratic, antigovernment, antiauthority, or simply bureaucrat bashing, we could see that its effects in the world of action were detrimental to our capacity to govern ourselves effectively.

Doubtless there were philosophical bases for the Manifesto, but in our view it was wrong to spend time trying to dredge them up retroactively. The Manifesto began in praxis, reflection, and in a struggle for reflexivity; in the personal reactions of all the co-authors to events; and, at least in my case, from the frustration of involvement with problems of public administration and governance "up close and personal."

It has grown increasingly clear to me that John Rohr is absolutely correct when he says that the nearest thing Americans have to any native exposition of a theory of the state can be found in the Constitution, the Federalist Papers, and the writings of the Anti-Federalists (Rohr 192: 1986). All three bodies of thought had their origins in practical, "dirty hands" problems of administration or governance. Without implying for a moment that our writings are in the same league, it seems to us that the "American State Papers" are eminently respectable exemplars of thoughtful persons beginning with practice and moving toward philosophy.

How had work on the Blacksburg Manifesto begun? In my own case I can no longer be sure, but I associate it with one of those wretched struggles to get through rush-hour subway traffic to National Airport and out of Washington on an unseasonably hot Friday in May of 1981. Such exits and entrances had become a mind-numbing feature of my life after 1977, when I began working with the President's Reorganization Project within the Office of Management and Budget during the Carter Administration. By 1981 I had gone on to involvement in several projects elsewhere in the government. On that particular Friday I felt more than the usual weariness and irritation of such circumstances, I was deeply depressed as well. It wasn't just another one of the little disappointments one inevitably encounters in governmental warfare, or a consultant's pique because one's work or ideas had not been used. I had tried to adopt the Beltway Bandits' credo when faced with vicissitudes such as those: "The money is all green, whether they use your stuff or not." This time, however, the problem I faced was different, and that bit of cynical bravado provided little comfort.

I had worked as a consultant to a relatively small, independent executive agency from the time it was known that Ronald Reagan had been elected our fortieth president. My task had been to assist the agency's overloaded, understaffed policy and program evaluation shop. It was staffed with career analysts and directed by a member of the newly formed senior executive service (SES).

We had worked long, hard hours preparing briefing books for the Reagan transition team. Every program in the agency had been analyzed and the available policy options carefully defined. We had been as thorough as time allowed and as nonpartisan as humanly possible. After the final frantic surge to get the books out, I returned to pressing matters at the university. Later, the agency called me back to Washington on another matter, and I asked how the briefing books had been received. I was told, in rather more pungent language than is appropriate for this book, that they had been "canned." I was dumbfounded. Relations with the transition team had seemed cordial, candid, and reasonable, but the takeover that followed assumed an altogether different tenor. The trashing of the briefing books was only the first of many traumas that the agency was to endure for several years.

The SESers of the agency who held important managerial positions were all called to a meeting at which they were informed that the agency had many problems, that they were to blame, and that "one way or another" they would all soon be "gone." The agency did indeed have many problems, not the least of which was the fact that it had been created by pouring a hodgepodge of programs from around the government into one new entity, but to accuse the SESers of being the cause was so ludicrous that it beggared the imagination. Just how ludicrous this was can be seen in the fact that several years later most of these same SESers were brought out of the various forms of exile to which they had been driven and asked to resume key positions in order to save the agency from a morass of fiscal, personnel, and legal fiascoes. These had even included a tawdry sex scandal. The overall effect was the near-total destruction of the agency's credibility in and out of the government.

But lest the reader assume the depression that overwhelmed me in May of 1981 was just another liberal academician's hand-wringing reaction to the Reagan "Revolution," let me add that it was depressing not because aspects of the Reagan transition were shockingly new, but rather because they were so shockingly familiar. Perhaps the Bush Administration will apply a more gentle hand to the bureaucracy, but in 1981 this was all painfully reminiscent of the Democratic Carter Administration and could be traced through the administrations of Ford and Nixon as well. In Yogi Berra's immortal words, "This was déjà vu all over again."

I had not been "on the ground" at the outset of the Carter Administration though I was often in touch with some of those who were. Instead, I had been called to Washington just as the administration began to really get underway in the summer of 1977. I had been asked to direct a study that would result in reorganization or the elimination of the Selective Service System. Like the Reaganauts that would follow them four years later, the Carterites had come to Washington as a victorious army conquering an alien city, intent on dealing bureaucracy and "red tape" (another man's "system," as Dwight Waldo has wryly remarked) a mortal blow. One of my SES acquaintances, with the kind of black humor that combat soldiers use to discharge anxiety, joked that both administrations had sounded like vengeful revolutionary forces — intent on capturing and occupying Washington and "making the Potomac run red with the blood of slain bureaucrats." Neither party allowed for the possibility that the so-called bureaucracy might just be the major factor in keeping our problems from getting worse or that it might, if properly led, be a major factor in their solution. Such thoughts have been as alien to our politicians for the last two decades as they were to the Huns or Visigoths when they seized other capitals in other eras. In point of fact, the case might well be made that the Huns and Visigoths showed more sense than their modern counterparts when it came to occupying capitals and governing.

The Carter Administration's attack on the government that it was simultaneously supposed to lead was symbolically embodied by the President's Reorganization Project (the PRP). I use the term *symbolically* because I feel many of the PRP staff, from Director Harrison Wellford on down, knew they had signed on for a "Kamikaze mission." Of course they wanted to believe that the government could be organized to be more efficient, and no one was absolutely certain it could not be; it was easy therefore to persuade oneself it was worth a try. Similarly, British horse cavalrymen must have convinced themselves they could successfully charge enemy barbed wire and machine guns in World War I. The naiveté of President Carter and his immediate staffers left PRP to make the doomed effort to reconcile the silly campaign rhetoric with the realities of our constitutional system. It had a few minor successes, among them the restructuring of the Selective Service System, in which I was lucky enough to have been involved. (It was small enough to get away with a realistic approach.) By and large, however, the PRP became a resounding "dud" of the first magnitude when the president and his top aides lost the will to press forward (*CQ Almanac* 1978; Sundquist 1979: 4-5). The bureaucrat-bashing rhetoric that seemed to play so well on the campaign trail proved difficult to translate into specific accomplishments once Jimmy and Rosalyn walked down Pennsylvania Avenue and took up residence in the White House. There turned out to be few supporters inside the Beltway for the reorganization that made such splendid campaign material (Dempsey 1979:75). When it moved from the realm of theory and down to practice, reorganization proved to be "about as popular as a bastard at a family reunion" as General Lewis Hershey had once remarked of the Selective Service (Wamsley 1969). Every proposal for reorganization seemed to generate legions of opponents — interest groups, congresspersons, Hill staffers, senators, and cabinet secretaries. The list seemed endless. If through sheer tenacity and savage will, some small victory was won against such overwhelming odds, it scarcely made the back pages of the *Washington Post*, not to mention papers across America. How much time, energy, and momentum of the Carter Administration was lost tilting at those windmills? There was no telling.

The Reagan Administration came to Washington with the same antigovernment attitude but perhaps with even greater intensity (Newland 1983:1). They did, however, learn from the Carter PRP debacle (Smith 1988). Their assault on the government was massive but it avoided the formal straitjacket of reorganization. Instead, they sought to cripple and dismantle the government by political penetration of levels of government formerly staffed by career civil servants. Concerns for competence went by the board. As presidential aid Lyn Nofziger said, "We have told members of the Cabinet we expect them to help us place people who are competent. . . . As far as I'm concerned, anyone who supported Reagan is competent" (Drew 1981). Equally important were massive budget and personnel cuts, and making drastic changes in program emphasis and direction but without resort to legislation and without putting things in writing (Durant 1987:180; Newland 1983: 2, 11, 12). They also used the aspects of the Civil Service Reform Act of 1978 that had been designed to make more flexible use of expert careerists as an instrument to get those same careerists out of the way "one way or another" (Newland 1983: 17-18)

The events that had occurred in the governmental unit to which I was a consultant were in no way unique; they happened throughout the government. All over town career executives were bullied or finessed into resignation, early retirement, some organizational "Coventry," or humiliating exile to some field office. The provisions of the Civil Service Reform Act were then used to fill the vacancies created with political appointees of certified "ideological purity." But all this was simply a slicker use of tactics than shown by the Carter Administration — the ends were the same and so were the devastating results (Newland 1983:3; Rosen 1986: 212-213; Gaertner 1983: 424). It was this realization, then, that led to the deep frustration and depression I felt in that sweaty exit flight from Washington in 1981. I was not such a poor student of history and government that all this was totally new to me. It was all familiar, of course, at a cognitive level of understanding, but it was the firsthand visceral experience that led me to approach my colleagues about the creation of the Manifesto.

I can no longer remember if I shared my troubled state of mind with any of my Blacksburg colleagues during the next few days or even months. I do remember that as the Reagan Administration proceeded, one horror story after another unfolded: faulty transitions, demoralization, erosion of effectiveness, decapitalization, conflict of interest revelations, scandals, criminal indictments, politicization of administration, and general disinvestment in the capacity to govern. It was not simply the stories of program cutbacks or turnarounds in programs that were depressing. Those no doubt bothered some of us because of where we stood politically, but some such changes were, after all, the due of anyone who had won the White House and could make that look like a "mandate" and get away with the claim. No, what depressed us as students of government were the chaos, confusion, the delegitimation of our institutions of government, the serious damage to the morale, the structures, and the processes of government — those things upon which the capacity to govern hinges, regardless of who occupies the machinery.

I recall that it was a conversation with Lester Salamon, who was at the Urban Institute in the summer of 1981, that finally stirred me to action. Lester probably cannot even remember the conversation, nor do I recall the specifics, but when I expressed my frustration at what was going on, he remarked something to the effect that maybe it was time to reconsider the way we thought and talked about government. He added, "A lot of people are going to do a lot of rethinking in the next few years." That led me to resolve to bring up the matter with my colleagues as soon as I returned to Blacksburg.

I suggested to them that perhaps we should try to articulate the kind of concerns we and other academics and practitioners of public administration seemed to share about the antigovernment tone of recent political campaigns and administrations. A faculty retreat was scheduled in the near future, and I was a bit surprised but pleased when my colleagues agreed that we should take up the matter at that time. None of us had any idea how we would do that or where it might lead. We simply agreed to "talk about it."

I imagine it will be easier to understand the context that produced the Manifesto if I explain that the Center for Public Administration and Policy (CPAP) of Virginia Polytechnic Institute and State University not only has a long name and is likewise part of a university with a name of mind-boggling proportions, but is atypical in other respects as well. It is a "center" only in the peculiar sense that politics, particularly those of higher education, can impart. It is "one center in three locations" where classes are conducted in vastly different settings by a faculty that teaches at all three sites. Some of us reside in Blacksburg, a university town located on the eastern flank of the Appalachian mountains, a place where one can hear a chamber concert by the internationally renowned Audubon Quartet, yet travel a few miles and be in utter wilderness or among residents of "hollers" who have never been out of the county and who will tell you they are "just as happy for it." Others of us reside in the fast-growing suburbs of Washington, like Tacoma Park, Reston, and Herndon — where freeway interchanges and shopping malls seem to spring up overnight like mushrooms and every conversation inevitably includes the "Skins" or the Orioles and commuter "war stories." Finally, all of us teach, though none of us reside, at the Naval Surface Warfare Center, Dahlgren, Virginia, where the Potomac River meets the Chesapeake Bay.

It is because of this anomalous distribution of sites and resources that we hold events such as faculty retreats at which we not only discuss the mundane business matters of any academic enterprise but also try to interact with one another socially and professionally. These retreats offer us an opportunity to mend our tattered social fabric and undo months of fragmented conversations and other forms of geographically induced miscommunication. Apparently, they serve their purpose, for CPAP has maintained a strong sense of community, both socially and intellectually. If the retreat provided the occasion for our coming together, it was the underlying sense of community that made it possible for us to engage in such an unusual task of co-authorship.

Our winter retreat was scheduled for January of 1982 in Charlottesville, a place having the advantage of being central to our three locations but the disadvantage that the University of Virginia — or "Mr. Jefferson's University" — is located there and considered to be Virginia Tech's arch rival. (A popular bumper sticker in Charlottesville reads: "All Dirt Roads Lead to Tech." A counterpart in Blacksburg reads: "How Do You Find UVA? Go North Till You Smell It and East Till You Step in It.") Despite this potentially inhospitable environment, we were to stay at a motel near the Federal Executive Institute (FEI) where Jim Wolf had made arrangements for our meeting. Charles Goodsell's book, *The Case for Bureaucracy* (1985), had just been published to excellent reviews. Much of what Charles had written had struck responsive chords in all of us. It matched our own longstanding concerns over the integrity of the public service. I suggested, therefore, that we all read or reread it and use it as a basis for "brainstorming" in an effort to see just what views we had in common on the nature of public administration and what had been happening to it under Carter and Reagan.

Five of us, Wamsley, Goodsell, Wolf, Rohr, and White, gathered that afternoon in the central meeting room of the institute, a room large enough to hold eighty or more people seated at tables. Around the vast room were the seals of the major departments and agencies of the federal government. The dates on some of the seals reminded me of the long history of some of the departments; at the same time it brought to mind the persistent rumors that Don Devine, the Reagan appointee favored by the American Heritage Foundation, was doing his best to shut FEI down. Clearly the physical setting was all wrong for us, but perhaps in a perverse sort of way it was both symbolic and conducive to what we were attempting to do. It both forced us to be informal and reminded us of the significance of our topic.

While the others sprawled on the carpeted floor, I used newsprint on an easel and a magic marker to try and capture our thoughts in some way. As the ideas started to flow, I scratched them out in notation form and stuck the newsprint up on the wall. I think we were all amazed at the energy that was being released and the ways the ideas seemed to be compatible. We did not become blocked or hung up by definitional problems, nor find it necessary to spend great amounts of time just trying to understand one another. I was writing and "sticking" as fast as possible but could barely keep up. The ideas continued to flow unchecked and the conversation continued over dinner and well into the night. The next day the dialogue kept on with increasing intensity over breakfast, through the morning, during lunch, and into the afternoon. Enthusiasm had reached the point where we were taking turns in seizing the magic marker from each other to make our points, and still we had no major disagreements.

We had always assumed that our intellectual differences were too great for this kind of agreement. Yet the way the ideas were coming together amazed us. We felt that something was emerging which was more than merely the sum of the parts we had individually contributed. We were on an intellectual high, and I for one felt caught up in one of those rare existential moments that has happened only a few times in my academic career.

It is impossible for me to speak for the others concerning the events at the FEI. John Rohr has said that the first time he realized there was a fundamental agreement among us which went beyond cordial collegiality was when Orion White pointed out that we all seemed to have something of a "structuralist" approach to the field. Some of us might be more comfortable being referred to as "institutionalists," but we understand that those terms and the intellectual space they connote are closely related. But in any event, as John Rohr has pointed out, it would be an error to think that we began with structuralism or institutionalism as first principles and then proceeded neatly, deductively, and logically. As he has noted, "We spoke explicitly of 'structuralism' hardly at all, but we spoke a great deal about administrative agencies as institutions of government. If we were structuralists, it was in the spirit of Moliere's 'M. Jourdain' who had to be told he was speaking prose" (Rohr 1986).

Discussions of authority, capitalism, the public interest, agency perspective, disinvestment, morale, and administrative capacity were all mixed together. In addition to a common ground in structuralism or institutionalism, we were surprised to discover that none of us was embarrassed to talk seriously about authority. Again John Rohr described this better than I can and with more wit.

At first, we were quite tentative; trying each other out in something of a "you too?" spirit—as though at once to our relief and chagrin we had discovered that an old friend shared a hidden vice. The reference to "vice" is not altogether inappropriate. We are loyal citizens of the Republic and as such share the national trait that disdains authority. We are also card-carrying members of the academy where such disdain is de rigueur. Our willingness to question the received wisdom of both polity and profession signalled an important step in collective self-revelation. (p. 6)

Toward the end of our efforts we struggled to find some orderly arrangement of ideas in the maelstrom of newsprint. It was stuck on the walls, on flip charts, strewn on the floor, wadded and tossed in corners. We tried to arrange ideas in piles of paper. But most interestingly and importantly, it was fun; no one complained of being tired.

Since I had called for the meeting, it was probably inevitable that I would be stuck with the chore of trying to make some sense of our intellectual binge. I was conscripted for the task of writing the first draft, and all the others as it turned out. Actually I did not mind. As a "pracademic" I had been involved in enough struggles over staff work and policy analysis to have adopted as a central tenet the notion that "the last pencil gets the final word," and candor compels me to admit that being "last pencil" on the Manifesto met many of my personality needs.

During the rest of 1982, we worked through several drafts and revisions of the Manifesto. It went slowly because my role as director at CPAP constantly crowded out writing time, but it also took time to circulate a draft among four other co-authors. As spring of 1983 rolled around, we wanted to try our ideas on other colleagues around the country but realized that the program for the annual convention of the American Society for Public Administration (ASPA) had long ago been finalized. Deciding to make a virtue of a necessity, we determined to set up our own unofficial "panel" outside the program and invite people whose opinions we particularly valued to a suite of rooms we rented for just this purpose. We needed a setting that would allow more discussion than the cramped timeframe of a panel, and we wanted the discussion to be more focused than seems possible with a panel. (Panels, as most academic readers know, sometimes unfold like a presidential news conference — each person asking a question has a different agenda and things can ricochet from one topic to another in a random and sometimes shallow fashion.) We also wanted to assure some stability of focus by inviting persons who would be basically sympathetic with what we were trying to do but would also respond critically. And, of course, it must be said that we were still rather tentative about our ideas. We were not quite ready to face colleagues who might be fundamentally opposed to our line of thought. We preferred to work up to that gradually, since we were still discussing and making revisions the very week the Manifesto was to be presented.

We hoped to make the invitation to listen to the paper easier to accept by offering free drinks and snacks. (I can no longer remember how I justified this to the university's accounting office, but that is just as well, given how "creative" it must have been.) I do remember deciding that the only way to get a full discussion of the many ideas in the paper was to read it in its entirety rather than "talking about it" as we customarily do on panels. I also recall vividly that I repeatedly read it aloud to my long-suffering wife, in an effort to get the right inflection, flow, and timing. She not only had to listen and criticize but stay awake as she drove toward New York. Finally I was able to get the reading down to twenty-two minutes and remarked that I was beginning to feel somewhat more secure about it. Susan renewed my angst, however, by dryly (and wisely) suggesting that it might be best to hold off on the drinks until after the reading.

About thirty-five persons crowded into our New York Hilton suite for the presentation. In addition to our invited guests, there was a handful of our graduate students and a surprise guest, Luther Gulick. We had not been bold enough to think of inviting him, but he was in the hotel participating in a Kettering Foundation Conference. Charles Goodsell had run into Gulick on an elevator and with his customary aplomb had immediately invited the worthy gentleman.

Not since I had played the lead in my high school senior play had I experienced such a dry mouth and knotted stomach. I recall thinking this had better be good or we were going to look very foolish. I finished reading the paper and was stunned when the room broke into applause. I was flustered and embarrassed and mumbled, "Will this get us labeled as New Left, New Right, Pinko . . . Proto-Fascist?" "Just Fascist," teased a grinning John Nalbandian, seated behind me on the room's air-conditioning unit.

I was momentarily drained and therefore grateful when Charles Goodsell took charge and asked Luther Gulick if he would like to make the first comment. Gulick's remarks were generous and encouraging but, as those who know him might have predicted, he criticized us for not being bold enough to have explored the significance of our ideas for international administration. That was certainly not a criticism we had anticipated.

After Gulick's comments, the ideas in the paper were analyzed and discussed in a more searching and critically thoughtful manner than anyone has a right to expect. My energy returned, and the next few hours were glorious fun. There were demands for clarification of our meaning of "agency perspective" and our positions toward capitalism. There was criticism of our reliance on the idea of the public interest and the way we used it. Some thought the role we prescribed for The Public Administration in the governance process relied too heavily on authority; others saw it as a thinly veiled statement of self-interested professionalism. Discussion continued in earnest for over two hours. Although there was a plentitude of criticism, it was generously sprinkled with encouragement. Most surprisingly, many of those present expressed their thanks for our bringing together ideas that they had been struggling to articulate on their own.

We gave everyone present a copy of the paper as they departed and asked for any written responses they were willing to provide. Upon our return from New York, we began to send it out to an ever-widening net of people across the country. It was, for example, mailed to anyone we felt might be interested whether potentially supportive or critical, to members of ASPA's Executive Council, to most of the principal representatives of the National Association of Schools of Public Affairs and Administration, to a sizeable number of the members of the National Academy of Public Administration, and to a number of persons running for public office. The response was astounding.

We had never imagined that people would take the time to respond so thoughtfully and carefully. People whom we had never met, with schedules that must have been hectic, took time to write, two, three, four, or more single-spaced pages of response. Although we never sent it outside the United States nor intended to speak to circumstances outside the American system, we soon began to receive responses and requests for the paper from such places as Australia, the Netherlands, and Canada. (We still do not know what to make of this phenomenon but find it interesting.)

Between the time we gave the paper in New York and its first publishing in Ralph Chandler's edited volume, *A Centennial History of the American Administrative State* (1987), we not only distributed the paper as described above but also presented somewhat modified versions of it at several regional ASPA conferences and the American Political Science Association's convention. We have tried to place excerpts from all written reactions in the appendix to this volume. There were a few instances where responders did not feel their remarks were prepared for publication and did not wish to take time to modify them. A few thoughtful letters were from prominent persons who were out of government at the time they responded but who have since gone back to high-level posts. They now wish for various reasons to withhold publication of their responses. We have honored those wishes. Some responses were specifically invited after we learned that the person had read the Manifesto and responded to it verbally or in writing. Herbert Kaufman's critical paper falls into that category. All in all, we feel that if the Manifesto accomplished nothing else it served well the purpose of stimulating dialogue and debate on a topic that is crucial at this juncture in history — the role of The Public Administration in the governance of America.

Even if we are correct in our presumption that the Manifesto has been a useful "invitation to dialogue," does it represent anything else in the development of public administration theory? Clearly we think so or we would not have taken the trouble to organize this volume and to expand on the ideas we could only touch on and infer in the shorter document. This book attempts to be more than just a response to the challenge of critics to elaborate upon our abbreviated ideas contained in the Manifesto. We have come to feel that to pull together the various ideas in the Manifesto — ideas that are not unique but are extant in the body academe and the practicing body of public administration — is to create a conceptual "critical mass" that points toward a normative theory of American public administration and to a theory of the American state, one that is positive in outlook and normative in nature. In other words, to engage that critical mass is to start down a road toward such theories. There are far too many people due thanks to undertake a listing of them here. Some of them are mentioned in the notes to the Blacksburg Manifesto as reprinted here from the Chandler volume in Chapter 2. Perhaps it is appropriate, however, to mention a few others who were not thanked there.

Special thanks are due to my colleagues of Troy State University of Alabama's European Division. Dr. Robert Kelley and Dr. Charles Connell provided me with a special appointment as a Distinguished Professor of National Security Management during 1986-1987. This appointment and the interaction with TSUA faculty and students provided a stimulating and supportive environment in which I could recuperate from too many years of being a public administrator and work through what amounted to a writing block.

Special thanks are also due to my CPAP colleagues for their patience and cooperation while I bowed out of my role as director and then took a long time regaining my forward momentum as a scholar. No words can cover my debt to Charles Goodsell who was willing to step into the role of director, at first temporarily and then permanently. Only the two of us can fully appreciate his sacrifice.

Thanks are also due to my many friends and colleagues who are practicing public administrators and have been willing to share their thoughts with me. They have suffered through trials, tribulations, and degradations to which I have largely been only a close-at-hand witness. (I could always retreat to the mountains of Appalachia when things got rough, but they had to show up every day.) In spite of what our political dialogue says of them and our political system does to them, they continue, amazingly, to give us some of the finest public service in the Western democracies, far more than we have a right to expect, far more than we pay for or deserve. They are the true heroes and heroines of constitutional governance. I hope they will recognize themselves and their influence in this book, even if not named.

Finally, my thanks to my wife Susan for her saucy but unwavering support, to my son Jonathan for his technical assistance with computer glitches, and to Linda Dennard who played a role that was more that of a helpful colleague than graduate assistant.

Gary L. Wamsley
Blacksburg, Virginia

Bibliography

Chandler, Ralph. *A Centennial History of the American Administrative State*. New York: Free Press, 1987.

Congressional Quarterly Almanac 50 (1979): 549-550.

Dempsey, John R. "Carter Reorganization: A Midterm Appraisal," *Public Management Forum*, Jan.-Feb. (1979): 74-78.

Drew, Elizabeth. Portrait of an Election: The 1980 Presidential Campaign. New York: Simon and Schuster, 1981.

Durant, Robert F. "Toward Assessing the Administrative Presidency: Public Lands, the BLM, and the Reagan Administration," *Public Administration Review* 47, 2 (1987): 180-189.

Gaertner, Gregory H., Gaertner, Karen N., and Devine, Irene. "Federal Agencies in the Context of Transition: A Contrast Between Democratic and Organizational Theories," *Public Administration Review* 43, 5 (1983): 421-432.

Goodsell, Charles. *The Case for Bureaucracy: The Public Administration Polemic, 2nd Ed.*. Chatham, N.J.: Chatham House Publishers, 1985.

Newland, Chester. "A Mid-Term Appraisal—The Reagan Presidency: Limited Government and Political Administration," *Public Administration Review* 43, 1 (1983): 1-23.

Rohr, John. "Background Comments on the Blacksburg Manifesto," Unpublished, n.d. Virginia Polytechnic and State University.

———. *To Run a Constitution: The Legitimacy of the Administrative State*. Lawrence, Kans.: University Press of Kansas, 1986.

Rosen, Bernard. "Crisis in the U.S. Civil Service," *Public Administration Review* 46, 3 (1986): 207-214.

Smith, Hedrick. *The Power Game: How Washington Works*. New York: Random House, 1988.

Sundquist, James L. "Jimmy Carter as Public Administrator: An Appraisal at Mid-Term," *Public Administration Review* Jan.-Feb. (1979): 3-11.

Introduction

GARY L. WAMSLEY

In this introductory chapter, permit me to switch from the personal "voice" of the preface to one that is more analytically detached, as I try to spell out what the ideas of the Manifesto and their exegesis in this volume represent in the relatively short history of theoretical development in public administration. Where do the ideas fit in the larger intellectual ecology? As I indicated in the Preface, we recognized a common intellectual strand among ourselves that might be called structuralism, institutionalism, or neo-institutionalism. But where does neo-institutionalism, if that label makes any sense, fit in the theoretical landscape of public administration theory?

Although there have been many exciting advances in organization theory since World War II, it seems to us that public administration theory has been trapped in an intellectual cul-de-sac created by behavioralism, the micropolitics of the discipline of political science, and the power of Herbert Simon's writings. There has been no major advance in public administration theory per se beyond the writings of Appleby, Waldo, Redford, Long, Price, Selznick, Sayre, and others. Although some of these theorists (most consistently, Long) have continued to expound on themes that should be central to public administration theory, those themes have not stirred nearly the interest in serious theory-building efforts that we feel they warrant. They seem never to have gained the kind of recognition and adherents they enjoyed in the late 1930s or 1940s. There are, no doubt, several reasons for this, but foremost among them has been the suffocating hold of behavioralism and positivism upon the social sciences in general. That hold has begun to loosen in the past two decades, but very slowly.

Unfortunately for the development of public administration theory, those who have led the way in challenging behavioralism and positivism have been people that Burrell and Morgan would likely label radical humanists or interpretivists. Though these paradigmatic approaches have many virtues, they are far more useful in rethinking human relations and the role of management in organizations than they are in rethinking the role of public administration in constitutional governance. Those theorists operating out of what Burrell and Morgan label the radical-structuralists paradigm (which draws heavily on a Marxist intellectual tradition) may yet have contributions to make to public administration theory, but to date they have not, for reasons too recondite to unravel here.

The landscape of public administration theory has thus been markedly bleak. The sole exception and signal event in public administration theory since World War II was the first Minnowbrook Conference and subsequent volume titled *The New Public Administration*. It therefore seems relevant to indicate how our neo-institutionalism, our so-called Blacksburg Perspective, relates to that first Minnowbrook Perspective.

The short, impressionistic answer might be — the Manifesto and its extended ideas are a "Minnowbrook I with institutional grounding." That is to say we hold important the same values as those often attributed to the so-called New Public Administration or the Minnowbrook Perspective: a commitment to greater societal equity (Wilbern 1973: 377; VrMeer 1973: 10; Marini 1971: 15); a concern for wider participation (Wilbern 1977: 377; VrMeer 1973: 10; Marini 1971: 15); a desire to move values and norms to a central position in theory and practice (Wilbern 1973: 376; VrMeer 1973: 10; Marini 1971: 15); a concern for the relationship between knowledge and action (Marini 1971: 311; Wilbern 1977: 377; VrMeer 1973: 10); and a critical outlook toward the shortcomings of pluralism (VrMeer 1973: 10; Marini 1971: 15; Wilbern 1977: 377); and those of logical positivism and empiricism (VrMeer 1977: 10; Marini 1971: 311).[1]

But what the Minnowbrook Perspective[2] seemed to lack was an awareness that more was needed than simply commitment of individual administrators to such values. Although all decisions and action must in the final analysis come down to individual responsibility (White 1973), as "structuralists" or "institutionalists" we are reluctant to rely *solely* on individual responsibility and commitment as the basis for action and social change. Humans are *social* creatures; we live, work, quarrel, construct reality and attribute meaning, cooperate, and act purposively in social constructs. We are of the opinion that relying solely on transformations in the "hearts and minds" of individuals to bring about social change is, to put it diplomatically, unrealistic (Denhardt 1981: 131). The morality and responsibility of individuals are socially shaped, constrained, nurtured, activated, buttressed, and reproduced by social constructs. We do not think or act as isolated individuals.

Moreover, we hold that societal problems are so "wicked," to use the apt word of Harmon and Mayer '1986: 3', that amelioration is only possible if they are approached from both directions: by seeking to change individuals, their perceptions, attitudes, and behavior, but at the same time by working to change structures or institutions — the embodiment of *collectively held and reproduced*

values, perceptions, attitudes, and behaviors (Douglas 1987). It is these collectively held and reproduced values that comprise structures; and it is these that
mold, shape, and reinforce the values and behavior of the individuals who
occupy roles within those social constructs, which are the necessary "tools" of
social action. Thus it seems to us that the Blacksburg Perspective differs from
that of Minnowbrook in a crucial aspect: the recognition of the need to work to
change values and to bring about social change from *both* ends of the structural-
individual continuum. If, however, one must choose (and inevitably life forces
choices on us about how and where we will concentrate our efforts), as
structuralists or neo-institutionalists we would throw our efforts into improving
American society and bringing about nonviolent social change by means of
improving and changing the social constructs by which we seek to govern
ourselves.

This speaks of a certain confidence on our part that the constitutional system
designed by our founding political elites can still be made equal to the challenges of the next two hundred years. It also bespeaks a confidence that if our
constitutionalism works effectively it will enable us to govern in a way that will
not only sustain the individualism and material aspects of our way of life but
also produce greater social equity and community.

When we say that the Blacksburg Perspective is an "institutionally grounded
Minnowbrook Perspective," we are, of course, suggesting that we feel the
values and implied action associated with Minnowbrook needed "institutional
grounding," that is, embodiment in the cultures of those social constructs of
government in order to be most efficacious. Whatever our commitment to
individualism may be, we must live and work in an organizational society, one
in which "the major actors in modern economic and political systems are formal
organizations, and the institutions of law and bureaucracy occupy a dominant
role in contemporary life" (March and Olsen 1983: 734). Further, all social
constructs develop cultures that shape individual behavior whether or not we
will it or intend that this happen. The important point for us is whether they will
manifest a culture with values that enhance our well-being and are a result of
our conscious, purposive, and socially constructive design or a culture that is
simply a collection of unanticipated consequences that may harm us (Selznick
1972; Peters and Waterman 1982). For we would hold with March and Olsen
(and historically, with classical theory) that political institutions determine,
order, and modify individual motives and that the "causal arrow" is much
stronger in that direction than it is from individual to institution (March and
Olsen 1983: 735)

Interestingly many students of public administration do not deny the importance and efficacy of institutions, but they seem to see their characteristics only
in negative or pathological terms. That is to say the importance and efficacy of
institutions is viewed alarmingly because of the harm they can do to individuals
who populate them and because of their presumed inertia and resistance to
social change (Denhardt and Hummel 1987: 247-269; Burrell and Morgan

1979: 279-325). We, the co-authors of this volume, are by no means insensitive to these aspects of institutions (Wamsley 1972; Wamsley and Salamon 1975). Some of us have contributed to the literature describing them. But from our perspective, seeing only the negative aspects of institutions and organizations is like seeing only the negative aspects of oxygen — it makes things burn faster, rusts steel, degrades paint, and so on. With such a focus we lose sight of its essentiality to life.

It hardly goes without saying that our stance as neo-institutionalists contrasts sharply with the approach of public choice theorists to organizations and public administration. The methodological individualism that is at the heart of much of economics, but especially of public choice, has generally blocked serious thinking on their part about collectivities like institutions (Ostrom 1986: 4, 22; McKean 1979). But despite the fact that a few public choice theorists have urged that serious attention be given to collectivities, the results in our estimation have been mixed at best. Too often they have developed elaborately logical and deductive microconceptualizations based on assumptions individuals would make if guided by a hypereconomic rationality. They have then sought to extrapolate from the behavior of individuals to that of collectivities (Rhoads 1985).

Some of these works have had their heuristic value but, as a few students of public choice are now trying to point out, this extrapolation from one level of analysis to another is simply not tenable. Collective behavior that occurs in social constructs is not merely individual behavior aggregated (Kelman 1987). Although self-interest calculations of individuals are by no means irrelevant in analyzing social constructs, the latter generally function, survive, and prosper best when they succeed in harmonizing or blending self-interest with collective interests, or when collective and self-interest can no longer be easily distinguished from each other (Barnard 1938: 122-123). They also function, and more often fail to function as we hope, precisely because logico-deductivism and hyperrationality do *not* prevail in social constructs.

Herbert Simon won a Nobel Prize at least in part for his efforts in elaborating on the point that organizations are staffed by "administrative man" who "satisfices" rather than "economic man" who theoretically maximizes (Simon 1955: 39). Therefore, whatever may be gained in clarity and simplicity by the application of rigorous logico-deductivism at the individual level of analysis is usually lost by inapplicability and irrelevance when we attempt to shift to the level of collectivities (Rhoads 1985; Buchanan 1978). If a "new economics of organizations" (Moe 1981) is on the intellectual horizon as some have proclaimed, it will have to indeed be a "*new* economics," for the old needs drastic overhauling if it is to be useful in analyzing social constructs like institutions.

Also fundamental to the Blacksburg Perspective is an acceptance of authority as an inescapable aspect of human society. To simply say we are positive toward authority might imply too much, but it is fair to say that we feel it has its positive as well as its negative aspects. Furthermore, we would support Orion

White's contention in Chapter 6 that the conventional wisdom that assumes that authority and participation are antithetical and mutually exclusive qualities in organizational/institutional life is dead wrong. It takes nothing from Orion's excellent discussion to point out that it echoes the much earlier work of Carl J. Friedrich. Friedrich, who was dealing with the starker alternatives that underlie authority, cautioned that in thinking of political leadership and power it was important "to realize that coercion and consent are not mutually exclusive" (Friedrich 1961: 7, 8). And, he continued, "coercion has a force of its own, as has consent; and in most power situations both are operative in varying degrees and combinations" (Friedrich 1961: 8). So it is with authority and participation within more limited social constructs.

As noted above, many academicians and amazingly, many political scientists and even public administrationists are either tentative or negative toward authority; others seem uninterested or even embarrassed to deal with it (Zald 1971). But to us public administration is part of the governance structure and process and as such there is no ducking the importance of authority, nor is there any place for squeamishness about it. It is as essential to governance as water is to life on the planet earth. More on authority and governance at a later point.

Another way in which the Blacksburg Perspective can be viewed as an "institutionally grounded Minnowbrook" is in our concern with history and the founding of public administration and with the Constitution and the founding period of America. We have been led in this by John Rohr who has done a great deal to awaken the field of public administration to the importance of the Constitution and the founding period. His chapter takes further steps in that direction. Here I only want to indicate in what way all of us involved in developing the Blacksburg Perspective are oriented toward the history and founding of public administration, to America's founding, and to the Constitution and how such an orientation contrasts with the rest of the field. With a few notable exceptions public administration has been dismayingly ahistoric and both ignorant and indifferent to its origins (Fesler 1988: 894; Gladden 1972). For most of the field public administration begins at the turn of the century, connected vaguely with Progressivism and civil service reform (Gordon 1986: 23). Woodrow Wilson's article (Wilson 1887) is perfunctorily assigned and, although the student may be impressed that a former president was concerned with public administration, he or she is probably left puzzled about how Wilson's rather enigmatic article represents a "founding" — something that has puzzled more careful students of our history as well (Van Riper 1983: 479; Van Riper in Chandler 1987: 3-36). Our introductory courses quickly move on to discuss the politics-administration dichotomy in condescending terms (Gordon 1986: 44-47). But this casualness toward the founding of our field is a terrible mistake on our part. The way we define our founding makes all the difference in the way we view ourselves and our place in the political system, or the way we are viewed by others. It is a matter of overwhelming importance to us (Rohr 1986; Arendt 1963: 214).

Adopting Woodrow Wilson (1887), Frank Goodnow (1900), and Frederick Taylor (1911) as Founders gives us the following pieces of debilitatingly irrelevant intellectual baggage we must drag about the academic and practical landscapes:

> — An outlook that is focused on management rather than governance; one that has borrowed heavily from private-sector management's concepts, techniques, and even its negative attitudes toward public administration; one that has therefore failed to develop its own theories, concepts, norms, or techniques suited to administration qua governance in a constitutional system of polycentric power.
> — An ignorance of the importance the Founding Fathers accorded administration in the republic they fashioned and of the important role effective administration has played at key points in our development; thus a lack of a sense of legitimacy that could come from such knowledge.

Our ignorance of the Constitution is equally egregious and the consequences equally disastrous. Because of that ignorance:

We fail to fully understand separation of powers and its implications for public administration.

We perceive the discretion that falls to public administration as a consequence of separation of powers as a threat rather than an opportunity.

We tend to view the Constitution's dispersal of powers as a problem or possibly a design flaw that impedes good management.

We view the politics-administration dichotomy as devoid of theoretical significance but continue by default to foster the establishment of its functional equivalent in the plebiscitory, integrative, personal, or administrative presidency. (Choose your adjective for more powerful and more expectation-burdened presidency.)

In one sense the "grounding" of the Blacksburg Perspective in comparison to Minnowbrook's is more clearly a matter of degree than kind. We refer to our epistemological stances toward the field of public administration. We are perhaps more clearly postbehavioral, postempirical, postpositivist than were those who gathered at Minnowbrook in 1968, but there is nothing remarkable or unique in that — so is most of the field today. Though there was by no means total unanimity on epistemology at the first Minnowbrook gathering (Wamsley 1976), most of the participants clearly saw the need and possessed the willingness to move beyond the constraints of behavioralism or empiricism and positivism. We have only followed the lead they established and (1) grown more convinced of the need for normative theory and impatient with the limitations of behavioralism and empiricism narrowly defined, but (2) have become more sensitive to the need to focus attention on institutional grounding of normative theory.

Whether or not we are any less functionalist than those at Minnowbrook I is a more difficult question to answer, indeed, is not one I wish to try to answer at this point. Clearly, however, there is more willingness to explore different ontological and epistemological bases for our work or other paradigmatic stances, particularly interpretivism, but also stances Burrell and Morgan label radical humanism and radical structuralism. In general, we have grown in our willingness to seek to understand and appreciate the contributions other paradigmatic stances make to the field. Orion White and Cynthia McSwain have captured the epistemological stance with which most of us involved in the Blacksburg Manifesto would resonate.

> We take it as the task of the academic wing of public administration to provide the public administrator with a solid grounding in modern structural analysis and in general to reorient the field away from complete reliance on the behavioralist model of organization theory and behavior. Drawing from structural anthropology, structural linguistics, depth psychology, and a broad concern with myth and symbolism, a new way of understanding administrative life — as the Traditionalists did but more grounded and more intellectually sophisticated — must be developed. By doing this, public administrators will become enabled, as the Traditionalists were, to take into account the irrational aspects of social life and to apprehend and respond to the large and important structural, symbolic, mythic forces that shape and energize it. (White and McSwain forthcoming: 50)

Finally, the Blacksburg Perspective is "institutionally grounded" in the sense that we prefer to see public administration as governance rather than merely management or administration in the public sector. It is my guess that many of those at the first Minnowbrook would have been acutely uncomfortable with such a way of thinking of public administration. Or they might simply have been puzzled by it — the term is neither well understood nor popular. More will be said of the concept of governance in Chapter 4. Here I need only point to a few implications of treating public administration as governance.

First it reminds us of the full dimensions of our role and its challenges. Managing in the public sector is challenge enough, but we are called on to do much more than that. Governance connotes the use of authority in providing systemic steering and direction. That is what our political system so desperately needs and which has been made so challenging by the democratization of the compound and extended republic bequeathed us by our Founders. Pendleton Herring once captured the conundrum faced by the democratic republic in a disturbing paragraph written in 1936:

> When a democratic government undertakes to alleviate the maladjustments of the economic system, it stirs up a greed that it may lack power to control. The "voice of the people" sometimes suggests the squeal of pigs at the trough. The regulation that a democracy can enforce is based upon the self-discipline of its people, and

this in turn demands the guidance of wise leaders who hold on high a clear vision of the public interest. But proper administrative tools are essential. (Herring 1936: 3)

It is our belief that given the growth of technicism we will continue to witness the atomization of our social and political lives and the consequent growth of hyperpluralism (McSwain and White, forthcoming). This means that we cannot expect to see strong political parties as a source of governing impetuses. We can probably expect to see further efforts to remake the presidency of the Constitution into a plebiscitory chief executive, but we feel that there is real peril in moving in that direction. The only possible source of governing impetuses that might keep our complex political system from either a dangerous concentration of power on the one hand, or impotence or self-destruction on the other, is a public administration with the necessary professionalism, dedication, self-esteem, and legitimacy to act as the constitutional center of gravity. That is a stark statement that some will find shocking, but it is said not for its shock value but in the interest of plain speaking and candor. Without such a public administration, one dedicated to discovering the public interest in the midst of conflicting demands and clashing interests, we cannot expect the outcomes of our political system to be more than the lowest common denominator of the most powerful interests, the result of presidential aggrandizement, and/or the consequence of the denigration of public service. We can also expect more scandals such as Watergate, GSA, Iran-Contra, HUD, the savings and loan industry, or Pentagon Procurement. Which brings us to the final point that distinguishes the Blacksburg Perspective from Minnowbrook I or other theoretical thrusts in public administration today — our concern for revitalizing the concept of the public interest.

As the reader will see, all the chapters are concerned with this idea of the public interest, but particularly Charles Goodsell's and mine. We refuse to accept the murder of a perfectly useful concept by Glendon Schubert (Schubert 1957). We hold with Pendleton Herring who over a half-century ago said, "This concept is to bureaucracy what the 'due process' clause is to the judiciary," or as James Fesler has said more recently — "It is for administrators what objectivity is for scholars." It is a crucially important ideal, and as Fesler says, "If there is not a public interest then we must denounce the idea of ideals — if it is illusory, so are justice, liberty and integrity" (897). If the concept is not alive and well, we must make it so and quickly.

Is this concern for resuscitating the concept of the public interest another example of "groundedness"? We think so. The normative impulses the academic wing of public administration had to suppress during the height of the behavioral revolution emerged clearly enough in Minnowbrook but suffered for lack of any conceptual or normative lodestar like the public interest (Hill 1988). Clearly it was needed. We will leave the explication and resuscitation of the concept to Charles Goodsell's able pen in Chapter 3.

We hope this attempt to contrast the Blacksburg Perspective with the writings to emerge from the first Minnowbrook Conference is not misinterpreted as invidious. Nothing could be further from the truth. Minnowbrook I stands as the only significant event in public administration theory in nearly a half-century. Two of us were participants in Minnowbrook I, and six of us were invited and five of us were able to attend the second Minnowbrook conference that occurred as this chapter was written. The comparison is made solely for purposes of trying to locate the Blacksburg Perspective within the intellectual ecology of public administration during the past few decades. In point of fact, I believe that when comparisons of Minnowbrook I and II are made we will see the same shift to "groundedness" in the second conference. We hope so, and we hope that our ideas in this volume are not too far from the intellectual mainstream of public administration thought. We will be happy if the chapters that follow merely catalyze, sharpen, or give voice to manifest concepts that are latent or only partially articulated in a body of scholarship and the related world of practice.

The chapter that follows sets forth the Blacksburg Manifesto. It is very close to the form that was first read in a New York hotel suite. There is one major difference — one that did not change many of the words but which made a significant shift in the substance. We are speaking of the addition of Camilla Stivers's ideas on the role of citizens in the The Public Administration. Cam, who was one of our doctoral students, was such an intelligent critic and her ideas so consonant with our own that it seemed only sensible to add her as a co-author. Our reaction to her ideas was, "We *knew* something was missing! We wish we could have had your input from the beginning." Fortunately, it was not too late to add her ideas to this book.

In Chapter 2 John Rohr sets forth the constitutional case for The Public Administration that we prescribe. We have made it clear in the preceding pages why we feel this constitutional grounding is crucial for public administration but especially for The Public Administration. This is as good a place as any to indicate that we will use capitals when we mean to refer specifically to the prescribed ideal we advocate in contrast to the field as currently constituted.

In Chapter 3 Charles Goodsell does an excellent job of administering intellectual CPR to the long-comatose corpus of theory (pun intended) known as the public interest. We think it is the kind of rejoinder many of us have felt for years should have been made to Glendon Schubert's brilliant butchery but that we had come to assume we would never see. The Public Administration could never come into existence without a viable normative concept and powerful political symbol like the public interest. We doubt that one will often see Schubert footnoted from now on without its being accompanied by a Goodsell cite. More importantly, readers of the Goodsell chapter will never again be able to think about the concept in the cramped, negative, and narrowly positivistic way Schubert's work depicted it.

In Chapter 4 I have taken on a task that proved much larger than I had foreseen: the conceptualization of a social construct that could serve as an institutional ground-point for the practicing public administrator in efforts to involve citizens (organized and unorganized) in developing a policy community and defining the public interest. The agency and agency perspective is as crucial to The Public Administration as is constitutional grounding and a revived concept of the public interest. Modesty requires that I leave to the readers any judgments about whether or not I succeeded.

In Chapter 5 James Wolf and Robert Bacher explore the "worlds" of public administration: the vocation, the job, and the career. Although this chapter is, like the others, prescriptive, it also rests on some sobering demographic analyses of general population trends and of related trends in the public-sector "workforce." Wolf and Bacher leave us ample reason to hope that The Public Administration can be developed and contain all three "worlds" but also ample understanding that it will not be easy.

Chapter 6 by Orion White is the longest of the chapters but his task is one of the most demanding. The Public Administration we seek to foster must develop and husband authority that will be viewed by citizens as legitimate — and that means it must evoke more than acquiescence and habitual compliance. That will not be easy to achieve, but it must start by building legitimate authority within the social constructs of the public sector. If public administrators within government cannot view the authority of their own bureaucracies/organizations/institutions as legitimate, then lay citizens can hardly be expected to view that same authority as legitimate. Nor is it likely that public administrators who feel debased by acquiescence to illegitimate authority exercised by their superiors, will turn about and exercise authority toward lay citizens in a way that fosters legitimacy. Considerable rethinking will therefore be required concerning the meaning of authority and how it relates to participation. Our efforts will be confounded rather than facilitated by the bulk of the existing literature of organization behavior and theory. Orion's deeply thoughtful and highly personal attempt to critique the inadequacy of that literature and to rethink these crucial concepts of authority and participation and their interrelationship is, in my opinion, a groundbreaking work.

Following logically from White's chapter must be an effort to rethink the meaning of citizenship in America and the way citizens and public administrators relate to one another. Camilla Stivers's Chapter 7 is a bold effort in this regard and one that challenges much of the negative conventional wisdom concerning citizen participation. It seems to us inevitable that it will play a significant role in shaping future dialogue on this subject.

Finally, we have an important effort by Phil Kronenberg in Chapter 8 to apply the concept of agency to the Department of Defense. One of the several interesting aspects of this chapter is the way in which it has developed. Phil was on leave from Virginia Tech at the time the Manifesto was developed. (He spent a year as a research associate at the Air War College and a year as a program analyst in the Office of Program Analysis and Evaluation, Office of the Secretary of Defense.) We all missed his participation in an event that was intellectually important to us, and we were interested to see how he would react to the Manifesto and whether or not he would be willing to be included in whatever projects might later evolve. Appropriately, Phil has taken a more detached perspective toward the Manifesto and some of the ideas derived from it. That, as it has turned out, has been good for us and comfortable for him. Phil's questions and prodding have helped the rest of us discover commonalities in our thinking that we might otherwise have been much slower to discover, and he has made us sharpen and clarify our thinking. In that same vein he agreed to attempt to apply the concept of agency to a key component of American government with which he is intimately familiar. The results are interesting and show both the strengths and problems of operationalizing the prescriptive concept.

Let us refer the reader again to the appendix where we have reproduced the wide-ranging reactions to the Manifesto that have come from both practitioners and academicians. Here the reader may find some of his or her own doubts, criticism, or positive feelings expressed by others. On balance the reactions are more positive than negative, but all treat our effort seriously and endeavor to be constructive. For that we are sincerely appreciative.

Notes

1. On the last point it is probably fair to say that we, like most of the field, have become aware of the limitations and inadequacies of pluralism, logical positivism, and empiricism, but that does not mean that we reject any of these outright.

2. As this is being written a second Minnowbrook Conference has been held. Unless I indicate otherwise, I will be referring to the first Minnowbrook Conference held in 1968.

1. Public Administration and the Governance Process: Shifting the Political Dialogue

GARY L. WAMSLEY[1]
CHARLES T. GOODSELL
JOHN A. ROHR
CAMILLA M. STIVERS
ORION F. WHITE
JAMES F. WOLF

Introduction

Nearly a century has passed since the appearance of Woodrow Wilson's essay "On the Study of Public Administration." Some of what he wrote seems to have a disturbingly prophetic quality. For example:

> The weightier debates of constitutional principle are even yet by no means concluded; but they are no longer of more immediate practical moment than questions of administration. It is getting harder to *run* a constitution than to frame one.[2]

If those words have such a disturbing quality today it is doubtless because they have proven so painfully true for us as the twentieth century draws to a close. We have accomplished administrative wonders since Wilson penned those words: dug a canal connecting the world's great oceans; organized, equipped, and deployed millions of men and women to win two global wars; saved from collapse and altered the nature of the American political economy by massive administrative intervention during the Great Depression; organized scientists and workers in a secret and desperate race with Nazi Germany to develop a nuclear weapon; we built an interstate highway system of unmatched size and capacity; we have put together hundreds of organizations both public and private involving thousands of scientists and engineers and billions of dollars to place American footprints on the moon. The list could and should go on and on. Yet despite these and many other accomplishments, it "gets harder to run a constitution." All our administrative accomplishments do not add to, and some wonder if in fact administration even contributes to, the stable and effective functioning of our political system. The essence, we believe, of what Wilson meant by "running a constitution" is a public administration that *does* result in the stable and effective functioning of our political system — in a way that steadily improves the quality of our lives and expands both equity and opportunity.

The problem then lies not simply in a lack of organizing and managerial skills, though we still have plenty of room for improvement. Rather it goes beyond, to the problem of governing a modern republic with a commitment to freedom and justice on the one hand and a commitment to a complex mixture of capitalism and state intervention on the other. Several contradictory pressures are thus generated. The commitment to freedom and justice creates pressures for equity but commitment to state capitalism creates a counterpressure for economic and social differentiation. The requirements of maintaining a vigorous economy in an increasingly competitive world and of maintaining world-power status in an increasingly dangerous environment create pressures for a rational, comprehensive, planning and policy process while our historical and constitutional tradition is based on fractionated power, overlapping jurisdictions, and disjointed incrementalism. The problems of public administration in America result from the difficulty of governing effectively such a political system; hence the difficulties of governing such a political system are not the result of, or caused by, public administration.

Rowland Egger sums up American history in a way that places our governance problem and the problems of bureaucracy in perspective. He points out that America has experienced four great social revolutions. The first was the revolution for independence, which set in motion forces of social change only partially crystallized and reflected in the great compromises of the Constitution; the second was the Jacksonian era, which marked our changed conceptions of who was entitled to participate in republican government; the third was the Civil War, which redefined the nature of the federal Union and further altered our definition of citizenship by making it national in character. There is, however, a fourth social revolution that is still in progress according to Egger. It began with the New Deal's response to the Great Depression and was given further impetus by the Civil Rights Movement now augmented by the Women's Movement. This revolution is in the process of redefining our concepts of justice and equity and our expectations of government's role in our efforts to find a uniquely American definition for these abstract concepts.

If this is a meaningful synopsis of our history then it becomes understandable, though no less lamentable, that America's public administration is caught in the eye of recurrent political storms: reviled by some because it does too much in pursuit of equity and justice, and by others who perceive it as doing too little. Both ends of the political spectrum have seen it at times as the ominous instrument of their opponent's will. Not only has it been forced to bear the opprobrium of being seen as the "opponent's instrument," but it has also become the scapegoat for the general problems of what Theodore Lowi has aptly labeled "interest group liberalism": the parochialization of the public interest, the fragmentation and erosion of public purpose and the centrifugal pressures that have franchised pieces of public authority to policy subsystems. Although American public administration is not without blame for some of these maladies, it has as often as not been victim rather than perpetrator, "compliant with" rather than "cause of," and, indeed, it can be argued that it has often served as the strongest available counterweight to these disturbing tendencies.

Be that as it may, political leaders have increasingly used "bureaucracy" as an epithet. Presidents of both parties have made attacks on it the centerpieces of their campaigns, only to find that this tactic, so useful in getting elected, becomes a self-inflicted wound in the subsequent struggle to govern. The gap between our system's need for effective governance and the capacity of our elected officials to provide it widens at an alarming rate.

Government and the American Dialogue

Much of the denigration of bureaucracy has been a natural outgrowth of our politics. Jacksonian democracy was heavily freighted with negativism toward government because new groups wanted both access to it and control of it. Even though the Progressive movement ran counter to this, the residual negativism has been amplified by contemporary conservatism and by political actors from all parts of the spectrum who are frustrated by the problems that derive from interest group liberalism but that are blamed on government or, synonymously, bureaucracy. *Thus our political culture has come to include a pernicious mythology concerning the public sector and public administrators which needs to be corrected before the American dialogue can enter a new and meaningful phase.* Items:

Most clients of bureaucracy are not dissatisfied; in fact the vast majority of them are very pleased with the services and treatment received.

The rate of productivity increase in the public sector is not clearly lower than the private sector; it is probably higher overall.

The federal government has not grown in number of employees since the early 1950s.

The bureaucracy is not a monolith; it is composed of many small and diverse bureaus and offices.

Public agencies stimulate and implement change; resistance to change is no more endemic to the organizations in the public sector than to the private.

Studies have shown that the private sector is more top-heavy with administrative personnel than the public sector.

Waste and inefficiency are no more prevalent in the public sector than the private; but in the former it is seen as waste of the taxpayers money while in the latter we fail to see that it is passed on to us in the prices we pay as consumers.

But our purpose is neither to bury bureaucracy nor to praise it; rather we hope to take a step toward reconceptualizing it as The Public Administration. *Bureaucracy* in its technical sense refers to a form of social organization that is not confined to the public sector. We carry no brief for any particular organizational form. Our focus is on the *functions* of government agencies and not on how they might be organized. Thus we speak of "The Public Administration" as an institution of government rather than of bureaucracy as an organizational form.

We see no way of arresting the pathologies of our political system and coming to grips with the sizeable problems of our nation's political economy without a new way of thinking about, speaking of, and acting toward The Public Administration. This will not be a sufficient condition for the challenges we face, but it will assuredly be a necessary one.

There must be, then, a significant change in both the content and breadth of the American Dialogue. This dialogue juxtaposes, on the one hand, ideas associated with broadening and deepening personal liberty and, on the other, ideas associated with social equity, public order, fiscal soundness, and capital accumulation. Inevitable tension between these two sets of ideas has meant that disagreement about the nature and role of government has always been central to that dialogue, though it has worn different masks at different times. During the last half-century the disagreement has become particularly acute as we have sought to redefine liberty and equity while carrying out our fourth social revolution.

We have been socialized, for complex reasons that have to do with the nature of capitalism, to fail to see this as the core issue of the dialogue. Nonetheless the great national debates of our history have as often as not involved questions about the nature and role of "government" in the struggle between democracy and order. Today we feel it is imperative that an important shift take place in the dialogue. Our political rhetoric and symbols have become too far divorced from reality and the conditions we face. *We cannot preserve and revitalize American industry and our natural resources in the face of increasing global interdependence nor improve the quality of our lives, if our public dialogue is focused on* whether *or not government has any role in these matters or on how to* reduce *its role, while the reality of our world, our behavior, and our actions is of necessity trying to grapple with questions of "How?" and "What form is most effective?"*

As Dwight Waldo reminds us, only in America did we create such rhetorical and symbolic disjuncture between the concepts of "good government" and "good management". In the rest of the Occident there is a profound and natural linkage resulting from legal concepts and institutions rooted in Roman law. Americans sharply attenuated that linkage when they revolted against the British monarchy and then, a century later, "invented" what Waldo calls "self-conscious administration," which strove to be "scientific" with empirically discoverable and generally applicable principles. We believe that attenuation and rediscovery were and are far more impressive in our rhetoric than in actual fact. This is not to say they were less important for being rhetorical; indeed they may be more important for that very reason. One point, however, is that the nature and role of public administration were never far from the center of America's public dialogue; they were only camouflaged as questions about "government" rather than "public administration." Beginning with the Articles of Confederation and continuing down to this day, we have been arguing about liberty and order and the nature and role of "government" in the pulling and hauling between these polar abstractions. From the suppression of Shays's Revolt and the Whiskey Rebellion, the assumption of the states' debts by the national government, the building of post roads, the national roads, the granting of land by the government to railroads and canal companies, the Northwest Ordinance (which dedicated land in each territory to support public schools), through the Interstate Commerce Act, down to current debates over the sale of government-developed communication satellites to private enterprise, in all these we have been engaged in a national struggle to define the nature and role of "government" in the perilous evolution of some kind of ordered liberty. *We must therefore refocus the American dialogue from questions about the nature and role of "government" to questions about the nature and role of "public administration." This would be a subtle but crucial shift in the American dialogue from questions of "whether" there should be a role for The Public Administration to questions of "what form?" that role should take.*

Finally, as part of an effort to shift the American dialogue, we need to assert that The Public Administration, with the managerial skills which lie at its core and its experience in applying those skills in a political context, is, despite its problems, a major social asset. As a major social asset it should be subjected to constructive criticism but not diminished, denigrated, or decapitalized lightly or for short-run partisan advantage. There may well be a direct relationship between the attacks on The Public Administration and the erosion of civic morality evidenced in behavior ranging from corruption and tax evasion to vandalism and littering. Those who attack The Public Administration for partisan advantage are no friends of the Republic; indeed they inflict considerable harm on the body politic. Similarly, those engaged in decapitalizing and disassembling administrative capacity should recognize that subsequent ruling groups (some of them of their own political persuasion), and all citizens will have to pay the price of such foolish disinvestment. Though The Public Administration needs many improvements and alterations, the need for administrative capacity will only increase, not diminish. *One of the major political economic questions confronting the American political system, one that needs to be at the center of a refocused American dialogue is: which (not whether) government intentions and actions should be pursued through the public sector, that is, be a part of The Public Administration and therefore have its authority and legitimacy behind them while at the same time being subject to its constraints.*

The Public Administration's Distinctive Character

The Public Administration is, of course, centered on the executive branch but includes segments of all branches of government to the extent that they relate to the constitutional mandate of the executive: the faithful execution of the laws through our multileveled governmental system. Our position is pointedly historical and includes not only those things we might point to with pride, like the Hatch Act, but also those of which we are justly ashamed, like the Teapot Dome Scandal.

The Public Administration is distinctive in character. It has at its core generic management technologies that comprise its "administrative capacity." These are a vital part of its expertise and they closely resemble the technologies of management in the private sector. But Wallace Sayre puts it aptly when he says that business and public administration are alike in all *un-important* respects. For the Public Administration is more than generic management. It is the administration of public affairs in a political context. As Carl Friedrich noted a half-century ago, administration is the core of modern government; it is an application of state power for what we hope are moral and humane ends, but always with the possibility of being used otherwise. Since governance entails the state's rewarding and depriving in the name of society as a whole, and since politics is the art of gaining acceptance for those allocations, administration is an inextricable part of both governance and politics. Because of its role in rewarding and depriving, redistributing, distributing and regulating, and because it is the only set of institutions that can rightfully coerce to achieve society's ends, it is seldom viewed dispassionately. Rather it is, as Murray Edelman reminds us, an object against which the people displace fears, hopes, and anxieties. The Public Administration is inescapably fundamental to this displacement and therein lies its distinctive character. Its part in governance and the resultant political context means that: (1) the Public Administrator must engage not in a struggle for markets and profits but in a struggle with other actors in the political and governmental processes for jurisdiction, legitimacy, and resources; (2) those persons with whom he or she must interact possess distinctive perceptions, expectations, and levels of efficacy toward The Public Administration (e.g., the differences between consumers and citizens or suppliers and interest groups are profound); and (3) the requisite skills, foci of attention, and perceived tasks of The Public Administration differ markedly from private-sector management. These differences are so great that a manager successful in one sector will not be as successful in the other without considerable adaptiveness. To the degree that we lose sight of that distinction, to the same degree do we lose our vision of what The Public Administration is or can be.

The Public Administration is also self-consciously derived from, and focused upon, what we shall call an Agency Perspective. By agencies we mean those institutions that have grown up in the executive branches at all levels and that are the instruments of action in pursuit of the public interest. A better understanding of the distinctiveness of The Public Administration must be built upon a greater appreciation of the institutional histories of agencies — their histories in a broad contextual sense — the history of an agency's political economy.

We feel this is appropriate and necessary because many of these *agencies are repositories of, and their staffs are trustees of, specialized knowledge, historical experience, time-tested wisdom, and most importantly, some degree of consensus as to the public interest relevant to a particular societal function.* Indeed the persons staffing these agencies have been charged with acting in the public interest and in executing the popular will in ways that sustain and nurture legitimacy for generations. The Agency Perspective is thus based on many years of struggle within the larger political system and the more limited governance process to achieve and enact some kind of consensus over specific aspects of public policy. Surely this unique task and experience is worth far more than we have been willing to acknowledge up until now.

That is not to say that the agencies have not been misdirected or misused by others or that they have not operated at times in self-serving ways. Indeed, as acknowledged earlier, agencies have contributed at times to the centrifugal pressures in American government, and in some respects they may have aided those who aimed to reduce their legitimate sphere, by neglecting substantive relationships with the ultimate source of legitimacy in governance, that is, the citizenry. But the dangers of parochialism are endemic to all organizations and they are, in the final analysis, perversions of the Agency Perspective. The Agency Perspective is intended only to serve public administrators as a "center of gravity" or a "gyroscope" as they go about their duties. On this solid foundation they must build a concern for broader public principles and values; in other words, a concern for the public interest.

As Max Weber pointed out, bureaucracy can be used for good or evil; how it is used depends on the human beings who staff it and direct it. Fortunately, over the grand sweep of American history, with exception made perhaps for the period between the election of Jackson and the passage of the Pendleton Act, agencies have for the most part been staffed by persons who have taken seriously the task of faithfully executing the popular will and the public interest. Although some have no doubt been concerned with a broader public interest, most have viewed that task through the lens of their agency and assumed, like the rest of us, that the broader public interest would emerge from the governance process as a whole. The point is that few groups in our society have been given as demanding a task as executing the public interest from any perspective. That task and the special skills and knowledge acquired by The Public Administration in performing it are worth far more than our present political dialogue allows.

Political elites have failed for self-serving reasons to credit agencies and those who staff them with distinctive characteristics and legitimacy, therefore the public at large, cut off from the realities of administrative practice, has also failed to credit them. Most lamentably, The Public Administration has been too timid in pressing its rightful claims to legitimacy of which the Agency Perspective is the basic foundation, and too hesitant about building the sense of trust among citizens that would justify such claims.

Most recently we have also allowed The Public Administration to be diminished by the headlong rush to adopt a policy or program perspective with an excessive focus on output without balancing it by concern for the public good. The two are often erroneously assumed to be synonymous, when in fact they are not. An agency can produce outputs inimicable to the long-range public interest; as well as short-run "results" that can have devastating effects on its infrastructure and capabilities and, most importantly, the future public good. A park service, for example, can process a larger number of visitors through facilities that it is overloading and allowing to decay through lack of maintenance. It is therefore possible for an agency to be "responsive" to immediate pressures while simultaneously being irresponsible with regard to the public interest. One of the characteristics of the Agency Perspective and of The Public Administration therefore should be a prudent and reasoned attention to agency performance, one in which consideration is given both to the short *and* long-run consequences, qualitative as well as quantitative measures; and one which rejects "the bottom line" as a slogan antithetical to good public administration.

Although public policy analysis and program evaluations used wisely can be valuable in carrying out the public business and in demonstrating agency performance, they are not ends in themselves, and simplistic use and clever abuse must be constantly guarded against. In executive agencies these techniques make sense only when viewed as part of the ongoing processes of administration. *Policy analysis, program evaluation, and decision sciences when applied within executive agencies should be subordinated to an agency perspective and to core management process. Too often the former have been allowed to intrude upon this perspective and these processes and have been detrimental to good public administration and inconsistent with their own aims.*

A particularly corrosive influence on the Agency Perspective came from humanistic psychology and a variety of cultural dynamics during the 1960s. We refer to the denigration of the role of authority in the administrative process and management relationships. The adolescent texture of the 1960s cultural upheaval wore heavily on our traditional concepts of authority within agencies. Now, in cooler retrospect, it is time to correct the misconceptions that arose from the debate of the traditionalists and the humanists in organization theory on this issue.

We need to note, first, that the traditional point of view was incorrect to the extent that it sought to base obedience to authority purely on the principle of deference and depicted the use of managerial authority as a tool by which managers could improve performance (the "shape up or ship out" position). This perspective was correct, however, in depicting the human situation as one requiring authority to check our sometimes capricious tendencies. In particular, the traditional view is correct in seeing that encounter with authority is an essential and positive part of the maturation process, not only in adolescence but throughout life; and for superiors and subordinates alike.

By the same token, the humanists were incorrect in carrying their attack on authority to the point of denying that it plays a needed role in institutional life — implying that it can thereby be replaced completely by processes of participation. They were, however, providing a helpful corrective to the traditional view by their call for more openness in the use of authority and for the establishment of a greater degree of mutual confidence in organizations.

What we can distill from this debate is the idea that authority is not as useful as feedback and other "humanistic" communication devices for improving performance in administration, but it is essential for dealing effectively with the intractable problem of compliance on issues wherein reasonable persons can disagree. It is these issues of compliance on which hinge both the personal development of managers and the people they manage, as well as the effectiveness of agencies in implementing public policies and programs. In sum, the message here is that *the vitality of the Agency Perspective, the health of The Public Administration, and the self-concept of the Public Administrator hinge upon our return to a fuller appreciation of the positive role of authority in administration.* This appreciation, in essence a form of trust, will develop among citizens to the extent that administrators communicate the realities of administrative practice so that citizens can understand them, and ultimately acknowledge the legitimacy of administrative authority.

The distinctive Agency Perspective is one that deserves greater legitimacy than it has received from our political culture. The very nature of the role the Agency plays in governance leads it inevitably to develop a distinctive perspective on the public interest. The Public Administration which rests upon the Agency Perspective as a foundation thus has an historic, covenantal, organic, and constitutional legitimacy that needs illumination. Many agencies at all levels of our political system have been with us from our genesis as a nation; some are even suggested in the text of the Constitution.

The distinctive nature of The Public Administration lies in the fact that it is a part of the governance process, that it is administration in a political context and competence directed *toward the public interest.* This sets it apart from management in business and provides the basis for a truly distinctive claim to status that has been too long ignored. The claim ought to rest, however, on more than competence to manage in a political context. It must also rest on a claim of competence in the maintenance of (1) the Agency Perspective; (2) the broadest possible public interest; and (3) the constitutional governance process.

The "public interest" has, of course, long been derided, particularly by social scientists, as a meaningless concept at best, a mask for arrogant despotism at worst. But setting aside for a moment the difficulties of defining its contents precisely, it is ironic that many social scientists prefer to be concerned with behavior but ignore the fact that the concept has a day-to-day, commonsensical, practical salience for the behavior of hundreds of thousands of Public Administrators. Caught as they are in the struggle of conflicting interests—sometimes as interpreters, other times as decision makers, and even at times as victims—they understand intuitively that the containment if not the resolution of that conflict is rooted in some notion of the public interest even though some may use the concept cynically or self-servingly. It is therefore a concrete, living, behavioral reality in spite of our problems in defining its specific content.[3]

The approach traditionally imposed for defining the concept has, however, led us astray by making a definition impossible. This approach has been to ask, "What is the public interest in terms of the *content* of given policy situations?" This question may never be answered. But, by shifting our perspective from specific content to an *ideal* and a *process*, and the emphasis from a search for certainty to recognition of the problematic nature of the public interest, the problem is no longer insoluble. In this vein, the "public interest" refers to a combination of several habits of mind in making decisions and making policy: attempting to deal with the *multiple* ramifications of an issue rather than a select few; seeking to incorporate the *long-range* view into deliberations, to balance a natural tendency toward excessive concern with short-term results; considering *competing* demands and requirements of affected individuals and groups, not one position; proceeding equipped with *more* knowledge and information rather than less; and recognizing that to say that the " public interest" is problematic is not to say it is meaningless.

Although this type of definition will not satisfy those who have been accustomed to posing the issue in substantive and finite terms, an ideal and process-defined norm is not that unusual—either as practical guidepost or positive symbol. The democrat endorses majoritarianism; the civil libertarian extols due process; lawyers cherish an adversarial legal process. We recommend approaching, if not defining, the public interest in the same spirit. Even the strongest opponent of the public interest concept, the economic conservative, is committed to an ideal and process-oriented norm, the competitive market.

Because this definition does not provide us with given policy or option answers, it invites the charge that the public administrator who lays claim to protecting the public interest is merely insisting on his agency's definition of what is "right." Such misplaced absoluteness constantly occurs on the part of public administrators as well as others. All must recognize the subjective elements in any conclusion as to which choice is "right," and indeed that "certainty" about the public interest is a dubious and perhaps dangerous posture. (Many of those involved in the Watergate Affair were certain that the public interest was embodied in the president's position.) At the same time, it can be said that all decision criteria are ultimately matters of agreement among relevant individuals. The key to the legitimacy of any criterion, including the public interest, is not whether it is subjective but whether all those who have a stake in the matter at hand have had the opportunity to share in defining it.

Although we feel that a commitment to a public interest viewed as an ideal, a process, and a habit of mind is the soundest ground for the concept, we would not preclude others. For example, the search in a positivist tradition for the specific content of the public interest has blinded us to another possible approach regarding its nature. It can be argued that we have already learned, believe, and know a good deal about what the public interest is *not*. Defining something negatively may be unsettling for those of us educated in contemporary social science, but it is commonplace in our everyday lives and in such diverse fields as theology and developmental psychology. In theology, for example, the transcendent is often undefinable and is therefore discussed in terms of what it is not. And in what may be a meaningful analog for The Public Administration and the public interest, Rollo May suggests that the human capacity to say and mean "no" is the most significant first statement of self-discovery — that is, knowing what we are not must, of necessity, occur well before knowing what we are.[4] Thus although we ought to continue to define the public interest in terms of a process, the pursuit of a positive but ever-problematic public interest could conceivably begin by explicating it negatively. We know, for example, that racism is not in the public interest. We may well debate what constitutes a manifestation of racism, but even on that issue we already have considerable definition in statutes, administrative regulations, and court interpretations. We probably have even more consensus on what constitutes racism than we realize; it is simply not well explicated. Starting with the negative as a means of explicating the public interest may yield more insight than a positivist approach has admitted thus far.

In speaking about The Public Administration's distinctive relationship to the "public interest" we thus wish to remain open to the idea that its content, however elusive and problematic, might yet to some degree be definable. But more important we think is the point that although the content of the public interest remains problematic, when an institutionalized tradition and support system exist to nurture a process *emphasizing* the relatively comprehensive, long-term, deliberative, and informed efforts essential *to the search for* the public interest, the chances increase that action will follow in accord with these values. Whatever the weaknesses of The Public Administration, it provides more of an institutionalized tradition of this kind than other elements of society or other actors in the political process, certainly more than political parties, interest groups, or mass media. Surely The Public Administration does not "know" the content of the public interest; but it is in a relatively good position to nurture the kind of process essential for its ongoing pursuit, particularly when it takes the enlarged view of the process that encompasses efforts to render faithful interpretations of the interests of all relevant stakeholders, including citizens at large.

The practical and beneficial consequence for The Public Administration of accepting the public interest as ever problematic may be a perspective that fosters: (1) tentative steps and experimental action rather than our typical "solutions" for this or "wars" on that; (2) curiosity and dialogue about ends as well as means; (3) individuals and institutions that "learn" as well as respond; (4) humility and skepticism about "grand designs"; (5) greater awareness of the unique responsibility and potential contribution of each individual to a national dialogue about the public interest; and (6) a greater attentiveness to the words of public discourse.[5]

Recognition of the distinctive character of The Public Administration can also be greatly enhanced if its academic community comes to a new and important point of resolution and clarity in the venerable question of whether or not there is a politics-administration dichotomy. First we must acknowledge that public administration theory detoured sharply into an intellectual cul-de-sac when some of us followed Herbert Simon's attempt to establish a fact-value dichotomy. We also erred in following too closely the organizational sociologists in their narrower quest to understand complex organizations. Both efforts led us astray from the important debate over a politics-administration dichotomy that had been carried on by Wilson, Goodnow, Gaus, White, Appleby, Waldo, and others. Our temporary obsession with behavioralism and our attempts to stay in step with political science, which was in the heat of its own behavioral fad, delayed moving on to a clearer resolution of the politics-administration dichotomy. Organizational sociology and business administration were never interested in questions of governance, and political science drifted farther and farther from such concerns and pulled public administration with it.

The path to a point of clarity on the dichotomy rests on grasping that the distinction between the two phenomena must be understood on three different levels. First we need to recognize that at the highest level, speaking descriptively and conceptually, there is no dichotomy. Public administration at this level of abstraction is an integral part of the governance and political processes. We need to comprehend this point as the beginning of our understanding of The Public Administration's role in the political system and the governance process. But in establishing that point over several decades, we have lost sight of the fact that at a second level of meaning (again speaking descriptively), at a less abstract level of behavior and action, there is, and always has been, if not a dichotomy, at least a considerable distinction. Persons in the governance and political processes seek to make and maintain a distinction between roles, behavior, situations, and phenomena that are political and those that are administrative. Sometimes the distinction is made self-servingly or even cynically; but it is made nonetheless. To ignore it is to ignore behavioral and empirical reality, and to do that is to thwart description and understanding of the behavioral phenomena we label public administration.

Finally, at a third level of meaning, if we speak prescriptively and normatively to those persons involved in ruling and governing, we feel we should acknowledge, elucidate, and extend the distinction between politics and administration. We need to help clarify and nurture the distinction between political and administrative roles and better understand and elaborate upon the distinction between ruling and governing. That distinction, at this third level of meaning, is crucial if The Public Administration is to be accepted, not least by the public at large, as a legitimate and valued part of the political process in general and the governance process more particularly.

The emergence of judges and courts as legitimate and valued actors and institutions in the governance process ("of" but not "in" politics) can serve as an analog. In the evolution of the English political system judges began as agents of the king, traveling the realm settling disputes in his name. Their work might best be looked upon as an early form of nation building. Their reputation for fairness fixed in the public mind a well-founded belief in the superiority of royal justice over the justice administered in the courts of the barons. These royal judges developed the common law — a law that was common throughout the realm and of a higher quality than the particularistic law of the feudal manors. Eventually, however, these royal officers developed distinctive symbols, ritual, language, a way of reasoning, and a claim to expertise and legitimacy that gave them a stature and role distinct from the king's — one that would lead them to use the law and their claim to be its legitimate interpreters to stand in opposition (but a loyal opposition) to the king. This development was taken even further on this side of the Atlantic when Chief Justice Marshall's adroit handling of *Marbury* v. *Madison* established the basis of the Supreme Court's claim to judicial review of the constitutionality of acts of Congress.

Like the judicial system, *The Public Administration needs to assert, but also to be granted, its propriety and legitimacy as an institution. It should assert the value of the Agency Perspective in effective functioning of the political system, the value and legitimacy of the Public Administrator as an actor in the governing process, and the distinctiveness and worth of his or her role — competence directed to the maintenance of: the Agency Perspective, the broadest possible understanding of public interest, and the constitutional governance process.* If this is done, and done far more successfully than it has been to date, it is conceivable that civilian Public Administrators, like judges before them or like their military colleagues today, could question a directive of their political superiors and have the question regarded as a sober second thought rather than as an act of bureaucratic sabotage. When that can happen The Public Administration, the Public Administrator, and our political system will have come of age. It may be, however, that just as the judicial agents of the king developed their reputation by going out among the people and visibly demonstrated the superiority of their practice, The Public Administration's assertion of legitimacy will need to be founded on more direct linkages with the people, in order to win their trust.

The Public Administration and Capitalism

In *The Administrative State*, Dwight Waldo questioned whether the rationalistic mentality reflected in the literature of public administration to that point could sufficiently comprehend what he called the "imponderable emotional substructure" of society. His point seems to have been that this aspect of social life had to be adequately understood if general social health were to be ensured. We wish to address this question in its current form in the United States, though we feel that our suggestion might have more general implications.

In our view social health, as with individual health, depends critically upon the existence of a reflexive relationship between the emotional substructure or unconscious and the conscious side of the human process. This reflexive relationship requires on the one hand a relative openness to the designs of the unconscious that emerge in ambition, pursuit of personal agendas, risk, and adventure. On the other hand, it also requires that these designs of the unconscious be juxtaposed with collective needs and concerns and with needs for introspection, judgment, and moral reasoning applied to matters affecting others beyond the expression and gratification of selfish impulse. In the case of the United States, it seems that capitalism as an institutional form has well provided for one half of the reflexivity equation. The genius of the market is that it can so quickly and easily give expression to emergent needs, tendencies, and tastes that are constantly forming and seeking vent in the collective unconscious. It is this aspect of capitalism that leads advocates of laissez-faire to equate (and to some degree correctly so) capitalism with freedom. In this sense at least, suppression of the emotional substructure is hardly a problem in capitalist society. Growth and development, stemming from unconscious impulses whether economic, social, or psychological, can take place relatively unimpeded for most of our people with the exception perhaps of a disturbingly persistent "underclass."

But capitalism has been notably less successful in providing the other side of the reflexivity equation. The marketplace can so facilitate the expression of the unconscious or emotional substructure that it can overwhelm the conscious side of society. As wants are expressed and satisfied with increasing speed and facility, a point can be reached where new wants are created by the process itself. Gratification divorced from content and substance becomes the motivating orientation of individuals and eventually of society itself. When this happens, societal bearings are lost, points of reference, both moral and practical, become obscure, and public standards that are essential for the exercise of collective human discretion and judgment fail us. Hence, the market is a necessary but insufficient device for maintaining our social well-being. Public authority, expressed through stable institutions of the Public Administration, is essential as a cooling, containing, and directing foil to the capitalist marketplace. Such institutions, indeed, must represent the collective consciousness of our society and serve as the vehicle for our efforts to bring to bear knowledge, reason, and moral judgment on both our problems and the design of our future. Capitalism in our case has been helpful in releasing the energy required to move our societal ship. It cannot by itself, however, give it adequate navigation. We must look to The Public Administration, under the captaincy of our political institutions, for this.

The Public Administration and the Constitution

Our political rhetoric and symbols are badly out of synchronization with our "enacted constitution" or at least with a Federalist interpretation of it. For that interpretation encouraged and anticipated The Public Administration. Unfortunately existing public administration theory is distressingly weak on this point and members of The Public Administration have themselves forgotten or failed to grasp it. Instead they have sought simply to emphasize their nonpartisan instrumentalism and to emulate management practices of business. Valuable though a claim of nonpartisan instrumentalism was in the emergence of The Public Administration at the turn of the century, it is neither well grounded in the Constitution nor adequate to the role demands of the late twentieth century. The Constitution to some extent explicitly and to a greater extent implicitly and through historic practice has assigned a more demanding and significant role to The Public Administration. We have all known since our first civics class that our Constitution is designed to preserve freedom by dividing power, but we do not always connect that profound truth with our circumstances as public administrators. It means, of course, that in the never-ending battle between the chief executive, the legislature, and the courts, The Public Administration is a "free-fire zone" and that the Public Administrators serve as targets of opportunity for the combatants.

When we assert that the Constitution, or at least a Federalist interpretation of it, anticipated The Public Administration, do we mean that the framers thought of it in the bleak metaphors of war used above? Assuredly not. With the possible exception of Hamilton at his most prescient, they did not foresee The Public Administration of today anymore than they could have foreseen the myriad changes in other institutions that have come to pass. But the history of the earliest days of the Republic (and indeed the actions of some of the framers themselves) show that as soon as the constitutional drama began to unfold, the Public Administrators were the persons in no-man's land who were left with ambiguities and a discretion that was viewed, on the one hand, as a threat to them (and to others) and, on the other, as a challenging opportunity to keep the constitutional process from becoming a stalemate in which the public interest would be the ultimate casualty.

In dealing with its constitutionally derived ambiguity and discretion The Public Administration must always act within the constraints imposed by its origin in covenant, a covenant manifested in the Constitution, the Civil Service Reform tradition, and historic experience. The word covenant has sacral overtones that are not altogether inappropriate for our purposes. But its secular usage preserves its fundamental sense of a solemn agreement on obligations between parties, and that would seem to capture what The Public Administration was, is, and ought to be: a solemn agreement between the Public Administrator and the citizens he or she serves; an agreement to serve the public with competence directed toward the public interest and the maintenance of a democratic process of governance; competence constrained by the vitality of the constitutional heritage, the law, and our common history as a people. The Public Administration therefore should look to the past as prologue to the great public dialogue that inspirits a free society. The Constitution should thus be viewed not as "The Word" but as "The Living Word."

The Public Administration should be neither monolithic nor homogeneous. It must assume a rich diversity of perspectives born of differentiation and specialization and ought to welcome constructive criticism from within and without. Differing perspectives ought to be granted a legitimacy, that is, they ought not to be judged as *ipso facto* self-serving, but as a part of the constitutional heritage of robust public dialogue. In this respect the Public Administration is an analog to the pluralism of the larger political process with all the attendant assets and liabilities plus one: the opportunity and the moral obligation to strive explicitly to achieve the broadest possible public interest, something theories of pluralism trust to an invisible hand. Thus the conflict among the differing perspectives of The Public Administration is a valuable part of the creative tension so essential to a healthy American dialogue.

If The Public Administration asserts and accepts its moral authority and rightful claim to be a constitutionally legitimate participant in the governance process, it can contribute to the correction of a major defect in the Constitution: its unsatisfactory resolution of the problem of representation. This problem was the centerpiece of George Mason's brilliant argument against ratification and was a source of embarrassment to such staunch Federalists as Washington and Hamilton. Both friends and foes of the Constitution wondered how the 65 members of the House would represent more than 3 million people. Today we ask how 435 members can represent a nation of more than 246 million people. Pluralist theory and the bureaucratic-politics school of thought have tried to suggest that the competition of interest groups is the best assurance of representation of all the people and that the public interest emerges as the vector sum of all interest group pressures. Although such a claim is not without merit, it has never been convincingly demonstrated and has been subjected to devastating criticism. It remains all too painfully clear that not all citizens and interests are represented by interest groups.

In light of this constitutional defect, The Public Administration as an institution of government has as valid a claim to being representative of the people in both a sociological and functional sense as a federal judge appointed for life, a freshman congressman narrowly elected by a small percentage of the citizens in southeast Nebraska or a senator from Rhode Island. For that matter The

Public Administration may be as representative of the people as a whole as a president elected by a coalition of voting blocs and interest groups claiming victory based on less than 51 percent of the popular vote and 29.9 percent of the eligible voters, which in turn is approximately 19 percent of the total populace. Political commentators have erred in looking for representation from elected officials alone.

It is time for us to advance the proposition that the popular will does not reside solely in elected officials but in a constitutional order that envisions a remarkable variety of legitimate titles to participate in governance. The Public Administration, created by statutes based on this constitutional order, holds one of these titles. Its role, therefore, is not to cower before a sovereign legislative assembly or a sovereign elected executive. Our tradition and our constitution know no such sovereign. Rather the task of The Public Administration is to share in governing wisely and well the *constitutional order* that the framers of the Constitution intended as an expression of the will of the people who alone are sovereign.

The Public Administration and the Public Administrator

We have spoken at length of The Public Administration—we now wish to speak more specifically of how it relates to our ideas about the Public Administrator.

As a critical first point, we need to remind ourselves that the Public Administrator takes an oath to uphold the Constitution of the United States—not the whims of the powerful. This oath initiates administrators into a community created by that Constitution and obliges them to know and support constitutional principles that affect their official spheres of public service. When law empowers rather than commands, that is, when it confers discretion upon administrators instead of issuing specific orders to them, the administrators' oath obliges them to exercise their discretion in a manner that is informed and guided by broad constitutional values as well as more immediate, short-term considerations.

Much has been said in recent years on the development of professionalism in the public administration and its meaning. What is important from the point of view of this essay is not so much whether the Public Administrator is or is not a member of a profession, or whether he or she has achieved a right to claim professional status. Rather, what is important is that the Public Administrator acts in a professional manner in the sense of a concern for the development of competence and standards, an orientation toward service, and a set of values that regards the broadest possible definition of the public interest as a real although problematic trust, and, above all, which holds the maintenance of the constitutional order as a fundamental duty. To act in a professional manner, for the Public Administrator, is to use expertise and competence toward these ends.

The more significant perspective on professionalism is thus to see the Public Administrator *as a* trustee *and a legitimate and significant participant in the governance process of society.*

As a trustee the Public Administrator must strive to look beyond both the political pressures of the day and a degrading self-image of mere instrumentalism. He or she should strive for a role that is "critically conscious": purposive in pursuit of the public interest and in maintaining the democratic governance process but disciplined by the rule of law and constitutional tradition of limited government; and conscious of the need at times to prudently accommodate powerful forces that may represent a temporary retreat from, or pause in, pursuit of the broadest possible definition of the public interest. Progress toward both the agency perspective and the broader public interest may not always be steady or forward.

The Public Administrator, however, must be steadfast and persistent, heeding Hamlet's advice to "play to the judicious few," rather than the vociferous many or the powerful few, to play to the long-term public interest rather than the most immediate and powerful pressures. And we need to remind ourselves that the "judicious few" need not be a small, closed, elite group. It has no preordained limits to its size. It is after all, an article of democratic faith — or at least an object of democratic hope — that the judicious few might become the judicious many. It is the duty of the Public Administrator to work to expand the ranks of the judicious few — by stimulating reasoned debate on the meaning of the public interest and by taking advantage of opportunities to facilitate substantive involvement by citizens in the governance process. The judicious few will only become the judicious many when more of the people develop the practical wisdom that is the essence of politics. This wisdom is best learned in the course of public-sphere activity itself. As the success of numerous publicly funded programs run by citizens attests, the administrative state is neither too big nor too complex for meaningful citizen involvement.

In large measure, it is the bureaucrat's faith in technical expertise and in the possibility of comprehensive solutions that makes him or her hesitant to turn to citizens. But the uncertainty and complexity of modern-day governance demand not comprehensiveness but tentative strategies, social interaction, and frequent feedback and adjustment. From this perspective, the postindustrial administrative state is *not only inconsistent* with involvement by citizens, *but it positively discourages it.*

Much has also been written about making the bureaucrat responsive and responsible. The Public Administrator must indeed act responsibly, and this means being responsive to constitutionally and legally valid orders that are specific. Responsiveness also means being attuned to the clientele that are served. The responsiveness of the Public Administrator to either elected officials or clients should not, however, be "seismographic" nor that of a "hired lackey," nor even that of a "faithful servant," for it must be more in order to be responsible in the highest sense of that word. Nor should it be the responsiveness of an artful dodger working between and among the forces resulting from interest group pressures, for it must be more than that. Rather the Public Administrator can only be responsible if his or her responsiveness is that of a trustee of that special perspective shaped by the agency's point of view, a public interest perspective and fidelity to the constitutional heritage.

This means that the responsiveness called for is one that conforms to the Public Administrator's ultimate responsibility, which like that of all governmental officers is to the constitutional order and the democratic governance process. This means that in their role as trustees the Public Administrators may have to incline their agencies' responsiveness toward the president at one point and toward Congress at another, or at other times toward the courts or interest groups that are likely to serve the long-term public interest as the agency sees it. Less often, it may mean that the Public Administrators must act on behalf of a public interest defined more broadly than the Agency Perspective, or on rare occasions they may have to act on behalf of the maintenance of the democratic governance process. This means, in essence, that the Public Administrators may have to play the role of balance wheel in the constitutional order, using their statutory powers and professional expertise to favor whichever participant in the constitutional process needs their help at a given time in history to preserve the purposes of the Constitutions itself.

Inevitably some will view The Public Administration merely as a means to status and power and some will pervert their duty into a sinecure. In spite of the inevitable human frailties of a few, despite its erosion by careerism and the fragmenting pressures of specialization, and in spite of its current detractors, The Public Administration has been, and remains, a vocation given meaning in the service of a "cause." In the everyday words of public administration, this cause is characterized as being a "civil servant," "career executive," or "public employee." With a self-conscious shift in the American dialogue we feel that the sense of a calling will grow and flourish in The Public Administration and Public Administrators as never before — more will live "for" it as a "cause" and fewer "off" it from less noble impulses.

Certainly the founders of the Republic viewed public service as a "calling" and as a trusteeship; so did the idealistic reformers who came later in our history: the Populists, the Progressives, and the New Dealers. If we have not yet lost that vision, it is certainly in grave peril.

Much of our loss of transcendent vision has been brought on by our concern for professional status. We have paid a heavy price for adopting too slavishly the trappings of science believed essential to a claim of expertise. A focus on the *means* of governance — as in management science, systems analysis, PPBS, and program evaluation — is important to a claim of expertise. But when we focus on these means to the exclusion of claims of transcendent purposes and moral commitment to community building, or of enhancement of freedom and dignity and the improvement of the quality of citizens' lives, we erode the legitimacy of The Public Administration and reduce the Public Administrator to just one more profession or interest group. We have let our vision slip from transcendent purposes and moral commitment to a narrow focus on the application of "value neutral" instrumentalism. It has cost us and the nation dearly.

The code of behavior of the Public Administrator must be broadened to include approaches to practice that will support this transcendent commitment. First, as we have said, administrators must seek to expand opportunities for direct citizen involvement in governance, so that citizens develop the practical wisdom that is the ultimate basis of trust in administrative good faith. Also, administrators must develop personal reflexivity, that is, consciousness of their own values and assumptions and how they affect daily decision making. Such consciousness will enable them to become critical of established institutional practices that inhibit the expansion of freedom and justice, and work toward change where it is possible. Finally, administrators, must be able to give reasons for what they do. Though established practices may frequently preclude direct dialogue with relevant stakeholders, it is the administrator's responsibility to consider who all these stakeholders may be, what their concerns are, and what reasons he or she would give for a decisive action if dialogue were possible.

The Public Administrator must assume that the human condition can be improved though never perfected. He or she should work for the amelioration of societal problems without expecting quick, cheap, or permanent solutions. The Public Administrator should work with the knowledge that some problems can best be alleviated by outcomes of the market or the use of marketlike devices whereas others can best be met by some form of state intervention. Although Public Administrators must be responsive to ideological or party-based views of elected officials on social problems, they must also provide them with sound analysis and feasible options based on their special competence. The Public Administrator should thus be both an analyst and an educator but *not* a philosopher-king or mandarin. He or she must work for the long-term education of elected officials, other actors in the governance process, and citizens at large on matters of public interest, and assume that this will often be a thankless and arduous task.

The Public Administrator should be committed to (1) praxis, critically conscious action or pursuit of goals; and (2) reflectiveness, thoughtful and critical assessment of action taken, in order to learn from experience. Both praxis and reflectiveness are essential to a role that directs its competence toward the kind of transcendent purposes we have outlined. They are also essential to more specific, day-to-day goals of serving the public with grace and dignity, of respecting the public while at the same time respecting one's self and one's peers.

Conclusion

Whether or not the Public Administrator and The Public Administration are living up to the prescriptive ideals we have outlined is a question that must be repeatedly asked and answered as honestly as possible. There are inherent problems and pathologies that we deny or ignore at our peril. Thus, those of us in the academic community associated with The Public Administration have a special task that goes beyond producing the necessary skills and expertise in new members or even helping instill the transcendent purpose. It is the special task of constructive and friendly criticism. It requires caring enough to be critical in a constructive way.

We also have a special responsibility to play a leading role in refocusing the American dialogue, a duty all too neglected of late by most of us. Accordingly we hope this paper will serve in a small way to initiate the desperately needed refocus of the American dialogue, a change essential if we are successfully to conclude Egger's fourth revolution to redefine equity and justice. Seeking to redefine equity and justice in a system that remains in large part capitalistic, which derives much of its momentum from that part, and which has considerable socioeconomic differentiation as both a consequence and catalyst, will be as great a challenge as any democratic society has ever faced. If we are to have any chance of meeting that challenge, our political dialogue must shift from "whether" there ought to be a public administration to what the role of The Public Administration and the Public Administrator should be in the governance of the Republic — as it enters its third and perhaps most perilous century.

Notes

1. The co-authors of this paper bear equal responsibility for the ideas it contains and with one exception are listed alphabetically. Wamsley's name appears first simply because he was assigned the role of faithful scribe.

Camilla Stivers was not one of the authors of theory in the original manuscript that received considerable circulation. As one of our students she criticized the original manuscript because we failed to consider the crucial role citizens should play in The Public Administration and in the shift of our political dialogue. The list of persons whose ideas we have drawn upon is too long to present here, but surely it would begin and end with the names of Dwight Waldo and Norton Long. We decided the best way to deal with the criticism was to include her as co-author and to become her students in this matter.

We wish to thank our many colleagues who provided criticism and encouragement. Particularly helpful were the comments of Phillip Cooper, Bayard Catron, Linda Wolf, Fred Thayer, Philip Schorr, and Eugene Lewis. The faults that remain belong to us; they did all they could to save us. Obviously we are drawing on the thoughts of many other persons in the intellectual community associated with public administration. With a few exceptions noted below, however, we have chosen not to use notes. We do not intend this to be an academic paper but a statement (a manifesto?) that we hope will encourage dialogue.

2. Wilson, Woodrow. "The study of Public Administration," *Political Science Quarterly* 56 (June 1887).

3. We are especially indebted to Professor Bayard Catron for this point. Indeed, most of the words of the foregoing three sentences are his. We could do little to improve on them. Source: correspondence with the authors.

4. Our thanks to Linda Wolf for this point. Correspondence with the authors.

5. Ibid.

2. The Constitutional Case for Public Administration

JOHN A. ROHR

> Men are not corrupted by the exercise of power or debased by the habit of obedience, but by the exercise of power which they believe to be illegitimate, and by obedience to a rule which they consider to be usurped and oppressive.
>
> ALEXIS DE TOCQUEVILLE

The purpose of this chapter is to elaborate and support the constitutional considerations touched upon in the Blacksburg Manifesto. More specifically, I intend to defend on constitutional grounds the Manifesto's claim that The Public Administration should take its rightful place in the governance of the Republic. I shall do this in four steps: (1) a brief introductory examination of the role of administration envisioned in *The Federalist Papers*; (2) an extended argument that shows how certain prominent features of the modern administrative state fulfill the political vision of the framers of the Constitution; (3) a response to the objection that administrators cannot share in governance legitimately because they are not elected; and (4) a statement of a constitutional theory of Public Administration derived from the three previous considerations.

I. Administration in *The Federalist Papers*

It has often been observed that the word *administration* does not appear in the Constitution of the United States. From this correct observation there often follows the erroneous conclusion that the framers of the Constitution did not care about administrative institutions. If *The Federalist Papers* are taken as a reliable guide to the thinking of the framers of the Constitution, sound public administration must be looked upon as one of their most serious concerns. *Administration* is one of the few words "Publius," the pseudonymous author of

The Federalist Papers, bothers to define.[1] Indeed, he distinguishes two meanings of the word to enable the careful reader to follow his extensive treatment of this topic in numbers 68-77 of the *The Federalist Papers*. These ten essays are often looked upon as the first and perhaps the best treatise ever written on public administration. The word *administration* and its cognates appear 124 times throughout *The Federalist Papers*; more frequently than either "Congress," "President," or "Supreme Court."[2]

An important characteristic of Publius's treatment of administration is his effort to weave administrative considerations into the fabric of his argument in defense of the Constitution. For example, the first argument he gives to defend the important constitutional principle that enables the president to be reelected is that it will enhance the likelihood of "permanence in a wise system of administration."[3] He recognizes that incoming presidents will be likely "to promote a change of men to fill the subordinate stations."[4]

This prospect does not please Publius. Frequent changes in presidential subordinates "could not fail to occasion a disgraceful and ruinous mutability in the administration of the government."[5] Hence, the Constitution wisely permits the president to be reelected indefinitely and thereby reduces the likelihood of frequent changes in high-ranking presidential subordinates.

When a new president does come into office, Publius hopes the Senate will exercise some control over the president's desire to being men of his own choosing into the highest positions. Although the first Congress decided otherwise, Publius thought the Senate's concurrence would be necessary before the president could remove a subordinate from office. He applauded this arrangement as one way to safeguard "the value of a steady administration."[6] Contrary to the spirit of today's constitutional practice that encourages the president to appoint his own "team," Publius condemns an executive who appoints those "whose chief merit is their implicit devotion to his will."[7] Sound public administration requires that a chief executive appoint or retain in high office "men who are best qualified for them."[8] Publius supports a senatorial check on the president's removal power because he thinks this will enhance administrative stability.

Publius's interest in administration is not confined to such structural matters as duration in office. He sees in administration a dynamic force destined to play a vital role in the regime of liberty he envisions. Publius looked upon sound public administration as the way to attract popular support away from the state governments and toward the new federal government.

This consideration had to be advanced cautiously because Publius's Anti-Federalist adversaries would pounce upon any suggestion that ratification of the Constitution signals the demise of state governments. Publius is a model of circumspection when he discusses the capacity of administration to wean public affection away from the traditional state loyalties to the advantage of the new government.

Despite this caution, however, his point is quite clear to the careful reader. In *Federalist 17* Publius gives his first hint on the important role he assigns to administration. The context involved his reply to the charge that the proposed federal government would eventually overwhelm the states. He dismisses this fear by arguing that the states will always enjoy greater popular support than the federal government because of the day-to-day interaction between the people and their state governments. He hedges this soothing assurance, however, with the caveat that the states will lose their advantage if it should turn out that the federal government provides "a much better administration."[9]

The significance of Publius's caveat emerges in *Federalist 27* where he predicts that the federal government will be better administered than the states and that this is one very important reason why the new Constitution should be approved. Prudently, he makes no mention of his earlier argument that superior federal administration is the only way in which popular esteem for the states might be weakened to the advantage of the new government.

The mask is dropped in *Federalist 46* where Publius boldly asserts that if the people should ever "become more partial to the Federal than to the state governments, the change can only result . . . from manifest and irresistible proofs of a better administration."[10] To this he adds the normative consideration that this is only right because the people "ought not surely to be precluded from giving most of their confidence where they may discover it to be most due."[11]

The argument culminates in *Federalist 68* where the prosaic Publius turns to poetry to buttress his case for the importance of administration in the new government. Wisely, he rejects as "political heresy" the couplet from Alexander Pope:

For forms of government let fools contest —
That which is best administered is best.

Publius will not allow his esteem for administration to trump his commitment to republican principles. Administration is instrumental for higher political ends such as winning popular support for the new government. He admits, however, that Pope's heresy, like all heresies, is but a distortion of the truth. "We can safely pronounce that the true test of a good government is its aptitude and tendency to produce a good administration."[12] Publius, the first and most authoritative commentator on the Constitution, unequivocally attests to the importance of administration in the Constitution he supports.

II. The Intent of the Framers

The previous section presented a brief statement on the importance of public administration in *The Federalist Papers*. In the present section I shall make a more elaborate and detailed argument to defend the constitutional legitimacy of the contemporary administrative state. In using the word *legitimacy*, I do not mean mere legality. Administrative institutions are quite legal, but so are the American Nazi Party, the Flat Earth Society, and *Hustler* magazine. By legitimacy I mean more than a grudging acceptance of the inevitable. To me the word suggests at least confidence and respect and at times even warmth and affection. Publius was speaking the language of legitimacy when he noted in *Federalist 27* that a well-administered government would win the affection of the people.

In American politics questions of legitimacy frequently lead to discussions of the principles of the "founding fathers" of the Republic. Our public dialogue often judges policies, practices, and institutions in terms of their fidelity to "the intent of the framers." I shall follow this well-trod path in my effort to legitimate administrative institutions in terms of constitutional principle.

To undertake this task we must examine the Constitution rather than simply revere it. We shall examine it less as the product of the framers' will than as a centerpiece of the great public argument of 1787-1788. Our task is to see how the administrative state can fit into American political orthodoxy — an orthodoxy that is found not in a set of approved propositions but in the limits of the public argument itself.

In emphasizing the public argument of 1787-1788, careful attention must be given to the vanquished Anti-Federalists as important participants in the great debate. They lost the argument, but in so doing they pointed to the glaring weaknesses in the Constitution — some of which are still with us today. It is for this reason that Herbert Storing, the leading Anti-Federalist scholar, insisted that the Anti-Federalists be numbered among the founding fathers of the Republic. He candidly acknowledged that they lost the ratification debate because their arguments were not as strong as those of their Federalist opponents.[13] Nevertheless, their searching criticism of the Constitution has taught us the invaluable lesson of where to look for likely shortcomings in the regime envisioned by the triumphant Federalists. They structured subsequent constitutional debate.

When we return to the founding fathers we find not dogma but arguments. In stressing the *argument* of the founding rather than its outcome, I follow Hannah Arendt's observation on American politics that more fundamental than the written Constitution itself is the "principle of mutual promise and common deliberation" that made the Constitution possible.[14]

Specifically, three points will be made concerning the administrative state and the Constitution: (1) that administrative institutions are not inconsistent with the constitutional principle of separation of powers; (2) that the higher reaches of the career civil service fulfill the framers' original intent for the Senate; (3) that the entire career civil service provides a remedy for a serious defect in the Constitution — the inadequate representation that so distressed the Anti-Federalists of 1787-1788. Thus I shall argue that the administrative state is consistent with the Constitution, fulfills its design, and heals a longstanding, major defect.

Separation of Powers

> To what purpose separate the executive or the judiciary, from the legislative, if both the executive and the judiciary are so construed as to be at the absolute devotion of the legislative? Such a separation must be merely nominal and incapable of producing the ends for which it was established. It is one thing to be subordinate to the laws and another to be dependent on the legislative body. The first comports with, the last violates, the fundamental principles of good government; and whatever may be the forms of the Constitution, unites all power in the same hands. (*Federalist 71*)

One of the earliest criticisms of the governmental institution considered by some as the harbinger of the administrative state — the independent regulatory commission — was that it violates the principle of separation of powers. Interestingly, Publius had to answer a similar attack against the Constitution itself: "One of the principal objections inculcated by the more respectable adversaries to the Constitution, is its supposed violation of the political maxim, that the legislative, executive, and judiciary departments ought to be separate and distinct."[15] Our problem in defending the blending of powers in administrative institutions is much easier than Madison's. We need only show that such blending is not contrary to the spirit or letter of the Constitution, whereas Madison had the more fundamental task of defending the blending in the Constitution itself. Our task is simply discharged by pointing to the Senate as a body that exercises powers that are (1) legislative (when it joins the House of Representatives in approving a bill); (2) executive (when it "advises and consents" to a treaty or to appointments of high-ranking federal officials); and (3) judicial (when it sits as a court to try impeachments).

The blending of powers in the Senate was a cause of considerable concern to the Anti-Federalists.[16] History has taught us to look upon the Senate as almost exclusively a legislative body. As we shall see below, this was not what the framers had in mind. The development of the executive agreement in foreign affairs and the merit system in personnel management have considerably reduced the significance of the Senate's constitutional powers over treaties and appointments. Impeachments have been so infrequent that we hardly ever think of the Senate as a judicial body. The judicial character of the Senate is dramatically clear, however, in the provision in Article I that the chief justice will preside over the Senate when it tries a presidential impeachment.[17] Since, fortunately, this has happened only once in our history, the awesome scene of a chief justice presiding over a Senate that can remove a president from office is more a majestic museum piece than an operating principle of government.

For the framers, however, this was not the case. Impeachment was discussed in remarkable detail at the Philadelphia Convention and during the ratification debate. It is surprising to note that the impeachment power was a central consideration in the creation of the electoral college. Throughout the Convention, the method of selecting the president was a matter of stormy controversy.

At various times the Senate or the Congress as a whole were considered among the possible candidates for this responsibility.[18] Toward the end of the Convention, a committee report came forward with what we know today as the electoral college. When Edmund Randolph and Charles Pinckney asked "for a particular explanation and discussion of the reasons for changing the mode of electing the Executive," Gouverneur Morris responded with an account worthy of the complexity of the college itself.[19] He began by stating the committee's reasons for deciding that the Senate was the proper institution to try causes of presidential impeachment. This power could not be given to the Supreme Court because a president removed from office might still be tried in the federal courts for the offense that led to his removal. Since the Senate would try the impeachments, the House should bring them. Since, then, both houses of Congress would be involved in the removal of the president, neither should be involved in selecting him. Here the Convention's reasoning seems to have been that a body that had chosen an officer would be likely to consider impeachment and conviction an adverse reflection on its earlier judgment. Hence, the committee recommended that a body of special electors (the electoral college as we have come to call it) should select the president. Only if this body failed to agree upon one person should the legislature — whose houses impeach and try presidents — be permitted to enter the presidential selection process.

I mention this arcane point only to support my contention that the judicial power of the Senate was not a bizarre aberration, but an aspect of constitution making that was solidly integrated into the overall design of the document. The framers found it easier to achieve consensus on how to get rid of a President than on how to select one.

The salience of the impeachment power in the constitutional design provides *textual* evidence that the framers were quite willing to place all three powers of government in one institution when circumstances so required. Hence any argument that administrative agencies act in a constitutionally suspect manner simply because they exercise two or even all three governmental powers can be refuted from the text of the Constitution itself.[20]

The separation-of-powers attack on administrative agencies is usually based on an excessively rigid interpretation of this venerable doctrine. One careful student of the history of separation of powers has described the "pure position" as separation of functions, exercised by separate organs of government, with no overlap.[21] This is helpful as an ideal type, but it is far removed from the understanding of separation of powers that was common among the framers. Madison's position is instructive. He acknowledges the importance of the principle of separation of powers when he allows that "the accumulation of all powers legislative, executive, and judiciary in the same hands . . . may justly be pronounced the very definition of tyranny."[22] After acknowledging "the celebrated Montesquieu" as "the oracle who is always consulted and cited on this subject," Madison maintains that Montesquieu "did not mean that these departments ought to have no *partial agency* in, or control over, the acts of each other." He meant, "no more than this, that where the *whole* power of one department is exercised by the same hands which possess the whole power of another department, the fundamental principles of a free constitution are subverted."[23] This is not the place to evaluate Madison's reading of Montesquieu.[24] What is important for our purposes is that no less an authority than James Madison in *The Federalist Papers* subscribes to a remarkably relaxed view of separation of powers. Clearly no administrative agency ever has or ever could function as a "department" that exercises the "whole power" of another department. (By "department" Madison here means the three great constitutional branches of government — not the "executive departments" of Article II.) In effect, Madison has defined any possible violation of separation of powers out of existence for the entire government as well as for any administrative agency we know today. Even Lincoln during the darkest days of the Civil War did not come close to appropriating the "*whole* power" of either Congress or the courts.

In making this point, I do not suggest that Madison is the most reliable guide on the correct understanding of separation of powers. Nor do I suggest that his position is representative of the framers. Certainly he is not alone in his relaxed point of view, but other framers were a bit more moderate. Rufus King and James Wilson, for example, stress the independence of one department from another as the heart of the separation-of-powers doctrine.[25] This follows Madison's position without going to the extreme of saying the principle is breached only when the "*whole power*" of one branch has been taken over by another. Hamilton, too, somewhat uncharacteristically, is less exuberant than his *Federalist* co-author on this point of separation of powers. In *Federalist 66* he gives a subdued summary of Madison's earlier statement.

> The true meaning of this maxim [of separation of powers] has been discussed and ascertained in another place and has been shown to be entirely compatible with a partial intermixture of those departments for special purposes, preserving them in the main distinct and unconnected. This partial intermixture is even in some cases not only proper, but necessary to the mutual defence of the several members of the government against each other.[26]

Madison would agree with Hamilton that a "partial intermixture" of the departments' powers is at times a good thing. Indeed, the main point of *Federalist 48* (written by Madison) is a positive defense of a blending of powers to preserve the principle of separation. It is not enough to rely on "parchment barriers" to keep the great branches independent of one another. The Constitution wisely preserves its intended balance by an elaborate series of "checks" that allow one branch to exercise in part the powers of another — for example, the president's legislative power of a conditioned veto over acts of Congress. Thus for both Hamilton and Madison, a discreet blending of powers is the best way to preserve their sensible and effective separation.

With this relaxed teaching of the framers in mind, we can see how wide of the mark are those formalistic attacks on the administrative state that are aimed at the mere existence of a combination of powers in administrative agencies. The problem is not one of doctrine, but of prudence. A partial blending of powers does not violate separation of powers and, according to Publius, it may at times enhance it.[27]

The Senate

And when I behold the Senate, . . . wielding in the one hand the strong powers of the Executive, and with the other controlling and modifying at pleasure, the movements of the legislature, I must confess that not only my hopes of the beneficial effects of the government are greatly diminished, but that my apprehensions of some fatal catastrophe are highly awakened. (James Monroe)

The previous discussion was intended to show that the blending of powers in administrative agencies is not inconsistent with the principle of separation of powers. The focus of the present section is the Senate. Here I shall escalate my position from the negative statement that the administrative state is not inconsistent with the framers' intent to the positive affirmation that it fulfills their design. I shall do this by examining the sort of institution the participants in the founding debate had in mind when they discussed the merits and defects of the proposed Senate. With allowance in mind for the havoc two hundred years will wreak on anyone's intent, my point in this section is that the function of the higher reaches of today's career civil service is in broad outline a reasonable approximation to what the framers envisioned as the function of the Senate in the proposed regime. This section has two parts. The first maintains that the Senate was intended to be part of an executive establishment and not simply a second house of a national legislature. The second examines certain salient characteristics the proposed Senate was expected to have, which, when combined with its participation in the executive establishment, suggest some striking similarities to today's higher civil service.

Executive Establishment

The first point in establishing the executive character of the Senate is to note that it was not seen by anyone as *simply* a second house of the national legislature. This perception was universal; it was shared by friend and foe alike of the proposed Constitution. Publius is unequivocal on this point.[28] So are the Anti-Federalists. At times they list the legislative function of the Senate as but one of several powers they find objectionable.[29] At other times they use such terms as "veto" and "negative" to describe the Senate's legislative role. This language appears not only in the context of "money bills," which must originate in the House of Representatives, but in general discussions of the Senate's legislative powers as well.[30] Perhaps the clearest Anti-Federalist statement on the nature of the Senate's legislative power appears in the quotation from James Monroe cited at the head of this section. He describes the Senate as "wielding in the one hand, the strong powers of the Executive, and with the other controuling and modifying at pleasure, the movements of the legislature."[31] For Monroe, the House of Representatives is the *real* legislature; the Senate's role is to control and modify it.

This view of the Senate can be found in the language of the framers of the Constitution at Philadelphia. Roger Sherman,[32] Gouverneur Morris,[33] and James Madison,[34] are explicit on this point.[35] The Senate is part of the legislative branch, but the nature of its legislative power is somewhat different from that of the House. Bicameralism did not mean simply that one house would check the other. As Gouverneur Morris put it, the Senate was to be "the checking branch" of the legislature.[36] The reason this function fell to the Senate was because of its executive character. Just as the president, the chief executive officer, had a conditional veto over both houses, so also his executive partner, the Senate, had a more extensive veto over the House of Representatives.

Thus far I have tried to show that the Senate was intended to be something other than merely a second house of a national legislature. Was it also seen as part of an executive establishment? A strong indication that this is the case appears in the development of the text of the Constitution during the Philadelphia Convention. On August 6, the Committee of Detail reported a draft of the Constitution that referred to the Senate "when it shall be acting in a legislative capacity."[37] This clearly implied that legislation was but one of its functions.[38] The same draft included earlier agreements that the Senate should have *exclusive* power over treaties and the appointments of ambassadors and judges of the Supreme Court. When the Senate exercised these powers, the August 6 draft would have exempted it from a prohibition against adjourning "to any other place than that at which the two Houses are sitting."[39] Thus this draft would have allowed the Senate to meet in a place other than its ordinary legislative location to conduct such executive affairs as making treaties and appointing officers. The language of the final version of the Constitution is not explicit on this point, but it is open to this interpretation. The fourth clause of Article I, Section 4 reads: "Neither House, during the Session of Congress, shall, without the Consent of the other, adjourn for more than three days, nor to any other place than that in which the two Houses shall be sitting." The immobility of the two houses applies only when *Congress* is in session. It is possible, of course, for the Senate to be in session without Congress being in session, namely, when the Senate conducts its executive affairs. If such business were to be conducted in a place other than the chamber in which the Senate legislates, its executive character would be dramatically heightened. An early draft of the Constitution made an explicit provision for this possibility and the final version at least implies it. This textual argument is offered to support the point that the executive character of the Senate was not simply an afterthought but was an integral part of the constitutional plan. Indeed, the fact that earlier drafts of the Constitution gave the Senate even more executive power than the final version shows conclusively that these powers were no afterthought. It is not as though the Senate were given a share in the treaty and appointing powers simply to provide a legislative check on the president. It was the other way around. The president was eventually given a share in the Senate's hitherto exclusive power over treaties and the appointments of ambassadors and Supreme Court judges.[40]

A profile of the Senate as an executive establishment emerges with striking clarity in the arguments of the Anti-Federalists. This is true even though the Anti-Federalists differ sharply in what they find offensive about the Senate. One group fears a Senate-presidential cabal. For William Grayson, the senators are the president's "counsellors and partners in crime."[41] "To gain his favor, they will support him" and will unite with the president "to prevent a discovery of his misdeeds."[42] Cato complains that in trying an impeached president the senators "are to determine, as judges, the propriety of the advice they gave him, as senators." They will not "be an impartial judicature." Instead, they will serve as a screen to great public defaulters.[43] Luther Martin[44] and James Monroe[45] voiced similar concerns.

A second group of Anti-Federalists feared the executive powers of the Senate were so great that they would overwhelm the president.[46] The Federal Farmer, for example, feared that "this sexennial senate of 26 members . . . will not, in practice, be found a body to advise, but to order and dictate in fact; and the president will be a mere *primus inter pares*.[47] Centinel sees the Senate as "the great efficient body in this plan of government" with the result that: "The President, who would be a mere pageant of state, unless he coincides with views of the Senate, would either become the head of the aristocratic junto in that body, or its minion."[48] The Anti-Federalist minority at the Pennsylvania Ratifying Convention voiced a similar concern: "The president-general is dangerously connected with the senate; his coincidence with the views of the ruling junto in that body, is made essential to his weight and importance in the government, which will destroy all independency and purity in the executive department."[49]

A third group of Anti-Federalists criticized the Constitution for failing to provide an executive council to the president.[50] The Senate, they maintained, is a poor substitute. At the Virginia Ratifying Convention, George Mason, after noting his fear of Senate-president conspiracies against the people, proposed a remedy: "a constitutional council, to aid the President in the discharge of his office." The Senate should have the power to impeach the president and his council. "Then we should have real responsibility. In the present form, the guilty try themselves. The President is tried by his counsellors."[51]

Mason's position on the executive council issue is important. As a delegate to the Philadelphia Convention, he had originally favored a plural executive. When this measure failed,[52] he took as his backup position an executive council that would not only assist the president but would check him as well.[53] In wanting to put the check *within* the executive branch, Mason hoped to recoup some of his losses from having the plural executive rejected. The idea of a council within the executive branch serving as a check on the president suggests interesting parallels with the contemporary bureaucracy. For the present, however, our main point is that Mason saw the Senate as a close executive partner of the president — "The Constitution has *married* the President and Senate,"[54] he tells us. He objects to the relationship and proposes an executive council in its stead. A similar position is taken by Anti-Federalist Richard Henry Lee in a letter to Governor Randolph[55] and by Samuel Spencer at the North Carolina Ratifying Convention.[56]

From a variety of adherents to the Anti-Federalist persuasion, the image of the Senate as an executive establishment emerges clearly. The Federalists do not contest this point. They grant it. Their counterattack is aimed at Anti-Federalist positions that find the Senate's role in executive matters excessive, unwise, or inappropriate.[57] Thus there was no dispute in 1787-1788 over the *fact* that the Senate was intended to serve as part of the executive. The dispute centered on the propriety of the arrangement.[58]

Attributes of the Senate

The founding argument highlights certain attributes of the Senate. Again, the argument was not so much over what these attributes were but whether they were desirable. The following attributes are important for our purposes:

Duration, Expertise, and Stability. These are actually three attributes, but Publius sees one leading to the other and discusses them all in *Federalist 62*. The six-year term of office will give the Senators the firmness they need to resist "the impulse of sudden and violent passions" by which "factious leaders" might try to induce them to approve "intemperate and pernicious resolutions." The Senate must "possess great firmness and consequently ought to hold its authority by a tenure of considerable duration."[59] The six-year term would also give the senators time to develop the expertise they would need to master the intricacies of public life; especially the complexities of foreign affairs.[60]

When the Anti-Federalists looked at the six-year term, they tended to emphasize the indefinite reeligibility of the senators. This, they feared, would lead to a lifetime in office that would lay the foundation for an eventual American aristocracy. The Anti-Federalists argued that because senators can be chosen again and again by their state legislatures, it is inevitable that they actually will be so chosen. For Centinel, this inevitability would come from "their extensive means of influence."[61] Brutus feared that "it will before long be considered as disgraceful not to be re-elected. It will therefore be considered as a matter of delicacy to the character of the senator not to return him again." Senators would in effect serve during good behavior. They would always be returned "except in cases of gross misconduct."[62]

Melancton Smith, Hamilton's great adversary at the New York Ratifying Convention, conceded the importance of stability in the Senate and agreed that a six-year term was not excessive. Reeligibility was the problem for Smith and, consequently, he proposed an amendment that would enable the state legislatures to recall any senator they had chosen and would prohibit them from selecting any one man to serve for more than six years out of any twelve. This would head off the possibility of the Senate becoming "a fixed and unchangeable body of men."[63]

The Federalists could not deny the possibility that some senators would probably serve for life. The text of the Constitution clearly allows for this. Instead, they spoke warmly of the lifelong tenure of the venerable senators of Sparta and Rome. This was not an embarrassment for the Federalists. At the convention, both Hamilton and Gouverneur Morris had supported a life tenure for senators.[64]

Continuing Body. The Anti-Federalists feared that the Senate would become a continuing body. Section 3 of Article II states that the president "may, on extraordinary occasions, convene both Houses, *or either of them*" (emphasis added). The most obvious situation in which the president would want to convene one house but not the other would be when he wanted the advice and consent of the Senate on a treaty or an appointment. The Anti-Federalists maintained that the "extraordinary occasion" of Section 3 would in practice become quite routine and, as a result, the Senate would be in session permanently.[65] Thus for George Mason, the Senate would be "a constant existing Body almost continually sitting."[66] For Luther Martin, it would be "in great measure, a permanent body, constantly residing at the seat of government."[67] Cato maintained that the powers of the senators were so extensive "that it would be found necessary that they should be constantly sitting."[68]

Personnel Management. The Senate's role in appointments received considerable attention during the founding debate. As we have seen above, earlier drafts of the Constitution had given the Senate exclusive power over the appointments of ambassadors and Supreme Court judges. Thus the framers were quite serious about including the Senate in the appointing power. Indeed, so serious were they that it was not until the penultimate session of the Convention (September 15) that the framers got around to giving Congress the power to vest "the appointment of such inferior officers as they think proper, in the President alone, in the courts of law or in the heads of Departments." Had this clause not been added to the second section of Article II, a literal reading of the Constitution would require senatorial approval for *every* federal appointment.[69]

The Federal Farmer was one of the strongest critics of the Senate's role in appointments. He feared the Senate would not approve legislation vesting the appointing power in department heads but would jealously guard this power for itself. He did not think the Senate itself would constantly be in session, but the demands of its personnel responsibilities would prompt it to select from its members a "council of appointment" which "must very probably sit all, or near all, the year."[70]

The Anti-Federalists tended to emphasize the extensive intervention of the Senate in what we might call today an aspect of personnel management. Hamilton took some trouble to deny this; such senatorial intervention would run counter to his cherished principle of unity within the executive.[71] In his eagerness to downplay the Senate's role in appointments, however, Hamilton proved a poor seer. He noted that the Senate's power to advise and consent referred only to *appointments* — not to nominations.[72] Thus, although the Senate can approve or reject, it cannot choose. Apparently, Hamilton would not have approved of what we have come to know as senatorial courtesy.

There was another matter touching the Senate's power over personnel matters in which history confounded Hamilton's crystal ball. This was the issue of removal from federal office which we mentioned briefly above. Aside from the impeachment clauses, the Constitution is silent on this topic. Hamilton argued in *Federalist 77* that the Senate would have to concur in a presidential decision to remove a federal officer. In making this argument, however, Hamilton compromised his belief in unity in the executive branch; but in this case it was a good bargain. Hamilton's commitment to stability in the public administration triumphed over his belief in unity. Presidents (especially after Washington) might come and go, but the Senate, with its staggered six-year terms, would provide stability. The passage is worth quoting in its entirety:

> It has been mentioned as one of the advantages to be expected from the co-operation of the senate, in the business of appointments, that it would contribute to the stability of the administration. The consent of that body would be necessary to displace as well as to appoint. A change of the chief magistrate therefore would not occasion so violent or so general a revolution in the officers of the government, as might be expected if he were the sole disposer of offices. Where a man in any station had given satisfactory evidence of his fitness for it, a new president would be restrained from attempting a change, in favour of a person more agreeable to him, by the apprehension that the discountenance of the senate might frustrate the attempt, and bring some degree of discredit upon himself. Those who can best estimate the value of a steady administration will be most disposed to prize a provision, which connects the official existence of public men with the approbation or disapprobation of that body, which from the greater permanency of its own composition, will in all probability be less subject to inconstancy, than any other member of the government.[73]

Hamilton's image of the civil servant whose tenure rests on "satisfactory evidence of his fitness" is instructive for our purposes. It fits neatly with the views of one of Hamilton's most formidable adversaries, the Federal Farmer. The latter, as we have seen, objected to the Senate's role in appointments because he thought it unlikely that the senators would yield their appointing powers to department heads — as the Constitution permits but does not command. This the Federal Farmer found unfortunate because he envisioned the department heads as "well informed men in their respective branches of business," who "will, from experience, be best informed as to the proper person to fill inferior offices." Appointments of department heads "will not often occur." The Federal Farmer thinks we can count on the department heads to make "impartial and judicious appointments of subordinate officers." In addition, the Federal Farmer finds in the presence of these well-informed, experienced, stable, impartial, and judicious department heads a further, but decidedly un-Hamiltonian, advantage: "an executive too influential may be reduced within proper bounds by placing many of the inferior appointments in courts of law and heads of departments."[74]

The idea of subordinate executive officers checking the president is strictly Anti-Federalist.[75] Hamilton would reject it out of hand. Despite this important difference, however, Hamilton and the Federal Farmer agree on a rather lofty image of the civil service. This agreement is somewhat remarkable since the contexts of the discussions are (for the Federal Farmer) how to get the senators out of appointments and (for Hamilton) how to get them into removals. Their agreement on the common end of a stable and competent civil service is all the more instructive because of their total disagreement over how to achieve it. A high-minded civil service is the intent of both supporters and opponents of Senate activism in personnel administration.

"Due Sense of National Character." In *Federalist 63*, Publius looks to the Senate to fill the need for "a due sense of national character." The expression occurs in the context of foreign affairs, but similar language in other parts of the *Federalist* and in speeches by both Madison and Hamilton at Philadelphia suggests a broader application of these intriguing words. In *Federalist 75*, Publius credits the Senate with "a nice and uniform sensibility to national character" and in number 65 he calls the senators "the representatives of the nation."[76] At the Philadelphia Convention Hamilton had looked to the Senate, whose members in his plan would serve during good behavior for life,[77] as embodying "a permanent will," a "weighty interest" in the government that would give them a reason to endure "the sacrifice of private affairs which an acceptance of public trust would require."[78] Also at the Convention, Madison had looked to the Senate as an institution that would "protect the people against their rulers."[79] By "ruler," the context makes clear, he meant the elected representatives in the House. As Publius, Madison echoes this theme in *Federalist 63* where he looks to the Senate for that "cool and deliberate sense of the community"[80] that will safeguard against the danger that the country "may possibly be betrayed by the representatives of the people."[81]

There may be some significance in these references to the Senate as (1) providing a "due sense of national character"; (2) embodying a "permanent will"; and (3) enjoying some special insight into the "cool and deliberate sense of the community." Perhaps these characteristics prompted Publius to use the rather extraordinary image of the senators as "the representatives of the nation." This language is extraordinary not only because of the rather exalted position it suggests for the Senate—a position not easily squared with Publius's understanding of checks and balances[82] — but also because it implicitly denies a role for the senators as representatives of the states. Quite clearly, the Senate does not "represent" the people. All are agreed on that; but, interestingly, many Anti-Federalists join Publius in denying that the Senate represents the states. Since the Senators will vote per capita, that is, as individuals, they cannot be said to represent their respective states. One Senator may cancel the vote of his colleague who has been chosen by the legislature of the same state. The state legislature cannot dismiss, impeach, or recall senators whose votes fail to reflect the state's interests. As A Federal Farmer, a leading Pennsylvania Anti-Federalist, put it: "It is not the power of choosing to office merely that designates sovereignty, . . . but the power of dismissing, impeaching, and the like those to whom authority is delegated."[83] In an effort to make sure the senators did represent their states, Anti-Federalist George Livingston introduced an amendment before the New York Ratifying Convention that provided in part:

> and that it shall be in the power of the legislatures of the several states to recall their senators, or either of them, and to elect others in their stead, to serve for the remainder of the time for which such senator or senators, so recalled, were appointed.[84]

This amendment was eloquently defended by Melancton Smith precisely on the grounds that it would insure that the Senate would be an institution that represents the states.

If, as all agree, the Senate does not represent the people; and, if, as the Anti-Federalists maintain, it fails to represent the states as well; then what does the Senate represent? Perhaps Hamilton's expression, "representatives of the nation," is meaningful.

In reviewing our examination of the Senate in the founding debate, what emerges is an institution:

1. in which legislative, executive, and judicial powers are combined;
2. which functions as part of an executive establishment; working (or conspiring) with the president and checking him as well;
3. whose members will serve for a long period and possibly for life or during good behavior;
4. whose members are expected to have a wisdom and expertise not found in the House of Representatives;[85]
5. whose members will have the institutional support to resist popular whims of the moment;
6. which could be constantly in session;
7. which may conduct its affairs in a place other than the legislative chamber;
8. which exercises some supervisory power over federal personnel matters;
9. which expresses a permanent will and national character.

I do not suggest that all the participants in the debate anticipated any one of the above characteristics, nor that any one of the participants saw all of them. What I do contend is that an institution with these characteristics can be found in the great normative act of founding the Republic.

Today's Senate, of course, resembles hardly at all the institution envisioned in the debate of 1787-1788. The adoption of the Seventeenth Amendment (direct election of senators), a wise and long-overdue recognition of the democratic spirit of the United States, formalized the role of the Senate as almost exclusively a second legislative chamber—a role that had characterized the Senate long before the amendment's adoption in 1916. Executive agreements in foreign affairs and a merit system in personnel administration considerably reduced the Senate's executive powers under the Constitution as well. Today's Senate is not an executive council in any sense; its judicial powers are hardly ever exercised; it is not notably more effective at resisting popular whim than the House; it is not constantly in session; relatively few of its members serve for more than twenty years; its wisdom and expertise may not be greater than that of the House; and so on. In a word, today's Senate is not the sort of institution the Federalists wanted and the Anti-Federalists feared.

The closest approximation to such an institution today is the career civil service and especially its higher reaches. I resist the temptation to point to the Senior Executive Service (SES) because I do not want to burden my argument with all the problems that face that unhappy institution. The pre-SES writings on some sort of Senior Civil Service seemed closer on paper than the SES does in fact to the sort of institution that is revealed in the founding argument.[86] This, however, is not the place to call for specific institutional reforms. My argument has been aimed at legitimacy, not reform. Neither a Senate nor a bureaucracy which resists popular whim is a likely candidate for plaudits today. We call such institutions unresponsive. I am not addressing the issue of how to make bureaucracy more responsive—nor even whether it should be. What I do suggest is that there are aspects of the administrative state that roughly fulfill the vision of the framers. Today's Administrative State is fair game for criticism, but not on grounds of constitutional legitimacy.

Representation

> To make representation real and actual, the number of Representatives ought to be adequate; they ought to mix with the people, think as they think, feel as they feel, ought to be perfectly amenable to them, and thoroughly acquainted with their interest and condition. (George Mason).

The third aspect of the founding argument that we shall consider is the debate over the number of representatives in the House. The Anti-Federalists had a powerful argument and they knew it. The Federalists knew it too; they put up only token resistance.

The Constitution provides that when the first Congress would meet there should be 65 men in the House of Representatives apportioned as follows: New Hampshire 3, Connecticut 5, New York 6, New Jersey 4, Pennsylvania 8, Delaware 1, Massachusetts 8, Rhode Island 1, Maryland 6, Virginia 10, North Carolina 5, South Carolina 5, and Georgia 3. The text of the Constitution makes it clear that this distribution was merely provisional. "Within three years after the first Meeting of the Congress," there was to be an "actual enumeration" that would redistribute representatives (and liability for direct taxes) in accordance with the standards of apportionment mentioned in Article I, Section 2.[87] The process of reapportioning representatives was to be taken up every decade after the constitutionally mandated decennial census. The ultimate size of the House was not fixed in the Constitution. The only provision was that, "The Number of Representatives shall not exceed one for every thirty Thousand, but each State shall have at least one Representative."

The Anti-Federalists attacked this arrangement. They maintained that there were too few members in the House to provide adequate representation and that the provision that there can never be more than one representative for 30,000 persons insured the perpetuation of the problem. Their argument was solidly grounded in a theory of representation that was held by nearly all Anti-Federalists who addressed the issue and, at times, by some Federalists as well.[88] The theory held that a representative assembly should be a microcosm of the society as a whole. With so few representing so many under the proposed Constitution, it was likely that very few men "of the middling sort" would ever be elected. This basic theme is captured in the quotation from George Mason at the heading of this section; representatives ought to think and feel the same as those they represent.

The theme is played throughout the Anti-Federalist literature with only minor variations. For example:

Centinel links inadequate numbers of representatives with safeguards against corruption:

The number of the representatives (being only one for every 30,000 inhabitants) appears to be too few, either to communicate the requisite information, of the wants, local circumstances and sentiments of so extensive an empire, or to prevent corruption and undue influence, in the exercise of such great powers.[89]

The Federal Farmer connects the representation issue with the Constitution's failure to provide for jury trials in civil cases:

The essential parts of a free and good government are a full and equal representation of the people in the legislature, and the jury trial of the vicinage in the administration of justice — a full and equal representation is that which possesses the same interests, feelings, opinions, and views the people themselves would possess, were they all assembled — a fair representation, therefore, should be so regulated that every order of men in the community, according to the common course of elections, can have a share in it — in order to allow professional men, merchants, traders, farmers, mechanics, etc. to bring a just proportion of their best informed men respectively into the legislature, the representation must be considerably numerous.[90]

Brutus finds it impossible to have adequate representation in a nation as large as the proposed United States and gives this as one of his reasons for opposing the Constitution:

If the people are to give their assent to the laws, by persons chosen and appointed by them, the manner of the choice and the number of the chosen, must be such, as to possess, be disposed, and consequently qualified to declare the sentiments of the people; for if they do not know, or are not disposed to speak the sentiments of the people, the people do not govern, but the sovereignty is in a few. Now, in a large extended country, it is impossible to have a representation, possessing the sentiments, and of integrity, to declare the minds of the people, without having it so numerous and unwieldy, as to be subject in great measure to the inconveniency of a democratic government.[91]

Samuel Chase fears that the House of Representatives will be dominated by the rich:

I object because the representatives will not be the representatives of the people at large but really of a few rich men in each state. A representative should be the image of those he represents. He should know their sentiments and their wants and desires — he should possess their feelings — he should be governed by their interests with which his own should be inseparably connected.[92]

Anti-Federalist literature abounds with similar attacks on representation in the Constitution.[93] As we have just seen, the argument may be paired with fear of corruption, opposition to an extended republic, and so forth; but the common thread in the Anti-Federalist attack is the need for the representation to reflect (to *re-present*) the society as a whole. "The representation ought to be sufficiently numerous to possess the same interests, feelings, opinions, and views, which the people themselves would possess, were they all assembled."[94]

The Federalists' reply to this argument was weak, confused, and disorganized. The reason for this was that many Federalists were quite sympathetic with their opponents on this issue. This was true even of Madison whose view of representation as "filtering" and "refining" public opinion was the most serious principled reply to the Anti-Federalists' microcosm theory.[95] Despite Madison's theoretical differences with the Anti-Federalists' position on representation, as a practical matter he agreed with them that the number of representatives in the proposed House was too small; there were limits to filtering and refining.[96] At the Philadelphia Convention, Madison had argued on several occasions that the number of representatives ought to be substantially increased.[97] Interestingly, Hamilton agreed with him. As Madison relates in his notes:

Col: Hamilton . . . avowed himself a friend to a vigorous Government, but would declare at the same time, that he held it essential that the popular branch of it should be on a broad foundation. He was seriously of opinion that the House of Representatives was on so narrow a scale as to be really dangerous, and to warrant a jealously in the people for their liberties. He remarked that the connection between the President and Senate would tend to perpetuate him, by corrupt influence. It was the more necessary on this account that a numerous representation in the other branch of the Legislature should be established."[98]

Since both Hamilton and Madison were displeased with the size of the House (Madison wanted the number of representatives doubled),[99] it is no wonder that as Publius they approached the defense of the actual number of representatives with little zest. Madison's discussion of representation in the *Federalist* is brilliant and justly famous;[100] but on the sixty-five member House, he is disappointing.

Concern over the size of the House was widespread at the Philadelphia convention. James Wilson explicitly defended the microcosm theory of the legislature.[101] So, of course, did George Mason, who as an Anti-Federalist after the Convention, hammered away at the representation issue mercilessly. Having been one of the most active delegates at the Convention, he knew the weak spots of the Constitution better than any other Anti-Federalist.[102] The most dramatic moment in the Convention's discussion of representation came on the very last day, September 17. The final version presented to the delegates provided that there could not be more than one representative for every 40,000 persons. With a motion on the floor to approve the entire document, Nathaniel Gorham of Massachusetts said that "if it was not too late," he would like to see the number 40,000 reduced to 30,000 "for the purpose of lessening objections to the Constitution."[103] The reduction would not affect the 65 members approved for the first Congress, but it would give Congress greater discretion to *increase* the size of the House in the future. One can imagine the anger of the weary delegates when literally at the last moment, Gorham raised this intractable issue which, by his own admission, "had produced so much discussion."[104]

Whatever restlessness the delegates might have felt was summarily quashed when General Washington, the president of the Convention, rose and, for the first time during the four months of the Convention, expressed his opinion on a substantive matter on the floor. Madison reports Washington as stating that "the smallness of the proportion of Representatives . . . had always appeared to himself [Washington] among the exceptionable parts of the plan and late as the present moment was for admitting amendments, he thought this of so much consequence that it would give him much satisfaction to see it adopted."[105]

Madison hastens to add: "No opposition was made to the proposition of Mr. Gorham and it was agreed to unanimously."[106]

The consensus that settled around the inadequate representation in the House of Representatives has a normative bearing on today's administrative state. No one would seriously contend that today's House of Representatives is in any sense a microcosm of American society. Its elite character is obvious. It has developed in a manner consistent with the worst fears of the Anti-Federalists.

The House appears in a better light if one follows Madison's filtering and refining view of representation. A charitable observer of American politics might find a certain human excellence in the men and women who sit in the House today. Even if this point is conceded, however, today's House with its 435 members representing over 200 million people does not meet an important precondition of Madison's filtering theory. In *Federalist 58*, Madison argues convincingly against a legislature that is too large. Without deciding how large is too large, he warns against adding members to the legislature; but he cautions that his warning should be observed only *"after securing a sufficient number for the purpose of safety, of local information, and of diffusive sympathy with the whole society."* The italics are Madison's; this is his generous concession to the Anti-Federalist microcosm argument. It is a concession, but not a surrender. Information and sympathy in the representatives is not the same as thinking as the people think and feeling as they feel. Throughout the representation debate, Madison tended to stress the *knowledge* the representatives should have of the people's circumstances; the Anti-Federalists tended to stress their feelings and character. Madison's reference to "sympathy" in *Federalist 58* is not as common in his writings on representation as his references to knowledge and information.[107]

Given a ratio of 435 to over 200 million, it is quite doubtful that today's representatives could meet the Madisonian criterion of information *and* sympathy. Indeed it is doubtful that they could meet the criterion of information alone. It is absolutely certain that they cannot meet the Anti-Federalist standard of feeling and character.

If one takes the founding argument as normative, it seems fair to conclude that the House of Representatives presents a serious defect in the Constitution; a defect that has been with us from the very beginning. There is a certain illegitimacy about the House of Representatives; not in a technical, legal sense, of course, because the House exists as the text of the constitution clearly permits. The illegitimacy is at a deeper level. The formal constitutional provision for apportionment belies the principles of representation that dominated the founding debate. The House of Representatives is at odds with what the founding generation thought representation should be. This defect is serious and perennial.

It is no answer to call for a larger House of Representatives. Publius argued convincingly against that approach: "The countenance of the government may become more democratic; but the soul that animates it will be more oligarchic."[108] Any freshman congressman would surely agree. In calling for a larger House of Representatives in 1788, the Anti-Federalists knew there was an outer limit. A mob was not what they had in mind. As Melancton Smith noted: "ten is too small and a thousand too large."[109] The Anti-Federalists had no intention of destroying the deliberative character of the legislature. In all likelihood, they would have been appalled at a legislature with 435 members.

If the House is too small and yet cannot be increased, the solution to the representative problem may lie elsewhere. During the past two decades, considerable professional attention in Public Administration has been given to the question of representative bureaucracy.[110] The literature is rich and varied. Sometimes it raises questions of equity; the distribution of jobs in the career public service should bear some resemblance to the makeup of society as a whole — an interesting reprise on the Anti-Federalist microcosm theme. Sometimes it stresses control; a truly representative public service is the most effective safeguard against a runaway bureaucracy. Again, the echo of the Anti-Federalists is heard; it is important to have in *government* (if not in the legislature) people who think as we think, feel as we feel. Sometimes the literature makes the bold claim that in certain circumstances the bureaucracy can *govern* more effectively than Congress because it represents important interests and attitudes that are nearly always excluded from Congress.[111]

If one combines the representative-bureaucracy literature with the literature that stresses the discretionary power of the modern administrative state,[112] what begins to emerge is the image of a *governing* (because of discretion) institution whose personnel distribution comes much closer to the microcosm the Anti-Federalists had in mind than the House of Representatives ever could. This is not to say that the bureaucracy *is* a microcosm; only that it comes much closer than the House of Representatives. Although the bureaucracy is not and perhaps should not be a microcosm of American society in any exact sense, it may be the sort of microcosm the Anti-Federalists had in mind. The Anti-Federalists were not doctrinaire. They were more interested in making the rather easy point that the House of Representatives is *not* a microcosm than in explaining the fine points of what they meant by thinking as the people think, feeling as they feel. There was no need for them to develop the point. The Federalists' attack was not coming from that flank. A careful review of the Anti-Federalist literature, however, suggests a rather clearly middle-class idea of microcosm. Though they fear "the better sort" as a fledgling aristocracy, it was "the middling sort" they favored.[113] Little is said about the poor.

Thus even if today's bureaucracy can be justly faulted for not being "truly" a microcosm, it may well meet the more relaxed, middle-class standards of the Anti-Federalists. With its merit system, it aspires at least in principle to achieve the filtering and refining effect of representation that Madison envisioned without sacrificing the "diffusive sympathy" with society as a whole that was also part of Madison's view. With its affirmative action policies, it is driven — again at least in principle — to seek out those qualified persons who have been excluded from serving in a governing institution where they *and people like them* will have a choice, not just a job, in the public service. The House of Representatives simply cannot do this. For this reason, I would suggest that the

Administrative State with its huge career public service heals a defect in the Constitution of the United States.[114]

I shall conclude this argument with the hope that administrators will not look upon legitimacy as an opening for professional arrogance. On the contrary, I would hope that constitutional legitimacy will tame the excesses of the administrative state. Legitimation has a civilizing aspect about it. In grounding the nature and function of the administrative state in constitutional principle, we invite administrators to assimilate the values salient in the constitutional heritage. If they do this, they will find at the center of their heritage a profound belief in individual rights and in the securing of these rights as the great, overarching purpose of government. If administrators look to this heritage to legitimate their activities, they will find what they seek; but they will find much else besides. They will find principles capable of instructing them on how to avoid the worst excesses of the administrative state. To legitimate is to tame, to civilize.

III. Governance by Unelected Officials

Critics of the Blacksburg Manifesto might be willing to admit that administrative institutions have some constitutional legitimacy without accepting the Manifesto's claim that administrators should rightfully share in *governing* the Republic. Objections of this sort are usually expressed in terms of democratic principles that will permit only elected officials to govern. In this section I shall respond to this argument by showing that for the framers of the Constitution popular election was but one of many titles to ground a legitimate claim to govern. To do this, I must present in some detail the theoretical background of the Federalists' understanding of the Constitution as a document that creates a "popular government."

For our purposes the central issue is the framers' innovation in constructing a regime that was democratic in principle but was not endowed with a supreme legislature. During the ratification debate of 1787-1788, many Anti-Federalist critics of the Constitution found this no innovation at all but simply an impossibility. As Herbert Storing observes: "The Anti-Federalists were . . . the conservative believing that the framers of the Constitution had fallen awkwardly and dangerously between the two stools of simple, responsible government and genuine balanced government."[115]

The Anti-Federalists maintained there were only two ways to design a government that could legitimately be considered popular. What Storing calls "simple, responsible government" was republican in spirit and featured a unicameral legislature that was directly responsible to the people. The "genuine balanced government" came out of the Whig tradition and attempted to balance the various orders in society — king, lords, and commons in the British experience — in the legislature.[116] What both systems had in common was the principle of legislative supremacy. With this principle as a starting point, the Anti-Federalists had considerable difficulty grasping the theoretical foundation of the new Constitution.

Nowhere is this clearer than in the interminable debate over sovereignty which the Anti-Federalists linked to their belief in legislative supremacy. Sovereignty is supreme and undivided power and the legislature, as Blackstone had insisted, is its accustomed place.[117] Since the proposed Constitution created a legislature whose acts would be the supreme law of the land, the Anti-Federalists argued that the new government would be sovereign and therefore its nature would be national and consolidated rather than federal. Hence, the rights of the states and perhaps even their very existence were in jeopardy.

The Federalists' reply in defense of the Constitution rested on an appeal to sovereignty in the people with a consequent denial of legislative supremacy. The object of the people's choice was not a supreme legislature that embodied their will, but a constitutional order, an arrangement of offices, a "system" that would provide efficient government and protect individual rights.

James Wilson was perhaps the most articulate spokesman of this Federalist theme during the ratification debate. Speaking in support of the Constitution at the Pennsylvania Ratifying Convention, Wilson argued that the sovereignty of the states was not destroyed by the new Constitution for the excellent reason that the states had never been sovereign. The people had always been sovereign. At one time they chose to delegate some powers to their state governments and others to Congress under the Articles of Confederation. Now they wished to rearranged this distribution of powers. As Wilson put it:

> When the principle is once settled that the people are the source of authority, the consequence is that they may take from the subordinate government powers with which they have hitherto trusted them, and place those powers in the general government, if it is thought that there they will be productive of more good. They can distribute one portion of power to the more contracted circle called State governments: they can also furnish another portion to the government of the United States. Who will undertake to say as a state officer that the people may not give to the general government what powers and for what purposes they please? how comes it, Sir, that these State governments dictate to their superiors? — to the majesty of the people?[118]

Throughout the process of shifting these powers from one level of government to another, it is the people alone who possess that power "from which there is no appeal and which is therefore called absolute, supreme, and uncontrollable."[119] Although the principle of popular sovereignty was invoked most frequently in debates over federalism, it is the application of the principle to the structure of the federal government itself that is of interest to students of Public Administration. On the issue of federalism, popular sovereignty nullifies state sovereignty; the states are not supreme because the people are. On the issue of separation of powers within the federal government, the legislature is not supreme because the people are. The object of the choice of the sovereign people is not a group of legislators who will carry out their will. What the people have chosen is a constitutional order that balances the powers they have delegated to three equal branches. In describing "the Federalist Persuasion," historian Gordon Wood notes that because "the Federalists were equating representation with the mere flow of authority, every officer would be in some way a representative of the people."[120]

Every *officer* a *representative*? Here is interesting language for students of Public Administration. It is pregnant with a legitimating argument for the nonelected official to participate in rule.

Herbert Storing makes the same point from a different angle. Because it exists as *part* of a constitutional order that the people have chosen, "[t]he legislature is a body of constitutional *officers*, not a microcosm of the sovereign people." Members of Congress "like *other officers* of government, derive their authority from the Constitution, not from their election." Elections are "merely a method of choosing, not a method of authorizing."[121]

Although Storing speaks of *officers* and Wood of *representatives*, they are at one in leveling the differences between elected and nonelected government personnel. For Storing, elected officials are officers; for Wood the nonelected officials are representatives. What both men imply is the *irrelevance of election* to ground a superior claim to speak for the people. This is an important consideration in any effort to legitimate the administrative state. It provides the beginnings of a principled response to the congressman who would raise doubts about the legitimacy of monetary policy by asking, "Who elected Paul Volcker?"

The tendency of the language used by Storing and Wood to level the difference between elected and nonelected officials is not a recent innovation of their own. Frank Goodnow used similar language and, more importantly, so did such significant figures of the Founding period as Publius, James Wilson, John Adams, Thomas Jefferson, Alexander Hamilton, Elbridge Gerry, Hugh Williamson, and the participants in the Pennsylvania Ratifying Convention of 1787. In England, Edmund Burke spoke of both elected and nonelected officials as "representatives."[122]

Although there are important differences between Storing and Wood, they are at one in interpreting the Federalist argument as pointing to ratification as the decisive act of the sovereign. Wood notes that the Federalists "were equating representation with the mere flow of authority," whereas Storing describes the Federalist theory of election as "merely a method of choosing, not a method of authorizing." The emphasis is different but the main point is the same. It is the act of ratification that initiates the "flow of authority" for Wood and that is "authorizing" for Storing.[123] The authoritative act is the people's ratification of the distribution of various offices in the proposed Constitution. The fact that some offices are filled by election and others by appointment says nothing about the connection between the people and the occupant of a particular office. The senators and representatives of Article I; the president, department heads, and inferior officers of Article II; and the judges of Article III are all the objects of a popular choice that determined how each officeholder would be selected — some by popular election, some by indirect election, some by appointment. They are all *equally* the object of popular choice because their offices are equally created by the Constitution that the people have chosen. They are equally provided for in the Constitution even though they are most emphatically unequal in the scope and nature of their constitutional duties. The "inferior officers" of Article II are indeed inferior to the president and the heads of the executive departments. Their offices, however, *ultimately* depend upon the same authoritative source that has created the office of the president. The difference is not one of more or less constitutional legitimacy but rather of explicit and implicit constitutional authorization.

When Wood maintains the Federalists "were equating representation with the mere flow of authority," he is distinguishing the innovative Federalist position on representation from the traditional understanding that through representation in a legislature the entire society was *re-presented*, that is, presented a second time on a smaller scale. Storing speaks to the same point when he maintains that for the Federalists "[t]he legislature is . . . not a micro-cosm of sovereign people." It was the microcosm view of representation in a legislature that grounded the case for legislative supremacy. That is why Wood refers to the *Federalist* interpretation of representation as "a *mere* flow of authority."[124] It is "mere" because it is a purely juridical act that lacks the rich sociological flavor of the legislature as microcosm. If the legislature is a microcosm of society as a whole, then, of course, it should be supreme. There is no principle of popular government that would allow an executive or judici-ary that is *not* part of the microcosm to "check" a microcosm of society itself. If the legislature is supreme, the executive and judiciary are inferior to it. This the Federalists denied. The three branches are equal. The only way to justify their position was to consider the Constitution as a whole with its separate and balanced powers as the object of sovereign popular choice.

In putting forward this theory, the Federalists were departing from the traditional idea of mixed regime. James Madison notes this departure explicitly in *Federalist 14*. The theory of mixed regime was based on the British experi-ence wherein the various orders in society — king, lords, and commons — came together in Parliament. This was balanced government, but the balance was struck *in the legislature*, in Parliament which was sovereign.

In republican America, where there were no "orders" in society, the mixed-regime theory continued to flourish because of a belief in a "natural aristocracy" that would have to be represented and balanced in the legislature. John Adams, of course, is the most famous advocate of this position. His celebrated *Defense of the Constitutions of Government of the United States of America* presented an elaborate justification of the need for a balanced legislature in a republican society. His adversaries were Turgot in France, and Franklin and Paine in America. All three of these men had argued that under republican government there was no need for a bicameral legislature because there was only one order of society — the people themselves. To speak of an "upper" and "lower" house was inconsistent with the genius of republicanism. Where there was only one order in society, there should be a unicameral legislature.

Adams's rejoinder to this argument was that every society had an inevitable tendency toward aristocracy. If the aristocrats are not recognized as a class by law, they will find other ways to assert themselves. They would quickly dominate a unicameral legislature in such a way as to deny the common people an effective voice; and this while paying homage to the principles of republicanism. For Adams, the path of wisdom was to maintain bicameralism as a way of constitutionally confining the natural aristocrats in a legislative chamber of their own which would be part of the legislature as a whole. This would preserve one house for the people and thereby assure a balanced constitution.[125]

The argument between the unicameral republicans and the advocates of the balanced constitution as an American version of the mixed regime became inextricably entwined in the argument over the ratification of the Constitution. Many Anti-Federalists attacked the Constitution as an expression of Adams's version of the mixed regime. Indeed, Adams himself supported the Constitution because of its similarities to his own position. This similarity, however, was only on the surface. President, Senate, and House in the Constitution were by no means the same as king, lords, and commons in Parliament.[126] Nor were they the same as the aristocrats and common people of the American version of the mixed regime. The Federalists' theory of the Constitution challenged *both* the unicameral republicans *and* the advocates of a mixed regime on the issue of legislative supremacy. The unicameral republicans saw the legislature as the supreme institution of government because it was chosen by the one social order in a republic, the people. They hailed Pennsylvania's unicameral legislature as comporting with sound republican doctrine. The advocates of the mixed regime saw Parliament (or the bicameral American state legislatures) as supreme because the various social orders had a voice in Parliament. The constitutional balance was struck in Parliament itself. There and only there *all* of society was represented and hence Parliament was supreme.

In preferring constitutional supremacy over legislative supremacy, the Federalists bypassed the unicameral-mixed-regime argument and broke new ground. Instead of balancing social orders in a legislature, they would balance *interests* in the Constitution itself. Congress, the legislative branch, was not where the balance would be struck; it was itself part of the balance.

Herbert Storing captures the spirit of the Federalists' argument when he describes their handiwork as "a balance of constitutional orders or powers . . . requiring only the impulse of popular consent to breathe life into it." This breath of popular consent is the taproot of the democratic character of the regime. It allows James Wilson to say of the government created by the Constitution: "In its principle it is purely democratical."[127]

Throughout the Philadelphia Convention, the proponents of a strong central government consistently maintained that it was "indispensable that the new Constitution should be ratified in the most unexceptionable form, and by the supreme authority of the people themselves."[128] From Edmund Randolph's submission of the Virginia Plan at the Convention's beginning to the polished language of the final product, popular ratification was defended time and again as a principle of the highest order.[129] This principle was solidly integrated into the overall strategy of the nationally minded delegates. For example, when James Madison attacked the New Jersey Plan, he noted its provision that "all Acts of the U. States in Congress . . . shall be the supreme law of the respective states."[130] He argued that this provision was incompatible with the New Jersey Plan's reliance on the several state *legislatures* for formal approval. Ratification by the state legislatures would be in accord with the Articles of Confederation, but no act of a legislature can bind a future legislature to agree that acts of Congress will be superior to its own acts. The "supreme law" clause of the New Jersey Plan showed that its supporters correctly understood the need for a considerably stronger federal government, but they erred in thinking they could reach this goal simply by amending the Articles of Confederation. What was needed was a new form of government and this required action from the people as a whole.[131]

An interesting exchange between Oliver Ellsworth and Edmund Randolph shows how crucial the principle of popular ratification was for the delegates of a nationalist persuasion. On June 20, the Convention took up a revised version of the Virginia Plan Randolph had originally submitted on May 29. The first resolution of the revised plan proposed "that a national government ought to be established consisting of a Supreme Legislative, Judiciary, and Executive."[132] Ellsworth objected to the word "national." He felt if this word were dropped, the plan could still "go forth as an amendment to the articles of Confederation."[133] The state legislatures, he thought, could still ratify it. This, for Ellsworth, would be a welcome alternative to submitting the plan to the people in a ratifying convention. Madison reports that Ellsworth acknowledged his dislike for these popular conventions because "they were better fitted to pull down than build up Constitutions."[134]

It fell to Randolph to reply to Ellsworth. Although Randolph would eventually become an Anti-Federalist, he was at this point in the convention a strong nationalist. He said he had no objection to deleting the word *national* but added the significant caveat "that apprised the gentlemen who wished for [the change] that he did not admit it for the reasons assigned; particularly that of getting rid of a reference to the people for ratification."[135] Thus Randolph drew a sharp distinction between an essential and nonessential matter as far as the nationalist cause was concerned. The word *national* was expendable; popular ratification was not. Randolph and his fellow nationalists had a clear-headed understanding of what they were about. The creation of a new form of government requires the consent of the governed. The new government will govern not the states but the people as individuals. Therefore the people themselves must ratify the Constitution.

In *Federalist 78*, Publius justifies his remarkable defense of judicial review of acts of Congress on the grounds that the Constitution, if approved, will be the immediate object of popular choice and therefore superior to any enactments by elected legislators. He goes on to argue that not only is the Constitution superior to a statute, but it is in a sense superior to the people themselves. For even if the people should approve of a congressional action contrary to the Constitution — for example, an ex post facto law — the judiciary should nevertheless void the statute. Such a statute should be looked upon as the product of a "momentary inclination" or of "ill humors" and should be resisted by the judiciary until "the people have by solemn and authoritative act, annulled or changed the established form."[136] The Constitution is to be preferred to an unconstitutional but popularly acclaimed statute because the people as authors of "a solemn and authoritative act" are to be preferred to those same people when they are under the influence of a momentary inclination. This is a republican remedy for a republican disease.

If we apply the framers' position on popular ratification to public administration, we can begin to see administrative activities in a new light. For example, all would agree that an employee of the Department of Transportation should obey the will of Congress as manifested in public law. He or she should do this, however, not simply because members of Congress are elected by the people but also because the Constitution — that supreme object of a popular choice that is direct, immediate, and abiding — vests the commerce power in Congress. At a behavioral level, it would ordinarily make no different how the employee looks upon Congress; what is important is that he obeys. However, a complex view that sees in a particular Congress both the result of an election and a temporary trustee of abiding constitutional powers, gives administrative action a richer perspective. This perspective could have important behavioral consequences in those interesting situations when a president, also an elected official, signals to an executive department an enforcement policy that seems to be at odds with what Congress has mandated by law. In such a situation, an administrator with a principled belief in his duty to carry out the will of elected officials will receive no guidance from his principles. To break the deadlock he must choose between competing elected superiors on some grounds other than the fact that they are elected. If these grounds are related to his oath to uphold the Constitution, he could justify preferring one elected official to another on a democratic principle that is deeper than mere election. This principle is, of course, the framers' principle that grounds the constitutional order in a popular choice of a most fundamental nature. When such difficult choices are called for, unelected administrators must decide what course of action is best suited to preserve the constitutional order.

IV. A Constitutional Theory of Public Administration

> It is constantly assured, especially in our Tolstoyian tendencies, that when the lion lies down with the lamb the lion becomes lamb-like. But that is brutal annexation and imperialism on the part of the lamb. That is simply the lamb absorbing the lion instead of the lion eating the lamb. The real problem is — can the lion lie down with the lamb and still retain his royal ferocity. (Gilbert K. Chesterton, *Orthodoxy*)

In the final section of this chapter I shall present a normative theory of Public Administration that is based on the constitutional considerations examined in the previous sections.

If the administrative state is indeed compatible with constitutional principles, it is necessary to make some sort of statement on how we might expect administrative institutions to sustain these principles. In a word, there is need for a normative theory of Public Administration that is grounded in the Constitution. This final section outlines such a theory. The theory proceeds mindful of Chesterton's advice that when we summon the lion to lie down with the lamb, we should not expect the lion to become a lamb. That, as he says, would be imperialism on the part of the lamb. The administrative state must not forfeit its administrative character to achieve constitutional legitimacy. As Woodrow Wilson counseled, administration "must learn our constitutions by heart; must get the bureaucratic fever out of its veins; must inhale much free American air"; but — as Wilson insists — all this without ceasing to be administration.[137]

The constitutional theory of Public Administration that I propose is intended to enable administrators to fulfill the objective of their oath of office: to uphold the Constitution of the United States. This means that administrators should use their discretionary power to maintain the constitutional balance of powers in support of individual rights. This, of course, is what the Congress, the president, and the courts are supposed to do as well. This unity of purpose is as it should be because the Public Administration, like Congress, president, and courts is an institution of government compatible with the constitutional design of the framers. Congress, the president or the judiciary, taken discretely, each either comprises or heads one of the three great "branches" of government.[138] Each contributes in its own peculiar way to the grand end of maintaining the constitutional balance of power in support of individual rights. The Public Administration neither comprises nor heads any branch of government but is subordinate to all three of them. Like Congress, president, and courts, the Public Administration makes its distinctive contribution in a manner consistent with its peculiar place, which is one of subordination.

The image of a balance wheel best captures the distinctive contribution of the Public Administration. The Senate originally intended by the framers (as opposed to the Senate of history) is the constitutional model for the Public Administration as balance wheel because the Senate, like the Public Administration, was intended to exercise all three powers of government. Unlike the Senate of the framers' intent, however, the Public Administration exercises all three powers in a subordinate capacity and must make its peculiar contribution in conformity with that subordination. It does this by choosing which of its constitutional masters it will favor at a given time on a given issue in the continual struggle among the three branches as they act out the script of *Federalist 51*, wherein ambition counteracts ambition and "the interest of the man . . . [is] connected with the constitutional rights of the place."

This, of course, is what the Public Administration has been doing ever since Alexander Hamilton's fascinating effort to position the Treasury Department he headed and himself as secretary of the Treasury as a buffer (or perhaps a conduit) between President Washington and the first Congress.[139] He knew he and his department were subordinate to both the president and Congress, but he had the statesmanlike vision to see in that dual subordination the opportunity to shape events. Examples as recent as the "Superfund" scandal point to the perennial practice of administrators choosing constitutional masters. Career civil servants at the Environmental Protection Agency (EPA) tilted toward Congress and against the president in that newsworthy battle.[140] Without political support from Congress, EPA career personnel could not have executed the agency's statutory responsibilities. Without an aggressive and cooperative civil service, Congress could not have uncovered the depth of the scandal.[141]

The normative theory I am suggesting deals more directly with attitudes than behavior. Administrators often do choose among constitutional masters, but they usually do so as a matter of fact and seldom as a matter of constitutional principle. Their preoccupation with the low arts of organizational survival blinds them to the brighter angels of their nature. They should lift their vision to see themselves as men and women who "run a Constitution."[142]

The normative theory I propose is intended to encourage administrators and the public to think about administrative behavior in constitutional terms. There is no need to ridicule as lackeys those administrators who zealously support the president; nor to condemn as obstructionists those who oppose him. Civil servants who provide Congress or the courts with vital but embarrassing information need not be "whistleblowers" to their friends and "leakers" to their enemies. By grounding our thinking about the Public Administration in the Constitution, we can transform erstwhile lackeys, leakers, obstructionists, and whistleblowers into administrative statesmen.

We can do this without any substantive policy implications. The constitutional approach to Public Administration is suitable for administrators who think we do too little for the poor as well as for those who think we do too much;

for those who support a nuclear freeze and those who oppose it; for supply-side economists and for advocates of industrial policy. The Constitution is permissive on these issues. Administrators will not be without firm, perhaps passionate, convictions on matters of this sort. They should certainly use their discretion to favor those policies they think are most likely to promote the public interest; but they should assess the public interest against the broad background of constitutional principle.[143] The Constitution transcends a given tax policy, a weapons system, or food stamps. It cannot be confined to any such particulars. The constitutional word becomes flesh in stature, rule, and policy. Constitutionally motivated administrators, like lobbyists, may be policy advocates; but their advocacy, unlike that of lobbyists, should be tempered by the imperatives of the constitutional order. They do not differ from lobbyists in the sense that lobbyists are committed to causes and they are not. Administrators differ from lobbyists because they take an oath to uphold the Constitution and lobbyists do not. For public administrators, the Constitution is the cause above causes. In exercising discretionary authority to support this policy or that one, their judgment should be informed by the constitutional needs of the time as well as by the needs of the poor, the environment, the Air Force, the housing industry, the economy, the Third World, and the myriad of other matters that clamor for the attention of the Public Administration.

The link between subordination to constitutional masters and freedom to choose among them preserves both the instrumental character of Public Administration and the autonomy necessary for professionalism. In this way we can reinstate the great insight of the discredited politics-administration dichotomy. This tired old warhorse still plays the mighty stallion despite academic efforts to put him out to pasture. Every student of Public Administration denies the possibility of making a distinction between politics and administration; but everyone else continues to make the distinction. Although the attack on the dichotomy is well grounded in social science literature, it always fails to persuade because the dichotomy holds the high ground from which administration can be seen as both subordinate to the political leadership of the day and professionally exempt from political interference. By suggesting a theory of Public Administration that combines constitutional subordination and autonomy, I hope to preserve the enduring insight of the venerable dichotomy without succumbing to its naive view of administration as apolitical. Administration is political; but, like the judiciary, it has its own style of politics and its distinctive functions within the constitutional order.

The idea of the Public Administration choosing among competing constitutional masters may overstate the competitive relationship among the three great branches. The competition never ends, but it is not all-consuming. The relationships can be harmonious and in some policy areas often are. Louis Fisher's *Presidential Spending Power* describes convincingly a political world in which "moral understandings" and "gentlemen's agreements" penetrate the constitutional barriers between the legislative and executive branches.[144] Administrators facilitate these mollifying arrangements and are at times themselves parties to such understandings and agreements. This is but another way of maintaining the proper constitutional balance of powers. Rather than choose between the Congress and the presidency, the Public Administration may at times look for suitable means to bring them or keep them together.

When it does this, the Public Administration plays a crucial role in softening the harsh logic of separation of powers and proves itself a worthy successor to the courts and political parties which provided the same service in the nineteenth century.[145] Parties, courts, and agencies have emerged as the institutional expression of Publius's caution against a doctrinaire interpretation of the principle of separation of powers.

Thus far we have spoken of the role of the Public Administration in maintaining the appropriate balance of power. This is not an end in itself. Constitutional powers are separated, checked, and balanced to protect individual rights, which is the purpose of American politics. In discussing the appropriate balance, we concentrated on the legislative and executive branches. The judiciary asserts its role in the constitutional balance through the doctrine of individual rights. This doctrine enables the courts to compete with the legislative and executive branches for the grand prize of contemporary politics: the control of the Public Administration.[146]

Because the administrative process affects individual rights in so many important ways, the Public Administration is no less subordinate to the courts than it is to the "political" branches. Judicial intervention in the administrative process can have profound and devastating effects on program management precisely because the intervention is made in the name of individual rights. Rights trump utility. Judicial intervention in defense of rights — for example, the rights of prisoners or patients in state mental hospitals — can irrevocably destroy the most careful long-term planning and the most elegant cost-benefit analysis. There is a natural and understandable tension between the courts with their commitment to rights and the managerial ethos of public administration that is deeply committed to utility.[147] A normative theory of Public Administration that is grounded in constitutional principle must not collapse into managerial utilitarianism. The courts must be considered serious competitors for the favorable exercise of administrative discretion. This is because the overwhelming majority of claims of individual rights begin and end in administrative agencies. It is not enough for public administrators to obey court orders; they should also take seriously the judicial values that are revealed in court opinions.[148] They should learn to think like judges as well as legislators and executives, because they are all three of these. In a regime of separation of powers, administrators must do the work of statesmen.

The claim for the important role of choosing one's constitutional master follows the argument in the third section of this chapter. The Public Administration is part of a constitutional *order* that was chosen by the people in the great ratification debate of 1787-1788. The fact that administrators, like judges, are not elected in no way diminishes their constitutional stature. Popular election is simply one of at least twenty-two ways that have been or still are approved for holding office under the Constitution. The other twenty-one are:

1. Selection of a president or vice-president by the electoral college;
2. Selection of a president by the House of Representatives voting as states;
3. Selection of a vice-president by the Senate;
4. Appointment by the president with the advice and consent of the Senate;
5. Appointment by the president alone as provided by law;
6. Appointment by the head of an executive department as provided by law;
7. Appointment by a court of law as provided by law;
8. Election to the Senate by a state legislature;
9. Selection as a presidential elector in such manner as a state legislature shall choose;
10. Selection by the House of Representatives as an officer of that body;
11. Selection by the Senate as an officer of that body;
12. Selection as an elector for the District of Columbia "in such manner as Congress may direct" (Amendment XXIII);
13. Selection as vice-president upon nomination by the president and conformation by both houses of Congress (Amendment XXV);
14. Discharge by the vice-president of presidential powers and duties as acting president upon the president's written declaration of inability to discharge the powers and duties of his office (Amendment XXV);
15. Discharge by the vice-president of presidential powers and duties as acting president upon written declaration to the president pro tempore of the Senate and the Speaker of the House from the vice-president and a majority of the principal officers of the executive departments that the president is unable to discharge his powers and duties (Amendment XXV);
16. Discharge by the vice-president of presidential powers and duties as acting president upon written declaration to the president pro tempore of the Senate and the Speaker of the House from the vice-president and a majority of a body designated by law for this purpose that the president is unable to discharge the duties and powers of his office (Amendment XXV);
17. Congressional resolution of a dispute between president and vice-president over the president's ability to discharge the duties and powers of his office (Amendment XXV);
18. Accession by the vice-president to the presidency upon the president's removal, death, resignation, or inability to discharge the powers and duties of his office;
19. Accession to the position to act as president in such manner as Congress may by law provide in the case of the removal, death, resignation, or inability both of the president and vice-president;
20. Accession to office by presidential appointment when a vacancy has occurred during a recess of the Senate;
21. Temporary appointment as senator by the governor of a state.

The provisions of the Twenty-fifth Amendment are particularly significant because this amendment was ratified in 1967, long after the president had been recognized as a man of the people. Although the framers of the Constitution did not see the president in these terms, the popular character of the office can be traced at least as far back as the presidency of Andrew Jackson. Despite this long tradition, the Twenty-fifth Amendment excludes the people from having any voice whatsoever in resolving whatever crisis might arise over presidential succession. Here is a legitimacy question of the first order that as late as 1967 is left to the experts to settle. The Senate has an equal voice with the House in settling a dispute between president and vice-president even though senators are chosen on the basis of the constitutional equality of the states rather than by population. Nevertheless, the "malapportioned" Senate is the constitutional peer of the House in selecting the president. Other significant actors in resolving the crisis envisioned in the Twenty-fifth Amendment are the unelected heads of executive departments and the enigmatic "such other body as Congress may by law provide."

In all this the spirit of the framers reasserts itself. The Twenty-fifth Amendment reaffirms Madison's "filtering" view of representation. If the people have chosen their congressmen and senators wisely, they have nothing to fear from letting these experts or those whom the experts designate decide the great matters of state anticipated in the amendment.

To counteract our excessive reliance on election as the entitlement to govern, we would do well to recall that a great constitutional scholar, Edward S. Corwin, once reminded Franklin Roosevelt that the president has his powers not from the people but from the Constitution. It is only the Constitution that has power from the people. Theodore Roosevelt announced in his *Autobiography* a "stewardship theory" of the presidency by which he meant that "it was not only his [the President's] right but his duty to do anything that the needs of the Nation demanded unless such action was forbidden by the Constitution or by the laws."[149] Although this view of the presidency is not without support in some Supreme Court opinions,[150] the threat it poses to the rule of law is apparent. If the American people have a "steward," it is their Constitution, not their president.

The Public Administration is no monolith. Throughout the Blacksburg Manifesto, "Public Administration" is prefaced with the definite article to underscore the Manifesto's effort to discuss an institution of government rather than process and behavior. When I speak of "The Public Administration" choosing among its constitutional masters, I do not envision every agency of the government rising as one man in support of, say, Congress against an overbearing president. The pluralism that dominates American politics is reflected in the Public Administration just as it is reflected in the Congress, the presidency, and the courts.[151] I carry no belief for pluralism in its manifestation as the interest-group liberalism so soundly criticized by Theodore Lowi.[152] A legitimated Public Administration could be helpful in taming some unhappy pluralist excesses; but this is action at the margin of affairs. If pluralism is a problem and not the solution that some think it is, a prescription for political medicine much stronger than administrative reform is indicated.[153] The Public Administration, faithful to the prevailing pluralist structure of American politics, will choose its constitutional masters on an agency basis. It will do this only after bitter internal wranglings. At times it will make its choice in the lonely and desperate action of an alienated individual who is either a hero, a fanatic, or both.

The literature in public-personnel management has at times called for an elite corps of unified, high-ranking senior career executives.[154] The Senior Executive Service (SES) created by the Civil Service Reform Act of 1978 is but a dim shadow of earlier suggested reforms. There is insufficient institutional support in the legislation to give the SES the kind of government-wide perspective the literature envisioned. An important by-product of the widespread disappointment within the SES has been a marked increase in the tendency of senior career personnel to come together to protect their interests.[155] The SES has proved a disappointment because it has been all stick and no carrot, all risk and no reward. Since the passage of the Civil Service Reform Act, congressional support for bonuses and salary increments has been so niggardly as to demoralize the senior executives and bring them together primarily for their financial self-interest. Now that they are increasingly organized, however, there is nothing to keep them from discussing issues of broader interest than their own finances. Indeed, they often do so in a public-spirited manner.[156] Perhaps these organizations will eventually develop into influential professional associations that will take positions on policy issues of the day in the name of nonpartisan managerial expertise.[157] Then, of course, it would be quite meaningful to speak of "The Public Administration" as an identifiable force unified in its leadership and ready to influence public opinion on specific issues of current interest. Should such a formal embodiment of the Public Administration emerge, it would not be the first time that self-interest planted the seed of high-minded public service. Publius would approve.

Notes

1. *Federalist* 72, p. 486-487. Page references to *The Federalist Papers* are taken from Jacob E. Cooke's critical edition. (Middletown, Conn.: Wesleyan University Press, 1961, 1982.) As a general rule I refer to the authors of *The Federalist Papers* as Publius rather than as Madison, Hamilton, or Jay. My reason for doing this is that the book as a whole has a consistent argument that is distorted by a close examination of who wrote which paper. At times I depart from this rule, but only when it is necessary to compare Madison or Hamilton as Publius with statements these men had made in other situations.

2. The number of times certain works are used in *The Federalist Papers* can be found in Thomas S. Engeman, Edward J. Erler, and Thomas B. Hofeller, eds., *The Federalist Concordance* (Wesleyan University Press, 1984).

3. *Federalist* 72, p. 488.

4. Ibid., p. 487.

5. Ibid.

6. *Federalist* 77, p. 515.

7. Ibid., p. 518.

8. Ibid.

9. *Federalist 17*, p. 106-107.

10. *Federalist 46.* p. 317.

11. Ibid.

12. *Federalist 68*, p. 461.

13. Herbert J. Storing, *What the Anti-Federalists Were FOR* (Chicago: University of Chicago Press, 1981) p. 71.

14. Hannah Arendt, *On Revolution* (New York: Viking Press, 1963) p. 214.

15. *Federalist 47.*

16. Herbert J. Storing, *The Complete Anti-Federalist*, 7 vols. (Chicago: University of Chicago Press, 1981). Brutus 2.9.197, 202; Mason 2.2. 7-8; Federal Farmer 2.8.86, 175; Old Whig 3.3.31; Officer of the late Continental Army 3.8.3; DeWitt 4.3.12-14; Agrippa 4.6.73; Brutus 5.15.1; Patrick Henry 5.16.7-14; Cincinnatus 6.1. 26-32; Plebeian 6.11.16. For a more relaxed Anti-Federalist stance on separation of powers, see Penn 3.12.16-17 and Watchman 4.22.4. Subsequent reference to *The Complete Anti-Federalist* will be listed as Storing, CAF. This reference will be followed by the name or pseudonym of the Anti-Federalist author and 3 arabic numbers. The first number indicates volume; the second the author's position in the volume, and the third the paragraph in the author's pamphlet or speech. Thus, Federal Farmer 2.8.86 refers to the Anti-Federalist writer who calls himself the Federal Farmer. He is the eighth author to appear in the second volume. The statement cited can be found in the 86th paragraph of his writings. All paragraphs in CAF are numbered. References to volume 1 (Storing's introductory essay) and to Storing's notes will be by volume and page. The introductory essay also appears in paperback under the title *What the Anti-Federalists Were FOR*. (See note 12.)

17. Since the vice-president of the United States is president of the Senate, it was essential to go outside of that body for a presiding officer at the impeachment trial of a president. Otherwise the vice-president would find himself in a severe conflict of interest.

18. In his remarks of July 26, George Mason provided a nice summary of the Convention's efforts to find a suitable way to elect a president. See Charles C. Tansill, ed., "Debates in the Federal Convention of 1787 as reported by James Madison." *Documents Illustrative of the Formation of the Union of the American States* (Washington, D.C.: Government Printing Office, 1927), p. 456-457.

19. Tansill, p. 662-663.

20. This is not to say that separation of powers can be disregarded at will. My point is simply that the mere presence of all those powers of government in one agency is not of itself constitutionally suspect. The responsible exercise of these powers is another matter. See *Wong Yang Sung* v. *McGrath* 339 U.S. 33 (1950).

21. M.J.C. Vile, *Constitutionalism and Separation of Powers* (New York: Oxford University Press, 1967), p. 13.

22. *Federalist 47*, p. 324.

23. Ibid., p. 325-326. Madison's position on separation of powers in *The Federalist* is quite consistent with his remarks at the Philadelphia Convention. See Tansill, p. 423-424; 166; 397-398; 412-413; 423-424.

24. For full discussions on separation of powers, see Vile *op. cit.* and W. B. Gwyn, *The Meaning of the Separation of Powers* (New Orleans: Tulane University, 1965).

25. For Rufus King's position, see Tansill, p. 419. For James Wilson's position, see Tansill, p. 444-445.

26. *Federalist 66*, p. 445.

27. The powers of administrative agencies, unlike those of Congress, president, and courts, are always "partial" in the sense that they are exercised over a narrowly defined scope of governmental activity — e.g., TV licenses, railroad rates, food stamps, etc. Not only are these powers partial but, unlike those of Congress, president, and courts, they are formally subordinated in their entirety to one or other of the traditional constitutional branches. Thus even egregious abuses by administrative agencies are far removed from "tyranny." There is, of course, a great difference between

avoiding tyranny and providing good government. When the attack on the administrative state is launched from the high ground of separation of powers, the entire argument has an upward tilt toward high politics— like questions of tyranny. If administrative agencies were spared the sort of attack that questions their legitimacy, they might be as successful in providing good government as they are in avoiding tyranny.

28. *Federalist 65*, p. 439.

29. Storing, CAF: Mason 2.2.4.

30. Storing, CAF: Monroe 5.21.32; Montezuma 3.4.2. See also the comments of William Grayson on June 14, 1788, at the Virginia Ratifying Convention. Jonathan Elliot, ed., *The Debates in the Several State Conventions on the Adoption of the Federal Constitution as Recommended by the General Convention at Philadelphia in 1787*, 5 vols; 2nd ed. (Philadelphia: J.P. Lippincott, 1836). Grayson's comments appear in volume 3, p. 375-377. Subsequent references will be listed as "Elliot" followed by volume and page.

31. Storing, CAF 5.21.37.

32. Tansill, p. 609.

33. Ibid., p. 319.

34. Ibid., p. 324.

35. See also the colloquy between Edmund Randolph and George Mason in Tansill, p. 528-529.

36. Ibid., p. 319.

37. Ibid., p. 474.

38. When this clause was eventually deleted, it was not because of any hesitation over the nonlegislative character of the Senate. The reason for deleting the clause was to *include* the executive functions of the Senate in the general congressional rule that a journal of proceedings should be published. Some framers wanted to exempt the Senate from this obligation when it was acting in a nonlegislative capacity. See Tansill, p. 519.

39. Tansill, p. 474.

40. Ibid., p. 661.

41. Elliot, III, p. 491.

42. Ibid.

43. Storing, CAF: Cato 2.6.45.

44. Ibid. Martin 2.4.42 and 2.4.48.

45. Ibid. Monroe 5.21.35; and Elliot, III, p. 220-222.

46. Some supporters of the Constitution shared this fear; see remarks of James Wilson in Tansill, p. 674.

47. Storing, CAF: Federal Farmer 2.8.170.

48. Ibid. Centinel 2.7.23.

49. Ibid. Minority of Convention of Pennsylvania 3.11.45. Several Anti-Federalists referred to the president as "president-general" because of his constitutional position as commander-in-chief of the army and navy. For a further discussion of the Anti-Federalists who favored a strong executive, see Storing, CAF I, p. 49 and note 5 on p. 94. The Federal Farmer was one of the staunchest Anti-Federal champions of a strong executive. See 2.7.128 where he follows Adams closely.

50. Some Federalists shared this concern. See comments of Wilson in Tansill, p. 684, and Ellsworth, p. 537.

51. Elliot, III, p. 494.

52. Tansill, p. 671.

53. Tansill, p. 686-687.

54. Elliot, III, p. 493-494.

55. Storing, CAF: Lee 5.6.5.

56. Elliot, IV, p. 116-117.

57. *Federalist 62-65*.

58. A final indication of the executive character of the Senate can be seen in the evolution of the office of vice-president. He is a late-comer to the convention; no mention of the office is made until September 4 — less than two weeks before the four-month convention would adjourn. Today we tend to think of the vice-president's role as president of the Senate as rather strange, but it made good sense to the framers. An earlier draft of the Constitution had the Senate selecting the president. This arrangement was rejected as an excessive threat to the independence of the president. The Senators would be all too likely to select one of their own number and then control the man they had selected. Since the president was not to be elected by the Senate, the framers logically concluded that the vice-president should not be elected in this way either. Since, however, they had given some thought to the Senate as a possible institution for selecting the president, it was only natural that they should look in this direction for a successor to a deceased president. So natural was this that Gouverneur Morris could assure critics of the office of vice-president that if there were no such office, the president of the Senate would become a "temporary successor" to the presidency anyway. Roger Sherman agreed and supported the creation of the office of vice-president in order to avoid forcing one state to lose the full voting power of one of its senators who would be elected president of the Senate. Tansill, p. 659-664; and p. 682-683.

Throughout the entire Convention there was never any discussion of the Speaker of the House succeeding to the presidency. If the successor was to have any connection with Congress, that connection would only be with the Senate. The fact that the Presidential Succession Act of 1947 puts the Speaker of the House right after the vice-president and before the president *pro tempore* of the Senate is consistent with the democratic evolution of the office of the president and the decline in awareness of the executive character of the Senate. It is interesting to note that in the 1792 Succession Act, the president *pro tempore* of the Senate was placed ahead of the Speaker of the House and right after the vice-president of the United States. This suggests that the executive character of the Senate was quite clear to the men of the founding generation.

59. *Federalist 62*, p. 418-419.

60. This point is also made by Rufus King in the Massachusetts Ratifying Convention, Elliot IV, p. 47-48; and by James Iredell in the North Carolina Ratifying Convention, Elliot IV, p. 41, 133.

61. Storing, CAF: Centinel 2.7.23.

62. Ibid. Brutus 2.9.201.

63. Ibid. M. Smith 6.12.27.

64. Tansill, p. 222, 319. Enough senators have served for twenty or even thirty years that the lifetime senators of Hamilton and G. Morris have not proved altogether fanciful. Since, however, the Senate never achieved its potential as an executive institution, this senatorial longevity has done little for *executive* stability. The twenty-second amendment, which prohibits a third presidential term, is a further limitation on executive stability. Today the career civil service is the most likely institution to fulfill Hamilton and Morris's view of *executive* stability through a lifelong career.

65. The fear of the Senate's treaty power was the basis of another Anti-Federalist argument. Article VI of the Constitution provides that treaties shall be the Supreme Law of the land. The Anti-Federalists maintained that this could lead to *legislation* without concurrence from the House of Representatives. A generous definition of "treaty" could put the entire legislative power in the hands of the Senate. This danger was combined with the fear of the proposed "federal city" where the Senators would live all year round. Their distance from home and their six-year term would threaten republican virtue. On the dangers of the federal city, see the following Anti-Federalist writings in Storing, CAF: Federal Farmer 2.8.222-223; Aristocrotis 3.16.2; Brutus 2.9.200; Columbian Patriot 4.28.8; Cato Uticensis 5.7.7.

66. Storing CAF: Mason 2.2.24.

67. Ibid., Martin 2.4.42.

68. Ibid., Cato 2.6.45.

69. See colloquy between Madison and G. Morris in Tansill, p. 733.

70. Storing, CAF: Federal Farmer 2.8.170.

71. *Federalist 66* and *76*.

72. *Federalist 66*, p. 449.

73. *Federalist 77*, p. 515-516.

74. *Storing CAF: Federal Farmer 2.8.173.*

75. George Mason is the leading Anti-Federalist on this point. See his remarks at Virginia Ratifying Convention. Elliot III, p. 494-496.

76. *Federalist 65*, p. 440. The quotation appears in the fifth paragraph of 65. The references to the Senate in the two preceding paragraphs and the one following the quotation indicate that Hamilton was referring to the Senate and not to the entire Congress when he speaks of "representatives of the nation."

77. Tansill, p. 222; but see also p. 283 where Hamilton is resigned to a shorter term for senators.

78. Tansill, p. 222.

79. Tansill, p. 279.

80. *Federalist 63*, p. 425.

81. Ibid., p. 426.

82. See Section IV: The Constitutional Theory of Public Administration, this volume.

83. Storing CAF: A Farmer 3.14.15.

84. Ibid., Livingston 6.12.25.

85. For further remarks on the Senate's expertise in foreign affairs see *Federalist 64*.

86. An excellent discussion of this literature can be found in Chester A. Newland, "Professional Public Executives and Public Administration Agendas" in Chester A. Newland, ed., *Professional Public Executives* (Washington: American Society for Public Administration, 1980), p. 1-29.

87. The full text of Article I, Section 2 reads as follows:

Section 2. [1] The House of Representatives shall be composed of Members chosen every second Year by the People of the several States, and the Electors in each State shall have the Qualifications requisite for Electors of the most numerous Branch of the State Legislature.

[2] No Person shall be a Representative who shall not have attained to the Age of twenty five Years, and been seven Years a Citizen of the United States, and who shall not, when elected, be an Inhabitant of that State in which he shall be chosen.

[3] Representatives and direct Taxes shall be apportioned among the several States which may be included within this Union, according to their respective Numbers, which shall be determined by adding to the whole Number of free Persons, including those bound to Service for a Term of Years, and excluding Indians not taxed, three fifths of all other Persons. The actual Enumeration shall be made within three Years after the first Meeting of the Congress of the United States, and within every subsequent Term of ten Years, in such Manner as they shall by Law direct. The Number of Representatives shall not exceed one for every thirty Thousand, but each State shall have at Least one Representative; and until such enumeration shall be made, the State of New Hampshire shall be entitled to chuse three, Massachusetts eight, Rhode Island and Providence Plantations one, Delaware one, Maryland six, Virginia ten, North Carolina five, South Carolina five, and Georgia three.

[4] When vacancies happen in the Representation from any State, the Executive Authority thereof shall issue Writs of Election to fill such Vacancies.

[5] The House of Representatives shall chuse their Speaker and other Officers; and shall have the sole Power of Impeachment.

88. See comments of James Wilson in Tansill, p. 160.

89. Storing CAF: Centinel 2.7.22. Centinel weakens his argument by assuming that the Constitution required one representative for every 30,000 persons. Article I, Section 2 provides that there cannot be *more* than one representative for every 30,000 persons. Thus the situation, from Centinel's point of view, was even worse than he thought.

90. Ibid., Federal Farmer 2.8.15. Federal Farmer's reference to jury trials in the vicinage touches on another important Anti-Federalist theme. Article III, Section 2 of the Constitution provides for a jury trial in criminal cases but not in civil cases. This was changed by the seventh amendment. Article III, Section 2 also specified that jury trials shall be held "in the state where the said crimes shall have been committed." Many Anti-Federalists found this provision inadequate. They demanded a trial in the "vicinage" of the offense, not merely within the state where the offense occurred. Modern readers might be surprised at Federal Farmer's willingness to rank trials in the vicinage as one of the two essentials of a free government. Many of the writers of the founding period stressed the important *political* function of juries. It was a way of including the people at the termination of the governmental process where laws are being applied to individual situations; just as the representatives of the people can be found at the beginning of the political process when the laws are made. If we were to use a contemporary analogy, the jury of the 1780s might be defended on the same grounds as popular participation in governmental decisions (e.g., rule-making under the Administrative Procedure Act) is defended today. There is an important difference, however. In contemporary rule-making procedures the participants are usually interested parties. The jurors were supposed to be disinterested. De Tocqueville saw great possibilities for the jury as an institution that develops civic virtue in the citizens because of the disinterested judgments they are asked to make. We seem to have lost something important along the way. Today jury duty is looked upon as a burden that shrewd citizens skillfully avoid. Nowadays popular participation in government decision making is justified on grounds of self-interest, not disinterested judgment.

In any event, the jury of the 1780s provides some help for those who look to the framers to support a modern argument for participatory democracy. The view many Anti-Federalists had of juries might somewhat soften the harsh language of Publius in *Federalist 63* where he celebrated "*the total exclusion of the people in their collective capacity* from any share in [America's] Governments." (Publius's italics.)

91. Ibid., Brutus 2.9.14. Obviously, Brutus would not be reconciled to the Constitution if a few more representatives were added to the House. His point is that republican principles cannot be satisfied in an extended republic — the point Publius attacks so brilliantly in *Federalist 10*. George Mason makes a somewhat similar argument when he uses the impossibility of meeting republican standards as the basis for his position that the federal government should have more restricted powers in very important matters such as navigation. CAF 5.17.1.

92. Ibid., Chase 5.3.20.

93. Melancton Smith is perhaps the most effective Anti-Federalist spokesman on representation. See CAF 6.12.1-40. passim. See also CAF 5.14.27-34; Storing's introduction to "Essays by A Farmer," CAF 5. p. 6; for further statements by Federal Farmer, see CAF 2.8.97, 106-107, 114, 117-118. For statements by George Mason, see CAF 2.2.2; 5.17.1; Tansill p. 161; Elliot III, p. 262, 265, 266.

94. Storing CAF: Minority of Convention of Pennsylvania 3.11.33.

95. For a recent discussion of Madison's views on representation, see Garry Wills, *Explaining America: The Federalist* (Garden City, N.Y.: Doubleday, 1981), p. 177-264. Wills argues that Madison looked to representation as the governmental institution that would refine not only public opinion, but civic virtue as well. Wills finds in Publius a more generous attitude toward the ordinary citizen than most commentators in the past have found.

96. At the Virginia Ratifying Convention, Patrick Henry offered the following *reductio ad absurdum* to Madison's filtering and refining: "If ten men be better than one hundred seventy, it follows of necessity that one is better than ten — the choice is more refined." Elliot III, p. 167.

97. Tansill, p. 349-350; 694.

98. Tansill, p. 694. Hamilton's candid fears of presidential corruption may stand as a monument to the wisdom of secrecy in some forms of decision making.

99. Tansill, p. 349.

100. See *Federalist 10* and *55-58*; also Tansill, p. 162-163.

101. Tansill, p. 160-161; see also statements by John Dickenson (Tansill, p. 168) and Hugh Williamson (Tansill, p. 668, 694, 720). Williamson raised the issue of representation on three occasions at Philadelphia. He seems to have been more interested in increasing the size of North Carolina's delegation than in a theory of representation.

102. Mason, Elbridge Gerry, and Edmund Randolph were the only members of the Convention who stayed till the end but refused to sign the Constitution. All three were quite active participants during the Convention, but Mason was more effective after the Convention than either Gerry or Randolph.

103. Tansill, p. 741.

104. Ibid.

105. Ibid.

106. Ibid.

107. For examples of Madison's emphasis on knowledge and information, see *Federalist 10, 35, 36,* and *57.*

108. *Federalist 58,* p. 396.

109. Storing CAF: M. Smith 6.12.14.

110. Harry Kranz, *The Participatory Bureaucracy* (Lexington, Mass.: Lexington, 1976); Kenneth Meier, "Representative Bureaucracy: An Empirical Analysis," *American Political Science Review* 69 (June 1975): 526-542; Kenneth Meier and Lloyd Nigro, "Representative Bureaucracy and Policy Preferences," *Public Administration Review* 36 (July/August 1976): 458-469; V. Subramaniam, "Representative Bureaucracy: A Reassessment," *American Political Science Review* 61 (December 1967): 1010-1019; and Samuel Krislov and David H. Rosenbloom, *Representative Bureaucracy and the American Political System* (New York: Praeger, 1981).

111. Norton Long, "Bureaucracy and Constitutionalism," *American Political Science Review* 46 (September 1952): 808-818.

112. Kenneth C. Davis, *Discretionary Justice: A Preliminary Inquiry* (Baton Rouge: LSU Press, 1969); Jeffrey L. Jowell, *Law and Bureaucracy: Administrative Discretion and the Limits of Legal Action* (Port Washington: Dunellen, 1975).

113. Storing, CAF: M. Smith 6.12.16-17.

114. Further "healing" may come from congressional staff. By a judicious use of patronage a public spirited congressman could come into close contact with those who think the way the people think and feel the way they feel.

115. Storing, *What the Anti-Federalists Were FOR,* p. 59.

116. A good comparison of the Whig and Republican positions can be found in Gordon S. Wood, *The Creation of the American Republic* (Chapel Hill: University of North Carolina Press, 1969), chaps. 1 and 2.

117. See the report of the Pennsylvania ratification debate in John B. McMaster and Frederick D. Stone, *Pennsylvania and the Federal Constitution 1787-1788,* 2 vols. (New York: Da Capo Press, 1970), I. p. 229. The Da Capo edition is a reprint. The book was originally published in one volume in Philadelphia in 1888.

118. Ibid., I, p. 302. Wilson's position is interesting. He was among the most democratic members of the 1787 Convention and hence it is not surprising that he should take the lead in developing a popular sovereignty interpretation of the Constitution. During that Convention he held a microcosm view of the legislature, but he had abandoned this position by the time of the ratification debate in Pennsylvania. For Wilson's microcosm statement during the Convention, see Tansill, p. 160. A discussion of Wilson's position on sovereignty at the time of the Revolution can be found in Bernard Bailyn, *The Ideological Origins of the American Revolution* (Cambridge: Harvard University Press, 1967), p. 224-226. For a thorough critique of Wilson's political thought, see Ralph A. Rossum, "James Wilson and the Pyramid of Government: The Federal Republic," in Ralph A. Rossum and Gary L. McDowell, eds., *The American Founding: Politics, Statesmen and the Constitution* (Port Washington, N.Y.: Kennikat Press, 1981), p. 62-79.

119. McMaster and Stone, p. 229.

120. Wood, p. 547. See also p. 532:

Relocating sovereignty in the people by making them "the fountain of all power" seemed to make sense of the entire system. Once the Federalists perceived "the great principle of the primary right of power in the people," they could scarcely restrain their enthusiasm in following out its implications. One insight seemed to lead to another, until the Federalists were tumbling over each other in their efforts to introduce the people into the federal government, which they had "hitherto been shut out of." "The people of the United States are now in the possession and exercise of their original rights," said [James] Wilson, "and while this doctrine is known and operates, we shall have a cure for every disease."

121. Herbert J. Storing, "The 'Other' Federalist Papers: A Preliminary Sketch," *Political Science Reviewer* (1976): 230 (emphasis added.)

122. For the pertinent language used in Pennsylvania Ratification Debate, see McMaster and Stone, 1970, vol. 1: 229, 250, 260, 270. See also *Federalist 27* where Publius refers to "all officers legislative, executive and judicial" and *Federalist 28* and *46* where all government officials are called representatives. Frank J. Goodnow refers to both elected and appointed personnel as "officers" in *Principles of the Administrative Law of the United States* (New York: Putnam, 1905), p. 257. He tends to blur the distinction by using the expression "the official relation" to describe both elected and appointed personnel, p. 222-315 *passim*. During his presidency, Jefferson referred to both legislative and executive personnel as "officers" and to elected officials as "public functionaries." Jefferson, *Works* IX 392-393; James D. Richardson, ed., *A Compilation of the Messages and Papers of the Presidents, 1789-1897* (Washington: GPO, 1899), p. 98-99. John Adams was the principal author of the Massachusetts Constitution of 1780 which includes members of the legislature within the term "officer." On James Wilson, see Tansill, p. 126. See Tansill, p. 433 where both Williamson and Gerry include legislators in the term "officer." On Edmund Burke, see Hanna F. Pitkin, *The Concept of Representation* (Berkeley: University of California Press, 1967), p. 172. Storing and Wood are not the only contemporary scholars who describe nonelected officials of the eighteenth century as "representatives." See Martin Diamond, *The Founding of the Democratic Republic*, p. 79; and Martin Diamond, "The Federalist" in Leo Strauss and Joseph Cropsey, eds., *History of Political Philosophy*, 2nd ed. (Chicago: University of Chicago Press), p. 643 and 645. Matthew Crenson speaks of "the Republic's Administrative Representatives" in *The Federal Machine: Beginnings of Bureaucracy in Jacksonian America* (Baltimore: John Hopkins University Press, 1975), p. 6. This language is consistent with Hamilton's use of the terms "representative democracy" to describe the government created by the Constitution. In using this expression, Hamilton was referring to the constitutional order as a whole and not just to its directly elected officials. Diamond, *The Founding of the Democratic Republic*, p. 69.

123. Storing, *What the Anti-Federalists were FOR*, p. 62.

124. Emphasis added. Storing notes that for the Federalists, elections were "*merely* a method of choosing, not a method of authorizing." (Emphasis added; see p. 70 above.)

125. A crude version of Adams's argument was stated by Gouverneur Morris at the Constitutional Convention in 1787; see Tansill, p. 319-321.

126. An argument affirming a mixed regime in the Constitution can be found in Paul Eidelberg, *The Philosophy of the American Constitution* (New York: Free Press, 1968).

127. Storing, "The 'Other' Federalist Papers," p. 231.

128. Tansill, p. 156.

129. Ibid., p. 229, 240-241, 244, 275, 325.

130. Ibid., p. 206.

131. Ibid., p. 226-234.

132. Ibid., p. 234.

133. Ibid., p. 240.

134. Ibid., p. 241.

135. Ibid.

136. For a discussion of *Federalist 78*, see David F. Epstein, *The Political Theory of The Federalist* (Chicago: University of Chicago Press, 1984), p. 186-190.

137. Woodrow Wilson, "The Study of Administration," *Political Science Quarterly* 2 (June 1887): 197-222.

138. Publius uses "department" where we use "branch" today. Contemporary usage is preferable for the present discussion in order to avoid confusion between the three great departments in Articles I, II, and III of the Constitution and the Executive Departments of Article II.

139. Lynton K. Caldwell, *The Administrative Theories of Hamilton and Jefferson* (New York: Russell and Russell, 1964), p. 36, 99-100.

140. The story was literally front page news for the first few months of 1983. A particularly insightful story about a central figure, Rita Lavelle, appeared in *The Washington Post* of 5 March 1983, p. C1.

141. The Superfund scandal was the most notable example during President Reagan's first term of politically appointed officials trying to change administrative practice because of the results of the presidential election of 1980. It was not the only example. The "Air Bags" dispute over Department of Transportation regulations on passive restraints ended up before the Supreme Court of the United States where Justice White gave a firm endorsement to the integrity of the administrative process against presidential claims of a popular mandate. *Motor Vehicle Manufacturers of the U.S. v. State Farm Mutual Automobile Insurance Co.* 103 S.Ct. 2856 (1983). Writing for the Court, Justice White reaffirmed the doctrine of the first *Chenery* case, 318 U.S. 80 (1943), that the administrative process must be governed by *reasoned* decision making. For a discussion of the Reagan administration's efforts to change coal surface-mining regulation, see Donald Menzel, "Redirecting the Implementation of a Law: the Reagan Administration and Coal Surface Mining Regulation," *Public Administration Review* 43 (Sept-Oct. 1983), p. 411-430.

142. The expression is taken from Woodrow Wilson's famous essay, "The Study of Administration," *Political Science Quarterly* 2 (June 1887). It was in that essay that Wilson said, "it is getting to be harder to run a Constitution than to frame one."

143. Throughout this discussion the focus is on the *discretionary* authority of the Public Administration. Where ministerial functions are involved, administrators should execute legally correct commands. The rule of law demands nothing less. This principle, however, is not terribly helpful because the most important issues for administrators concern discretionary matters wherein the law empowers rather than commands. There may still be considerable administrative discretion even after a clear and legally correct command has been given because such a command may contradict another clear and legal command from a competing institution of government. An executive order at odds with its alleged statutory foundation is the classic case. For a good discussion of the impact of executive orders on the administrative process, see Phillip J. Cooper, "By Order of the President: Administration by Executive Order and Proclamation," *Administration and Society* 18 (forthcoming, 1985).

144. Louis Fisher, *Presidential Spending Power* (Princeton: Princeton University Press, 1975), p. 73, 76. Fisher's discussion of impoundment under President Nixon shows the limitation of gentlemen's agreements when one of the parties to the agreement is no gentleman. (See chap. 8.) The discussion of "reprogramming" in chap. 4 suggests opportunities for the sort of administrative statesmanship envisioned in the theory of Public Administration I have in mind.

145. Stephen Skowronek, *Building the New American State: The Development of Administrative Capacities 1877-1920* (New York: Cambridge University Press, 1981), p. 24-35.

146. An excellent discussion of the role of the judiciary in the administrative state appears in David H. Rosenbloom, *Public Administration and Law: Bench v. Bureau in the United States* (New York: Marcel Dekker, 1983), chap. 7.

147. John A. Rohr, "Public Administration and the Constitutional Bicentennial: An Essay on Research," *International Journal of Public Administration* 4 (1982): 349-380.

148. This point is developed in the second chapter of John A. Rohr, *Ethics for Bureaucrats: An Essay on Law and Values* (New York: Marcel Dekker, Inc., 1978).

149. Edward S. Corwin, *The President: Office and Powers*, 4th ed. (New York: New York University Press, 1957), p. 153.

150. The leading cases are *In re Neagle*, 135 U.S. 1 (1890); and *In re Debs*, 159 U.S. 564 (1895). *Myers* v. *U.S.*, 272 U.S. 52 (1926), somewhat ironically supports Theodore Roosevelt's exuberant view of presidential authority. The irony comes from the fact that the opinion was written by Chief Justice Taft whose own writings on the presidency were critical of Roosevelt's position.

151. It has often been noted that the "Madisonian Model" of pluralism was intended to exist only in Congress and not in the executive branch. Among the delegates to the 1787 convention, George Mason was the strongest proponent of pluralism in the executive branch. He opposed the one-man executive. When he lost on this issue, he argued for an executive council to limit the president's power. His loss on this issue as well was one of the main reasons why he eventually joined the Anti-Federalist opposition to the Constitution. Publius, of course, speaks often of "unity in the executive." Care must be taken in interpreting his position in this matter. Unity in the executive does not always mean rigid hierarchy as in the managerial textbook notion of unity of command. At time Publius's target was the plural executive favored by some Anti-Federalists. Unity in the executive at times means nothing more than a defense of a one-man presidency. Pluralism in the executive may be looked upon as a contemporary expression of the Anti-Federalist heritage.

152. Theodore J. Lowi, *The End of Liberalism* (New York: Norton, 1969).

153. Three recent books in administrative history bring out just how deeply the pluralist tradition is embedded in the American tradition. See Barry D. Karl, *The Uneasy State* (Chicago: University of Chicago Press, 1984); Stephen Skowronek, *Building a New American State*; and William E. Nelson, *The Roots of American Bureaucracy: 1830-1900* (Cambridge: Harvard University Press, 1982). Nelson makes a provocative argument that traces the origins of American bureaucracy to the fundamental American commitment to pluralism. The connection between anti-slavery sentiment and Civil Service Reform has often been noted. The strength of Nelson's book lies in its explanation of how anti-slavery moral principles rallied to the support of bureaucratic structures. The deed was done in the name of pluralism. See especially Nelson's fifth chapter, "Building Bureaucratic Authority Structures."

154. A good survey of this literature can be found in Chester A. Newland, "Professional Public Executives and Public Administration Agendas," in Chester A. Newland, ed., *Professional Public Executives* (Washington, D.C.: American Society for Public Administration, 1980), p. 1-30.

155. Two particularly impressive organizations are the Federal Executive Institute Alumni Association and the Federal Executive and Professional Association. Their articulate newsletters provide considerable insight into the current mood of senior civil servants. Other groups include the Federal Managers Association, the American Foreign Service Association, the Federal Executive League, the Executive Women's Group, the Senior Executive Association, and Federally Employed Women, Inc. For an account of the formation of the Federal Employees' Roundtable, see *The Washington Post*, September 9, 1982, p. C2. For examples of "Federal Workers . . . Fighting Back," see *U.S. News and World Report*, August 29, 1983: 53-54. A good overview of these organizations appears in Eileen Seidman, "Hanging Together: Federal Executive Associations," *The Bureaucrat* (Winter, 1983): 40-43.

156. The survival of the Federal Executive Institute as a training facility for senior executives is due in no small part to organized pressure brought by career personnel in the SES. See David T. Stanley, "Civil Service Reform: Then and Now," in Patricia W. Ingraham and Carolyn Ban, eds., *Legislating Bureaucratic Change: The Civil Service Reform Act of 1978* (Albany: SUNY Press, 1984), p. 282.

157. The need for the SES to develop a sense of community for public-spirited purposes is discussed by Norton Long, "The S.E.S. and the Public Interest," *Public Administration Review* 41 (May-June 1981): 305-312.

3. Public Administration and the Public Interest

CHARLES T. GOODSELL

In 1936 one of the founders of modern political science, Pendleton Herring, published a book with the title *Public Administration and the Public Interest.* Written at the height of the New Deal, Herring's concern was that "special interests" had captured the legislative process, making it difficult for Roosevelt to create a positive American state. To him the only adequate counterweight to particularized, self-regarding rule via Congress was a large, competent, and responsive public administration. "Can we," he asked, "build up within our administration a rallying point for effective opposition to the selfishly organized groups that terrorize our representative assemblies into granting them special favors?"[1]

Herring was, in effect, asking whether The Public Administration could be considered a legitimate, balancing, constitutionalized institution of governance in the spirit of this book. If this thoughtful intellectual were still in our midst we would certainly ask him to engage in the revitalized dialogue called for in Chapter 1. One issue he would surely raise is that of an appropriate normative basis for public administration. Herring believed this matter was still unresolved despite the exuberance of New Deal governance. In rising above the special groups the civil servant "has no clear standard upon which to act," he wrote. The president cannot give him personal direction, he added, and administrative law provides only procedural guidance. But nonetheless there *is* a lodestar available to the public servant:

> What criteria are to guide him? The *public interest* is the standard that guides the administrator in executing the law. This is the verbal symbol designed to introduce unity, order, and objectivity into administration.
>
> This concept is to the bureaucracy what the "due process" clause is to the judiciary. Its abstract meaning is vague but its application has far-reaching effects.[2]

Unfortunately we have not, in the fifty years that have gone by since the publication of Herring's book, pursued the full implications of his position.

Theorists in public administration have tended instead to (1) ignore "the public interest" as a concept relevant to administrative behavior; (2) define administrative competences and values in terms of economic efficiency and managerial control; or (3) regard public bureaucracy itself as captured by special interests. Although it is true that some in the field still discuss the notion of public interest, they do so with none of the intellectual excitement and implicit promise of Herring's work. One recent analysis assumes the public interest can be found through periodic citizen surveys; another portrays public interest rhetoric as camouflaging special favors to groups; a third discussion calls for systematic inclusion of the public interest in a "Public Service Model" of administration, but concludes that defining the term is still an unsolved problems.[3]

One wonders if public administration theorists abandoned serious inquiry on the concept of public interest simply because the notion fell from academic favor. Always on the defensive intellectually it seems, public administration scholars are terrified by the prospect of being perceived as old-hat or not sufficiently rigorous. Indeed, as Richard Stillman has written, a notion of generic public interest almost had to be passé in the 1960s and 1970s, in view of enthusiasm for such specific "good causes" as the plight of the poor, minorities, consumers, and environment. In Stillman's words,

> The Public Interest became the public interest: i.e., clouded, more fragmented, less easy to know or act upon and, hence, it became a subject few administrative theorists addressed or even tried to assert as an important or worthy guide for administrators' action . . . . The public interest became a poor road map to follow in the turbulence of the times. Indeed the subject was something of an embarrassment for serious students of the field to "take seriously."[4]

Yet, as mentioned in Chapter 1, the words *public interest* — despite their poor academic reputation — remain in use in the realm of *practical* government. They are found sprinkled throughout the statutes practitioners administer, the memoranda they write, the testimony they give, and the verbal speech with which they articulate their points of view. Should academics in the field blithely disregard or reject outright a notion that is at the heart of normative considerations in the practice of public administration? I propose that they should not.

The Schubert Critique

In searching for a meaningful concept of public interest let us begin by retracing our intellectual steps to the point where academic interest in the public interest seriously wavered. The event that seemed to destroy the confidence of public administration theorists with respect to the intellectual value of the concept was Glendon Schubert's article of 1957. I have found no serious advocacy of the notion in the literature which is avowedly public administrationist since that time. Schubert ridiculed the field's writings on the subject and concluded that the public interest notion is close to useless in the development of a true social science. Making sure in his analysis that the phrase was always surrounded by deprecating quotes, Schubert divided writers on the public interest into three categories.

"Proponents of Administrative Rationalism" are characterized as positivists who believe the public interest is what the legislature says it is. The task of administration then becomes efficient implementation of this will. "The model constructed by the positivists," he said, "is a sausage machine, into one end of which is poured the public will and out of the other end of which drop neat little segments of the public interest, each wrapped in its own natural casing." Schubert's second group is the "Advocates of Administrative Platonism." They are depicted as "social engineers" who mystically speak of professionalism, empathy, and conscience, but are in effect exhorting: "Be clever!," "Be wise!," "Be good!," and even "Be God!" The third category is the "Administrative Realists," who define the public interest in terms of process. "The principal difficulty of their theory," writes Schubert in a delightful mixing of metaphors, "lies in its generality, for they describe wondrous engines (including the human mind) into which are poured all sorts of miscellaneous ingredients which, after a decent period of agitation, are spewed forth from time to time, each bearing a union label which reads: 'Made in the Public Interest in the U.S.A.' "[5]

In addition to the apparent efficacy of Schubert's attack, this author's review of the literature led him to a second conclusion. It was unexpected, due I suppose to a combination of bias and ignorance on my part: despite rejection of the notion by Schubert in the name of scientific study of politics, other political scientists outside public administration were not frightened off at all! To the contrary, they proceeded in the years following 1957 to develop a number of creative ideas on the subject. Let us review these ideas for possible use to American public administration.

An Inventory of Public Interest Ideas

Of course, not all political scientists have been warmly attracted to the idea. In their writings on the subject they often devote more space to criticizing others' theories of public interest than presenting positive alternatives. A case in point is a 1957 article by Frank Sorauf. He categorizes several approaches to defining *public interest* and then concludes that because of the term's imprecision it is useless for purposes of scientific analysis. Yet, at the conclusion of his piece, Sorauf admits that the notion serves positive functions in American politics, even though these fall short of desired standards of intellectual rationality. These functions are four — unifying, legitimating, delegating, and representing. To recapitulate Sorauf:

1. The public interest "serves as a unifying symbol, a mutually congenial slogan, under which differing groups may compose their differences and join in

political coalition. As a 'binder' it welds majorities because so many groups can subscribe to it in the abstract and profit from the prestige it carries."

2. The public interest reassures citizens that the balance of interests achieved in formulating any given public policy "is something more worthy, and more deserving of our support, than the mere triumph of one or a number of powerful interests." In this way it legitimizes policy outcomes.

3. The very lack of clarity as to what public interest means permits a legislature "to frame a vague, undefined delegation of authority for an administrative agency that will later be expanded and explicated by the agency itself. The public interest becomes a means by which the necessity of specific definition, and the conflict of interests that would invite, is postponed to more propitious times and circumstances."

4. The public interest serves a "hair-shirt" function. "It has offered many a public servant and citizen an uncomfortable and persistent reminder of the unorganized and unrepresented (or underrepresented) interests in polities. It directs our attention beyond the more immediate and toward the often ignored interests." Thus the public interest "may represent the interests of freedom, equality, and opportunity — the widely-held and unorganized interests . . . that might be forgotten or overlooked in the pressure of political combat."[6]

Not all political scientists are as worried about recognizing the irrationality in politics as is Sorauf. In a little-noticed book published in 1960, Howard Smith argued that the public interest is a myth, but a "good" myth. It is useful because it creates pressures in behalf of the two social habits that Smith believes are essential to democracy: (1) a habit of responsiveness to the public by policy-makers and (2) the habit of making policy within a built consensus in accord with the preferred method and accepted rate of political change. The public interest notion promotes responsiveness, Smith believes, by pressing policy-makers to keep their minds open until decisions are made. This is accomplished by the inevitable variety of values that can be espoused under the broad rubric of public interest. The public interest also encourages consensus by requiring those in the society who make policy demands to address their justification of preferred policies to the sense of the community. Smith argues that in so doing it is difficult to ignore, at least blatantly, the need to resolve political conflict harmoniously.[7]

A well-known anthology on the public interest is volume 5 of *Nomos*, published in 1962.[8] Some nineteen writers discuss the topic from a variety of perspectives, including Schubert and Sorauf. C. W. Cassinelli, addressing the topic of political ethics, points out that just because a public official exercises discretion to interpret the public interest in a concrete situation does not mean that the official then becomes arbitrary or uncontrolled. In Cassinelli's view all the usual standards of official responsibility must be seen as embraced by the standard, including requirements to observe the constitution and conduct business honestly and efficiently. However open-ended the notion, he concludes, it carries with it obligations as well as rights.[9]

In the same volume Stephen Bailey comments on a paradoxical aspect to public interest. While on the one hand public officials utter the phrase with great ease to justify what they wish to do, on the other hand its symbolism requires them to provide a reasoned basis for their aims in the first place. Thus, although the public interest may be "balm for the official conscience" and "one of society's most effective analgesics," to be used for this rationalizing function "public servants must be able to give it a rational content anchored in widely shared value assumptions." As a consequence, Bailey concludes that the public interest is no less than "the central concept of a civilized polity. Its genius lies not in its clarity but in its perverse and persistent moral intrusion upon the internal and external discourse of rules and ruled alike."[10]

A third idea of importance in the *Nomos* volume is related to Bailey's but emphasizes how the meaning of the public interest accumulates over time. Roland Pennock makes this point in the administrative context by noting how a vacuous "public interest" statutory provision that is given over to an agency to interpret does not remain an empty receptacle for administrators to fill and refill at their convenience. Rather, it emerges and develops as an evolving, ever more specified and elaborated guiding concept. "A legislature that delegates to an administrative agency the power to regulate in accordance with the public interest is not merely 'passing the buck'; it is providing the means for applying a dynamic and increasingly precise policy based on experience."[11]

Also appearing in 1962 was an article on the public interest by Anthony Downs. Although a founder of what we today call public choice theory would seem to be the last to contribute to public interest theory, Downs's article is full of provocative ideas on the subject. He explains that the reason he is writing the piece is that his book *An Economic Theory of Democracy* had been criticized for lacking a theory of the public interest, which he proceeds to supply.[12]

Downs contends, like those mentioned above, that just because the content of the public interest is unclear does not mean it cannot serve useful functions. One of these is to serve "as a guide to and a check on public officials who are faced with decisions regarding public policy but have no unequivocal instructions from the electorate or their superiors regarding what action to take." Downs states that the phrase forces the official to show the logic of a policy position and to tie that position to a reasonable value orientation. Further, it requires the official while defending a position to articulate its value base more clearly than would otherwise be the case: "the necessity of defending himself in this manner checks each public official from totally disregarding the welfare of potential questioners."

A second line of argument by Downs approaches the task of clarifying the public interest indirectly rather than directly. In the manner of much of the Bill of Rights and many doctrinal arguments in theology, he states what the public interest is *not* rather than what it *is*. One thing it is not, Downs contends, is a departure from the "minimal consensus" that holds a democracy together. This includes agreement on a vague image of what a "good society" consists. Also it incorporates policy principles, for example, that government ought to prevent depressions, and rules of policy making, such as majoritarianism. Downs concludes that "anything that is in the long run detrimental to the majority of citizens cannot be in the public interest, unless it is essential to the protection of those individual rights included in the minimal consensus."

Finally, Downs assigns a leadership function to the public official in regard to defining the public interest. Since there must be "at least a little bit of idealism in every government decision-maker" because of the above points; and because the official, "acting as a specialist in the division of labor, is usually in a far better position than the average citizen to know what alternative policies exist and what their consequences might be," the official should not stand aside while citizens make mistakes. Rather, the official "can attempt to change their views through information and persuasion, so that they will prefer the actions he believes best for them, and meanwhile carry out those actions." The key to such leadership, according to Downs, is the notion of public interest: "only because a government official has developed, however cynically, some concept of the public interest independent of current public opinion will he be able to make such judgments."[13]

Probably the most serious theorizing with respect to the public interest from a normative standpoint has been done by Richard Flathman. In a book published in 1966, Flathman points out that what we do when we utter the phrase and associate our views with it is to claim that a policy should be commended because its full impact on all affected persons has been considered and has been found desirable. If the espoused position is merely a personal opinion or a purely self-regarding view it does not deserve to be so labeled. The public interest is attained only when what Flathman calls the "universalizability principle" is observed, which requires us to seek not idiosyncratic benefits but to act in behalf of the entire class of persons similarly affected. Such positive effects include both factual, objective benefits and cognitively perceived or affectively desired outcomes.

In short, the public interest, unlike older concepts such as "public good" and "common weal," embraces subjective *interests* as well as objective *goods*.[14]

Flathman believes that observance of the concept of public interest requires those in governmental office who pronounce the term to search constantly for common ground among external demands being made on the state. Unanimity in this search is an impossible goal and should not be expected; in fact the very plurality of demands being reviewed will enrich whatever definition of the public interest that emerges. Ultimately someone must decide the definition for all, and this must be the government official since government acts in the name of all and its actions apply to all. But to *be* in the public interest the official must consider the implications for all, in a spirit of goodwill and in an attempt to utilize the knowledge, information, and judgment "which only wide knowledge and information make possible."

This latter capacity, Flathman goes on, rests in an institutional context: "We establish central authority not merely to enforce decisions against recalcitrant citizens, but in order to build institutions which facilitate the gathering and assessment of the complex information necessary to proper judgments concerning public policy." The active pursuance of such a concept of public interest fosters what Flathman calls the "politics of public interest," that is, a politics where other-regarding benefits are widened and common ground is enlarged.[15]

In a volume published in 1970, Virginia Held gives an example of Flathman's "politics of public interest." She describes the public controversy over the quality of television programming that followed Newton Minow's "vast wasteland" speech of 1961. The positions taken by the Federal Communications Commissioners and industry spokesmen alike were forced by the FCC Act's public interest standard to address more than personal taste, broadcaster demands, and even audience ratings. Held concludes that "clearly a substantive discussion, capable of affecting governmental decisions, took place in which the phrase 'in the public interest' meant more than a preponderance of individual preferences, and the discussion was in large measure about what more it meant."[16]

The Public Interest as Public Discourse

We turn now from a review of public interest ideas from political science to possible application of these ideas to public administration. The following discussion is composed of two parts. We first consider how the public interest, as a verbal symbol, brings to the fore certain values when employed in the oral and written discourse in which public administrators engage. Second, we contemplate how bureaucracy itself relates to public interest values. The thesis that emerges is that the values inculcated into administration by the verbal symbol are in turn inculcated into the polity by bureaucracy, at least as it obtains in America.

Sorauf refers to public interest as a symbol, in that it unifies diverse groups around a common slogan and legitimizes public policy outcomes as something more worthy than a resultant of group forces. When we think of public interest as a symbol, it should be noted, we are relieved of the obligation to define clearly what public interest "means." Indeed, a verbal expression *cannot* be a symbol if its substantive content is overtly manifest; in that instance it would be a sign, not a symbol. The meaning of a symbol is, by definition, obscure, only partially understood, and felt emotionally rather than known in a precise cognitive way. The symbol's distant and shrouded referent is, in fact, a basic explanation for its power and mystique. When social scientists such as Schubert demand that the public interest be explicitly defined in order to have any methodological usefulness they fail to understand this fundamental point. If a symbol can be precisely operationalized its "content" has either been destroyed in the act of explication or not captured at all.

The public interest is obviously a *political* symbol. Cobb and Elder classify political symbols in three categories: (1) Community, or symbols that invoke feelings about the entire polity (e.g., democracy, constitution); (2) Regime, a less general type that specifies accepted rules of governance (such as due process, majority rule); and (3) Situational, a still more specific category that refers to political actors or policy issues (Ronald Reagan, gun control).[17] Within this typology, public interest would probably be classified in the second category. Another typification could be what Merelman calls "metasymbol." By this he means especially important higher-order political symbols that permit lower-order legitimizing symbols to come into being. "Metasymbols are legitimacy symbols which indicate the proper circumstances under which new symbols of legitimacy may be introduced, the criteria of acceptability for such symbols, and possibly, the method by which they may become legitimate."[18] Perhaps its status as metasymbol is why Bailey considers public interest to be "the central concept of a civilized polity."

As a *verbal* symbol, it is in *discourse* that the concept makes its impact. Following the thinking of Downs and Flathman as well as Bailey, we can assume that in the formal language of officials the words *public interest* constitute more than propaganda or analgesic balm. Within the American context, they convey, perpetuate, and inculcate certain values. Flathman notes the emphatically commendatory valence of the term; hence use of the symbols endorses specified values by commending behavior that can be defended as in accord with them. Obviously mere utterance of a phrase does not determine commendable behavior or enforce desirable values. The contribution is, rather, one of establishing a normative frame of reference, of subtly conditioning the terms of public policy discussion, and of giving higher-order purposiveness a more elevated position of attention than it would otherwise occupy. As the philosopher of language John Searle points out, the very fact that we employ certain words commits us to underlying value premises that derive from them. Searle calls these the "constitution rules of the institution." The constitutive rule of "private property," for example, is that one should not steal; the rule of "public debt" is that the government should repay its creditors.[19]

Let us now entertain the issue of the constitutive rules or values that are reinforced by the verbal symbol "public interest." Drawing upon the ideas of the authors reviewed above, six suggest themselves.

Legality-Morality

As Cassinelli points out, the lack of specific content in the standard of public interest does not grant the official an open invitation to exercise untrammeled discretion. It implies, at the very least, adherence to law, the constitution, and the basic precepts of moral behavior such as honesty and integrity. Being lawful and moral are commonly seen as "good"; and lawful and moral conduct by public officials would no doubt fall into what Downs calls the society's "minimal consensus." Thus, to employ Downs's indirect method of thereby defining interest, it would not normally include lying, cheating, grossly ignoring the courts, or blatantly violating statutes. Hence discourse peppered with the phrase "in the public interest" would not, perforce, be the language of conspirators and plotters. An action like shredding evidence or calculating how to circumvent a statute is more likely planned with such phrases as "You know what you have to do." Use of the term *public interest* implies that, at the very least, the user is *claiming* to be law-abiding and decent. In this respect it differs strikingly from such phrases as "reason of state" or "military necessity."

Political Responsiveness

A second value stressed by the term is conformity to the overriding wishes of citizens or relevant groups. Such responsiveness is once again within the bounds of Downs's minimal-consensus notion for a democratic society. Indeed, he is quite explicit in arguing that any step contradictory in the long run to preserving majority rule and minority rights must be contrary to the public interest. Smith reminds us that the very open-content nature of the public interest encourages officials to weight external opinions other than their own. Flathman points out that the multiplicity of external demands made in the name of public interest enriches its ultimate definition.

Hence consumer protection measures or steps against child abuse can be easily defended in the language of public interest because of their broad popularity. Also varied interpretations as to what will best achieve the aims of actually protecting consumers and children can be discussed in such terms. Discourse directed at undercutting these efforts or substituting contrary aims must, by contrast, be talked of in such terms as "stopping big government," "promoting free enterprise," or "deficit reduction." This is, perhaps, why political reactionaries seldom use the term *public interest*.

Political Consensus

Public interest discourse not only requires officials to defend themselves in terms of what the public wants, it also requires contending groups within the public to defend their positions in terms broader than naked self-interest. Sorauf points out how the vague meaning of public interest permits policy differences between groups to be papered over. It is often observed that in pending legislation a generally phrased preamble or vaguely defined standard may assist in the formation of a coalition to support a bill. If more explicit language were used, the coalition would break apart because its separate elements would appear disloyal to their internal constituencies.

Yet something deeper than simple deception may occur. As Sorauf notes, the public interest label carries a certain prestige. Such appeal will extend outside the narrow circles of the group and its constituency. By donning the mantle of favoring the public interest, the group can claim a standing more important than is otherwise the case. Further, by helping to create an actual emerging common ground between itself and competing groups, the special claimant enlarges the opportunity for this elevation of importance. Since such common ground is "sacred" compared to the mere "secular" appeals of self-interest, occupying it can be helpful strategically. As Smith points out, the group can thereby associate itself with the broader sense of the community, especially if it displays a desire to resolve the conflict harmoniously.

Another author in this volume, Camilla Stivers, has pointed out how it is possible to think of consensus in policy debate at still a third level.[20] An interpretivist notion of constructed social reality, such as espoused by Berger and Luckmann,[21] leads to the conclusion that the formation of common ground does not require something as formidable as a shift in the objectively fixed positions of opponents. Rather, opposing positions can be subjectively reconstructed and thereby joined. That is to say, "intersubjective understanding" can be formed as contenders reshape what "they" want. Former positions are not forcibly abandoned or even compromised — they are substituted for in light of a newly perceived reality.

To the extent this is possible, the ideal of public interest then becomes a useful conceptual repository within which a merging intersubjective understanding can be lodged. It also serves as a binder for the reconstruction process and a rationalization for the new reality. This view is not as radical as it may appear; even an apparent positivist such as Flathman argues that subjective desires as well as factual benefits are embraced by the word *interest*. A notion of "common good," by contrast, must exist independently of the private worlds of individuals and thus does not serve in this unifying manner.

Concern for Logic

A fourth value propagated by public interest discourse is connectedness between advocated public policy and its underlying normative purposes. In this way policymakers are held accountable for what they advocate in ways that transcend legal or fiduciary accountability. Bailey contends that for the public interest phrase to have "analgesic" effectiveness, officials must avoid using it with complete cynicism, that is, as a mere facade of justification for unjustified acts. Instead they must take the notion seriously, which means giving it "a rational content anchored in widely shared value assumptions." Downs takes a similar position. He views the concept as imposing a check on officials by requiring them to justify their positions publicly as inherently logical and tied to reasonable purposes. In other words, since the *public* interest claim so clearly refers to fulfillment of broad societal purposes, it is incumbent upon those who use it in discourse to make a case, at least, that: (1) the societal purposes are valid as articulated; (2) the advocated policy will tend to advance these purposes; and (3) the advocated policy itself is reasonable and coherent.

To illustrate, the National Park Service recently announced that it planned to limit visitor access to certain national parks. In this announcement it (1) emphasized that (a) park ecosystems must be preserved over the "long run" and (b) visitors must be given a "quality outdoor experience." Further, the Park

Service (2) pointed out that closing the parks when they are full respects their "carrying capacity"; and (3) noted that (a) indirect controls had been tried in the past and had failed (e.g., limiting inns and campgrounds) and (b) in an experimental closing only one letter of complaint had been received.[22] One cannot envision a private campground or game preserve issuing such an elaborated justification for turning away customers!

Concern for Effects

A related value advanced by public interest discourse is concern for the effects of public policy. Appealing for support of policy on grounds that it is in the public interest implies that the policy is commendable because its probable effects have been investigated and found to be beneficial. This concern focuses not on traced connectedness, as in the previous concern, but on examined implications. In Flathman's language, the public interest defense says, in effect, that we have examined the future effects of the policy on all affected persons and have concluded that they are beneficial; that is, we are not proceeding blindly or projecting lack of concern about impacts — rather, we are proposing the policy knowledgeably and responsibly.

The *future* orientation of this impact value calls for long-term consideration of effects, with the park-visitor limitation policy given above illustrating this. Also involved is a *comprehensiveness* requirement, associated with Flathman's universalizability principle. When we claim a policy is in the public interest we are in effect maintaining that its effects on *all* affected persons have been considered. The Environmental Protection Agency, for example, could not claim that a water pollution measure is in the public interest without showing that in weighing its adoption the agency had considered the needs of municipalities, industry, workers, navigational interests, and recreational groups — and not just one or two of these categories. Another way of expressing the value is the assertion that the agency's policy making has been "even-handed" or "balanced." The public interest standard is, needless to say, open-ended as to which group's effects will be considered most heavily when the moment of decision making is at hand. But that is a different matter.

Agenda Awareness

A final value that is stressed by public interest dialogue is concern for inarticulated needs within the society. Whereas debate between private interest consists of making and exchanging articulated demands and is normally limited to that, discourse on the public interest allows consideration of issues or needs not yet advocated by any private interest. Stating the point another way, one can claim that it is in the public interest to place the interests of a certain group of ignored persons, who have been silent so far in the public debate, on the agenda of the political system and of government itself. This is the point made by Sorauf with respect to his "hair-shirt" function.

The very phrase *public interest* reminds us that interests exist other than private and that they may be unrepresented. It thus creates a generalized awareness that the public agenda is always unfinished. Unrepresented interests are likely to be, in a system of pressure politics, persons or groups too poor, too unorganized, or too unsophisticated to play the policy game well or even to try to play it at all. Examples from the past are migrant farm workers, teenage runaways, purchasers of used cars, and widows facing aggressive funeral directors at a time of bereavement. It is no accident that lobby groups that push for legislation or regulation in behalf of such organized interests call themselves "public interest" organizations or law firms. In this instance the verbal symbol is no longer a Regime symbol or Metasymbol but a Situational symbol, in Cobb and Elder's classification. It refers to a specific category of political actor, such as a Ralph Nader. The phrase would not be endlessly repeated by Nader if he did not regard it as bearing a legitimizing mystique for his work.

The Public Interest as Public Administration

We turn finally to contributions to public interest values made by public administration. As indicated, I am portraying the public interest as not merely a means of internalizing certain values in the minds of participants in policy making, but also as a means of externalizing certain values via the public bureaucracy. In short, the public interest is not only a verbal symbol but also an institutional force; public interest discourse becomes, in Flathman's language, public interest politics.

I realize that depicting such a role for public bureaucracy will strike many as unjustified and even ludicrous. "Bureaucracy" is of course a principal *bête noire* in popular and academic culture. Most discussions of its relationship to the public interest revolve around how bureaucracies become active proponents of a narrow point of view and then try to legitimate their activism under the guise of public interest. Alternatively, naive theories of a politics-administrations dichotomy are sometimes propounded in which administrators are seen as not even involved in policy making and hence not concerned with the public interest.

Contrary to these more orthodox views, public bureaucracy is regarded here as the leading institutional embodiment and proponent of the public interest in American life. It is, of course, not the only such proponent; the public interest groups mentioned above as well as other institutions also see themselves in this role. Yet, I would argue, in terms of "volume" of contribution if not intensity, the able, high-level, professional public administrator can outdo even a Ralph Nader. He or she can also surpass, in my view, the typical judge's and legislator's contribution to public interest values. This is not because the bureaucrat is more noble or intelligent, but because of characteristics of the administrative apparatus itself. Public administration's contribution is an *institutional* one.

Bureaucracy's public interest contribution can be considered in the framework of the six values reviewed earlier.

Legality-Morality

Public administration advances the cause of legality and morality in government in at least four ways. First, the professionalism brought to government by the civil service is itself a source of conformity to ethical and legal standards. Preprofessional, patronage bureaucracy is romantically viewed by some, but its standards of personal conduct are hardly worthy of emulation today. Second, a persistent theme in the culture of administration is the requirement of accountability. The recordkeeping, audits, accounting procedures, performance evaluation, and appeals channel abundant in modern bureaucracy are often chastised as "red tape," yet they impart to government standards of behavior that would otherwise not exist. When the accountability theme of modern administrative culture is absent, for example in informally run congressional offices or personalized local government fiefdoms, their absence is notable, with deplorable results.

A third contribution emanates from Pennock's point with respect to legislative delegation of policy making to administration by means of ambiguous public interest language. This kind of lawmaking, often necessary because of technical uncertainties, does not undercut constitutionalism since the undefined governmental authority is gradually replaced by the bureaucrats with an elaborated standard. This creates a continuing, narrowed interpretation that is then reviewable by the legislature and courts. Without such emerging guidance, the law's meaning would be subject to particularized, ad hoc manipulation.

Finally, administrators contribute legality and morality by being available to report partisan abuse of power without being in a position to gain from it. An attempt by elected officials to use administrative power for electoral advantage, whether in Nixon's White House or Daley's City Hall, is more likely to be known by the bureaucrats than anyone else. They are the supreme insiders, after all; and they are in a position to initiate external disclosure via formal or informal channels. In surveying democracies around the world, Eva Etzioni-Halevy concludes that developed, nonpartisan bureaucracies alone seem to serve as a bulwark against political corruption, thus ultimately preserving the democratic nature of these system.[23]

Political Responsiveness

The bureaucracy is of course not parliament, and the administrative agency is often cited as a danger to democracy because it possesses power and yet its department heads are usually not elected. With respect to the political responsiveness value, then, the public administration probably makes less of a contribution than the legislature. Yet, as was pointed out in Chapter 1, a large bureaucracy is itself representative of the people in ways that a legislature is not. Bureaucrats tend to be demographically more like ordinary citizens than legislators. Also their personal and political views are generally not unlike those of the electorate as a whole.[24]

In other ways as well a public bureaucracy embodies the value of responsiveness. Studies have shown that government has been far more responsive to demands for equal employment opportunity by minorities and women than has the private sector.[25] Many of the institutions of citizen participation that have sprung up within the American political system in the past two decades have been initiated by administrative agencies. Arrangements of advice and coproduction at the citizen level seem more meaningful and prolific within administration than other components of government.

Finally, bureaucracy is responsive in an expressive sense. A wave of sentiment passes through the population and it is responded to by legislative or executive organs of government, which pass appropriate statutes or issue appropriate orders. Political attention then turns elsewhere, with only the bureaucracy's methodical actions of implementation remaining to show that "someone cares." To illustrate, the elderly are naturally pleased when an Older Americans Act is passed, but it is the daily "meals-on-wheels" service that demonstrates the political system remains responsive.

Political Consensus

This expressive character of public administration, its concrete embodiment of the political consensus, also helps to bind the community together. Administrative activity is visible to all members of the population and is understood to affect all citizens. Hence it helps to form a sense of belonging to a collectivity; putting this in interpretivist terms, the reality of the "community" as intersubjectively understood is fostered. And the concrete visibility of administration is everywhere: buildings such as post offices, county extension offices, and district headquarters; sights and sounds like mail carriers on their rounds, children entering the public school, and the wail of police and fire truck sirens; and media expressions such as Armed Forces recruiting posters, television campaigns on hiring the handicapped, and "report drunk drivers to the police" bumper stickers. Aside from voting at election time, the citizen of a capitalist economy would scarcely know whether the government or even the state exists if it were not for the public administration.

Concern for Logic

Public bureaucracy propagates the value of logical public policy in two ways. First, it is the principal proponent of the disciplined process of examining alternative courses of government action that we call policy analysis. In recent decades policy analysis has assumed something of an exalted position in the field of public administration and in government itself. Although not capable of "scientific" or "objective" examination of issues, policy analysis does pursue the three elements of policy logic discussed earlier: (1) articulation of underlying purposes, (2) indication of how proposed actions advance these purposes, and (3) demonstration that the proposed actions are reasonable and coherent. Such outcomes of analysis, although unable to give "optimum" alternatives, at least try to fulfill Bailey's ideal of "rational content anchored in widely shared value assumptions."

Bureaucracy also acts as a force in behalf of logical policy by the way it is structured. One way purposes are refined and connectedness and reasonableness are pursued is to institutionalize disagreement between competing interests and points of view. The ensuing competition brings issues to the surface and winnows out arguments and counter arguments. To some extent all institutions of government structure disagreement, but usually on only one or two dimensions. Courts, for example, structure conflict between the opposing parties of plaintiff and defendant. Legislatures do so between political parties and among the various geographic regions represented. Bureaucracies, however, structure disagreement among rival agencies, hierarchical levels, subject-matter specialities, levels of jurisdiction (as in federalism), professions, areas (field offices), and dyadically opposing parties (as in the budget process). With so much structuring of conflict in so many ways, the public administration is not tightly integrated, as parodied versions of the Weberian model suggest, but is instead highly fragmented. This fragmentation is, however, corporately bound in systems of cooperation and decision making, thus making constructive exchanges of viewpoint possible.

Concern for Effects

Bureaucracy possesses, within government, unparalleled expertise, knowledge, files, experience, and technical skills; in this realm even parodied versions of Weber are not far wrong. By comparison, legislatures are amateurish whereas courts are narrowly based and elected executives superficially informed. It is the ability to amass information and mobilize specialized talent that enables bureaucracy to investigate the effects of public policy. Acquisition of knowledge of conditions around the country, appreciation of probable impacts on sectors of the economy, and prediction of resulting costs and benefits are better done in the public administration than elsewhere. Just as the field of policy analysis institutionalizes the search for policy logic, the field of planning institutionalizes consideration of the long view ahead. Similarly, the field of program evaluation institutionalizes the view back while the field of management information systems does so for the current situation. Without the public administration, government would indeed proceed blindly and unconcernedly; with it, it can act knowledgeably, responsibly, and in the public interest.

The writers reviewed at the beginning of this chapter endorsed, in effect, this view of public administration. Sorauf admits that the legislative delegation of authority to administrative agencies permits postponing specific definitions of the public interest to "more propitious times and circumstances." Downs agrees that governmental specialists will know more than the citizen as to what policy alternatives exist and what their consequences might be. Thus the official, in this case the public administrator, should assume the role of leader and attempt to persuade the citizen to follow what is deemed the most effective means to achieve a given end. Flathman, for his part, points out that the knowledge, information, and judgment needed to make decisions in the public interest cannot help but rest in an institutional context. He could be referring explicitly to bureaucracy when he says we must "build institutions which facilitate the gathering and assessment of the complex information necessary to proper judgments concerning public policy."

Agenda Awareness

Politicians, including elected executives and legislators, are always on the lookout for the new and attractive issue. But, for the most part, they are reactive politically. They respond to the demands of their constituents and those whose votes they are courting. If they did not do this, they would soon be out of office.

Bureaucrats, as a class, probably tend to be more proactive politically. For one thing, their jurisdiction may be, in one sense, less secure than that of the elected official. They do not have a fixed electoral district to represent which will persist indefinitely. Instead they depend on the persistence of a function of government. In traditional areas like law enforcement, public health, and transportation, these functions are never forsaken and hence the bureaucracies performing them are never abandoned. In social areas, however, a capitalist culture such as the American does not allow such permanence. Programs and agencies come and go, and are often funded poorly. As a result the bureaucrat must become an active entrepreneur, working hard to define problems and garner resources to ameliorate them. Like the business entrepreneur, the bureaucratic entrepreneur searches for "markets" and "customers." The consequence is the presence of institutions eager to represent unrepresented needs, including those of the underprivileged or disadvantaged. This allows needs to be represented as well as demands — Sorauf's "hair shirt" is institutionalized.

The uncomfortable side of bureaucratic entrepreneurship is a shameless catering to targeted groups ("needs assessment") and outright programmatic propaganda ("social marketing"). Certainly bureaucracy, like any human institution, is ambivalently motivated. Bureaucracies are self-interested, but they are not *based* on self-interest, as is the business corporation for example. Like philanthropic organizations, their raison d'etre is to assist others. This fact, plus the socialization of staff that takes place in many public service professions, creates an ethos of service within bureaucracy that is not found in the for-profit, private sector. The public administrations is, in effect, a kind of societal conscience, sensitive to underdogs and unrecognized problems.

The Public Interest in Summation

Pendleton Herring, writing at the beginning point of the modern administrative era in America, looked to public administration as the institutional means for stifling the "selfishly organized groups" that he saw to be "terrorizing our representative assemblies." He postulated that the concept of public interest could be conceived of as an adequate guide to the public administrator in this awesome civic task.

In the half-century since Herring expressed these aspirations, we have been accustomed to denying their feasibility. The public interest concept, while elaborated upon by several political scientists, was ridiculed or ignored in writing about and within public administration. Public bureaucracy has instead been regarded as either a neutral instrument or political activist in its own behalf.

In this chapter we reject these orthodoxies and contend that several of the political scientists' ideas on the public interest may be used to construct a model of the public interest that is particularly applicable to public administration. This model centers on six values that are posited as central to the public interest idea. These are: Legality-Morality, Political Responsiveness, Political Consensus, Concern for Logic, Concern for Effects, and Agenda Awareness. The model utilizes these public interest values in two ways. First, attention is drawn to how use of the phrase *public interest* in public discourse on governmental policy tends to insert these values more prominently into the political process because of the phrase's underlying premises and power as a verbal symbol. Second, it is shown how the public administration, because of its functions, structure, processes, and ethos, embodies and disseminates these values into the political system. In short, public administration is, on the one hand, affected itself, in favorable ways by public interest discourse; on the other hand, it in turn favorably affects the society through public interest politics. To quote Herring again, the public interest's "abstract meaning is vague but its application has far-reaching effects."

Notes

1. E. Pendleton Herring, *Public Administration and the Public Interest* (New York: McGraw-Hill, 1936), p. 5.

2. Ibid, p. 23.

3. A. W. McEachern and Jawad Al-Arayed, "Discerning the Public Interest," *Administration and Society* 15 (February 1984): 439-453. Barry M. Mitnick, "A Typology of Conceptions of the Public Interest," *Administration and Society* 8 (May 1976): 5-28, 23. Patricia W. Ingraham and Carolyn R. Ban, "Models of Public Management: Are They Useful to Federal Managers in the 1980s?," *Public Administration Review* 46 (March-April 1986): 152-160.

4. Richard J. Stillman, "The Romantic Vision in American Administrative Theory: Retrospectives and Prospectives," *International Journal of Public Administration* 7, 2 (1985): 114-115.

5. Glendon A. Schubert, Jr., " 'The Public Interest in Administrative Decision-Making: Theorem, Theosophy, or Theory," *American Political Science Review* 51 (June 1957): 346-368,

354, 357, 367. Schubert subsequently published a book generally attacking public interest theories, categorizing them as Rationalist, Idealist, and Realist. *The Public Interest: A Critique of the Theory of Political Concept* (Glencoe, Ill.: Free Press, 1960).

6. Frank J. Sorauf, "The Public Interest Reconsidered," *Journal of Politics* 19 (November 1957): 616-639, 638-639. Sorauf in a later piece attacks the vagueness of the term without acknowledging its contributions. See "The Conceptual Muddle," in *The Public Interest*, Nomos V, ed. Carl J. Friedrich (New York: Atherton, 1962), p. 183-190.

7. Howard R. Smith, *Democracy and the Public Interest* (Athens, Ga.: University of Georgia, 1960).

8. *The Public Interest*, Nomos V, ed. Carol J. Friedrich (New York: Atherton, 1962).

9. C. W. Cassinelli, "The Public Interest in Political Ethics," Nomos V, p. 44-53, 52.

10. Stephen K. Bailey, "The Public Interest: Some Operational Dilemmas," Nomos V, p. 96-106, 97, and 106.

11. J. Roland Pennock, "The One and the Many: A Note on the Concept," Nomos V, p. 177-82, 182.

12. Anthony Downs, "The Public Interest: Its Meaning in a Democracy," *Social Research* 29 (Spring, 1962): 1-36.

13. Ibid, p. 4, 9, 16-17.

14. Richard E. Flathman, *The Public Interest: An Essay Concerning the Normative Discourse of Politics* (New York: Wiley, 1966).

15. Ibid, p. 48.

16. Virginia Held, *The Public Interest and Individual Interest* (New York: Basic Books, 1970), p. 1.

17. Roger W. Cobb and Charles D. Elder, "The Political Uses of Symbolism," *American Politics Quarterly* 1 (July 1973): 305-338, 326. See also Elder and Cobb, *The Political Uses of Symbols* (New York: Longman, 1983), p. 36.

18. Richard M. Merelman, "Learning and Legitimacy," *American Political Science Review* 60 (September 1966): 548-561, 557.

19. John R. Searle, *Speech Acts: An Essay in the Philosophy of Language* (Cambridge: Cambridge University Press, 1969), especially chap. 8. The private property example is Searle's, the public debt example is mine.

20. See also Camilla Stivers, "The Need for 'The Public Interest' in Health Policy Debate," unpub. MS, Center for Public Administration and Policy, Virginia Polytechnic Institute and State University, March 1985, p. 9.

21. The reference is to Peter Berger and Thomas Luckmann, *The Social Construction of Reality* (New York: Doubleday, 1966).

22. *Washington Post*, June 8, 1985, p. A5.

23. Eva Etzioni-Halevy, *Bureaucracy and Democracy* (London: Routledge & Kegan Paul, 1983), p. 227.

24. Charles T. Goodsell, *The Case for Bureaucracy*, 2nd ed. (Chatham, N.M.: Chatham House, 1985), p. 82-88.

25. Ibid, p. 157-160.

4. The Agency Perspective: Public Administrators as Agential Leaders

GARY L. WAMSLEY

Introduction

The challenges facing the American political economy in its third century of nationhood require an effective Public Administration now more than ever. The expectations of government and its administrators are staggering. Working within a constitutional structure in which power is overlapping and shared, both horizontally between branches and vertically between levels of government, public administrators are expected to: develop and implement programs that further social change, equity, and justice; ameliorate the externalities and shortcomings of a market economy; and preserve economic dynamism and growth in the face of an aging infrastructure, mounting urban problems at home, and tougher international competition abroad. All this to be done, of course, without eroding civil liberties and while advancing equal opportunity. Public administration at all levels of government is unavoidably at the center of these daunting and conflicting challenges. The challenges would threaten any democratic republic, any political economy, and any public administration. It is unsettling to contemplate what it may do to ours.

At the same time, the longing for a sense of community and "connectedness" grows acute, yet community needs seem always to be overshadowed by individual and group demands (Bellah et al. 1985). At a time when public administration might be a force for generating community, the credibility of public institutions is crumbling, and the public confidence in public administration has seldom been lower (Farazmand forthcoming; Levine 1986).

Clearly the challenges ahead require "governance" (choosing, prioritizing, directing, and steering) as opposed to drift or gridlock (Wamsley et al, forthcoming). Yet governance requires a better and more dedicated public administration at all levels of government, one which plays an effective role in governance. Such a public administration is possible only if the respect for public institutions and the self-image of public administrators are restored.

114

An effective, competent, and respected Public Administration is a vital necessity for meeting the challenges of "running the American Constitution" today. The Constitution, however, not only makes effective and efficient administration difficult, it fails to resolve basic questions of administrative power in a clear and unambiguous way. When the troublesome question is asked, "To whom or what is the Public Administrator responsible and/or responsive?" The answer is a relatively long list including the Congress, the president, the courts, interest groups, the people, and the public interest.

Such an answer runs directly counter to our historic and popular conceptions of how administration and management should be structured — monocentrically and hierarchically. The answer infers that the Public Administrator's role requires little less than superhuman qualities in exercising statecraft in a field of clashing interests and values. The role demands a super-statesperson willing to accept pay and status geared to the merely "competent" (Culler 1986). Perhaps because of the idealism of those who have chosen to pursue a career with public service, we still have better public administrators than we deserve. Nonetheless, public administrators will need a refurbished self-image and relief from the bureaucrat-bashing that has been a prominent part of our contemporary political culture. Such refurbishment will be essential if public administrators are to meet the demanding role necessitated by the Constitution.

It will be difficult to enhance the self-image of public administrators and give them an enlarged role in the governance process without also recognizing their discretion and power. Clearly there is a need to simultaneously empower and constrain them. We suggest that a part of the answer lies in a normative guide.

A normative guide, of course, is not a novel idea. The founding fathers (both Federalists and Anti-Federalists) knew that cultivation of public virtues in administrators must be a key element in the survival and success of the Republic (Richardson and Nigro 1987: 369, 373). This was to be accomplished by relying on "the law of honor and outward esteem" (Forrest McDonald 1985: 189-199) as well as by public opinion and special education. The cultivation of public virtues in public administrators was an interest expressed by Woodrow Wilson a hundred years later (Richardson and Nigro 1987: 373). The interesting question is what should this normative guide for the cultivation of public virtues be?

Clearly this normative guide should *not* be something that suggests that public administrators should be anything more than a subordinate of other actors in the governance process. The guide *should* be something that conceptualizes the public administrator as an agent acting on behalf of others, yet doing so in a vigorous and thoughtful manner. It should build an autonomous agential role based on unique claims for a special role in governance. These claims should include: (1) expertise in operationalizing policy in the form of specific programs; (2) expertise in creating and sustaining processes and dialogue that results in the broadest possible definition of the public interest; (3) skills in community-building politics and the fostering of active citizenship; and (4) guardianship (along with other constitutional officers) of the Constitution and constitutional processes.

Developing a concept and norms with appropriate connotations, requires *pre*scription — not description. There must be a return to the spirit that existed when students and practitioners of public administration dealt unabashedly with norms and values and could be unapologetically positive toward The Public Administration and the Agency they served. Leonard D. White (1939), Paul Appleby (1949), John Gaus (1957), Norton Long (1949), and Emmette Redford (1958), for example, evince the mood and tone to be recaptured.[1]

Searching for a Word and Concept with Positive Connotations

Conceptualization of a normative guide for a more respected public administration requires a name that is not specific to, or synonymous with, some level of government or a structure like a cabinet-level department, a bureau, or a regulatory commission. It is important, however, to avoid the negative connotations attached to alternative words and to find one with special positive meaning. To answer Shakespeare's venerable question "What's in a name?," the answer is sometimes "A great deal." As Ralph Hummel has said,

> What has to be remembered is that in a very exact sense even a word is a theory. When you label something you not only raise what is labeled out of the dark or out of the chaos unto the light or into an order within which it can make sense, you also direct thinking along a certain path, and you foreclose other paths (Hummel 1985: 58; see also Habermas 1979).

> Beyond the dynamic nature of a word as both creator and activator in language is its related influence as maintainer and reinforcer of attitudes. As Murray Edleman has said "language dispels the uncertainty in speculation, changes facts to make them serve status distinctions and reinforces ideology," (1967: 48), or as Benjamin Whorf puts it, "there is no way we can get out of a perceptual set imposed by language without speaking another language (in Edelman 1976: 82).

> Agency and the Agential Perspective is an attempt to change our language, and therefore our thinking, to embody, in a more positive and prescriptive voice, the multiplicity of expectations and attitudes we have of public administrators. Simply exchanging the word agent for bureaucrat and Agency for bureaucracy, however, does not change the larger context in which the words are used. (A rose by any other name . . . ?) But the change does serve as a catalyst, a bump in the road that realigns our thinking towards more positive and helpful frames of reference which focus more on what we want from public administrators and what they are capable of doing and less on the negative, limited visions of the word "bureaucracy."

Agency and the Agential Perspective: An Overview

A word that offers some promise is the term *agent. Webster's Third New International Dictionary* (1981) defines *agent* as follows:

> ... (1) something that produces or is capable of producing a certain effect: an active or efficient cause; (2) one that acts or exerts power; (3) a person responsible for his acts; (4) a means or instrument by which a guiding intelligence achieves a result; (5) one who acts for or in the place of another by authority from him. (See also Giddens 1977).[2]

The first two definitions of *agent* are essential: acting and exerting power. Note, however, that the third definition introduces a different notion: that an agent is a "person responsible for his acts" or "one who *acts for*, or *in place of another by authority from him*" (emphasis added). These definitions begin to approximate the kind of concepts needed in the agential perspective we advocate; a perspective requiring the individual public administrator to see him or herself as a citizen agent standing in place of other citizens (principals), exerting power *for them and in their stead* to achieve an end, a collective purpose; but always consciously *responsible to them and acting by their authority*. The Public Administrator is thus a "special citizen"; not one with special status or privileges but rather one with special skills and responsibilities; standing in place of and acting for fellow citizens. The Agency is the bureaucratic/organizational/institutional embodiment of this concept.

In order for public administrators to be viewed as legitimate agents, the Agency must stand for: (1) the broadest possible definition of the public interest derivable from its statutory mandate, requirements for fiduciary responsibility, and consistent with the Constitution; and (2) a sincere search for a consensus on the "common good" within the realm of the substantive policy concerns that fall within the agency's ambit. It must not only satisfy or balance the most powerful interests impinging upon it as any successful institution would, but it also must seek to represent the unspoken interests of unwitting stakeholders and thus to invoke a higher common good. The agency thus must act as an agent for those citizens *not* present and indeed serve as the agent-trustee for all citizens of the nation, perhaps even those of future generations.

The Agency must therefore go beyond the mirroring of manifest and latent representation of interests suggested by theories of pressure groups or interest group liberalism. That would be a daunting enough task in itself. The Agency must, however, also pursue a common good — one that is distinguishable from what a society (even one faithfully represented) thinks it wants. Given a complex world and imperfect knowledge, a society faithfully represented may want something that in the long run may contribute to the "tragedy of the commons" described by Hardin (1968). In this classic example, it was to every individual English citizen's advantage to graze more sheep on the land held in common. Thus the individual wishes of all did not result in a common good but a common tragedy of overgrazing.[3] In such a case the responsibility of Agential Leadership is not to impose its notion of the common good in opposition to society's wishes, if these be manifest in constitutionally correct laws that are unswervingly clear. Granting that such conditions seldom obtain, nonetheless *should* they come to pass, agential leadership must follow the law but continue, to the extent possible, *educating citizens toward* the common good until such time as circumstances, the shape of the issues, or the collective wishes of society have changed, or until the folly or tragedy becomes clear.

The normative guide we need must take advantage of the strategic discretion that is the constitutional inheritance of public administration (Rohr 1986). The authors of the *Federalist Papers* spoke frequently of a vigorous and sound administration. Implicit in their conception of administration is the necessity to perform, in a subordinate and agential capacity, *all three* of the basic functions of government: making, applying, and adjudicating rules.

All three functions must be performed by administration in order to operationalize policies and programs that actually touch the lives of citizens. The allocation of values is embodied in the form of government programs. The president may bestow an occasional medal and the courts may fine or imprison, but even these acts result from systematic program activities, from administrative systems. Only the "private bill" introduced by a legislator to honor or reward a constituent and passed with the indifferent complicity of his or her colleagues represents a value allocation with nonprogrammatic origins. In allocating values (rewarding and depriving), Congress, the president, and often the courts must of necessity and by design leave public administrators discretion. Discretion is an inevitable consequence of guidance coming from three or more sources; some of it is bound to be contradictory. This clearly gives the public administration a strategic position at the confluence of powers and functions that the Constitution spread among branches in a sometimes maddeningly contrapuntal fashion. By strategic position we mean one that enables the Agency to behave strategically in its efforts to pursue a broad definition of the public interest and the common good. The position is strategic because of the discretion that follows from countervailing pressures from more than one locus of power. That discretion must not be used to serve the Agency's ends per se, but rather it should always be guided by the agential concept—"acting for"—"standing in place of" other citizens or other constitutionally empowered authorities.

The role that the normative guide must therefore encompass, is one which is subordinate, autonomous, agential, responsive, and responsible to the President, Congress, the courts, and the people. For those who have trouble conceiving of an autonomous subordinate, we would refer them to some homely examples. The "top" sergeant in a military organization has many line and staff officers superior to him (or her) and yet acts, of necessity, with a great deal of autonomy. Or academic readers might consider the similar role played by the indispensable head secretary in their department. The department, like an army unit, would have trouble functioning without its essential subordinate acting autonomously a great deal of the time within broad policy guidelines. The concept of lower subordinates who achieve unusually high informal status because of their essential activities has long been recognized in the literature of organization analysis (Mechanic 1962). We are simply suggesting the concept be recognized and extended.

The role our normative guide would prescribe for the Public Administrator provides the opportunity, along with others, to serve as an active catalyst for purposive, systemic direction in governance; a direction oriented toward the common good rather than simply the vector-sum direction implied by interest group theory. First, by serving as a point around which the powers and concerns of various institutions (or branches) can be initially brought to a focus upon issues of program design and implementation. Second, by setting the tone of the dialogue and *orienting the shifting coalitions* of interests toward a concern for the public interest broadly defined; toward a notion of the common good rather than the least common denominator of agreement among the most powerful. In other words, a respected Public Administration, subordinate but autonomous, agential, responsive and responsible to "everyone," with strategic discretion, not only could uphold constitutional values and processes, but could also achieve a definition of the common good with greater moral content than interest group liberalism has been able to achieve. The point may be further clarified by making a distinction between mediation and consensus. Mediation implies a bargained solution as the sum of the parts divided by the number of interests involved with some interests carrying more weight than others. The reference point is the end decision rather than the dialogue. The decision reflects a solution that contains only the artful rearrangement or equilibration of decision elements brought to the process by the self-interested participants. Mediation dialogue is aimed at finding that point of equilibration among competing claims. The consensual process relies on a creative synergism that results in an agreed-upon solution transcending the sum of the parts, that is, the self-interests brought by the participants. The synergism can be freed from the constraints of dialogue "management" by an administrator operating in a "facilitating" mode; one who assumes an equality among interests without reference to power, that is, who maintains the functional myth that there are no "special interests" only the public interest. Consensus may or may not reflect a specific interest but may create a solution not apparent before the dialogue began. The reference point is the dialogue as the search for a solution (or problem) in the general interest of the community; interest defined in the more traditional sense as "the totality of human aspirations, not just economic ones, which includes an element of reflection and calculation implicit in the notion of public interest dialogue (Stivers 1977: 32). Consensus is very similar to what the constitutional framers called "deliberation" (Cox 1985). In seeking consensus through public interest dialogue, The Public Administration may provide the key impetus and painfully lacking communitarian moral authority for our government of fractionated power and our culture of individualism. It requires a voice that speaks beyond the limiting confines of self-interest dialogue. As Bellah reminds us, that old dialogue is increasingly devoid of positive meaning.

> [P]olitics of interest provides no framework for the discussion of issues other than the conflict and compromise of the issues themselves. Visibly conducted by professionals, apparently rewarding all kinds of inside connections, and favoring the strong at the expense of the weak, the routine activities of interest politics thus appear as an affront to true individualism and fairness alike ... (Bellah et al. 1985: 201)

The metaphor of "main spring" and "balance wheel" may help our understanding but overstate what we seek to convey. The Public Administrator would never be the sole source of impetus, equilibration, and moral content; merely a significant and legitimate contributor, along with others, to these essential qualities of governance.

Governance is something that has never been easy because our complex constitutional system has been strained to cope with the moral dilemmas derived from slavery, the stresses of nation building and a role as superpower in an unstable world. Although governance was difficult in the eighteenth and nineteenth centuries, it seems impossible at times amidst the demands and extremities of the latter part of the twentieth century. A Public Administration with the qualities that make it a respected source of impetus and equilibration in quest of the common good can represent the crucial difference between effective governance and disastrous drift or gridlock for our political system. Let us try to conceptualize in more detail the combination of guide and self-constraint for this subordinate but autonomous agential role in governance. Such a normative guide is a necessary prerequisite to increased respect. By extension, it is also a prerequisite for the principled exercise of limited but crucial strategic discretion by The Public Administration in the governance process.

Correlates of an Effective Agency

Before proceeding to discuss the Agency more fully, we must recognize a fundamental point implicit in the discussion so far. Some of the terms used to describe social constructs associated with public administration (bureaucracy, organization, institution) convey a negative connotation or lack the developed normative dimensions required by our theoretical needs. Despite this limitation, a social construct worthy of being an Agency may, depending on the nature of its tasks and mission, need to simultaneously exhibit to varying degrees the positive aspects of bureaucracy, and organization, and an institution.[4]

Perhaps it goes without saying that an Agency must possess the positive attributes of a viable institution. Philip Selznick (1957) enabled us to see bureaucracies and organizations in a new light. He made us see that if they operate as we intend, they are value-free instrumentalities efficiently pursuing collective ends. But he also made it clear that they seldom operate as we intend or are prone to believe they should operate. Such social constructs of *intended* rationality are always in the process of becoming value-laden institutions as soon a they are staffed with humans.[5] He enabled us to see that social constructs of intended rationality become, and are, organic wholes with functions, structures, and processes that (1) work toward collective survival in a Hobbesian world; (2) struggle to maintain, by a variety of means, both the external and internal equilibria which Barnard had earlier described as essential for a functioning organization (1938: 157); and (3) seek to maintain crucial values, special competencies, and a distinct identity.

As Selznick described an institution, it can best be understood by attention to: (1) its history and the way it has been influenced by the social environment; (2) "how it is adapted to existing centers of power in the community, often in unconscious ways"; (3) where its leadership is drawn from the policy implications; (4) how its existence is justified ideologically; and (5) what underlying need in the larger community — not necessarily expressed or recognized by the people involved — is filled "by the institution and its practices" (1957: 16-18).

Selznick is therefore consistent with what Anthony Giddens many years later would call "structuration." Structuration is human social practices ordered across space and time, which reproduces the existing systems within which they take place; these social practices are in turn reproduced by them (Giddens 1979). According to Giddens, social systems are patterned activities situated within a particular spatial and historical context; their properties, or "structures," consist of rules and resources that act in a manner analogous to the syntax of a sentence, both enabling and constraining action (p. 33). Thus Giddens is explicitly doing what Selznick did implicitly: ending or at least avoiding the characteristic social science dualism that separates structure and action and thereby increases actors' perceived lack of control over societal structures (Stivers 1989: 21).

The most important normative aspect of an institution is its mission, which is cast in inspirational language and associated with powerful, positive symbols of the culture. The mission of the institution is, however, much more than mere symbolism. It is an adaptation without serious corruption of the general aims of the institution to the requirements of institutional survival (Selznick 1957: 66). It is based on: (1) considerations of the external political and economic forces mentioned above; (2) the institution's capabilities; and (3) the demands of forces within it (Wamsley and Zald 1973). Often the latter are comprised of factions within the internal polity struggling to define the mission differently. These factions range widely in size, numbers, the degree to which they are able to coalesce into alliances, and in the intensity of their conflicts (Wamsley and

Zald 1973; Cyert and March 1963). The nature of these are thus very important factors shaping mission. The mission may, for example, need to be defined with just the right degree of ambiguity to maintain a tenuous coalition of some of the institution's contending factions.

However tenuous and fragile a mission may be beneath its surface, its function is to invoke solidarity and commitment from institutional members and external supporters. It is intended to embody and articulate a set of shared values that evoke commitment. Commitment is, of course, at the heart of the notion of a "calling," and calling, as James Wolf will suggest in this volume, must be at the core of The Public Administration.

The second aspect of an effective institution's normative order is its "constitution" (Wamsley and Zald 1973). This refers to those aspects of the normative order that have to do with the "rules of the game" (including transition of power and succession) and the "rules of engagement," that is, the rules ordering internal conflict among individuals and factions, and the patterns of interest aggregation and articulation. Some tactics and maneuvers considered de rigueur in one institution would be seen as déclassé in another. Some institutions have worked out longstanding agreements among internal polity factions that do such things as specify the rotation of leadership among factions, prescribe rules for articulation of dissent, or define certain subjects and arrangements as outside the realm of bargaining.

A third aspect of an effective institution's normative order is *culture*. Institutional culture is broader than the "constitution." It involves shared beliefs toward both internal and external phenomena. It is simultaneously a manifestation of shared values and a reinforcer and maintainer of those values. Most importantly culture shapes attitudes, outlooks, and self-perceptions; the way events within and without are perceived, problems and impingements are defined, solutions are conceived, and clients are treated (Pondy et al. 1983; Smircich 1983a; 1983b). Culture is also manifest in such things as: physical surroundings (as Harold Seidman [1970] noted, the Department of Treasury looks and "feels" like a bank); in important symbols from departmental seals to letterheads; in structures such as "local boards composed of friends and neighbors in the old Selective Service System"; and even in key perception-shaping words and phrases such as "in line with the policy of the President" in the former Bureau of the Budget. There are also important rituals—an agency budget hearing, the annual awards ceremony, or the observance of an institution's founding as in the Marine Corps. Culture also includes myths, apocryphal stories and folklore, heroes and villains, the importance of which students of public administration have only begun to explore (Mahler, forthcoming).

The normative aspects of institution (missions, "constitutions," and cultures) admittedly cut both ways. As Seidman (1970) acknowledges, "programmatic goals [may be] displaced, and institutional, professional, or bureaucratic survival and aggrandizement [may] become the overriding objectives" (p. 107). But survival and aggrandizement are not the only manifestations of the normative aspects of institutions which warrant concern. The same forces that can lead to survival and aggrandizement behavior also foster program commitment and advocacy. All of the normative aspects of institution lead to behaviors we would consider positive, but at the same time they have their negative sides. For example the same things that foster commitment and advocacy lead an institution to resist program changes or reductions and efforts to coordinate several programs in a joint endeavor. Graham Allison (1971), for example, left us with a chilling picture of the consequences of such culture-induced program commitment in his study of the Cuban missile crisis. It was Allison's study that popularized the phrase "where you stand, depends on where you sit" among students of organizations and institutions. Efforts of President Kennedy and his ExComm to orchestrate the American confrontation with the Soviets were repeatedly jeopardized by biases and narrow perceptions stemming from institutional cultures. The Navy did not respond to direct orders to pull back its line of intercept for Soviet ships, and the Chief of Naval Operations refused to consider altering Navy SOPs (standard operating procedures) for operating a blockade. Air Force and CIA leaders engaged in a time-consuming struggle over whose U-2s and pilots would be used for reconnaissance (Allison 1971).

These are understandably disturbing manifestations of institutional culture, but two things need to be said in counterpoint. First, a national security crisis that has the world on the brink of Armageddon is not an appropriate circumstance to make judgments about whether or not institutional cultures have negative versus positive valences. Mercifully, such circumstances are rare. The need for, indeed the appropriateness of, such external, microcontrol by the president is rare. We cannot design either our policy-making process or other social constructs of intended rationality for such unusual circumstances because of the constitutional distortion that would be entailed. Second, the general design of the Founders still serves as a powerful antidote to parochial tendencies stemming from institutional culture. Steve Kelman acknowledges that the design of the political process (i.e., separate institutions sharing powers) —

> encourages "agency" officials to broaden their perspectives. Decisions must be supported by a statement of reasons based on arguments and evidence that appears on the record. Opposing arguments must be answered. Courts review them and elected officials examine them, all against a standard of adherence to a disinterested search for good public policy. (1987: 1, quotes added)

The design of our political system is not the only important antidote to the narrowing of perceptions and castellation that may result from institution's normative order. We can also depend on the dynamics of institutions (something Allison did not discuss) to work against closure and bias in the longer term. Fortunately, no institutional normative order is monolithic, static, or homogeneous. Most often they are multidimensional, rife with factional conflict over mission emphases, and laced with distinct subcultures in various states of congruity or tension with the dominant culture.

The structure of an institution's normative order is thus a dynamic and complex blend of adjustments to powerful forces within and without: powerful interest groups; other institutions of government such as congressional committees, White House staff, OMB, the courts and the like; capabilities of its technological core; divisions and/or alliances within its executive cadre which in turn reflect outside forces to some degree, ideals, and values of society. Although this resulting dynamism should not completely alleviate our concerns for the double-edged aspects of a normative order, it does put the problem in a proper perspective and admits of solutions.

A great deal of attention has been devoted here to institutions and their normative aspects because Selznick's conception of institutions comes closest to capturing some of the key aspects of an Agency. An Agency's normative order must be carefully developed and maintained with a distinct civic-spirited orientation. It must also sustain a level of complexity and dynamism that can offset potential pathologies.

Clearly in an Agency we need a social construct that is valued for more than itself. This required transcendence and more specifically its teleology is only suggested by Selznick in his work on the institution. In spite of several characteristics that approximate what we are seeking, the concept of institution can only be an important departure point for further normative conceptualizations about the Agency and the Agential Perspective.

The concept of institution was never developed in sufficient richness by Selznick to serve as the foundation for the kind of normative theory we want here. Selznick remains rooted in functionalism at a point when we need to transcend the bounds of that paradigm. We must move from an observer's descriptive understanding of how institutions adapt and survive to a participant's prescriptive insight of how to achieve what we want from institutions by transcending the confines of structural adaption. Giddens insists that it is this kind of knowledgability of human actors — a knowledgability based on shared consciousness and ongoing reflexivity — that enables them to be proactive, to be "purposive agent(s)" who have both reasons for their activities and the ability to elaborate discursively upon those reasons (p. 3). The idea is akin to Hannah Arendt's distinction between freedom and the constraints imposed on it by the rationality of administrative efficiency: Freedom gives men the chance to take the initiative, to begin something new in the world, according to Arendt. The use of the social sciences for the rational administration of men and things is, in effect, an extension of government as enforcer, the replacement of citizens by bourgeois followed by control by executive committees of technocrats. Denying the validity of political experience implies an attempt to turn the world into a "smoothly run household." (Hill 1984: 283,285)

Giddens structuration theory gives credence to the contextual dimensions of action, so that actors are seen as constrained by situated practices that have preceded and surround them (Stivers 1989: 22). But humans, as agents, have the capability to "intervene in the world . . . to make a difference" (Giddens 1979: 14)

To illustrate the distinction between consensual dialogue and mediation and the way the former can transcend structural imperatives, we can look to contemporary research into the way community organizations adapt to the bureaucracy with which they interact. Neighborhood organizations, initially commissioned with the task of providing avenues for citizen participation, tend over time, for example, to deemphasize participation and at the same time increase their levels of professionalism and bureaucratization. They thus became very much like the organization with which they interact in the larger society (Cooper 1980). Korten suggests this occurs because the emphasis is on the project. Projects require detailed upfront planning and rigorous adherance to implementation schedules and preplanned specifications; these he calls the "blueprint model" (1980: 483), which

> reinforces professionalization and bureaucratization. It perpetuates a view of citizens as merely the passive beneficiaries of change. In other words, social change is something which just happens (or more to the point does not happen), not something which citizens create for themselves. (p. 484)

In this model citizenship is only ancillary as a support for the achievement of the project goals. By contrast Korten's "learning" model places the assisting organization in a support role as facilitator of community dialogue. The focus then is on orchestrating dialogue in such a way that new insights appear. Administrators "learn" from the community and nurture the potential for participation as a means of broadening the base of understanding as to what the "public interest" may be. The "critical fit" between the community and the assisting organization is found when participants are able to define and communicate their needs and have those needs expressed in project methods and goals (p. 496). As such the learning model does not define organizational goals but provides a framework within which political choices can be made (Ventriss 1984: 229; Sabatier 1987).

Korten describes the nature of the interaction between organization and citizen group as learning to embrace error (i.e., not requiring citizens to have perfect knowledge of technical details and learning from mistakes); planning with people and linking knowledge with action. Linking knowledge with action assimilates what is learned through dialogue into the structure of the Agency. As such, the model potentially facilitates adaption to the community rather than adaptation of the community to the organization. It enriches the effectiveness of organizational structure and processes by providing an infusion of community insight. The blueprint model, in contrast, by directing outcomes and managing information, discounts the importance of citizen input in favor of compliance within the narrow range of options supplied by the Agency. The result is the adaptation of the community group to the Agency and eventual displacement of participation (Ventriss 1984; Cooper 1980). At the juncture between blueprints and community dialogue is the agential public administrator, who, in a reflexive manner, must make a link between the ambiguous nature of creative dialogue and the functional constraints of getting things done within the organization. He is guiding but constrained. To allow for these apparent incongruities we must free public administration from its narrow conceptual ancestry in management.

Borrowing from Existing Theory and
Moving into New Conceptual Ground

In our overview of the Agency and Agency Perspective we drew upon Webster's and Blackman's dictionaries for a definition. There are, however, serious efforts to adopt a theory of agency from the fields of finance, accounting, and the economics of information and organization. Essentially the effort is aimed at developing a descriptive/explanatory theory of the *relationship* between a principal seeking to exert power or achieve ends *through* an agent and the agent seeking to produce an effect or efficient cause on the principal's behalf. This approach to agency theory seeks to model relationships and explain behavior of the agent and principal by assuming all relations in bureaucracies, organizations, or institutions are a series of principal-agent contracts. The approach is thus one of examining: (1) their different perceptions; (2) the conditions (costs, constraints) surrounding the acquisition and maintenance of their respective information resources; (3) the differences in their reward and cost structures; (4) differences in effort levels; (5) what monitoring, policing, and enforcement mechanisms are available to the principal; and (6) what discretion, potential for evasion, or misperception are at work in the agent's role (Mitnick, 1985, n.d.; Fama 1980; Moe 1984). It recognizes the existence of costs of agentry that lead to deviations by the agent from the principal's exact preferences, but it also recognizes that the costs of monitoring and enforcing compliance of agents may lead principals to the acceptance of agency deviations.

Many of these ideas may well be important and highly relevant for building a descriptive/explanatory theory not only for regulation, as Mitnick has sought to do, but for public administration in general. Our immediate concern, however, is for developing a normative/prescriptive theory.[6] For that purpose we need for now to draw upon only a few of the central concepts of economics-derived agency theory and elaborate upon them. The most important of these is obviously the "means" of agentry. Someone (an individual Public Administrator or an Agency) seeking to act responsibly for a principal may do so by a variety of "means": supplying information, offering expertise, extending the principal's range and presence, providing a process that benefits the principal, insuring the coordination of group activity in which the principal has a stake, and so on (Mitnick 1985: 13). This "means" is analogous to the "special competence" that lies at the heart of Selznick's institutional mission. Obviously Agencies as we are prescribing them may operate on statutory authority that combines several of these means of agentry in their missions and goals.

The other key aspect of the descriptive/explanatory approach to agency theory important for our *normative* purposes is a crucial one pointed out by Mitnick: "*agency involves a game of principals*" (1985 19; emphasis added) as well as principles. A normative prescriptive theory must confront the issue of *providing principled guidance for an agent in situations of multiple principals which offset one another's influence with a resulting increase in the discretion on the part of the agent.* The need is obvious and acute in the American system of fragmented and shared powers. Who is the principal? The president? Congress? The courts? Clientele? Interest groups? As we noted at the beginning of this essay, this is a difficult question that admits of no ready answer. Ultimately, the answer must come close to being metaphysical in nature: the public interest or "the people"; for although the Constitution created a republic that did not make them the "firsthand" principal, today it is they who must ultimately be seen as principal by the Agency in our system. How the directions from such an abstruse principal along with the many other principals are to be interpreted and expressed is the stuff of a normative theory of agency.

One of our major problems in conceptualizing an Agency as a positive rather than a threatening force in governance and in developing the Agential Perspective in normative and prescriptive terms is that a conceptual no-man's-land exists between organization theory and political theory. Unfortunately, that is exactly where the concept of an Agency will have to be built. Traditionally we have approached these two kinds of theory very differently, and it is here that the block to our imagination and conceptualization lies. Political theory has focused on the state, a much more comprehensive entity and ontologically precedent to organizations. Yet in large part the differences in our approaches to these two theories also derive from contrasting epistemological traditions. Organization theory developed in the traditions of descriptive-explanatory theory-building in sociology whereas political theory has been largely in the tradition of normative theory derived from classical political philosophy (not political science as we know it today). If there has been a contemporary public administration theory, it has been largely unconscious and under the guise of "management" theory (Waldo 1948).

Other differences can be seen if we first contrast the way we view society and the way we think of organizations. As Harlan Wilson (1975) puts it:

> Perhaps the key aspect of "society," besides complexity, is its *unpremeditated* quality. Society consists of all the vast diversity of human activities and is not planned as a whole (although it may contain spheres such as organizations within which rational planning and premeditation exist). (p. 289)

Formal organizations, by contrast, are the most rational and premeditated of institutions; they are also much smaller and simpler than whole societies.

The political order, including the state, lies somewhere between the extremes of society and organizations. Clearly, though, it is much less premeditated, or much less an outgrowth of consciously intended means/ends rationality, than organizations. The degree of premeditation or intended rationality that should exist in the political order is an important issue in political theory. There has been, however, little contention until recently over whether these qualities should exist in organizations.

Organizational and political theories have also held quite different views of complexity. Although both organizations and polities may be complex, complexity is viewed positively as a check on power in the latter but as a "problem" in organizations. It is viewed as a problem for organizations because of the assumption that complexity confounds the coercive control or normative manipulations used to accomplish intended aims.[7]

In contrast, political theorists, at least more contemporary democratic theorists from Madison through Dahl, have viewed complexity in polities as positive. The more complex, the better the chance for conflicting interests to balance one another and avoid tyranny by a majority or a minority. Complexity is not seen so much a problem as a solution; complexity connotes a richness to be nurtured rather than something dysfunctional to be eliminated like static in radio transmission.

The point is that we have trouble conceiving of an Agency in a positive sense because it must of necessity be something that sits in the theoretical no-man's-land between organization theory on the one hand and political theory on the other. We must build upon the descriptive-explanatory approach to theory-building derived from the traditions of organization theory but use the insights we gain to develop (in the tradition of political theory) a normative concept and prescribe a social construct that has significance for the state and the values that surround.

We must also come to terms with duality and dichotomous tension in conceptualization. Thus, for example, the Agency we wish to prescribe would be: instrumental and technical but infused with value; based on both coercive and normative dependence; built and sustained by both selfish and altruistic motives yet dedicated as a collective to pursuit of the public interest and the common good; autonomous from other institutions of governance but subordinate to them; possessed of special knowledge and skills not found in most citizens but representative of, interactive with, and ultimately responsible to those citizens; and simultaneously an intended solution that presumably will have aspects that are problems.

These kinds of duality and complexity are extremely difficult for us to comprehend and appreciate. Decades of drift into technicism have made us dangerously prone to look for greater simplicity and instrumentalism in our social constructs and to simple and neat solutions to problems that at best may be only subject to amelioration. Our Founding Fathers left us with a complex system of governance for good reasons. We do them little honor if our only means of making it work is by misplaced oversimplification. We must cease to view complexity and ambiguity as problems and see them rather as natural and, indeed, strategically enabling conditions; as opportunity rather than threat.

Fostering Conditions Conducive to Creating Agencies and the Agential Perspective and to Governance

Many, perhaps most, of the characteristics of Agency can be the consequence of effectiveness as a bureaucracy, organization, or institution, but "acting *for* citizens by authority *from* them" reaches beyond these and requires new attitudes and actions. Clearly new conceptual ground must be covered if we are to develop an entity and an outlook that can contribute to governance, that is, to something more than is implied in the phrase political scientists traditionally use to describe politics: "the authoritative allocation of values" (Easton 1965). The latter is something done as a part of governance, but it lacks some important connotations of "governance." Specifically, Webster (1958) defines govern as "direct[ing]; in order to keep in a straight course or smooth operation *for the good of the individual and the whole*" (emphasis added).

The word derives from the Greek noun *kybernatas* (Latin — *gubernator*), a helmsman. The challenges we face require a government that can act as a helmsman rather than equilibrator of demands and distributor of values. Yet American officials (elected and career) do apparently everything but govern. They "serve," "hold office," "work for the government," "win elections," "represent," and so on, but one seldom hears of anyone "governing." Several American political dictionaries surveyed in 1985 did not even contain the word.[8]

Classical political philosophy was focused on questions of governance. It was Plato (1950) who gave us the metaphor of the "ship of state" in his *Republic*. Both he and Aristotle (1981) were deeply concerned with such questions as: "Who should govern?" "What happens when one group governs rather than another?" "What qualities are essential in those who govern?" American political scientists have shown little interest in such questions. In large part because of their captivation and, as Lowi (1976) says, their "corruption" by pluralism. As he puts it —

[P]olitical science embraced the myth of the automatic society granted us by an all-encompassing, ideally self-correcting, providentially automatic political process. (1967: 54)

Such a process may invite description and analysis of *politics*, but not of *governance*. After all, there is no need for governance in the automatic society.

As for public administration, governance was at least implied in Wilson's phrase "to run a Constitution," but unfortunately pluralism, the politics-administration dichotomy, and scientific management enabled public administration to duck any concerns with governance. These concepts allowed public administrators to say their only role was to "manage."

Wilson's (1887) and Goodnow's (1900) creation of the politics-administration dichotomy fitted nicely with the shop-floor focus of Taylor's scientific management (1947). The former assumed the ends would be "given" as in cabinet government with strong political parties and the latter assumed the ends would be "given" as in loading pig iron. But strong political parties still elude us and the tasks we face are seldom as simple as loading flat cars with ingots. Political scientists may be able to fiddle as the Republic crumbles, but public administration can no longer retreat to scholasticism. We must face the fact that our system does not allow us a role as comfortable as merely "managing." It needs governance desperately, and we cannot escape a key role in such governance. All the forces of a government of separated institutions with overlapping powers come to bear in our constitutional "space"; we cannot avoid a role in governance, nor did our Founding Fathers presume we could or should do so.

John Rohr (1986) has shown us that although the Founding Fathers did not speak specifically of administration in the Constitution, they *presumed* a great deal about it as evidenced by its prominence in the Constitution's major exegeses, the Federalist and the Anti-Federalist papers. Indeed, Rohr is convincing in his argument that the Senate envisioned by the Founding Fathers would have had many of the characteristics and performed many of the functions The Public Administration we are prescribing would play. Clearly a role for public administration in governance is not something that would have done great violence to their thinking. Much has happened, however, to make the assumption of that role less than easy. At the same time we endeavor to assume a role in governance we must work on helping to create the conditions that make such a role functional and respected by us and our fellow citizens. Not only must we learn to play a new role, but we must help build the stage and help write the play. Not only is life "not fair," as President Kennedy once remarked, but it is not easy either — surely a postscript he must have thought of more than once.

Rediscovering Communitarian Politics and Active Citizenship

Public Administrators must seek to create Agencies and foster an Agency Perspective. Central to the success of both endeavors is a rediscovery of a communitarian conception of politics and of active citizenship. Both notions require some explication.

Currently the "politics of interest" has become an amoral and barren swamp for our civic spirit. The bargaining inherent in this kind of politics does not, nor will it ever, result in a political equivalent of the economists' largely mythical market, guided by a beneficent invisible hand of even more mythic proportions.

The politics of interest have virtually annihilated the concept of active citizenship; reduced the majority of us to disillusioned apathetics or cynical spectators, and the minority to "claimants or bargainers for a share of a pie [we] feel little responsibility or capacity to help produce" (Long n.d.:20). As Norton Long observes of this kind of politics, it is "all too often organized on principles of xenophobic hostility and defended turf, [consequently] perceiving an interest shared with outsiders comes hard" (p. 21). This is not a circumstance that Public Administrators can avoid, but neither is it one they can continue to tolerate. They must help change it.

Our nostalgia for a legendary politics of community is only symptomatic of our deeply felt need for a real community. Individualism and rampant consumerism have left us with an aching void, a reduced sense of connection to our fellow citizens. Occasionally, we experience the illusion of connectedness in brief episodes of television-induced community: the bicentennial celebration in New York Harbor; the 1984 Summer Olympics finale in Los Angeles; the return of U.S. embassy personnel from Iranian captivity in 1980; and the Challenger space shuttle disaster and its aftermath. But for all the psychosocial babble about the "world village" of television these are not instances of real community. They are simply brief "electronic hookups"—episodes of human and machine interface involving "playlike" or "movielike" dramas somewhere else. We feel, emote, empathize in crowdlike unison but from the isolation of electronically enhanced individualism. Real community continues to be a chimera.

George Frederickson (1982) has placed the challenge of restoring community squarely with public administration:

> There has been a decided loss of sense of community in contemporary America. The single greatest conceptual and theoretical problem we [public administration] face[s] is the reconstruction of this sense of community. (p. 505)

Admittedly, politics is inescapably a matter of interests, and a struggle for power as well. To give Karl Marx his due, politics is to a large degree a product of history and economics and to some degree an instrument of class domination. Anyone who ignores or denies these aspects of politics is simply foolish, but anyone who thinks these aspects capture the totality of politics has an impoverished view of both politics and humankind. Politics is: therapeutic, developmental, curative, ameliorative, transformational, and yes, even ennobling. Ralph Hummel (1980) describes politics as "the way we bring human needs into accommodation with social facts." Ricoeur (1986) sees politics as an ongoing tension between the ideal of law and the "real" of administration. Yehezkel Dror (1971) speaks in a similar vein of the struggle to close the gap between the ideals of polity and the reality of government. George Will (1983) and Steven Kelman (1987) see politics as Plato and Aristotle did, as the noblest of human endeavors and a school for citizenship and ethical behavior.

These definitions all share a theme of striving and aspiration toward *communitarian* ends: they imply pursuit of a higher collective or common good even though it must be brought into resolution with reality — something, nonetheless, that goes beyond allocation or distribution, the focus of contemporary definitions. This communitarian theme is something neither new nor radical. It is as old as classical political theory of Aristotle and Plato and as conservative as George Will. We simply have lost a view of politics that has a higher purpose, something greater than the sum of its parts. Along with it, we have lost any meaningful conception of citizenship. Both our conception of politics and citizenship have turned toward a skepticism that now verges close to a corrosive cynicism.

Classical philosophers saw politics as a means of cultivating virtues in citizens. The state needed virtues in citizens who held office and the state's purpose was to help cultivate those virtues in citizens. Indeed the Aristotelian concept of citizenship held that "moral and rational faculties of individuals are developed fully only as they act as citizens" (Sinopoli 1985: 1). Thus, in the classic conception neither politics nor citizenship are a means to a higher end: they *are* the higher end. Politics in pursuit of the common good, mediated by reality and pursued by active citizenship, is the good life — is nothing less than to be fully human. Gawthrop (1984) has charged us squarely:

> In addition to ensuring that the laws are faithfully executed, it must also become the primary responsibility of the permanent career public service, at all levels of government, to ensure the vitality of citizenship in an active citizenry fully engaged in the art of government. (p. 106)

The need for a communitarian view of politics and active citizenship can be seen from yet another angle. An Agency Perspective can only be functional for the political system if agents and principals hold one another in mutual respect. Agents must respect their principal(s) whether that means "the people," voters, the legislature, the president, or some other constitutional superior. Similarly principals must see agents as trustworthy, as wise counselors, as experts in pursuing the principal's ends, and above all as loyally dedicated to their (the principals') interests. That does not mean the agent must be servile and never take issue with the principal. In short, the Agential Perspective is simply infeasible without politics in pursuit of the common good and the presence of active citizenship.

This means that we must continue to view those in governing roles as citizens and arrest the growing tendency to define them as "different" from the rest of us. Whether they are elected politicians or career civil servants we must retain the notion that they are, in Terry Cooper's (1984) terms, "special citizens," not special in privileges but in responsibilities and in willingness to serve the collectivity. They are "special" because they stand "in lieu of the rest of us" (p. 143). When citizens cease to view those in a governing role as citizens (albeit special ones), they impede a constructive relation based on mutual respect. When public administrators see lay citizens as merely clients or "consumers," they demean them and lay the basis for contempt. Such "consumers" are not beings, who rule and are ruled in turn; they do not take part in reasoned judgments for the common good nor take part in authoritative action; they simply consume, and demand more.

Mutual respect between "special citizen" and "lay citizens" is important to public administrators because it is crucial to sustaining legitimacy for their role in governance. One cannot demand respect from other participants in governance without according them the same. More is at stake, however, because both the functional and the moral basis for a democratic republic has to rest on a relationship between rulers and ruled that is one of genuine mutual respect. In fact the potential for community, for shared values, that will permit pursuit of a common good hinges on it. Economic reasoning applied to government has been pernicious precisely because it assumes away pursuit of a common good—after all, consumers need only continue to pursue their individual and insatiable ends. But Kelman reminds us this is errant nonsense. Citizens *will* accept "losing," cutbacks in programs that serve their interests—tangible material losses, individual sacrifice for a collective end—*if* they perceive that sacrifice is just and equitably distributed (Kelman 1987: 210).

Stivers (1988) notes that Aristotle (1981) seems to speak across the centuries directly to those subverting the classic conception of politics and citizenship with economic assumptions. She quotes Aristotle:

> ... the state is not an association of people dwelling in the same place, established to prevent its members from committing injustice against each other, and to promote transactions. Certainly all these features must be present if there is to be a state; but even the presence of everyone of them does not make a state ipso facto. (Stivers 1988: 43; Aristotle sec. 1280b 29)

What is lacking in the economic orientation toward politics is the very essence of politics: that in a zero-sum game in which some must win and some must lose, or some win more or lose less than others, this can be accepted—not without genuine conflict—but for a higher purpose: the common good. Cynics may insist that those who agree to sacrifice are either duped or "benefit" by feelings of martyrdom, but this "reasoning" (if it can be called that) adds neither truth nor insight and ends in mocking all human meaning and existence. What matters for our purposes, and those of the citizens involved (both "special" and "lay"), is that the sacrifices are accepted for a *perceived* common good. Such a conception is outside the bounds of economic rationality; it is unique to the realm of politics; it is essential to community.

Stivers (1989) makes a point concerning acceptance of losses for the common good that is essential to understanding communitarian politics and active citizenship. If politics is the tension between ideals and reality, then community only becomes possible with acceptance of that gap because of our mutual respect and trust for one another. Stivers says:

> Unless we understand that our intentions . . . the ends of which the state was formed . . . are ultimately out of reach, we will be unable to practice the trust in one another that enables us to accept the differentiations that policies make inevitable. (Chap. 7, p. 15)

In other words, we accept losing in the name of common good. We continue to see sufficient reason, justice, and good will in our fellow citizens acting as governors, in one another, "in the needs of strangers," and in the state generally, to accept a hard choice with grace. Our need to continue to belong to the larger social entity in point is stronger than negative feelings generated by our individual or group losses. That need hinges on communitarian politics reinforced by active citizenship.[9]

Overcoming Our Misunderstandings of the Constitution

Our unbalanced, largely negative view of bureaucracies/organizations and institutions and their processes, and our concerns about an Agency Perspective, stem in large part from misguided notions about our Constitution and particularly of the president as a chief executive. If we are to build Agencies, maintain an Agency Perspective, and develop a role in governance, we must gain a better understanding of the Constitution. Our misbegotten intellectual genesis, which drew too heavily from scientific management, administrative management, and our pervasive probusiness orientation, has led us to think of our president as a corporate chief executive and to think of the executive branch of our government as unitary or monocentric in form with the president as chief executive officer (CEO). Pfiffner and Presthus (1960) have labeled this kind of thinking as "the integrationist model," and it pervades the thinking of both academics and practitioners of public administration. More recently it has surfaced as the "administrative presidency" (Nathan 1983), or as the other side of the same coin: "political administration" (Newland 1983). Whatever we call it, it is assumed that in the name of effectiveness and efficiency (and now of policy control), administrative power must be centralized in the office of a chief executive. But administration is a broader concept, function, and activity than is encompassed in "executive." Article II states that the *executive* power shall be vested in a "President." Whatever that may mean, the most cursory reading of the Constitution makes it abundantly clear that the president must share administrative (and executive) power with other officers, such as congresspersons judges, and career administrators.

The trouble, of course, with the chief-executive concept, the integrationist model, the administrative presidency, and the "triple E management" that they are all supposed to make possible, is that, apart from their dubious feasibility and desirability, they distort our Constitution. It was not crafted with the intent that one branch or institution could provide sole policy direction to administration. Indeed, it was designed expressly to prevent it. For better or worse, our federal, and indeed our state and most local governments, are not, nor were they ever, structured monocentrically in the way we assume corporations, armed forces, or city-manager municipalities are. They are, no matter how we might wish otherwise, governments of separate institutions with shared powers intended to make clear policy development and implementation a complex and conflict-ridden process; one that the Founding Fathers hoped would promote prudent and reasoned decision making. Leaving aside the question of whether or not those hopes were or can be fulfilled, it is fair to say that such a conflict-ridden process inevitably confounds "triple E management." No amount of wishful thinking, misguided political science, errant conventional wisdom among political elites, or even proclivities of the mass public can make it otherwise.

Lester Salamon and Hugh Heclo (1981) have aptly conceptualized our unrealistic expectations of the CEO president as "the illusion of presidential government." As they put it,

> Presidential government is the idea that the President, backed by the people, is or can be in charge of governing the country. The President's national electoral mandate is translated into a superordinate responsibility over the machinery of government, and the President's job is defined as leading a followership. This is an "illusion" in the fullest sense of the word, for it is based on appearances that mislead and deceive. (p. 1)

According to both the "illusion," the integrationist model, and administrative presidency, our chief executives (mayors, governors, the president), because they are elected at large, can be looked to as the embodiment of the will of the people. The presidency is thus viewed as plebiscitory and as such can be entrusted with the kind of power we assume corporation executives possess. With such power the president can presumably provide the clearly defined policy guidance to administrators and, by using administrative discretion rather than statutory changes involving Congress, the CEO can supervise the implementation of policy. Given these dubious assumptions, it seems somehow subversive of democracy when a president sends his appointees out to do his bidding, to serve him "in directing 'his' administration," only to find that Congress has its own ideas about whose administration it is and who should direct it; or when a president learns that to be effective his appointees must adopt some of the major values of the departments they are supposed to "direct." The negative reaction created by these assumptions is captured in the remark of one White House aide who complained that the effort to gain presidential control of the bureaucracy was so frustrating because "the missionaries always seemed to end up marrying the natives" (Heclo and Salamon 1981: 3).

Unfortunately, the kind of thinking reflected above is not only simplistic and based on misperceptions but is based on dubious interpretations of the Constitution as well. To begin with, our electoral politics operate so as to assure that presidents will have a difficult time at best in creating a mythical mandate. Even when they are given something that looks like a mandate as a result of a crisis like economic collapse or war, or when they artfully create one with the help of republican artifacts like the electoral college and their own exceptional political talents, they still lack specific plans for action or even opinions or predispositions on the tens of thousands of issues that lie waiting for them or their appointees who are sent "out there" in the departments. Even if they, or more likely the more zealous of their appointees, do have specific programmatic dispositions, Congress will not allow these to go unchallenged if they trample on congressional intent. Presidents do not have the time or attention to devote to any but a small fraction of programmatic questions, and assuredly they do not have enough power to transmit to their appointees so as to back their every decision and move. As Norton Long (1969) put it,

> [P]ower is not concentrated by the structure of government or politics into the hands of a leadership with the capacity to budget it among the diverse set of administrative activities. A picture of the Presidency as a reservoir of authority from which the lower echelons of administration draw life and vigor is an idealized distortion of reality. (p. 7)

The political appointee, therefore, does not stride in the door of the government organization as the powerful proconsul of an emperor but more like a tentative and lonely ambassador appointed to a beleaguered foreign outpost. Many will have already received some sobering constitutional lessons on the shared aspects of power as a result of their confirmation hearings before the Senate and will learn more as they turn their attention to budget making and trying to secure confirmation for their deputies and assistant secretaries. It will become clear that their fortunes lie more in the hands of Congress, particularly its committees and subcommittees, and of interest groups than the president or White House staff. In fact they may find it very difficult to get on the appointment calender of anyone at 1600 Pennsylvania Avenue, but like it or not they will hear from, and be on the calendars of, persons on the Hill to an extent they may well find uncomfortable.

They find they are very much on their own in a hectic and conflict-torn milieu in which the president's power and prestige is as remote and lacking in warmth as the Crab Nebula. The reality of our system is described by Long (1949):

> [T]o deny that power is derived exclusively from superiors in the hierarchy is to assert that subordinates stand in a feudal relation in which to a degree they defend themselves and acquire support peculiarly on their own. A structure of interests

friendly or hostile, vague and general or compact and well defined, encloses each significant center of administrative discretion. This structure is an important determinant of the scope of possible action. (p. 258)

A government of separated functions but shared powers does not know a sovereign such as we are trying to make of the president or, to be more precise, we would make of the particular president for whom *each of us* voted. For every phrase in the Constitution that accords the president some power that might point toward a role as chief executive there is a counter phrase that shares the power with another institution and therefore detracts from that role.

The Constitution never refers to the president as chief executive though such a role is a plausible inference. Certainly it does little to describe a president's power vis-à-vis the officers of the executive branch. Although presidents appoint officers, this is only with the advice and consent of the Senate, and the power to remove them was never specified (nor has the custom that developed been successfully challenged); although they can require reports of officers, the Constitution does not say presidents can order them to do anything but report; and though presidents are commanders-in-chief of the armed forces, it is Congress which must levy taxes, provide for the "common defense," raise and support an Army, maintain a Navy, make the rules for the operation of the military, and call the militias of the states into national service. Although statutes (not the Constitution) have given presidents the power to develop an executive budget, the funds for running the agencies must be raised through taxes initiated in the House and funds appropriated by the Congress. These are all familiar constitutional "facts" we seem to forget. The point, of the above, is that the president is not by any stretch of the imagination a chief executive nor even commander-in-chief in the sense we seem to have attributed to him in recent decades. Is *any* "chief" executive or commander? Probably not so much as we imagine but assuredly not when we speak of the one residing in the White House, in fifty governor's mansions, or in countless mayoral residences, all of whom are constitutionally constrained to share power with other institutions and officers of the government. We simply have chosen to ignore the fact for five decades or more despite Richard Neustadt's reminder thirty years ago that the president's greatest power was the opportunity to persuade (Neustadt 1980).

Shrewd institutional entrepreneurs of the type Eugene Lewis (1980) describes have always operationalized "separation of power" so as to be responsive and responsible to a variety of other actors and institutions *in addition to* the president. General Lewis Hershey, who built and for decades directed the Selective Service System; Admiral Hyman Rickover, who directed the development of nuclear power in the Navy; J. Edgar Hoover of the FBI; General Billy Mitchell, the champion of air power within the Army; James Webb, who did so much to build NASA and place a man on the moon; David Lilienthal, who led the development of the TVA; General Curtis LeMay who built the Strategic Air Command; General Leslie Groves, who directed the Manhattan Project to develop the atomic bomb; and Gifford Pinchot, who led the way in developing our Forest Service – all, whether we judge them as heroes or villains, were more than simply subordinates of the president. Indeed, they could not have accomplished those things for which they are justly famous if they had been. They took seriously the Constitution's separation of functions and its sharing and overlapping of powers.

These men all realized and operated on the basis of the constitutional axiom Neustadt (1960) put so well when he said our government is "not one of separated powers but rather of shared powers" (p. 27). He might well have added – "shared grudgingly" (p. 27). Not all of these examples are success stories in terms of democratic government; and not all make a strong "agency perspective" look like an unmixed blessing. Worrying, however, that the officials appointed by the president will be shaped by the social constructs (or our prescribed Agency) to which they are appointed is a legitimate worry but one that is assuredly misplaced. The vast majority of appointed officials arrive with no clear policy guidance from the White House, nor any prospect for it. Moreover, there is no clear constitutional basis for following it if it should by some miracle be forthcoming. If there were such clear guidance, Harold Seidman (1970) offered a cautionary note:

> It may be doubted that either the national interests, or, in the final analysis, those of the President himself would best be served if departments were headed by agnostics who did not believe in the goals and values of the institutions they administered. (p. 107)

The political elites that engineered our founding could not, of course, foresee the development of the sizeable role for administration today. This does not mean, however, that they would have welcomed, nor that we are free to create, a public administration that knows the president as its sole master. Our constitutional structure is not that of a unitary government no matter how much Woodrow Wilson, the Presidential Commission on Administrative Management of 1937, and other commissions since, may have wished it. Public administration in America will have to look to some other model than corporate management, and political science will have to seek some other solution to the "deadlock of democracy" than the plebiscitory, Caesarian, or administrative president if we are to find a solution consonant with our constitutional tradition. It is we who have read "chief executive" and "commander-in-chief" as "sovereign executive"; and we who have assumed that administrators are solely the president's subordinates despite all constitutional and historic evidence to the contrary. In sum, our concern that bureaucracies, organizations, institutions, and Agencies may thwart responsiveness and responsibility *to the president alone* is illfounded for it presumes a condition never meant to exist under our Constitution. Our ill-founded concern further increases our negative perceptions of bureaucracy, organizations, and institutions and makes us worry excessively about the dysfunctional potentials in an Agency. Gaining a better understanding of the Constitution to offset this negative bias is a necessary step in building a concept of Agency.

Re-Thinking the Concept of the Public Interest and Its Relationship to the Public Administration

Creating Agencies, fostering the Agency Perspective, and playing a role in governance demand that we rethink the concept of the public interest and its relationship to public administration.

A Closer Look at the Public-Interest Concept

We can begin by taking a closer look at the public interest. First, we can state what it clearly is not. It assuredly is *not* something the public administrator is free to create from a vivid imagination, whims, or from his own personal "needs" or those of the social construct to which he or she belongs. Neither is it only specific, tangible, quantifiable goods and services, nor is it ever permanently and finally defined. It is largely, but not completely, a powerful symbolic concept that is both a means and an end. We can use the symbol to develop policies and programs that enhance values we associate with the symbol itself. Policies and programs that we can agree reflect the public interest are not easily achieved. They must be based on the Agency's statutory mandate and consistent with the regime values reflected in the Constitution. Furthermore, they should be consistent with the positive aspects of the Agency's history and traditions and congruent with the dominant forces of its micropolitical economy. It will also have to show a large degree of congruence with the micropolitical economy of its policy subsystem. Those traditions and political economies represent hundreds perhaps thousands of decisions, great and small, that have been made over many years of dialogue and debate within a delicate framework of consensus (Milward 1982; Keller 1984; Wamsley and Milward 1984; and Wamsley 1985).

Roland McKean (1979) points to an important aspect of the public interest as a symbol—they can "significantly lower costs of reaching agreement when bargaining costs are high by provid[ing] a conspicuous focal point that can convert unfocused goodwill into beneficial behavior" (p. 261). Goodsell (1989: chap. 3) makes the same point as McKean. Additionally he points out that the public interest as a symbol (1) legitimates by reassuring citizens that the compromises struck represent something more worthy than the triumph of the most powerful interests; (2) exhorts Public Administrators, that is, serves as a "hair shirt"—controlling, guiding, reminding officials of their agential role and their need to represent the under- and unrepresented interests in implementing the law; (3) reminds us that in making policy we must work within a "built" minimal consensus and in accord with accepted methods and rates of change (Goodsell 1989: 7-8); and (4) demands reasons, that is, it must be given "rational content anchored in widely shared value assumptions" (Bailey 1962: 97) or that we "show the logic of a policy position" (Downs 1962: 7). In effect it requires or permits public administrators to articulate a value base that rests on a higher plane than "victory for the most powerful interests," reinforces important values for Public Administrators such as "legality-morality," and evokes a commitment to look at the point of view of others and reminds them of their agential status on behalf of principals (Goodsell 1989: chap. 3, p.12).

Clearly then the public interest is something no less significant because it may be difficult to specify. Bailey (1962) suggested that the "genius" of the public interest concept "lies not in its clarity but in its perverse and persistent moral intrusion upon the internal and external discourse of rulers and ruled alike" (p. 106). It is what Cobb and Elder (1973) call a regime symbol or Merelman (1966) calls a metasymbol; a key element in stimulating and shaping dialogue, facilitating compromise by tempering the triumphs of winners and easing the defeat of losers, encouraging the search for broader common grounds for agreement and, in short, legitimating authoritative value allocation and making governance feasible. It is nothing less than, in Bailey's words, "the central concept of a civilized polity" (Bailey 1962: 6). Not an unworthy focus for an Agency's energies and aspirations.

A Hard Look at Hard Realities

This chapter has suggested that The Public Administrator or the Agency should look beyond the immediate stakeholders and parties of interest (even when broadly defined) to the *common good* that encompasses the well-being of all citizens, and even unborn generations.

With an exhortative prescription that goes so far, it is only prudent to acknowledge and accept the hard realities of the politics of governance and of human behavior as seen in social constructs of intended rationality and surely in the prescribed Agency as well. To wit: a policy equilibrium can only be achieved if it allows a modicum of satisfaction among the most powerful interests surrounding an Agency. This is prerequisite to survival and to discovering a broader public interest or the common good.

The earliest works on bureaucratic politics and pluralism rather naively assumed that the compromises worked out with interest groups in the process of turning statutes into programs represented a definition of the public interest. Leiserson (1942) for example, suggested that

> a satisfactory criterion of the public interest is the preponderant acceptance of administrative action by politically influential groups. Such acceptance is expressed through compliance on the part of such groups affected by administrative procedural requirements, regulations and decisions, without seeking legislative revision, amendment or repeal. (p. 13)

Written at a time when pluralism was in full flower, Leiserson's formula sounds naive to a later generation attuned to several decades of criticisms of pluralism. Writers like Bachrach and Baratz (1970) have now sensitized us to "nondecisions" that never make it on to the public agenda, either as a result of conscious suppression, unconscious avoidance of anticipated reactions by powerful forces of opposition, or because a policy so challenges existing political culture that is seems "preposterous" or is successfully defined by opponents as "not worth considering."

We are now much more aware of the special political resources necessary to give expression to interests in our system in a way that results in policy change, and of the uneven distribution of such resources in our population. We are no longer confident that a beneficent invisible hand produces the public interest from the milieu of struggle among the most powerful interests. We can now see that the earlier writers on the subject made the mistake of assuming that agreement among the most powerful culminated in the public interest when instead it was only the first step in its pursuit. Although it can be said that it is a necessary but not a sufficient condition, nonetheless, we must remember that it is assuredly a necessary condition.

An Agency as a Catalyst for the Public Interest

We have also come to recognize that, setting aside questions of public interest, we probably cannot even achieve a policy equilibrium simply by finding agreement among the most powerful interests with which an Agency interacts. We now recognize that policy is made in much more elaborate structures and processes of interaction than we previously comprehended. Initially these subsystems were described as largely "closed" and emphasis given to the efforts of members to maintain the status quo and exclude outside influence, for example, the iron-triangle metaphor (Davidson 1977; Jordan 1980; Gais et al. 1984). Later writings have revealed the complexity, diversity, and dynamism of these policy subsystems (Milward 1982; Keller 1984; Wamsley 1985. In this dynamic complexity an agreement of the most powerful interests is still a prerequisite to policy equilibrium and Agency survival, but it is only one crucial aspect of a very complex, unending process.

The government entity with a statutory authority in a policy realm may be only one of several with related authorities and one among an array of multifarious actors that comprise a policy subsystem. And although dominant coalitions of subsystem actors inevitably seek to maintain a policy equilibrium that they found congenial (or at least harmless) to their interests, and to suppress disturbing influences from within and without, these efforts can only be successful for limited time. Dissident factions and coalitions are just as diligent in their efforts to destabilize and undermine an equilibrium as the dominant coalition(s) are in trying to maintain it (Wamsley 1985).

If the Agency is only one of a multitude of actors, it nonetheless remains a key actor — usually the focal actor in a policy subsystem because of its statutory responsibilities. It also has some unique resources at its disposal for pursuing a broader definition of the public interest in the ongoing stuggles over policy making, implementing, and adjudicating. The "ordeal of the executive," as David Truman (1951) called it, is the struggle to reach and maintain a modicum of consensus on the allocation of values in the public interest but in a different arena from election campaigns, presidential news conferences, legislative bodies, and the courts. Inevitably, if legislation is to be translated into programs, the focus of action must shift to the administrative arena, which, like the courts, is less manifestly political in a partisan sense, and in which the useful fiction is maintained that what takes place is "merely administration" or "simply efficient implementation of the law." Here a new, and inevitably somewhat different, consensus must be built around the discretionary decisions incident to implementation and changing circumstances of program operations. In this arena actors are more inclined, and indeed are driven by imperatives of circumstance, to justify their actions in the language of triple-E management, cost-benefit analysis, rationality, science, data, procedural due process, and so forth. Public administrators must grapple with defining the public interest in a real and concrete sense in the heat of interest group and interorganizational warfare. There is little room left in these trenches for escape to comfortably fuzzy words as in the legislative or judicial arenas. It is in the discretion incident to building, adjusting, and maintaining that consensus of interests around program operations that the Agency Perspective can work toward a broader conception of the public interest.

Public entities are handed statutes, executive orders, or court opinions and orders with broad language calling on them to determine such matters as: what is primary as opposed to secondary medical care; or to "establish exactly what concentrations of harmful substances (such as sulfur dioxide, benzene, or hydrocarbons) are permissible in the air" (Kelman 1987:88). Similarly, in implementing the Trade Adjustment Assistance Act, the Department of Labor must "determine when workers in industries affected by foreign competition are eligible for benefits" (Kelman 1987:88). Millions of dollars and thousands of jobs and votes, as well as happiness or anxiety for millions of citizens, are riding on these concrete definitions incident to program implementation.

The Public Administrator and the Agency are thus involved in politics in a particular idiom, and in defining more concretely than anyone else the public interest and the common good. Kelman (1987) draws out the clear implications of this involvement: Generally, no part of government has more expertise about a policy area than the government "organization" involved in this area. It lives with that policy area and its problems full-time, whereas the attention of other participants in governance is fragmented and episodic. Kelman further notes:

> "Agency" officials are also closer to the situation. They get more ongoing feedback from the world outside government. Because of their experience they understand the political constellation surrounding an issue better than short-term

participants such as White House staff. The "bureaucracy" is also a unique source of information on whether production capabilities exist or can be created with regard to various policy alternatives [p. 90][10] (Quotes added.)

The Agency is thus better situated and equipped than any other actor in the process to play a key role in: (1) shaping the dialogue among powerful stakeholders in ways that constrain them to make some accommodations to a higher notion of the public interest; and (2) defining the public interest programmatically.

The Agency's Role in Focusing Policy Dialogue upon the Public Interest

Discourse that includes or focuses on the symbol of "the public interest" allows public administrators to focus the terms of dialogue in a policy subsystem on a higher plane by explaining their actions in terms of the public interest. The symbol also demands that contending groups defend their positions in terms broader than naked self-interest. The Agency's special role in the policy dialogue should be to constantly raise the debate to the level of the public interest and indeed the common good. As Stivers has pointed out—"the language we use shapes the manner in which we conceive of problems, design possible solutions, make choices, and act." As she says, economic (and one might add, unadulterated interest-group) language "cannot deal with and in fact eschews consideration of general interests, that is those that are not aggregations of individual preferences" (p. 310). The Agency by its agential concern for the public interest, by providing rationale and being reason-giving, thus becomes a catalyzer of the dialogue. Like a catalytic agent in chemistry, it sets in motion transformative changes that result in something new and different— something more than the sum of its parts. The outcome of the dialogue may be and should be a new perception of reality by all participants; a perception that is not coincidental with the views of any one participant, nor is it simply the sum of all their views. That holds out the prospects of forming a new intersubjective perceptual base, of shifting to a higher common ground that represents more than mere shifts or losses and gains from fixed positions of policy-process participants.

Discourse focused on the public interest facilitates losing or sacrifice. It enables someone to raise the rhetorical question, "How can anyone *really* lose if the larger collectivity—the 'public' benefits?" More importantly it offers public administrators the opportunity to explain just *how* the public will benefit. A discourse that treats the public interest seriously reinforces the need for public administrators and others to be logical, to be rational and, above all, to give reasons (Goodsell 1989:15). It also constrains them to be comprehensive or universalistic, that is, concerned for the effects of public policy on all people, at all levels, and in the long run as well as the short.

A dialogue built around the public interest sensitizes public administrators and other policy subsystem members to a concern for unarticulated needs within society — to an awareness, as Goodsell (1989) puts it, that "the public agenda is always unfinished" (p. 16). This fosters the long-range perspective that Public Administrators should have. They need to remind themselves that theirs is always the "long course"; that they will suffer many defeats and setbacks and must therefore play for an "averaging strategy"; and that when the immediate tumult is over they will be the ones who are still on the field, still the focal point of a policy subsystem, and will still bear the responsibility for the needs unmet and unspoken.

Steven Kelman (1987) reminds us of that which is easily forgotten because self-interest seems to readily explain so much of what we observe: "when people try to achieve good public policy, the results tend to be good public policy" (p. 210). It is perhaps sufficient for your present purposes to agree with his observations that "people choose different forums for the display of different types of behavior" including that of "other regarding" (p. 72). (Saracen [1972] refers to these forums as "created settings.") The market is viewed as a place for the expression of unbridled self-interest, but fortunately the public policy process has not been similarly viewed, at least not completely nor up to this point in our history.

Public Administration, Cognitive Competence, and the Public Interest

Norton Long (1987) has proposed another way in which public administration should seek to relate to the public interest within the policy subsystem. He feels public administration should use policy analysis in an action-theory mode; seeking to understand the consequences for the public interest of one policy over another, and changes in policy or program administration. He thinks we should strive to develop our "cognitive competence" relevant to the public interest. He reminds us that information is not a free good but rather a very expensive one. Still it is one that can make a tremendous difference in our understanding of public policy issues relevant to the public interest. Long draws on Richard Flatham (1966) who maintains we can subject policies to public interest tests of (1) generalizability; (2) the examination of consequences; and (3) community values.

Long (1987) maintains that we need only a commonsense list of the dimensions affecting the quality of human condition for use in assessment and evaluation relevant to the public interest. Among the dimensions he would use would be: life, health, security, self-respect, the respect of others, education, jobs, income, housing, and recreation. A policy or policy change, a lack of a policy, or a change in program administration could be appraised for its impact on "the significant dimensions of the lives of the individuals making up the relevant population" (p. 11).

Elected officials feel pressure to oversell the efficacy of policy initiatives; public administrators who do not feel this pressure to the same degree must act as a counterweight to this. They can do so by using policy analysis to effectively assess policy and policy changes and provide good information enabling midcourse corrections. They can also foster the idea of policy experimentation (Campbell 1971) to dampen the dipsomaniacal swings of public support for policies.

The strategic position of public administration in the policy process, its "cognitive competence," its proximity and longstanding experience with the issues, makes this special relationship with the public interest feasible and morally compelling. As Long (1987) puts it:

> It is an important task of public administration to work at developing a concep-tualization of the public interest both to evaluate policies and to direct research and practice. As long as our cases are determined to be successes or failures without driving the meaning of success and failure to the bottom line of their significance in the lives of real people, our appraisals will be lacking and in addition they will be inadequate to test the theories underlying policies by the consequence of acting on them. (p. 12)

Creating and Nurturing Legitimate Authority

Another condition essential to our being able to develop an Agency and to play a respected role in governance is a concern for developing and nurturing legitimate authority. This means a shift in our focus from power to authority. That is not to say that power should no longer be viewed as the "lifeblood of administration," to use Norton Long's famous words (1949). Rather it is to acknowledge and to act as though power of the kind we seek to gain and wield in Agential Leadership is *derived* from authority. Authority is linked inextricab-ly to legitimacy; power may or may not be linked to such a concept. One can have power (get another person to act in accord with your will rather than his or her own) by sheer force and still lack authority.

Power and authority have often been confused. Often it has been thought of as "formal" power or "rightful" power. Lately, Friedrich (1972) points out, it has come to be associated with the pejorative adjective "authoritarianism," or with such negative conceptions as the "authoritarian personality."

Friederich points out that the etymology of the word has been the subject of debate, but for most of modern history Mommsen's etymological analysis stood. Mommsen thought the word *power* to be derived from the Latin word *auctoritas*, which in turn developed from the verb *augere* (to augment or enlarge). He argued that *auctoritas* "implement[ed] a mere act of will by adding reasons to it" (Friedrich 1972:147). Such augmentation and enlargement oc-curred when the Roman Senate, composed of "seres" (the old ones), deliberated upon a matter. The "auctoritas patrium" they issued was "more than advice, yet less than command" (p. 47). It was advice that "could" not be safely dis-regarded. The Senate bestowed its blessing on the popular will, thereby making it law and thus acquiring authority. Friedrich concludes that "it was a matter of adding wisdom to will, reason to force and want, that is to say, a knowledge of values shared and traditions hallowed to whatever the people wished to do" (p. 147).

Whatever the etymological facts of origin may be, Friedrich's point is compelling. *Authority* should be distinguished from power and defined as "the capacity for reasoned elaboration" (1972:46). The "ability to gain another's assent" (p. 55) hinges on reasoning embodied in communication, "superior knowledge, insights and experience" (p. 18). Not simply superior knowledge based upon education or learning, but knowledge insights and experience based also on "established values and benefits having persisted over several generations" (p. 18). This is a kind of basis for reasoned elaboration an institution or an Agency can provide in the struggle and dialogue within the policy subsystem and the broader process of governance. How do we go about creating and nurturing authority within Agencies and between them and relevant others? Perhaps this can best be seen by examining the simpler notion of dependency.

All social constructs are held together through dependence or interdependence. They can, as Harlan Wilson (1975) points out, be held together primarily through *coercive* dependence in which one party depends on another because the party of the first part possesses a needed resource, coercive force, or controls a condition. Such dependence relations, he suggests, are characterized by mistrust, suppressed hostility or anger, and latent or manifest conflict. In contrast, *normative* dependence is quite different. As Wilson describes it:

> [It] is based on willingness of B to depend on A because that dependence is found to be *fulfilling* or *enabling* in some respect, not odious as the case may be in coercive dependence relationships. (1985: 285; emphasis added)

Of course, Wilson means to suggest that these differences in dependencies exist not only at the personal level but also interpersonally in larger aggregations or social constructs.

Normative dependence is thus a key moral aspect of authority; one that has roots in classical political theory. Its more contemporary expression, however, goes back at least to 1938 and Chester Barnard, who pointed out that most successful administrators seek to *blend* the two dependencies, alternating between the two depending on circumstances. Wilson, however, dichotomizes them to make a valid point: coercive dependence is perceived as constraining and tends toward alienation and viewing others as roles or objects; in contrast, normative dependence draws people closer to one another, can be enabling and liberating—permitting people to contribute and to act.

Wilson acknowledges that normative coercion is no less compelling and in that sense people's actions may be "involuntary." Nonetheless they are what we consider "willed" and the bonds of the relationship are not perceived as constraints but as supports. Orion White's notions from Chapter 6 are, of course, highly relevant here. We have tended to see authority and participation as mutually exclusive conditions and we have been dead wrong. They are mutually reinforcing or reciprocal conditions. In democratic-tending societies authority is legitimated by mature and responsible participation; one cannot have such constructive participation without maturity; and one cannot develop maturity without being able to encounter legitimate authority in the varying institutions of society from the family to the state. These three phenomena are thus locked in a seamless circle of relations.

An agency must encompass both forms of dependence but base the preponderance of its dependencies on normative grounds if (1) it is to develop the legitimacy demanded by its key agential role in the governance process; (2) it is to gain and keep the commitment of its members; and (3) it is to keep the respect of its relevant others, clientele, and other citizens in general.

Whether the Agency we prescribe is based on coercive or normative dependencies or a blend of the two, prudence dictates concern for the amount of influence it may have over our lives and actions. We must continue to concern ourselves with the historically validated tendency of power to "autonomize" itself. The typical American response has been to turn to structural solutions — more Newtonian mechanics of the kind on which our Constitution is based. The latest and most egregious example being the Gramm-Rudman-Hollings Act (Balanced Budget and Emergency Deficit Control Act of 1985). This may, however, be the wrong response for the world in which we live today. Increasingly, it has led to adversarial arguments not deliberation, the erosion of legitimate authority, and the growth of irresponsibility by various political actors.

Schaar (1981) suggests we must search for an answer that brings power together with authority in a way that creates legitimacy — "humanly meaningful legitimacy." He speaks approvingly of Rousseau, whom he feels

> was the first to understand fully — that ours is the task of developing the theory and institutions of community in which men can be both conscious and individual and share the moral bonds and limits of the group. (p. —)

This, of course, is the same point Orion White (1990: Chapters 6 and 7, this volume) makes when he says we must discover appropriate archetypes of authority that are combinations of authority *and* participation; archetypes in which we can find individualism by surrendering some of ourselves in effective participation and authentic interaction with others. By effective participation we do not mean the mere appearance of participation while power lies in the hands of superiors. We mean a real sharing of power and taking part in decision making within certain bounds. This kind of participation entails genuine respect for individuals, accepts conflict as a natural part of the process of deliberation, and then fosters conditions permitting the exercise of choice.

So the bringing together of power and authority to create legitimacy for action involves more than the additional ingenious counterbalancing of interest against interest and force against force; and more than different language and management styles, important though these are. It means that power, which relies so much on threat of force and habit, must be transformed by the addition of imagination and a "theory to buttress and justify" assent (Wilson 1975). The transformation can then take place from negatively based coercive dependence on power to positively based normative dependence on authority. Authority thus involves assent, trust, willingness to follow or emulate. In this way authority based on moral dependence can be a "source and augmenter of others' actions" by example — by showing the way and by the ability to assure that what is recommended will succeed and enlarge the actors (Wilson 1975). It can also augment others by creating the situations and circumstances for growth, learning, the exercise of citizenship, and the exercise of choice. As Preston (1987) reminds us, freedom is most meaningfully expressed through choice, but deliberate (free) choice requires knowledge, competencies, and resources — things that today can best be provided in and largely through an Agency.

Authority based on moral dependence is thus viewed not as depleting and confining but liberating, enriching, and nurturing. To do this successfully, authority must above all else have a theory — a rationale. It must "give reasons" — reasons that are accepted. Schaar (1981) states:

> As Plato put it, each law must have a preamble, a statement that walks before the law, justifying and explaining it. The rationale includes an account of reality, an explanation of why some acts are preferable to others, and a vision of a worthwhile future toward which men can aspire. Put differently, the rationale consists of a more or less coherent body of shared memories, images, ideas and ideals that gives to those who share it an orientation in and toward time and space. It links past, present, and future into a meaningful whole, and ties means and ends into a continuum that transcends a merely pragmatic or expediential calculation. Authorities at once personify or incarnate the rationale, this conception of legitimacy, and are justified by it. (p. 26)

Schaar is speaking generally of authority and legitimacy in the modern state, but we commonly refer to the presence of such phenomena, wherever they are found, as simply "community" — meaning by that a type of social relationship that is not geographically determinate. He never specifies but presumably is speaking of it at the level of the nation-state. It would seem, however, that efforts to develop humanly meaningful authority and legitimacy at that level in America will depend on our working to create enclaves of community wherever possible and at all levels within the various substructures of the state.

Finding an Appropriate Focus for an Agential Perspective

We must be able to create community at levels below and within a scope less broad than the nation-state. This is so because community requires considerable personal interaction and because authority and legitimacy are difficult to build and are fragile. There are very real problems of scale when dealing with such requisite ingredients of authority and legitimacy as salience of citizen interests, sentiment, and participation. Perhaps the less democratic republic envisaged by the authors of the Constitution, one with a limited franchise and participation, might have escaped the problems of scale and scope inherent in building legitimacy and authority. A compound and extended republic but of more modest democratic expectations might have been able to grapple with defining the broadest possible public good or public interest at the level of nation-state structures.[11] But we have grown into a democratic republic of fervent rhetoric, though our practices and our participation continue to decline. With our wants stimulated by the capitalist aspects of our economy we seem to demand more but participate less. Our government can respond but not govern; can say "yes" easily but only say "no" through obfuscation; but most importantly it cannot solve problems, prioritize, or plan. We must therefore search for a way to bring direct participation and demands into some better proportionate balance, to create institutions that can produce deliberation, that can educate us to what we can or cannot have, and enlighten citizens concerning the trade-offs.

We have tended to think that the way to do this was to make such efforts around a geographic point or area—around state or local government. Norton Long (1980), for example, has been an eloquent spokesman for a renaissance of civic citizenship. He notes that many years ago John Dewey argued that "only in the local community could the public discover itself and in doing so realize its shared common purposes that alone make possible real democracy" p. 17). Long admits, however, that:

> Dewey did not say how he saw the modern nation-state being transformed from the present mechanically organized Great Society into the Great Community. Perhaps the answer lies not in the nation-state becoming a single, unified community. *The community of the nation-state that is desirable may well be the community of communities.* (p. 17; emphasis added)

Henry Anna (1986) has shown that local government can be conceptualized as an Agency, and we feel that we must seek to establish Agency *wherever* it proves feasible to bring citizen salience and participation together in order to start the process of community building. Obviously, some of our larger social constructs of government are inappropriate candidates for building Agency. Most federal cabinet departments and many of their state counterparts are loose conglomerates of functions and mission patched together as a result of political expediency and misguided attempts to apply the integrationist model over the years. Most of our problems and solutions, and therefore most necessary value allocations, are not susceptible to delimitation by a handy formula for geographic or "organizational" bounding. Agency, community, and citizen development will be, not where we find them, but where we can create them.

The Agency wherever it is conceptualized exists in an elaborate policy subsystem or perhaps at the nexus of several subsystems. These contain both horizontal and vertical linkages to multifarious groups, individuals, organizational entities, and other subsystems with vested interests in policy outcomes. Though often depicted as static those linkages and relationships are most often dynamic. What we wish to suggest here is that the Agency can serve as a focal point of interest and participation, and as an access point for active citizen involvement not only in the Agency itself but in the policy subsystem as well. The policy subsystem becomes a setting for a dialogue about the particular policy with which members are concerned. Whether or not they are in agreement, subsystem members develop a common language and a predominant outlook on policy, a way of thinking and talking about it. Camilla Stivers (1988) provides insight into the importance of this shared language and outlook:

> In using a policy language, we can only, as in analysis, describe situations and state facts; we also do things by saying something. We put forward proposals; raise questions; launch attacks; mount defenses. These acts take place in existing (intersubjective) reality the result of many conversations. They carry this reality forward, but they also adjust it in light of new knowledge and changing values. (p. 318; see also Sabatier 1988)

In the rich normative aspects of Agency Perspective and the complex dynamics of policy subsystems lie the potential for the Agency to become the focal point of a community (not of harmony but consensus) within a "community of communities" to use Dewey's words. This community would not be fixed by a geographic locus but rather by "the coherent body of shared memories, images, ideas and ideals that gives those who share it" (and those who may take issue with it) an "orientation in and toward time and space" (Schaar 1981). Our political system desperately needs communities such as this wherever we can found and nurture them. In the absence of strong political parties, community built around an Agency and linked to a larger policy subsystem(s) may be one of our best hopes for meaningful citizen involvement and development. It is possible, indeed it is likely, that if we are to create humanly meaningful participation and interaction around issues of national or societal scope, and thereby also foster the authority and legitimacy needed to govern a political system as large and diverse as the American, we must turn to the Agency as a focal point within a policy subsystem and look to it as another important locus for community.

The Agency and the Agency Perspective: A Summary of Characteristics and a Look Beyond Power to Entitlement and Authority

We began this essay by the quest for a normative guide for public administrators; something to both empower and constrain. We have conceptualized the

Agency Perspective as such a normative guide. The essence of an Agency and the Agency Perspective is to be found in a set of attitudes. It is the presence of this set of attitudes that distinguishes the Agency from a bureaucracy, organization, or institution. The Agency may have some of the positive attributes of a bureaucracy or organization; and it must have the positive attributes of an institution; but it *must* still have something more—a normative order that is agential. Earlier we outlined the dimensions of an institution's normative order: mission; "constitution"; and culture. In an Agency all three must reflect a set of attitudes that are civic-spirited or "other regarding" but more specifically Agential. The mission must be framed from an agential perspective, and that framing must be more than a few glowing adjectives and rhetorical flourishes. The Agency's "constitution" must at least be neutral. That is to say, "constitutional" rules should not impede the advancement to top positions of cadre members who hold agential attitudes. Nor should the "constitution" work in some way to filter out interests that reflect agential concerns. Most importantly the overall culture must reflect civic spirit and agential values. These should include a commitment to:

Pursue the broadest and longest-range conception of the public interest and the common good in the dialogue within policy subsystems and in operationalization of programs.

Create and nurture legitimate, reason-giving authority by the development of normative dependencies.

Foster active citizenship and communitarian political values.

A fuller understanding of the Constitution and the polycentric nature of power it entails (i.e., multiple principals).

Uphold and defend the Constitution, and policy processes that conform to the Constitution and the regime values reflected in it.

We do not mean to preclude the possibility that an Agency may differ from other social constructs in some aspects of structure and process. But if this should be the case, these will be supportive of, correlative with, or derived from the all-important attitudinal differences that permeate an Agency's normative structure. While we agree with Mancur Olsen (1971) that structure and process shape behavior, it is still true that attitudes shape the outcome of structures and processes.

An Agency has been given trusteeship over maintaining the capacity to act as an agent for all of us, and this means maintaining the physical and political capacity to act on our behalf. This in turn necessitates the nurturing of legitimacy. As John Schaar (1981) reminds us, "Legitimacy is that aspect of authority which refers to entitlement," (p. 21). It is not power the American state or the Public Administration needs in the face of the challenges confronting them. Rather, it is the entitlement to govern that seems to be steadily eroding at the very time it is needed so desperately. Legitimacy that creates positive authority derives from attitudes on the part of governors and the governed to produce more legitimacy. Schaar describes legitimate authority as follows:

> An authority is one whose counsels we seek and trust and whose deeds we strive to imitate and enlarge . . . one who, while lacking most of the specific attributes of power as force, makes recommendations which cannot safely be ignored because they are usually right. (p. 26)

Such a person or Agency is not a constrainer, but instead "becomes a source and augmenter of others actions" (p. 26). Legitimate authority does this by example and by being able to assure others that the actions recommended "are rightful and will succeed" (p. 26). Schaar concludes that, "seen in this light, authority, far from confining and depleting men, liberates and enriches them by bringing to birth that which is potentially present." Such legitimate authority does not rely on force, manipulation, or propaganda (p. —). It may command and decide but more often it proposes, recommends, inspires, and creates conditions for the growth of individuals and for the confluence of self and collective interests — circumstances in which "interests can do the work of virtue." Above all, however, it persuades by being "reason giving" in a way that reinforces its legitimacy — fostering active citizenship, instilling confidence, and releasing citizens' potentialities. According to Schaar, this rationale or "reason giving"

> includes an account of reality, an explanation of why some [courses of action] are preferable to others, and a vision of a worthwhile future toward which men can aspire. . . .
>
> It links past, present and future into a meaningful whole, and ties means and ends into a continuum that transcends a merely pragmatic or expediential calculation. Authorities at once personify or incarnate this rationale, this conception of legitimacy, and are justified by it. (p. 26)

Plainly, the message in Schaar is that we need to drastically alter our conceptions of public administrative leadership whether by career civil servants or political appointees. There is absolutely no place in this concept for the "purging" of bureaucrats by political appointees or for mean-spirited "enforcing the law" or "holding clients to the rules" as a means of petty power wielding and ego-gratification by careerists. Nor is there any place for foot-dragging and buck-passing or a "cover your ass" mentality. Such behaviors are neither leadership nor administration but symptoms of bureaucratic and organizational dysfunction. The Agential Leadership we prescribe must be decidedly different in the way Schaar is urging whether it involves elected or career officials. At best, according to Schaar, we have tended to see leadership as little more than brokerage — "providing information, identifying possible coalitions, facilitating side payments and developing log rolls" (p. 38). Instead Agential Leadership must be the kind that "transform[s] preferences, both of the leader and the followers," interacts with other leaders, and is "capable of being co-opted into new beliefs and commitments" and so co-opting others. It must be "educational and inspirational; a stimulator and changer of world views; and a re-definer of meanings and stimulator of commitments" (p. 44).

Public administrators are not accustomed to thinking of themselves and their role in this way with perhaps the exception of a few who have risen to the top ranks. But self-conscious Agential Leadership must begin long before the apex of careers. Public administrators are exercising discretion and leadership that reach beyond the bounds of their organizational entity long before they reach the so-called supergrades. It is time they recognized it and set about reconceptualizing their roles.

This chapter has been an effort to prescribe a normative guide for Public Administrators that simultaneously empowers and constrains them to develop Agencies and administer and lead them so as to (1) maintain the capacity to act effectively as society's agent; (2) enrich participation in civic life; (3) enhance legitimate authority; and (4) thus promote our systemic capacity to govern. At the heart of such an effort is the building of community, not of place but of shared hearts and minds. Norton Long (1980) cites John Dewey's work on the public interest and says:

> Dewey is right that the principal problem of making a functioning democracy is the *rebuilding of community* in which publics may come to realize that they possess public, common interests which are shared goods that individuals value and energetically desire to maintain and enhance. (p. 19; emphasis added)

We clearly see the Agency as a potential focal point for building community at all levels of our government, a special social construct not simply of intended rationality but *intended community* as well. The Agency can and must be a social construct that "create(s) and confirm(s) interpretations of life" and which develops individuals, groups, community, and the public interest and common good. As Kelman (1987) puts it,

> [T]he policy making process is not just about producing visible, material outcomes. Through government people seek recognition of their dignity and worth. In addition, the process of government should serve to function as a school for teaching ethical behavior toward others, for molding character. (p. 210)

Agency members, however, are not simply mentors of fellow citizens in the process; rather *public administrators and their fellow citizens are both mentors and students of one another.*

Conclusion

The set of attitudes embodied in the Agency Perspective, and the Agency, do *not* call on us to abandon a concern for efficiency of output, *nor* to neglect the survival and well-being of the bureaucracy, organization, or institution as a whole. Rather it calls upon us to go beyond these with a concern that encompasses and transcends such social constructs — a concern for the public interest and the common good. It calls upon us to remember our agential role but to perform it strategically and pro-actively as a de jure subordinate with considerable autonomy and with different responsibilities from other officers but with a similar constitutional standing in the governance process. Finally it calls upon us to develop a new kind of leadership that fosters legitimate authority of the state and its "agencies" by maintaining the capacity to act agentially, by being reason-giving and by fostering participation, citizen development, and community.

The Agential Perspective does not provide a public administrator with all the answers to the problems he or she faces daily, nor does it call upon him or her to determine the public interest or the common good in terms as broad as the societal-wide community. It calls upon them to try to make the determination in the realms of the Agency and its policy community, grounded in their history, micropolitical economics, values, and cultures. It provides an attitude and outlook grounded in the normative structure of their Agency and its policy community that helps guide the way they perceive or encounter those problems, define them, and shape solutions. That attitude or outlook may be worth as much, and probably a great deal more, than additional skills, dollars, and information can ever provide. Contrary to the conventions of bureaucrat bashing, it is not management skills or "business know-how" we are lacking in the public sector. It is a set of "grounded" principles, an attitude or outlook that guides us as to when, how, or if we should apply such skills and, most importantly, toward what end — for that end is not clearly and unequivocally drawn for us as it is at least alleged to be in business.

In the final analysis, the agential attitudes we prescribe provide the "soul" of government. James Wolf has remarked that privatization or contracting out of governmental activity may be able to provide the service in question, but it becomes management without any "soul." "Soul," Wolf says, may not be crucial to many functions of government considered on an individual basis, but there are a host of activities in which "soul" *is* crucial, and it is absolutely essential to government as a collectivity. In government as a whole, "soul" is *the* essential ingredient that ultimately determines whether or not an "allocation of values" will be "authoritative," that tempers winners and consoles losers, that indeed blurs such distinctions, that is, it is the essential ingredient in governance. Soul is nothing less than the socially constructed community of shared values, among which is the key belief that the state acts *agentially* — for us, on our behalf, and for our welfare. The ability to construct such community and sustain such a belief is what The Public Administration must be all about. It is what George Will (1983) refers to as statecraft, and its purpose of providing for the development of citizens—physically, intellectually, politically, spiritually—is inseparably linked with constructing community. Its purpose is what he calls "soulcraft," and as he puts it—"statecraft *is* soulcraft."

Notes

1. For a fascinating analysis of the role and place of such persons in the development of public administration, see Orion White and Cynthia McSwain, "The Phoenix Project: Rising from the Ashes," a paper delivered at the first annual conference on public administration theory, Lewis and Clark College, Portland, Oregon, April 1988.

2. The definition of *agent* in *Black's Law Dictionary* (1968) is similar:

One who presents and acts for another under the contract or relation of agency; . . . one who undertakes to transact some business, or to manage some affair, for another, by the authority and on account of the latter, and to render an account of it . . . one who deals not only with things, as does a servant, but with persons, using his own discretion as to means, and frequently establishing contractual relations between [the] principal and third persons. (p. 59)

3. As sometimes happens in the history of ideas, Hardin's analog is extremely useful but may be based on a misinterpretation of history. See Cox, Susan Jane Buck, "No Tragedy on the Commons," *Environmental Ethics* 7 (Spring, 1985): 49-61.

4. Hopefully the foregoing discussion has made it clear that a serious theoretical discussion demands that we use the terms *bureaucracy, organization* and *institutions,* i.e., assign theoretically explicit meanings to the terms whenever it is meaningful to do so. However, this in turn means that we need a generic term that we can use more loosely when theoretical specification is unnecessary or cumbersome. One term I've considered but which I will not burden the reader with here is *social construct of intended rationality* (SCIR). It could be used to speak of either bureaucracy, organization, or institution without specifying to which form of social construct we are referring.

5. Over the years persons have persisted in interpreting Selznick as having said some organizations remain organizations—rational, technical instruments—while other organizations become institutions—social constructs with internal factions and an environment with which it must cope. See Perrow 1986, p. 167. Perrow says "the distinction is attractive." Yet Perrow, like others, makes too much of a distinction. Selznick clearly spoke of institutionalization as a "process" (p. 16) and said "no organization of any duration is completely free of institutionalization" (p. 16).

6. Whether or not a descriptive/explanatory approach to agency theory will prove of value will hinge on the ability of its advocates to escape the problems Ostrom (1986) and Perrow (1986) have identified. Foremost among these is the tendency to oversimplify and to model complex social relations as individual contractual exchanges. This tendency may have heuristic value, but it cannot be the basis for descriptive/explanatory theory. Whatever limitations the concept of agency may have as a basis for descriptive/explanatory theory in private-sector organizations, it seems to us that these may be offset for members by the utility it offers in getting at a key dimension of organizational behavior in the public sector. Agency—acting for another by authority from him or her—is what public-sector administration is "all about." The concept has a meaning of greater richness in the public sector than it can ever have in the private. It seems to us, however, that in the public sector it has even greater promise as a keystone in normative or prescriptive theory than it does in the service of description/explanation.

7. This view is basic to most organizational theorists. Theorists of the human relations tradition are unhappy with this but largely acknowledge its empirical reality. Perhaps it can be said

that it causes the most notable normative dismay among the more fervent radical-humanist segment of organizational theorists.

8. Under the G's in the *Dictionary of Political Analysis* one finds such interesting terms as *group, game theory, generalization,* and *Guttman Scale,* but nothing for *govern.* Raymond's *Dictionary of Politics* also has no entry for governance. The only political dictionary to come close to defining govern or governance is *A Dictionary of Political Thought* edited by Britisher Robert Scruton assisted by a British panel, only one of whom taught government. The latter book defines *government* as "the exercise of influence and control, through law and coercion, over a particular group of people, formed into a state" (p. 189).

9. We must leave the development and elaboration of active citizenship to Stivers in chapter 7. Our point here is that the Agency must seek ways to foster it. We need only repeat here that active citizenship is defined by: (1) decisive judgment; (2) concern for the common good; (3) practical wisdom; and (4) community (Stivers 1988: 89).

10. We use the quotes to indicate we feel these terms are used too loosely by Kelman (as by all of us). The terms ought to be used with more theoretic specificity. When we use "bureaucracy" it ought to connote Weber's image of a social construct of intended rationality. When we use "organization" it ought to connote Simon's, etc.; when we use "institution," Selznick's. Unfortunately that leaves us no generic term for use when we do not need nor wish to speak with theoretic specificity. I am still searching for a term and often use "social construct of intended rationality." So far I have persuaded no one that this is a useful, let alone a felicitous, phrase.

11. This, of course, is what the Founding Fathers had in mind. Jefferson felt something close to democracy would develop at the local and state levels while the national government would remain a more limited republic dealing with fewer matters — matters of importance but not of as great a salience for the populace.

Bibliography

Allison, Graham T. *Essence of Decisionmaking: Explaining the Cuban Missile Crisis.* Boston: Little, Brown, 1971.

Anna, Henry J. "The Agency Perspective and Local Government Administration." *Dialogue: The Public Administration Theory Network* 9, 2 (Winter, 1986) : 38-42.

Appleby, Paul H. *Big Democracy.* New York: Alfred A, Knopf, 1949.

Arendt, Hannah. *Policy and Administration.* University, Ala. : The University of Alabama Press, 1949.

— — — -. *The Human Condition.* Chicago: University of Chicago Press, 1958.

— — — -. *On Revolution.* New York: Penguin, 1963.

— — — -. *The Origins of Tolitarianism,* new ed. New York: Harcourt, Brace, and World, 1966.

Aristotle. *The Nichomachean Ethics,* trans. J.A.K. Thomson. New York: Penguin, 1976.

— — — -. *The Politics.* trans. T. A. Sinclair. New York: Penguin, 1981.

Bachrach, Peter, and Morton S. Baratz. *Power and Poverty: Theory and Practice.* England: Oxford University Press, 1970.

Bailey, Stephen K. "The Public Interest: Some Operational Dilemmas," *Nomos 5* (1962): 96-106.

Barnard, Chester I. *Functions of the Executive.* Cambridge, Mass.: Harvard University Press, 1938.

Bellah, Robert N., Madsen, Richard, Sullivan, William M., Swidler, Ann, and Tipton, Steven M. *Habits of the Heart: Individualism and Commitment in American Life.* New York: Harper and Row, 1985.

Black, Henry Campbell, ed. *Black's Law Dictionary,* rev. 4th ed. St. Paul, Minn. West Publishing, 1968.

Buchanan, James M. *Public Finance in Democratic Process: Fiscal Institutions and Individual Choice.* Chapel Hill, N.C.: The University of North Carolina Press, 1967, p. 299-300.

— — —. "Markets, States and the Extent of Morals," Papers and Proceedings of the Ninetieth Annual Meeting of the American Economic Association, (American Economic Association, May 1978).

Budziszewski, J. (1986) *The Resurrection of Nature: Political Theory and Human Character* (Ithica: Cornell University Press).

Campbell, Donald T. 1971. "Methods for the Experimenting Society," A paper delivered at the American Psychological Association, April 17, 1971.

Cater, Douglas. 1964. *Power in Washington* (New York: Vintage), p. 17.

Chomsky, Noam (1979) *Language and Responsibility* (Sussex: The Harbestor Press).

Cobb, Roger W. and Charles D. Elder. 1973. "The Political Uses of Symbolism," *American Politics Quarterly* 1 (July): 305-338.

Cooke, Jacob E., ed. 1961. *The Federalist* (Middletown, CT: Wesleyan University Press).

Cooper, Terry A. 1980. "Bureaucracy and Community Organization, *Administration and Society* 11 (Feb): 411-444.

— — —. 1984. "Citizenship and Professionalism in Public Administration," *Public Administration Review* 44 (Special Issue): 143-149.

Cox, Susan Jane Buck. 1985. "No Tragedy on the Commons," *Environmental Ethics* 7 (Spring): 49-61.

Culler, T. W. 1986. "Most Federal Workers Need Only Be Competent," *Wall Street Journal* May 21, 1986.

Cyert, Richard M., and March, James G. 1963. *A Behavioral Theory of the Firm* (Englewood Cliffs, N. J.: Prentice-Hall).

Dahl, Robert A. 1967. *Pluralist Democracy in the United States: Conflict and Consent* (Chicago, IL: Rand McNally).

Davidson, Roger. 1977. "Breaking Up Those Cozy Triangles: An Impossible Dream?" In Susan Welch and John Peters (eds.), *Legislative Reform and Public Policy* (New York: Praeger).

Douglas, Mary (1986) *How Institutions Think* (Syracuse University Press).

Downs, Anthony. 1962. "The Public Interest: Its Meaning in a Democracy," *Social Research* 29 (Spring): 1-36.

Dror, Yehez Kel. 1971. *Design for Policy Sciences* (San Francisco: Chandler).

Easton, David. 1965. *A Systems Analysis of Political Life* (New York: Wiley).

Edelman, Murray. 1967. *The Symbolic Uses of Politics* (Urbana: University of Illinois Press).

Fama, Eugene F. 1980. "Agency Problems and the Theory of the Firm," *Journal of Political Economy* 88: 288-305. C/r in org. theory.

— — — —, and Michael Jensen. 1983. "Separation of Ownership and Control," *Journal of Law and Economics* 26 (June): 288-305. C/R in org. theory.

Farazmand, Ali. "Crisis in the U.S. Administrative State," *Administration and Society*, forthcoming.

Finer, Herman. 1941. "Administrative Responsibility and Democratic Government," *Public Administration Review* 1 (Summer): 335-50.

Flatham, Richard E. 1966. *The Public Interest: An Essay Concerning the Normative Discourse of Politics* (New York: John Wiley).

Follett, Mary Parket (1924) *Creative Experience* (New York: Longmans Green).

Frederickson, H. George. 1982. "The Recovery of Civism in Public Administration," *Public Administration Review* (Nov./Dec.): 501-508.

Freeman, J. Leiper. 1955. *The Political Process* (New York: Random House).

Friedrich, Carl L. 1940. "Public Policy and the Nature of Administrative Responsibility," *Public Policy* 1 (1940): 3-24.

— — —. 1972. *Tradition and Authority* (New York: Praeger).

Gais, T. L., Peterson, M. A., and Walker, J. L. 1984. "Interest Groups, Iron Triangles and Representative Institutions in American National Government", *British Journal of Political Science* 14 (April) 161-185.

Gaus, John. 1957. *Reflections on Public Administration* (University, AL: University of Alabama Press).

Gawthrop, Louis C. 1984. "Civis, Civitas, and Civilitas: A New Focus for the Year 2000," *Public Administration Review* 44 (Special Issue): 101-106.

Giddens, A. 1979. *Central Problems in Social Theory* (Berkeley: Univ. of Calif. Press).

Goodnow, Frank J. 1900, 1967. *Politics and Administration: A Study in Government* (New York: Russell and Russell).

Goodsell, Charles T. 1982. *The Case for Bureaucracy: A Public Administration Polemic* (Chatham, NJ: Chatham House).

— — —. 1989. "The Public Administration and the Public Interest", Ch.III, in Gary L. Wamsley, ed. *The Public Administration in the Governance of America* (Chatham, NJ: Chatham House).

Graham, Cole Blease, and Steven W. Hayes. 1986. "Traditional Responses to American Administrative Discretion" from *Administrative Discretion and Public Policy Implementation*, Douglas II. Shumavon and Kenneth Hibbeln, eds. (New York: Praeger).

Griffith, Ernest S. 1939. *The Impasse of Democracy* (New York: Harrison-Milton Books), p. 182.

Habermas, Juren (1973) "Dogmatism, Reason and Decision: On Theory and Practice in our Scientific Civilization," *Theory and Practice* Trans. John Vierter. (Boston: Beacon Press) p. 255.

— — —, (1979) *Communication and the Evolution of Society* Trans. Thomas McCarthy. (Boston: Beacon Press).

Hardin, Garrett. 1968. "The Tragedy on the Commons," *Science* 162: 1243-1248.

Heclo, Hugh. 1978. "Issue Networks and the Executive Establishment", in Anthony King, ed., *The New American Political System* (Washington, DC: American Enterprise Institute), p. 88.

— — —, and Lester M. Salamon. 1981. *The Illusion of Presidential Government* (Boulder, CO: Westview Press).

Hill, Melvyn A., Ed. (1979) *Hannah Arendt: The Recovery of the Public World* (New York: St. Martin's Press).

Hummel, Ralph. 1985. "Organizing a debate: 'Resolved,' that there should be no theory or theorist in ASPA or the Profession," *Dialogue, The Public Administration Theory Network* 8 (1): 49-61.

Hummel, Ralph and Robert A. Isaak. 1980. *Politics for Human Beings*, 2nd ed. (Belmont, CA: Wadsworth).

Jordan, A. G. 1980. "Iron Triangles, Woolly Corporatism and Elastic Nets: Images of the Policy Process," *Journal of Public Policy* 1 (Feb): 95-123.

Keller, Lawrence F. 1984. "The Political Economy of Public Management: An Interorganizationl Network Perspective," *Administration and Society* 15 (4): 455-474.

Kelman Steven. 1987. *Making Public Policy. A Hopeful View of American Government* (New York: Basic Books, Inc., Publishers).

Korten, D. "Community Organization and Rural Development: A Learning Process Approach," *Public Administration Review* Sept./Oct.1980: 480-511.

Leiserson, Avery. 1942. *Administrative Regulation: A Study in Representation of Interests* (Chicago, IL: University of Chicago Press).

Levine, Charles H. 1986. "The Quiet Crisis of the Civil Service: The Federal Personnel System at the Crossroads", *National Academy of Public Administration*, Occasional Paper, December, 1986.

Lewis, Eugene. 1980. *Public Entrepreneurship: Toward a Theory of Bureaucratic Political Power* (Bloomington: Indiana University Press).

Long, Norton E. 1949. "Power and Administration," *Public Administration Review* 9 (4): 45-61..

— — —. n.d. "The Objectives of Administrative Reform in the Modern Democratic State," Missouri-St.Louis. C/R. in org. Theory.

— — —. 1969. "Reflections on Presidential Power," *Public Administration Review* 29 (5): — — —.

— — —. 1980. "Dewey's Conception of the Public and the Public Interest," University of Missouri, St Louis at the Mid-West Pol. Science Association, 1980, annual convention on April 24-26. C/R in org. theory.

— — —. 1987. "Power and Administration," in Classics of Public Administration, Second Edition, revised. Shafritz, J. M. and Hyde, A. C., eds. (Chicago: Dorsey Press) 203-212.

Lowi, Theodore J. 1976. *American Government: The Incomplete Conquest* (Hinsdale IL: Dryden Press).

— — —. 1979. *The End Of Liberalism: The Second Republic of the United States*, 2nd ed. (New York: W.W. Norton).

Mahler, Julianne. "The Quest for International Development: Identifying and Interpreting the Symbolism in Organizational Stories," *Administration and Society* Forthcoming issue.

March, James G., and Johan P. Olsen. 1983. "The New Institutionalism: Organizational Factors in Political Life," *APSR* 77: 281-296.

Marx, Karl. 19— . *Das Capital, 1* (New York: Modern Library), n.d. C/R in org. theory.

McDonald, Forrest. 1985. *Novus Ordo Sectorum: The Intellectual Origins of the Constitution* (Lawrence, KS: University of Kansas Press).

McGregor, Douglas. 1966. *Leadership and Motivation, Essays of Douglas McGregor* W.G. Bennis and E.H. Schein, eds. (Cambridge, MA: MIT Press).

McKean Roland. 1979. "Some Economic Aspects of Ethical-Behavioral Codes," *Political Studies* 27 (2) June: 251-265.

Mechanic David. 1962. "Sources of Power of Lower Participants in Complex Organizations," *Administrative Science Quarterly* 7 (December): 349-364. C/R in agency theory.

Merelman, Richard M. 1966. "Learning and Legitimacy," *American Political Science Review* 60 (September): 548-61.

Milward, H. Brinton. 1982. "Interorganizational Policy Systems and Research in Public Organizations," *Administration and Society* 13: 457-478.

Mitnick, Barry M. 1985. "Agency Problems and Organization Theory and Design: The Bureaucrat as Agent", paper delivered Acad. of Mgt. San Diego, CA Aug. 1985.

— — —. 1985. "Strategic Risk Reduction and the Creation of Agents in Regulation", Working Paper Series, Graduate School of Business, University of Pittsburg, N.D.

Moe, Terry. 1984. "The New Economics of Organization." *American Journal of Political Science* 28 (4 November): 739-777.

Narr, Wolf-Dieder (1984) "Towards A Society of Conditioned Reflexes," in obserations in *The Spiritual Situation of the Age* Editor Jurgen Habermas. (Cambridge, Mass and London: MIT Press).

Nathan, Richard. 1975. *The Plot that Failed: Nixon and the Administrative Presidency* (NY: Wiley).

— — —. 1983. *The Administrative Presidency* (New York: Wiley).

Nelson, Michael. 1982. "A Short Ironic History of American National Bureaucracy," *Journal of Politics* 44: 747-778.

Neustadt, Richard. 1980. *Presidential Power: The Politics of Leadership from FDR to Carter* (New York: Wiley).

Newland, Chester A. 1983. "A Mid-Term Appraisal—The Reagan Presidency: Limited Government and Political Administration," *Public Administration Review* 43 (January/February): 1-21.

O'Connor, James. 1973. *The Fiscal Crisis of the State* (New York: St. Martin's Press).

Olsen, Mancur. 1971. *The Logic of Collective Action* (Cambridge, MA: Harvard University Press).

Ostrom, Elinor. 1986. "A Method of Institutional Analysis", in *Guidance, Control and Evaluation in the Public Sector: The Bielefeld Interdisciplinary Project*, Franz-Xaver Kaufman, Giandomenico Majone, Vincent Ostrom, eds. with the assistance of Wolfgang Wirth (New York: W. de Grayter).

— — —. 1986. "An Agenda for the Study of Institutions," *Public Choice* 48: 3-25.

Ostrom, Vincent. 1974. *The Intellectual Crisis in American Public Administration*, rev. ed. (University, AL: University of Alabama Press).

Perrow, Charles. 1961. "Goals in Complex Organizations," *American Sociological Review* 26 (6 December): 854-865.

— — —. 1986. *Complex Organizations*, 3rd ed. (New York: Random House).

Pfiffner, John M., and Robert M. Presthus. 1960. *Public Administration*, 4th ed., (New York: Ronald Press Co.).

Plato. 1950. "The Republic", in *Dialogues of Plato*, Jowett trans,. (New York: Pocket Books, Inc.).

Pomper, Gerald M. 1981. "The Nominating Contests," in Marlene Michels ed., *The Election of 1980* (Chatham, NJ: Chatham House Publishers, Inc.)

Pondy, Louis, Peter Frost, Gareth Morgan and Thomas Dandridge (eds.). 1983. *Organizational Symbolism* (Greenwich, CN: JAI Press).

Preston, Larry M. 1987. "Freedom and Bureaucracy," *American Journal of Political Science* 31 (4) November: 773-795.

Prince, Carl E. 1927. *The Federalists and the Origins of the U.S. Civil Service* (New York: New York University Press).

Redford, Emmette S. 1958. *Ideal and Practice in Public Administration* (University, AL: University of Alabama Press).

— — —. 1969. *Democracy in the Administrative State* (New York: Oxford University Press).

Richardson, William D., and Lloyd G. Nigro. 1987. "Administrative Ethics and Founding Thought: Constitutional Correctives, Honor, and Education," *Public Administration Review* 47 (5 September/October): 367-375.

Rohr, John A. 1986. *To Run A Constitution: The Legitimacy of the Administrative State* (Lawrence, KS: University of Kansas Press).

— — —. 1987. "Constitutional Foundations of the Administrative State" in Ralph C. Chandler, ed. *A Centennial History of the Administrative State* (New York: Wiley).

Sabatier, P. 1987. "Knowledge, Policy-Oriented Learning, and Policy Change: An Advocacy Coalition Framework," *Knowledge: Creation, Diffusion, and Utilization* 8(4) June: 649-692.

Salamon, Lester M. 1981. *The Reagan Presidency and the Governing of America* (Washington, D.C.: The Urban Institute Press).

— — —., and Hugh Heclo, eds. 1981. *The Illusion of Presidential Government* (Boulder, CO: Westview Press).

Sandel, Michael (1982) *Liberalism and the Limits of Justice* (Cambridge: Cambridge University Press.)

Saracen, Seymour, B. 1972. *The Creation of Settings and the Future Societies* (San Francisco, CA: Jossey-Bass Inc., Publishers).

Sayre, Wallace, S. 1951. "Trends of a Decade in Administrative Values", *Public Administration Review* 11: 1-9.

Schaar, John. 1981. *Legitimacy in the Modern State* (New Brunswick, NJ: Transaction Books).

Schubert, Glendon A. Jr. 1957. "The Public Interest: Administrative Decision-Making: Theorem, Theosophy, Or Theory?" *The American Political Science Review* 5 June: 346-368.

Seidman, Harold. 1970. *Politics, Position, and Power: The Dynamics of Federal Organization* (New York: Oxford University Press).

Selznick, Philip. 1952. *The Organizational Weapon: A Study of Bolshevik Strategy and Tactics* (New York: McGraw-Hill).

— — —. 1965. *TVA and the Grass Roots* (New York: Harper and Row).

— — —. 1957. *Leadership in Administration* (New York: Harper and Row).

Sheldon, Garrett W. 1987. "Jeffersonian Constitutionalism," A paper delivered at the Annual meeting of the Southern Political Science Association, Charlotte, N.C.

Simon, Herbert A. 1957. *Administrative Behavior: A Study of Decision-Making Processes in Administrative Organization*, 2nd ed. (New York: The Free Press).

Sinopoli, Richard. 1985. "The Founders' Liberalism and the Problems of Civic Virtue" a paper presented at the annual meeting of the American Pol. Sci Association, New Orleans, August 29, 1985.

Smircich, L. 1983a. "Organizations as shared meanings," p. 55-65, in Louis Pondy, Peter Frost, Gareth Morgan and Thomas Dandridge (eds.), *Organizational Symbolism* (Greenwich, C.N.: JAI Press).

— — —. 1983b. "Concepts of culture and organizational analysis," *Administrative Science Quarterly* 28 (September): 339-358.

Stivers, Camilla M. (1989) Toward a Community of Knowledge: Active Citizens in the Administrative State, forthcoming in *Return from Oz: Refounding Public Administration* Gary Wamsley, Ed. (Newbury Park: Sage).

Stivers, Camilla M. 1988. "Reframing Health Policy Debate: The Need for Public Interest Language," *Administration and Society*, 20 (No. 3. Nov): 309-327.

— — —. "Active Citizenship In The Administrative State," Dissertation submitted to the Faculty of the Virginia Polytechnic Institute and State University in partial fulfillment of the requirements for the degree of Doctor of Philosophy in Public Administration and Policy, April 1988.

Taylor, Frederick W. 1947. *Scientific Management* (New York: Harper and Brothers).

Truman, David B. 1951. *The Governmental Process* (New York: Alfred A. Knopf).

Urwick L. and Elliot M. Fox. 1973. *Dynamic Administration: The Collected Papers of Mary Parker Follett* (Pittman Publishing), Ch. 5-6.

Ventriss, Curtis and R. Pecrella. 1984. "Community Participation and Modernization: A Re-examination of Political Choices," *PAR* 44 (3): 221-231.

Waldo, Dwight. 1948. *The Administrative State: A Study of the Political Administration* (New York: The Ronald Press).

Wamsley, Gary L. 1969. *Selective Service and a Changing America.* (Columbus, Ohio: Charles E. Merrill).

— — —. 1984. Policy Subsystems: Networks and the Tools of Public Managhement" in *Public Policy Formation and Implementation*, Part I, ed. by Robert Eyestone (JAI Press).

— — —. 1985. "Strategies in Implementation: Applying the Political Economy Framework to Policy Subsystems," paper prepared for Conference on Multi-Actor Policy Analysis: The Scope and Direction of Policy Recommendations, Umea University, Umea, Sweden, July, 23-26, 1985.

Wamsley, Gary L., and Brinton H. Milward. 1984. "Policy Subsystems as A Unit of Analysis in Implementation Studies," in *Policy Implementation in Federal and Unitary Systems*. Proceedings of the International Workshop on Interorganizational Implementation Systems in the Public Sector, eds. Kenneth Hanf and T.A.J. Toonen, Martinus-Nijhoff, Amsterdam, The Netherlands, 1984.

Wamsley, Gary, and Mayer M. Zald. 1973. *The Political Economy of Public Organizations* (Lexington: D.C. Heath and Co.). C/R in Comp.Org.

Wamsley, Gary L., et. al. "A Legitimate Role for Bureaucracy in Democratic Governance" in Larry B. Hill, *The Present State of Public Bureaucracy* (Baltimore, MD: Johns Hopkins University Press, forthcoming).

Wamsley, Gary L., et. al. 1990. *Refounding Public Administration* (Newbury Park: Sage).

Weber, Max. 1947. *The Theory of Social and Economic Organization*, translated and edited by A.M. Henderson and T. Parsons. (New York: Oxford University Press).

— — —. 1968. *Economy and Society*, vols. 1 and 3, 4th ed., edited by G. Roth and C. Wittich. (New York: Irvington Publications).

M. Weber, From *Max Weber: Essays in Sociology*, trans, Gerth and Mills (Oxford, 1946). M. Weber, *The Theory of Social and Economic Organization*, trans. Henderson and Parsons (Oxford, 1947).

Webster's Third New International Dictionary 1981. (Springfield, MS: Merriam).

Webster's New Collegiate Dictionary, 2nd ed. (Springfield, MS: Merriam) 1958.

White, Leonard D. 1939. *Introduction to the Study of Public Administration* rev. ed., (New York, NY: Macmillan.)

— — —. 1948. *The Federalists: A Study in Administrative History* (New York: Macmillan).

Will, George, F. 1983. *Statecraft as Soulcraft* (New York: Simon and Schuster).

Wilson, Harlan. 1975. "Complexity as a Theoretical Problem: Wider Perspectives in Political Theory," in Todd R. La Porte, ed. *Organized Social Complexity* (Princeton, N.J.: Princeton University Press). C/R in agency theory.

Wilson, Woodrow. 1887. "The Study of Administration," *Political Science Quarterly* 2: 197-222.

5. The Public Administrator and Public Service Occupations

JAMES F. WOLF
ROBERT N. BACHER

The Public Administrator: The Worlds of Public Service Occupations

In the Blacksburg Manifesto, the Public Administrator is identified as a critical point of focus yet recognized to be in a very ambiguous situation. Who are these people who grow up to become Public Administrators? What roles are available or could be developed to serve The Public Administration? Should this person be a professional? A seer? An anointed one? A hired lackey (if so, for whom)? A servant? A teacher? The Blacksburg Manifesto takes the position that professional status is not the answer and exhorts the Public Administrator to employ the metaphors of servants, vocation, and accountable teacher.

Any discussion about the proper role of the Public Administrator will need to take into account the world in which he or she lives. Although this world is principally the world of governance, politics, economy, and bureaucracy, in a very significant way it is also the world of occupations. Children grow up and become public administrators, as others become doctors, firefighters, mechanics, and computer experts. Through the dynamics of occupational structures, a person becomes part of The Public Administration. To a large degree, the world of the Public Administrator is given meaning through the particular occupational path that is chosen and pursued. An understanding and appreciation of the occupational worlds of the public administrator is essential if dialogue is to advance and if we are to understand how persons in these occupations can become the Public Administrators called for in the Manifesto.

This chapter will first present three occupational worlds in which public administrators exists — *vocation, job,* and *career.* Second, a brief demonstration is offered of how these vocation, job, and career worlds are played historically in American Public Administration. Finally, some prescriptions are identified for the future. We begin with a portrayal of the major forces at work in The Public Administration situation.

The Situation of the Public Administrator: Forces Affecting the Public Administration Occupations

Powerful forces are changing the nature of Public Administration occupations. These include: the questioning of the role of government in today's society, the devaluation and loss of legitimacy of public agencies, the rise of the professional state, and societal demographic changes that effect public service occupations.

The questioning of the role of government comes from both the left and right. An issue from the "left" focuses on the credibility and legitimacy of governmental institutions. Because of the blurring of state and corporate interest, the use of authority for the public interest is viewed with suspicion. From the "right" comes the challenge to the activist state and a demand for greater use of market mechanisms to fulfill social responsibilities.

A second yet related force is the devaluation and loss of legitimacy of public agencies. Public organizations have undergone a dramatic devaluation during the past decade. The last two presidential elections featured candidates who ran against the bureaucracy. The Reagan Administration was clear about its distaste for domestic federal agencies. Often there appears to be a conscious choice to destabilize and disinvest in the capacity of these agencies of government to act. This strategy in turn decreases public confidence in The Public Administration and leads to further loss of support. A major feature of this strategy for crippling public agencies is to undermine and sap the will and capacity of the public administrators within the agencies.

The rise of the professional state is a third force helping to shape the public administrator's situation. The professional state is characterized by Mosher as a government wherein many professions control critical positions within an agency (Mosher 1982). More importantly, the identities of many professionals employed in public organizations are more closely allied to the values and concerns of the profession than to the legislative mandates, presidential interests, or broader agency objectives. Perhaps the most significant result of this domination of agency agendas by professional interests is the equating of a public service career with the professional occupation. An important exception to this characterization is the elite corps that are tied to agencies rather than to broader occupational groups. Examples include the Park Service, the Public Health Service, the Foreign Service, and many of the military career corps.

The fourth force is a set of demographic changes that are altering the daily realities of the public service. The demographics of public organizations seem to be characterized by feast or famine. Following the dramatic rise in public sector employment during the 1950s, 1960s, and early 1970s, we now have an equally dramatic leveling off and, in some cases, decline in public sector jobs.

At the same time, the demographic bulge of the baby boom generation is causing distortions in the demographics of public sector employment. As the baby boom cohort moves into both middle age and into the middle level of the organizational hierarchy, employment opportunities for this group are severely diminished (Wolf 1983). The result is a disruption of normal occupational or career paths that an upwardly mobile generation had expected by this time in their work lives. No doubt, meanings given to work and to a personal sense of careers have been affected by this constricted sense of opportunity in public administration.

At the same time the public service will be facing severe problems of recruitment and retention of competent employees in the upcoming decade. This seemingly paradoxical situation of a crowd at the middle levels and too few at the entry levels results from several forces. The baby bust generation that followed the baby boom group will not fill the need at the entry levels. The changing nature of work of the public service forces agencies to search the job market for highly specialized and technically trained applicants. The unattractiveness of public service occupations compounds the effort to recruit in a very competitive job market. Finally, the composition of the workforce will change dramatically. There will be a far greater percentage of women, minorities, and foreign-born workers in the public service (Johnson et al. 1988).

These four forces combine to create pressures that contribute to a crisis in public service occupations. The heart of the crisis involves the ways public employees relate to their jobs and the processes that public organizations use to connect their employees to the organization. This chapter explores the nature of the crisis and its implications for the public administration. The approach taken is to describe and analyze the characteristics of occupations in the public service. Hopefully this can be done without slippage into the reductionist positions that come from an overemphasis on individual issues flowing from the psychological or "personal growth" perspective offered by much of the organization-behavior literature. At the same time, it is important to be equally wary of a management approach that tends to overemphasize the agency's strategic and control mechanisms for addressing the problem. By avoiding these two positions, we do not deny the possibility of personal or organizational action affecting occupations. Rather, our approach attempts to describe the strong societal forces that shape the context in which individuals engage in career-related activities.

Although the following analysis seems most applicable to public service occupations, we believe it also applies to other sectors, particularly the not-for-profit sector.

The Public Administration: Existing in Three Occupational Worlds.

Public service employment exists simultaneously in three different, yet sometimes reinforcing, social realities or "worlds." We have called these the worlds of job, career, and vocation. Before looking at each of these, some discussion of what is meant by the term *worlds* is needed. One way to understand this claim is to begin with the assumption that a special "lens" is needed to view each of these worlds. The notion of a lens represents an heuristic device to see and understand the three occupational worlds.[1]

We will also use the idea of "worlds" or paradigms as socially real, and therefore as a way of understanding. Occupations are the building blocks for understanding work in the public service and, at the same time, those in the public sector are embedded in the broader occupational groups in the societal-level workforce. Occupations provide the mechanisms to ensure that the there is an adequate supply of specialized work groups for an industrial society. Occupational paradigms are of the everyday world in that they provide logic for acting that individuals and organizations use to develop career decisions and processes.

What we are calling an occupational world seems to have certain features, and in the description of vocation, job, and career worlds that follow, four of these features are discussed. First, the occupational worlds have patterns of consciousness that consist of ideas, beliefs, values, and language. There is an interaction between these patterns and the occupational experiences of individual workers. One modifies the other. For example, a young Foreign Service officer may want to treat his new job as a nine-to-five experience, but the career traditions of the Foreign Service Officer Corps will not permit that kind of behavioral definition of the job. On the other hand, if the bulk of new recruits start to view their jobs in the same limited way, the structure of the Foreign Service Officer Corps will undergo significant change.

Second, the patterns resulting from the interaction of individual experiences and the structure of the occupational world provide a language of legitimacy that, in turn, supports the potency of each world. These legitimizing patterns also guide and control the *discourse* of each world. Perhaps one of the most important components of these patterns is their tacit and shared background knowledge. Shared background knowledge about what it means to be in an occupation provides a frame or logic for acting and interpreting social life within each of the three occupational worlds.

Third, sources for control and legitimacy of the occupational world come from patterns of authority that help to define the legitimate and illegitimate aspects of occupations, including career paths and rules. The patterns also provide credentials for signaling achievements and claims in each world, rules for moving among worlds, as well as rules for behavior within each. In addition there are public worlds that serve as sources of ideas for the patterns of consciousness, yielding accountability systems of persuasion and control.

Finally, the interaction seems to produce both positives and negatives — each has strengths and weaknesses. This is an important feature of the occupational worlds. We will see, for example, that the variation offers real opportunities to connect individuals to a broader community of purpose but, at the same time, poses the danger of blind commitment to unreasonable, illegal, or unethical organizational demands. An encouraging feature of the three worlds is that the practice of one can frequently ameliorate the damaging consequences of another.

Before describing each occupational world in its dynamic qualities, it should be noted that public sector employees are simultaneously buffeted by all three worlds and, within each world, experience dialectic tensions through time. One needs to be aware of the ways in which each occupational paradigm modifies the other at any particular time in history and that each is itself altering its own structures and patterns as it moves through time. Any analysis, including the following one, is not static. The worlds are not clearly formed but, rather, are emergent and powerful. Each results from different phases of historical development and is a significant force that continues to shape public service occupations. Each world offers a way to understand, to critique, and to imagine action possibilities for individuals, organizations, and society.

An Examination into the Three Worlds

The idea of the three worlds of vocation, job, and career are consistent with and supported by the recent work of Bellah et al. In the book *Habits of the Heart* (1985), these writers provide an important analysis of current American life in light of the deeper cultural traditions of individualism and community in our society. They also use the concepts of vocation, job, and career. Their idea of vocation emphasizes the biblical and republican strains in American life, which are concerned with linking a person to the larger community in which a "calling of each is a contribution to the good of all." The ideas of job and career are based on the powerful traditions of individualism. In the case of the job, the work is a way of making money and supports a self defined by "economic success, security, and all that money can buy." The career, rather than being defined by economic success, is rooted in the expressive individualism that is typified by the ideals of Emerson. The career "yields a self defined by a broader sort of success, which takes in social standing and prestige, and by a sense of expanding power and competency that renders work itself a source of self-esteem" (Bellah et al. 1985). Let us now turn to an examination of how these three ideas are manifested in The Public Administration.

The World of Vocation: A Calling to Public Service

Our popular notion of vocation builds on the German concept of *Beruf* or calling. During the sixteenth-century Reformation period, Martin Luther and others emphasized that vocation is played out in response to God's call through one's daily activities, especially occupational roles. A call implies a caller or source of call, thereby introducing a transpersonal aspect to the idea of vocation. Having a vocation is not entirely a matter of individual interests and pursuits but seems to connect one with larger forces — of God, nation, state, family, or profession. The idea of career or job becomes embedded in meanings beyond individual meanings, hopes, and experiences. Sources for a calling obviously do not have to be religious. Although the idea of *Stand* or order of creation implies a divine design for one's place in this world (Wiggens 1957), the source can also come from the social order and institutional patterns in society.

Vocation seems to carry a powerful transpersonal dimension and invokes an affirming and positive role for institutions. Within the American tradition, the sense of calling is closely tied to biblical and republican tradition. Bellah et al. demonstrate this thread through the *Episcopal Book of Common Prayer*. In the text, each is called to contribute to the good of the whole. In the collect for Labor Day there is the prayer to "So guide us in the work we do, that we may do it not for self alone, but for the common good" (Bellah et al. 1985). At the level of the Public Administrator, a public administrator's sense of calling is to the public service and is rooted in the U.S. Constitution and subsequent historical experiences. The Constitution acts as a beckoning or call toward a set of values and beliefs about our public order and institutions. John Rohr's chapter in this volume makes clear how the "founding" and Constitution provide this grounding. A sense of transcendence is added then by this "call" as one response to a sense of values and beliefs outside oneself. Although self-expression is involved, the response is primarily also a matter of the collective development of our society and institutions over time as expressed through constitutional order.

To avoid individual misuse, and the misuse of individuals, it is important to treat vocation as containing the idea that one's place is not fixed. Vocation implies a sense of order existing in society and a beckoning to a set of values that result from the "living world" of the Constitution and society, but the notion that individuals exist only to fulfill certain slots in a predetermined order of things must be rejected.

Some of the key *ideas* for this world of vocation include integrity, connectedness, a sense of self-transcendence, a focus on the role of work, and living for — not off — the public service (Wamsley et al. 1983). One powerful idea is that of a *commitment* to something: the public service, the client, or the broadest possible definition of the public interest.

The *language* of this world includes vocation, calling, commitment, a sense of purpose, public service/servants, trustee (Wamsley et al. 1983), career corps, and being in a significant human endeavor for more than self-expression and development.

The control and legitimacy patterns of this occupational world are tied closely to the career roles in the occupational structure of public organizations. Since there are so many different occupational groups employed in public organizations, there are a variety of sources for "calling" and control. It includes a general "public service" occupational group typified by the common response: "I am a civil servant." There are also more clearly identifiable groups including technical and administrative professions as well as the agency career corps found in military, foreign service, and some other public organizations. Embedded in these groups are institutionalized values of service, commitment, and professional competence. The professions provide standards, norms, status structures, and credentialing processes that tie one's occupational role to the broader societal context. The structure of these various public service occupations — organizational career ladders and career paths, compensation, job protections — all provide patterns for control and legitimacy in the world of the vocation in the public service.

The power and influence of vocation in the public service have ebbed and flowed. During the early days of the Republic, the emphasis, at least at the highest level, was on service by good public citizens of integrity. Although there was an elite focus during the Federalist period, there was also a belief that the call to service by the government was something that should be heeded by the best of the country's citizens.

This thrust was renewed during the Reform period. The need for good government was established and the primary way to secure it was through merit and nonpartisanship. The public employee was a public servant with a special mandate — to be an uncorrupted public servant.

The Depression saw a renewal of the idea of government playing a positive role in solving severe public problems. The government attracted talented people (in part because of fewer opportunities in the private sector) who were committed to working on a major public enterprise. This spirit of the public service was continued during World War II and to some extent in the optimism of the Kennedy years (the Peace Corps, the New Frontier). These were times in our history when a call seemed to go out for a creative and competent public administration that had a responsibility to be excellent in order to address a pressing public problem or challenge.

As we said, the vocation is enhanced by the affirming role of society and institutions. An affirmation of citizenship and a special group of citizens — public servants — is more possible in the world of vocation. The public servant is not afforded greater privilege than other citizens. Rather, public servants are special because they are deeply involved in a shared project of governance and common endeavor of the society. Public servants are presented with an opportunity for experiencing what many consider difficult to find in modern society, a sense of transcendence — a chance to be connected to the broader community through common purposes and efforts.

A key issue for vocation is the tension between critical commitment and blind commitment to the perceived responsibilities of the public employee. The tension operates at individual, agency, and societal levels. Will the public servant see his or her commitment to be one of unwavering obedience to responsibility and higher authority, or will a public servant's action be carried out with a critical sense of how actions affect not only immediate personal and organizational needs but also the requirements of the public interest?

The world of vocation offers the public servant some powerful opportunities: a chance to be part of a humanist social enterprise, to experience meaning in work, and the feeling of altruism. This world seems to help individuals achieve what Robert Lifton (Lifton 1976) calls *connectedness*, a powerful, formatic sense of belonging that overcomes separation and alienation yet respects integrity and individuality.

The down side to the world of vocation for the individual is the danger of overcommitment to job and career and the neglect of other aspects of a full and responsible life. The Nuremberg trials brought out the dangers of uncritical obedience to whatever the person sees as his or her *source* of calling—the agency, profession, nation-state in this context is an ever-present danger.

The world of vocation also offers an important positive force at the agency level; the possibility of a committed workforce. The sense of calling increases the attraction of staying with an agency and being committed to its goals. Another important benefit of vocation is the facilitation of an institutional memory that allows for changes without loss of those competencies and capacities that develop over time. With workforce anchored in the values of the public service and agency purpose, an agency is more likely to become an institution — one that is capable of developing and sustaining long-term strategies for attracting and keeping a talented and committed workforce (see Chapter 4).

Perhaps the world of vocation's most serious challenge to the agency is the counterforce that a professional identity frequently gives to its members. This becomes problematic when cosmopolitan professionals become grounded more in their relationships with the profession's standards and status structure than those of the agency. Such a way of thinking can represent a powerful challenge to the agency. If the sense of vocation is attached to the profession and not the agency, it is not difficult to see the potential difficulty in securing any allegiance to the agency purpose (Mosher 1982).

Society also benefits from the investment in its institutions created by public service vocations. Public institutions stand to gain through the psychological commitment of its employees to a public career in an agency, thereby increasing a capacity to use public instruments for social action. At the broadest level, there is greater occupational competency throughout the society when employees invest more of their time and energy in their work world. Finally, we should not underestimate the power that comes from a commitment to a larger enterprise. The psychic energy that results from commitment to a cause outside oneself can be a positive force for community action. The longing to be part of a societal effort, when enhanced through a sense of vocation, can be an enriching force throughout our society.

On the other hand, uncritical acceptance by public administration of demands from the agency or profession can lead to adoption of institutional values that undermine important societal or human values. The obedient institutional servant can be a source of societal harm.

Finally, the public servant is only one source of vocational identity. Other occupational professions also offer opportunities to be linked to broader communities of practice and service. Nevertheless, the public service does offer special opportunities for individuals to become part of important common enterprises — governances and efforts to achieve shared ideals in society.

The World of the Job: An Employee in the Public Sector

The world of the job began as the Western world moved from an agrarian to a capitalist society. During this transition, work became less related to one's place or *Stand* in the world. Individuals became interchangeable parts that could be exchanged with one for the other and which could be replaced by land or capital. A labor market allowed individuals to sell their competencies for the going price. The asking was a day's work for a day's pay. Development of Western capitalist society required at least two types of roles from its members: employees and consumers. As employees, we purchased goods and services. These two roles became the predominate way that individuals interacted with the economic world. Society also needs employees who are willing to do the pleasant and unpleasant jobs. A smoothly operating economy requires a competent and predictable workforce in order to meet the demands of production. The world of jobs provides it.

The central *idea* of the world of the job is that a "job is a job is a job." A job entails labor, principally as a way to gain enough money to live. One recognizes and accepts that a job is not coterminous with real *life work*, for which arrangements must be made outside and beyond employment. Little more than material remuneration is expected or obtained from the job. Neither psychic reward nor fulfillment is expected beyond the status associated with being able to afford a particular standard of living. In matters of personal fulfillment, what really counts are those times and places away from the job. Frequently the attitude employees adopt is either that of the obedient cheerful robot (Brown 1978: 372) or the passive worker who seeks to get away with doing the least amount of work acceptable.

The job world is not necessarily made up of meaningless exchanges of work for money. The market value of the exchange is what gives meaning to the work. Utilitarian individualism prevails. This value gives the worker an identity that is judged by economic success, security, and all that money can buy (Bellah et al. 1985). The job is the way we "get ahead" and is the way to define success. This almost ascetic posture holds that if one works hard, observes the rules, and learns to keep personal desires suppressed in the workplace, the rewards of morale self-esteem, respect from others, and worldly goods will follow (Yankelovich 1981). However, there is still no meaning derived from the work beyond the exchange value provided by the economy and occupational system.

The language of this job world includes: "It's just a job," "Nine to five," "Labor contract," "Avoid overcommitment," "Get ahead," "What really keeps me going is . . . " Many of the interviews by Studs Terkel of working people capture the flavor and language of this world (Terkel 1985).

The nature of the labor market — including wage scales, demands for specific jobs and occupations, legal and organizational standards for occupational entry and advancement, and the educational system and class structure — contributes to patterns of control that treat the job simply as a medium for exchanging labor for money.

The world of the job has always been strong. One expression has been the notion of the "adequate public service." The historical roots can perhaps best be traced to the Jacksonian tradition. As government became larger, so did the range and number of jobs. It is important to note that this tradition did not advocate that just anyone could hold a public job. "Jackson insisted that he sought men whose diligence and talent would insure faithful execution of duties" (Mosher 1982). There was a strong belief in the simplicity of public works. The jobs should be made simple enough so that anyone could do them. In this way the number of people who could qualify would expand. The concern then was not for excellence but for adequacy. The expectation for an adequate bureaucracy reinforces a resistance by the public and by politicians to invest in the bureaucracy through training, high pay, and so on. The bureaucracy is simply not valued that highly. Even recent efforts to gain more production do not get beyond the rather simple exchange notions embedded in the job paradigms — the public bureaucracies are seen in fairly simple machinelike terms. For example, the performance-pay thrust of many personnel "reforms" assumes that increased performance in the public service will result from economic incentives — not from a broader commitment to common purposes.

The most compatible occupational paradigm for these sets of beliefs is the world of the job. A person is simply a public employee who must do an honest day's work for an honest day's pay. For the vast numbers of occupations in the public administration, this world of the job has offered the most plausible explanation and grounding. During the last decade, the public professional and manager has seen the esteem of his or her world ebb. As the public service has become devalued, producing fewer desirable work motivations, the world of the job is becoming the predominate occupational paradigm for many at middle and even upper levels of the public bureaucracy. These managers are taking on may of the attitudes toward work that their co-workers at lower levels in the bureaucracy hold.

A key tension in this world centers on the problem of compartmentalization of the self. What does it mean when major time periods of an individual's life are spent on almost purely instrumental activity? Implications of this tension at the individual level include the following: the job can offer freedom and a financial base to pursue one's own interests outside the job; freedom from excessive psychological burdens that vocation places on the employee; and escape from overexpectations of work.

The negative side for the person who is presently detached from the "hassle" of the job is excessive compartmentalization of the self. The person "on the job" and the person "outside the job" can become strangers and suffer estrangement. The absence of an integrated social self can lead to stress and other psychological and spiritual costs. A related dynamic to the delimited notion of what one can get out of the job is the frustration of not dealing with core life processes within the work world when so much on one's time and energy are spent on the job. For the public organization certain gains accrue. If employees need to work to live but don't bring vocation-world expectations with them, it becomes possible to get the "dirty work" done. If the right wage is paid, the work can be done without worry about issues of job satisfaction or meaningful work. This outcome is particularly desirable in instances where organizational high performers are unnecessary or where extraordinary effort levels are not critical.

When there are requirements that employees go beyond the minimal expectations of the job, however, there is limited gain from the marginally involved worker. An important negative consequence is the loss of imagination and thus of creativity. Imagination feeds on enthusiasm, and enthusiasm is not one of the by-products of the job world. Finally, the world of the job misses an important opportunity that the world of the vocation offers — the chance to build institutional commitment or to foster the "good citizen" who is willing to invest in the agency (Bateman and Organ 1983).

The development of a sizeable, predictable labor market is crucial for a modern industrial society. The solution for getting the right labor to the right place at the right time is achieved through the market mechanism. By emphasizing the job, the taxpayers' money may be well used. There has been a longstanding belief that the bureaucracy does not have to be excellent; it need only be adequate to obtain the minimal level of public action. This attitude seems to have gained adherents common among public and political leaders, particularly with reference to domestic bureaucratic functions. The world of the vocation — and as will be presented next, the world of the career — requires more focus on the individual worker and thus is more costly. Perhaps, some reason, such an additional cost is not what society needs. The Reagan Administration was noted for this conclusion. The world of the job is very compatible with this perspective.

Perhaps the most troubling outcome of the job paradigm, particularly for The Public Administration, is the damage resulting to our institutions. The emphasis on exchange of labor for money as the basis for defining the relationship between the government and its employees adds to the limited involvement by these employees in their work lives. Public institutions form some of the most important of societal bonds. Institutions of The Public Administration represent a great deal more than the segmented interests that created them. The application of nonpartisan competence in pursuit of the public interest through The Public Administration can only exist if there is a public service. To weaken the public service by reducing it to a job also weakens our public institutions. Anemic public institutions in turn contribute to a loss of very important societal glue.

The World of the Career

The world of the career is the newest occupational paradigm. This occupational world, as a more recent arrival, is rooted in many of the social trends of the last three decades, particularly those centering on personal growth, self-actualization, and sometimes a "do your own thing" ethic.

The implicit logic of the world of career is a psychological and therapeutic imperative with an emphasis on personal growth, development, and mental health. The self-help activities of the 1960s and 1970s are other examples of this emphasis on personal development. To some extent, the world of career represents a counterforce to the world of vocation with its insistence on commitment to broader collectivities, and to the world of the job with its fixation on the instrumental character of the work world. The world of career is also a product of the existential movement that rejected many of the older Western traditions' focus on community and transcendent values.

A certain set of values seem powerfully related to this paradigm. In some instances, those values contribute to its formulation and may also be a catapult for extending it. These values are represented by the psychologists Karl Jung and Erik Erickson and the philosopher/theologian Tielhard de Chardin, who emphasize a dynamic and continual growth process. The universe is an evolving set of ultimately positive cosmic forces that call for a commitment to growth and development (Ferguson 1980). These ideas lend support to the belief that growth and self-development serve the needs of both individuals and broader social and indeed cosmic worlds.

According to this paradigm, the self is the legitimate focus for organizational involvement and commitment. Therefore the workplace should foster opportunities for personal growth as well as financial reward. Argyris's (1964) emphasis on the integration of individual and organizational goals is typical of this notion in organizational-behavior literature. The work is seen as a form of self-expression and not simply a labor shot.

Through the idea of career, work presents opportunities to develop one's identity and self. Implicit in much of this thinking is the belief that to remain one's self, one has to grow. Unlike the vocational world, there is little source of calling. If there is one, it is within the individual and his or her overcommitment to growth and development.

The focus on career sometimes places an excessive emphasis on the individual showing little interest in communitarian ideas; however, operating in this paradigm does not necessarily preclude recognition of community or societal roles for the individual. However, not all justifications for the world of career come from this more enlightened strain of argument. A great deal of the popular thrust for career comes from the value of "expressive individualism" (Bellah et al. 1985).

The values of this career world are self-development, individual and group development, and integration of the individual and the organization. The language contains references to learning and growing, environments for growth, self-actualization, the evolving universe, and beliefs such as, "to stop growing is to die." It is important to note that in moving from the individualistic strain of the career world to its more communitarian ones, there seems to be greater similarity to the vocational world.

The career paradigm suggests that the individual should use the job as a place to grow — to break out of the segmented world of work. The workplace can be a time and place (a way station) in pursuit of one's life project.

The world of the career is a more recent development taking shape in the public service only during the last few decades. During the late 1960s and 1970s, the career paradigm came to dominate the professional and administrative ranks of the public sector. The expansion of public programs required competencies from a vast range of college-educated, technically trained employees. Promotion was rapid and the public sector was a good place to find oneself and have a meaningful career.

It was not only a good place to get ahead but also a place where one could become a creative, autonomous self. Self-actualization was no longer impossible in the bureaucracy, so public managers were sent to training programs to learn about the hierarchy of needs and taught ways to tap into the energy potential of a motivated, self-actualizing employee.

What appeared to be the wave of the future now seems to be endangered. The career currently holds much less influence as the occupational environment becomes more hostile to those who seek professional growth through public employment. The public service is heavily peopled by upwardly mobile professionals who benefited from the growth of the postwar booms. They have made it on to rungs of the social ladder above those occupied by their parents. They have done this through education at universities and then through careers in professional, technical, and managerial occupations. The expansion of the role of government opened new occupations that absorbed many of the midlevel career seekers. It was this group that grabbed onto the promise of career growth — self-actualization through the job. Although this movement did have many of the characteristics of narcissism, there was also a genuine interest in seeking growth.

The difficulty for careers arose when the promise of continual growth ran aground on the shoals of declining government and the "inevitable" truth of hierarchy: there are only so many jobs at the top. A baby bust generation (a smaller cohort of Depression and World War II babies) moved into the top positions at relatively young ages, followed closely by a huge cohort that is not much younger (the baby boom born between 1946 and 1964). Large problems for the younger cohort will emerge. There are simply more people, who are relatively young, seeking fewer jobs that are held by those who are not much older. Although this situation does not exist in all public sector organizations, it holds true for the majority.

In addition to this demographic problem of too many middle managers and professionals competing for too few higher jobs, there is the additional pressure to limit and cut down the size of government. The goals of career growth, particularly defined in terms of increased opportunities for self-fulfillment, responsibility, and movement up the organizational ladder, are placed in great peril.

Perhaps the most negative consequence of the career world is the potential for narcissism. The responsibility of being connected to anything outside of the self is diminished. The focus on self-growth to the exclusion of anything else as a viable measure of worthwhile activity can lead to isolation and anomie. The career emphasis can also weaken Robert Lifton's observation that connectedness is essential to human life. The belief that to remain myself, I must keep moving, always in search of new opportunities, can weaken ties and bonds of commitment and belonging (Lifton 1976).

What do agencies gain from this culture of career? Workers in the agency who are committed to self-growth can contribute energy to enhance tasks. Tapping into one's developmental journey through opportunities for career growth can be a positive asset for an agency. An increase in personal energy, if compatible with agency directions, can increase productivity and creativity.

When the career world is dominant, however, opportunism can pervade the public organization. This may be avoided if there is enough slack in the agency's workforce requirements to meet the special growth needs of its employees. It is important to remember that the growth needs of each individual as defined through the career are unique to each person. However, to expect an exact match between multiple career needs of employees and work requirements of an agency is unreasonable, especially during periods of declining resources or excessive competition for higher positions. For much of the public sector at this time, it may simply be too difficult to deliver on the promise of meeting the career development needs of public employees.

When a society can meet the growth needs of its citizens through the workforce, there are obviously many benefits, such as individual fulfillment contributing to mental health, and enhancement of the development of society. A potential danger to society is that of a self-centered culture. A focus on personal growth as the major criterion for evaluating the quality of a job in the workforce, grants little sense of common purpose. Unless the assumption is made that we all grow when any one of us grows, there is little collective gain. Finally, the career world can lead to manipulation and exploitation similar to that of the vocation world. With vocation, the justification for excessive demands was based on commitment and common purpose. With the career, the justification is that the individual is foregoing an opportunity to grow. Growth opportunity becomes growth obligation. The seventy-hour-a-week job is per-used in the name of the cause of furthering one's career.

Prescriptions for the Future

What are the implications for The Public Administration of this weakening of both vocation and career and a simultaneous strengthening of the job world? As the opportunities for work being the source of vocation and career diminish, the alternatives can indeed seem bleak. For the public employee, a reappraisal of the significance of career and the potential of the vocation is suggested. Two reactions seem to prevail and neither seems to be entirely desirable. Both involve an emphasis on the job world.

Some will begin to seek a way out. As opportunities for public service and personal growth seem to diminish, the disillusioned public employee gives up on the public sector as a source for these on-the-job qualities and seeks employment in other sectors. Since the public at large and the dominant political leadership do not value the public service and see it as "the problem," there is an understandable desire to escape. Many are forced to leave, either through reductions-in-force or down-grading of positions.

A second group will learn to live with the situation by giving up on the career and vocation worlds and living entirely within that of the job. At most they hope for reasonable job satisfaction and, at worst, a tolerable workday with opportunities for seeking growth and commitment outside work. If they are able to accommodate to this world, they become "solid citizens" who are willing to do an honest job for a fair compensation. If not, they survive as unhappy, disillusioned, and perhaps as "dead wood," people who wait for the end of the workday, the holidays, vacation, and retirement without being challenged or hassled by the demands of the bureaucracy, the politician, or the public.

The dangers of a general retreat to the job level go beyond public service organizations. Yankelovich points out that values supporting this would simply no longer hold. Hard work resulting from a belief in self-denial and the giving/getting covenant has been undermined by the questioning of self-denial that began in the 1960s on campuses and spread to the me-generation of the 1970s. The belief in working hard to get ahead has been undermined, and little is left to support the job world beyond pressure for economic survival (Yankelovich 1981).

This retreat to the job world presents a severe problem for The Public Administration because its quality and capacity to play a role in the governance process is undermined. This may seem a matter of little moment at this time to those who seek a smaller role for the national government in the federal system. Just what such a smaller role would be is not clear. However, even if a smaller role is favored, the remaining institutions should be credible, competent, and infused with a commitment to achieving a broad definition of the public interest.

One result would be a crippled or less-capable bureaucracy brought about by employees either escaping to the private sector or becoming a disillusioned group of "dead wood" remaining in the public organizations. As bureaucracies become less capable, they become less credible, and it follows that they should be asked to do less, not more. Whether this is the intention or not, the outcome is the same: public organizations of declining competence because of decreasing credibility of the public service. We cannot accept this position as one that furthers the common good.

What can be done to strengthen the quality and capacity of The Public Administration to become a competent participant in our governance process?

1. The strength in each of the paradigms should be recognized. The current crisis provides an opportunity to draw on each of them. As our occupational world has emerged, the fact that three paradigms now exist offers the potential for a more humane occupational world for workers and a more adaptive and capable situation for The Public Administration. There is a danger in retreating to the world of the job. We are well served if all three worlds cooperate in a healthy way.

When the governing value of the job paradigm is that of competence and adequacy from the employees and fair compensation from the employer, there is a possibility of achieving justice for employer and employee. For those who seek less government, this may be the favored paradigm. If the norm is competence in return for just rewards and respect for the employee, then some justice is achieved. Admittedly not all jobs *can* offer opportunities for commitment (vocation) and growth (career). The career world also offers opportunities for individual growth and protection. After all, organizations are irrational — sometimes, including public organizations.

The career paradigm keeps alive the valid concerns for self as well as the important emphasis on growing in competence for the public service and effecting creative change. Finally, the notion of a vocation for the public service is also powerful, and can be of great value as the chances for career growth diminish in public sector employment.

2. There is also an opportunity to renew the call for a committed public service. A universal emphasis on the vocation of the public service is in the public interest. Whatever positive aspects they may hold, the worlds of job and career have been found wanting with regard to The Public Administration because of the lack of connectedness and community. They are totally lacking in transcendence from any broader effort or purpose. It is the vocation that links one to a community "of disciplined practice and sound judgment whose activity has meaning and value in itself, not just in the output or profit that results from it" (Bellah et al. 1985). This calling not only links a person to fellow workers but to the larger community. The calling becomes the crucial link between the individual and the public world.

One of the values now being sought by a seemingly contradictory public mood is a searching for commitments and connectedness. Perhaps, as we move beyond what seems to be a powerful mood of selfishness, this return to a more outreaching and giving mode — a search for community — will be conductive for a return to the ideals of a public-service calling of the kind prescribed in the Blacksburg Manifesto.

For this transformation to happen, however, changes are needed at the individual, agency, and national levels. For the individual, there needs to be a recognition that there is something beyond the more immediate and selfish gratifications of job and career. The acceptance of a community of purpose, and that one's work is a tie between personal and public lives, is essential. The capacity to see that one's work activities do affect the lives of others in the community is the key. Without this connectedness, vocation will be difficult to achieve.

This is where the agency perspective can be most helpful. Indeed, it is understandably difficult to see the connectedness between day-to-day actions and the broader community without a grounding in an agency perspective. An agency's historical tradition and current mission provide the most direct link between The Public Administration and the effort of a public servant. It is at the agency level where the relationship between the community and the government is most concrete. The streets are built, the national defense maintained, the welfare checks distributed, the environment protected, and public liberties guaranteed when agencies act. It becomes imperative that agency leaders help employees see this relationship and instill a sense of commitment to effective and efficient service to the community.

The agency perspective is also helpful in mediating some of the excesses of professions that also can create a sense of vocation but which erode a larger concept of the Public Administration. The emphasis of professions on a set of practices can be more positively directed toward the community that professionals serve if they become more willing to anchor practices in the collective commitments and actions that are represented in the agency perspective.

The emphasis on the individualism of the job and career worlds places everything up for sale. Everything has a price but nothing has a value if it is anchored solely in the calculus of individual preference. Unless we can ground the efforts of job and career in public purpose, we will lose more and more of the traditions of community to the excesses of individualism. Both tensions are needed if there is to be a creative and caring society. For the public servant, it is the calling to public service by doing the work of the agency that makes this balance more possible.

The Public Administration can gain from the mood that accompanies the world of vocation. The calling is embedded in the idea of Wamsley et al. (1983), that the vocation be based on

its fundamental sense of a solemn agreement on obligations between, and that would seem to capture what the Public Administration was, is, and ought to be: a solemn agreement between the citizens he or she serves; an agreement to serve the public with competence directed toward the public interest and the maintenance of democratic process of governance; competence constrained by the vitality of the constitutional heritage, the law and our common history as a people.

Perhaps a more powerful public service vocation anchored in the agency perspective can serve as a crucial link between individual effort and the broader community. The calling to the public service with the agency perspective offers a practical and concrete link among professional competence, individual effort and goals, and public purpose. Professional competence that is not grounded in service to community as represented by the purposes embodied in the agency perspective is without meaning. It has a connectedness to the community that the alternative sense of calling to professional competence cannot provide. It also expands the narrow focus on self and on features of the career and job.

"With a self-conscious shift in the American dialogue, we feel that the sense of calling will grow and flourish in the Public Administration as never before — more will live for it as a cause and fewer off it for less noble impulses." A strong sense of public vocation can lead to a more enriched sense of the public job and a more enlightened sense of public career.

Notes

1. The idea of a "lens" borrows from Richard Harvey Brown's concept of *organizational paradigm*. Brown asserts that an organizational paradigm consists of (1) structural patterns of consciousness (Weber, Schutz, Garfinkle, and Durkheim); and (2) notions of authority, domination, legitimacy, official ideology, and public worlds which serve as sources of ideas that create and sustain these patterns of consciousness. According to Brown, paradigm refers "to those sets of assumptions, usually implicit, about what sorts of things make up the world, how they act, how they hang together, and how they may be known. In actual practice, such paradigms function as means of imposing control as well as a resource that dissidents may use in organizing their awareness and action. That is, . . . paradigms . . . [are] . . . practical as well as cognitive, used as a resource as well as a constraint" (Brown 1978).

Bibliography

Argyris, Chris. *Integrating the Individual and the Organization.* New York: Wiley, 1964.

Argyris, Chris, and Schon, Donald. *Theory in Practice: Increasing Personal Effectiveness.* San Francisco: Jossey-Bass, 1974.

Bateman, Thomas S., and Organ, Dennis W. "Job Satisfaction and the Good Soldier: The Relationship Between Affect and Employee 'Citizenship,' " *Academy of Management Journal* 26, 4 (1983): 587-595.

Bellah, Robert N., Madsen, Richard, Sullivan, William M., Swidler, Ann, and Tipton, Steven M., *Habits of the Heart: Individualism and Commitment in American Life.* Berkeley: University of California Press, 1985.

Brown, Richard Harvey. "Bureaucracy as Praxis: Toward a Political Phenomenology of Formal Organizations." *Administrative Science Quarterly* 5, 23 (Dec. 1978): 365-381.

Durkheim, Emile, *The Division of Labor in Society*, Glencoe, Ill.: Free Press, 1947.

Erickson, Erik. *Childhood and Society.* New York: W. W. Norton, 1963.

Ferguson, Marilyn. *The Aquarian Conspiracy: Personal and Social Transformation in the Eighties.* Los Angeles: Tarcher, 1980.

Garfinkle, H. *Studies in Ethnomethodology.* Englewood Cliffs, N. J.: Prentice-Hall, 1967.

Gerth, H. H., and Mills, C. Wright., eds. In "Politics as a Vocation," *From Max Weber: Essays in Sociology.* New York: Oxford University Press, 1958, p. 77-128.

Henry, Nicholas. *Public Administration and Public Affairs.* Englewood Cliffs, N.J.: Prentice-Hall, 1975.

Johnson et al. *Civil Service 2000.* The Hudson Institute, June 1988.

Lifton, Robert Jay. *The Life of the Self: Toward a New Psychology.* New York: Simon and Schuster, 1976.

Mosher, Frederick C. *Democracy and the Public Service.* New York: Oxford University Press, 1982.

Schutz, Alfred. *Phenomenology of the Social World.* Chicago: Northwestern University Press, 1967.

Terkel, Studs. *Working.* New York: Ballantine, 1985.

Tielhard, de Chardin. *The Phenomenon of Man.* New York: Harper & Row, 1965.

Wamsley, Gary L., Goodsell, Charles T., Rohr, John A., White, Orion F., and Wolf, James F. "The Public Administration and the Governance Process: Refocusing the American Dialogue," A Centennial History of the American Administrative State. Chandler, R. C. NY: The Free Press. 1983.

Wingren, Gustav. *Luther on Vocation.* Philadelphia: Muhlenberg Press, 1957.

Weber, Max. *The Protestant Ethic and the Spirit of Capitalism.* New York: Scribner and Son's, 1958.

Wolf, James F. "Career Plateauing in the Public Service: Baby Boom and Employment Bust." *Public Administration Review* 43 (March/April 1983): 160-165.

Yankelovich, Daniel. *New Rules: Searching for Self-Fulfillment in a World Turned Upside Down.* New York: Random House, 1981.

6. Reframing the Authority/Participation Debate

ORION F. WHITE

Introduction

In the twenty years that I have now been a professional in the fields of Political Science and Public Administration, I have consistently — and persistently — encountered one, pivotal conceptual issue that has run like a mutable river through all the theoretical territories I have explored. Further, it has interested me to realize that there is more to this issue than its purely conceptual dimension describes. It carries an emotional loading that attracts personal involvement and brings the deepest beliefs of political and organizational theorists into question. This issue is what I shall call in this chapter the "authority problem." In the field of Public Administration it has most frequently been discussed, within the framework of organization or management theory, as the question of whether and/or to what extent *participation* is "better" or "worse" than centralized or unilateral decision processes. Much of the critique and discussion that the Blacksburg Manifesto has engendered has centered on what our colleagues in the profession have taken to be the commitment the Manifesto makes to elitism and authority as against democratic and egalitarian processes of participation.

My surmise is that few or none who come to read this chapter will be mystified or confused by the assertion that the authority problem is central to the field of Public Administration, or at least has held visibility as a central issue within it since the 1960s. My purpose here is to identify this problem by placing it in broad perspective, illuminate it by analyzing an important but largely undiscussed underlying dimension of it, and then present an "answer" to the issue — albeit an answer only in the sense that it may provide a new locus from which discussion can continue.

The Authority Problem in Perspective

First, let me make clear that I do not wish to discuss the problem of authority in what I would call merely technical terms, namely, as an aspect of the more general phenomenon of power and a "special case" in the application of power.

In my view, it is *authority* that is the more generic and important problem; authority, rather than power, is endemic to the question of social organization. I wish only to discuss authority in its broadest and most generic aspect, that is, as the core issue around which any approach to social organization must be configured. Considered in this light, the two identifiable positions in the traditional debate about authority are conservatism on the one hand, and liberalism on the other. I will begin with an exposition of these two positions.

The "Classical" Conservative View

I place the word *classical* in quotation marks in this subtitle because I mean to use it in a general, loose sense, that is, merely to indicate (1) that the view I am about to discuss should be disassociated from contemporary uses of the term *conservative*, and (2) that the view I will consider here seems to me to have pervaded, in one form or another, the history of civilization, at least at this history has been interpreted to us. The viewpoint I am naming classical conservatism is one that is centered around the following axiology: the primary axiom of *conservatism* is *distrust of self-conscious intellectualism as rationalism and the willful mastery of fate.* The world is seen as an imminently and immanently chaotic place where it is difficult to attain and sustain security, stability, and order. The imponderable forces of entropy, evil, or simple human emotionalism are viewed as persistently at work to bring about disruption if not chaos in human affairs. According to the conservative view, any program of action that does not sufficiently acknowledge this reality, and looks for guidance in rational designs, must certainly fail, leaving conditions as bad or worse than they were before the attempts at improvement were made.[1]

The axiomatic corollary to this most fundamental belief is prudence, if not caution, regarding all matters of social life. The best defense against disorder or chaos, since it cannot be overcome by conscious design, is to protect whatever gains have been made. That is, where agreement on social rules has been achieved and they are now "in the background," providing a stable basis for working institutions, the advisable course is to respect them and support their continued enforcement. Tradition is seen, therefore, as the best, most trustworthy basis for law and order, for social life as a whole.

The conservative point of view puts emphasis on the group, or *collective,* rather than the individual. *Community*, and the conformity to group norms that the word connotes, is the centerpiece of the conservative perspective. The individual is seen to have identity only through the group, by virtue of his or her identification with and deference to it. The "whole" is experienced as something real in itself, with an existence that transcends the sum of the individual parts.

It seems clear enough from this brief picture of the axiological foundation of the conservative perspective that a strong emphasis is given in it to the role authority is to play in social life. It is obedience to authority, indeed, that is the mark of good citizenship and good leadership. Both citizens and leaders are to defer to the set of traditions, and the stable institutions through which they are expressed, that define the social order.

The Classical Liberal View

The philosophical theory that stands most in contrast to the conservative viewpoint is *liberalism* or the contract theory of society. This perspective also is founded on the belief that the natural world tends toward chaos and violence, but its answer to this condition is the opposite of the conservatives'. The liberal viewpoint emphasizes rational, conscious *contract* as the basis for banding together into society so as to create order and the security that flows for it.[2] There is implicit in liberalism a belief that individuals are inherently rational and conscious and hence able to enter into a contract with each other as the basis for a society and state. (At the same time, rather inconsistent with this belief, there is the assumption that the human being is born as a tabula rasa, *without* an intrinsic structure of mind or consciousness.) To the liberal viewpoint, the best protection against capricious violence and domination in society is to regard the individual as the basic unit of society and limit collective or authoritative institutions in their relations to individuals. Hence, authority is seen as a necessary evil. Danger is seen as inherent in the act of granting authority to government and every precaution must be taken in doing so.

A Comparison

Where conservative philosophy emphasizes the group or the collective as the unit of society, sees people as incapable of designing rationally and mastering their affairs, and gives authoritative institutions a central role in enforcing traditions—which are seen by conservatives as the basis for meaning and order—liberalism places the individual in a position of preeminence and makes rational, explicit contract the basis for social relationship, such that meaning and order are seen as flowing from the pursuit by individuals of their own self-interested inclinations. The senses in which I have defined conservative and liberal, as I noted earlier, are not contemporary. They are the senses drawn from classical political philosophy. The use of these terms has become muddled in current American politics due, largely, to the development of welfare liberalism, southern conservatism, and what might be called free-enterprise traditionalism. For purposes of this present discussion, I am ignoring the contemporary overlapped and reversed usages of these terms.[3]

What seems clear about both of these positions, however, is that each is seeking to avoid the same thing—the outbreak of *social pathology*. They both want to avoid what they see to be an inherent tendency toward the emergence of disruptive or "evil" forces into social life. The conservative sees this tendency as most likely taking the form of anarchy driven by the eruption of individual or "selfish" motives, ideas, or desires. The liberal sees evil as taking the form of dominative, oppressive institutions that use authority either for their own purposes or to further the designs of despots within them.

From this perspective we can see that the difference between the two positions is *not basic but rather derivative,* that is, it derives from a difference in *how each position sees the etiology of social psychosis.* Again, the conservative sees evil as erupting through individuals, whereas the liberal sees it as erupting through the collective. If we view these positions as, in a sense, "faith commitments," we can say that conservatism put its faith in institutions whereas liberalism places its faith in individuals. Another way of viewing this would be to describe conservatism as according the group or the "collective" primary moral and ontological status, whereas the individual holds these places in liberal theory.

The Comparison Extended: Some "Profound Simplicities"

I would venture to assert that the dialectic that has continued over time between the conservative and liberal positions is based on a profound, indeed generic dichotomy in human thought about society and social process. Though I must commit a rather vast simplification and overgeneralization in doing this, I believe that if we view relatively each of these dichotomies (and not look for a totally consistent pattern across pairs) we can discern an underlying pattern that relates them to each other. It seems we can see the competition of conservative and liberal axiologies as underlying the distinction that Dwight Waldo had recently drawn between the Greek and Roman political systems.[4] It is similar to the distinction typically made between the concepts of *gemeinschaft* and *gesellschaft;*[5] It seems similar to the difference between *status* and *contract* theories of society; [6] or the difference between the *organicist* and *mechanicist* metaphor of organization.[7] It is like the difference that Alvin Gouldner and that Richard Sennet each see in social orders based on *esteem* versus *respect* and, similarly, that Berger, Berger, and Kellner make between *dignity* and *respect* as principles of social organization.[8] Broadly lumping them together, we can see this same distinction in the concepts of society and politics implicit in the Federalist-Anti-Federalist debate about the formation of the U.S. Constitution.[9] Last, I think we can see this sort of polarization in the distinction between, and debate about, "politics" and "administration" in the literature of political science and Public Administration.

In the polemic that this dialectic has produced, we can see each pole of the dichotomy characterized in both positive and negative terms. The positive characterizations use such labels as (following the order of conservative versus liberalism): community v. individualism and freedom; commitment v. participation; stability v. creativity; order v. change; security v. liberty; relationship v. rationality; and loyalty and commitment v. free speech and moral resistance to authority. Some negative characterizations of both sides include: conformity v. alienation; stagnation v. anomie; and — consolidating a few related labels and images — totalitarianism, authoritarianism, fascism, *1984* v. totalitarianism, technicist hyperrational authoritarianism, and *Logan's Run.*

The point of this inventory is to show, albeit in a shorthand, sketchy way, how this issue is generic and how pervasively it permeates our dialogues about social life. Also consolidated in this way, the issue reveals itself as probably not resolvable in its present form. What seems indicated is that we *reframe* the debate at a more fundamental level of analysis, particularly, a level that centers on the question of how social pathology develops and how it can be avoided.

The Third Alternative: Marxist Humanism

It is instructive in this matter to review the case of Marxist humanism, since this line of theory can be seen as representing an example of how the debate over authority can be *reframed yet misunderstood* in terms of the traditional dichotomization just described. In the evolution of his point of view on social dynamics for Hegel and through Feuerbach, Marx finessed the traditional theoretical dichotomy into which thought about social process typically becomes pressed.[10] He did this by positing an essentially relational and process-based image of human nature, one that shows human potential as being fulfilled through activity and unalienated human relationship, where activity serves as the vehicle for relationship. Under conditions where valid relationship prevails, social affairs are seen by Marx as *self-regulatory* and hence requiring no structures of authority or governance external to the individual. As such, his position seems to rely on a kind of communitarianism. It is decidedly *not* the communitarianism of classical conservatism, however, because its emphasis is on the individual and individual self-realization through free activity — activity that is not even tied to a fixed occupational role. Hence Marx seems to have one foot in both the camps created by traditional dichotomous thinking about authority. He engenders the enmity of both sides of the traditional debate because he seems, on the one hand, to wish to reject the stable institutions and conformity of the classical image of community and, on the other hand, he is construed as subordinating the individual to a collectivist "context" where everyone is the same and apparently is "lost in the crowd" of the collectivity.

I raise the case of Marx because it is illustrative of the fate of most humanist approaches to the authority problem — they have typically been appropriated into the dichotomous framework of thinking about the issue, identified with both sides of it in one way or another, and attacked from both sides. Indeed, even some Marxists (the so-called vulgar Marxists) have fallen prey to this tendency, in that they have adopted an interpretation of Marx that presents itself as a kind of radical communitarianism. This case is instructive in that it indicates to a degree what is the underlying problem with the traditional dichotomy and what is the source of the confusion that surrounds the issue.

The underlying problem to which I refer is the insufficient attention, in the traditional debate, paid to the question of *social process* or *social interaction*. The classical conservative and liberal position are both founded on differing assumptions about human nature and, in addition, the hidden assumption that

human nature is fixed or static, that is, a set of *traits*. To the conservative
viewpoint, human beings are beset with a great deal of irrationality and it is
therefore necessary to subordinate them to the discipline of community institutions and allow only slow, incremental processes of change. To the liberals,
people are rational but self-interested and hence do not need to be put under the
control of such institutions but must be allowed to establish instead a contractual basis for social relations. Neither side trusts social process. Each sees social
organization as a problem of how to establish stably functioning defenses for
man against other men as individuals or other men as agents of institutions. In
the liberal theory, men in institutions are held in check by law and institutional
structure; in conservative theory tradition limits them in the same way that it
regulates society generally.

The Marxist and humanist traditions seem to be founded on a concept of
human nature that differs radically from the conservative and liberal traditions
in that it posits a human nature that is in principle benign and that allows for
trust in social relations. If the correct set of social institutions take hold in
society, a liberated, responsible human nature will be evoked. Hence when
looked at from the poles of the traditional dichotomy, the idea of community
becomes not the hierarchically organized, tradition-bound form envisioned by
the conservatives, but an "encounter-group" type collectivity of open, shifting
relations which comes to agreements or decides things spontaneously. The
individual becomes not the rational self-interestedly calculating entity of liberalism but a relationship-oriented, feeling, sensuous person seeking union with
others. Given this image, it is easy to see how both conservatives and liberals
are repelled. What is puzzling (and interesting) is why it is that many Marxists
and humanists have adopted this distorted stereotype as their own and attempted
to defend it.

The trap into which all have apparently fallen hinges on the question of
trustworthiness as an aspect of human nature. In my view, as long as this
question is viewed through the frame of whether a fixed or immutable human
nature allows for trust in human relations the trap is unavoidable. Examples of
atrocities and evil programs pursued by both egomaniacal individuals *and* by
institutions as well are rife in human history. On this point evidence can be
pitted against evidence in an irresolvable cycle that does not yield a clear
victory for either the advocates of liberalism or conservatism. It is likewise not
a solution to bypass the issue, as the Chinese Communists and Russian Marxists
(using Pavlovian psychology and Lysenkovian genetics) have attempted to do,
by claiming that human nature is mutable and hence amenable to restructuring
into a form compatible with a given plan of social organization like com-
munism. The central problem with *this* answer is the question of where the
shapers of human nature would find a transcendant standpoint from which to
do their work.

As I see it at this point, the best way of obtaining movement on this issue is
to shift the focus of it *from* the question of how *human nature bears on it* to how

the dynamic of social process bears on it. It is *social process* that is the "missing link" in the debate as it has been carried to this point. The confusion I have been sketching above is largely a result of the conceptual leap entailed in jumping from assumptions about human nature to the level of making generalizations about necessary and/or desirable patterns in macrolevel social organization.

The Case of Fred Thayer — And Others

It is instructive to examine one other specific but more contemporary case in order to understand just how the traditional theoretical dichotomy truncates and distorts communication about the authority issue. For this purpose, the work of Fred Thayer, a notable theorist in the field of public administration, can serve well. In 1973 Thayer published *An End to Hierarchy: An End to Competition*, and by so doing moved, it seems fair to say, into a rather highly visible position as a critical theoretician of bureaucratic organization.[11] In the years subsequent to the publication of this book (it is now in a second edition) he has issued countless comments — published and otherwise — critical of the principles of hierarchy and competition and has detailed their negative effects in various organizational arenas, including that of the academic field of public administration and the university systems within which it resides.[12] This running critique and commentary has led many to view him as something of a gadfly in the field — in both the positive and negative senses of the term — and he has sometimes been the object of personal attack. Thayer recently published a second book of critique, this one explicitly focusing on what he sees as the weaknesses, if not absurdities, of economics as a paradigm for social philosophy and as a principle of social organization.[13] Though he disavows expertise as an economist, his background and mindset dispose him to the macrolevel of social analysis and to issues of economic process and organization.

Thayer's critique is novel and astute in that it steps outside the traditional dichotomies of conservatism and liberalism and points to a problem underlying both. As such, in my view, he has made the positive step of addressing the generic issue of social health and pathology and has, in the process, escaped the ontological, epistemological, and axiological assumptions, (and the emotional loadings that go with these) of the traditional dichotomy. The problem to which Thayer points, and he considers it not less than the root source of all social pathologies, is the principle of hierarchy. In the latest version of his analysis, hierarchy is a metaphor for a form of consciousness characteristic of the entire era of civilization, in that it probably, in his view, began to develop when the human race ceased hunting and gathering as its main form of food-generating activity.

It is obvious how his critique confronts (and affronts) the conservative image of social life, where central emphasis is placed on the creation and maintenance of stable hierarchical institutions. His critique of liberalism — as liberal capitalism — is somewhat more subtle. Put in sketch form, his argument is that liberal capitalism is a direct reflection of hierarchical consciousness, in that in principle it puts the consumer in a position of comparatively evaluating the products of competing producers, as a "boss" does with subordinates. Competition, as the device of hierarchy in the market, creates waste through overproduction and eventual disaster. In the meantime, however, it creates human alienation and general social disorder, primarily by pitting the consumer, who is in a hierarchical position, against the worker — the consumer seeking a low price, the worker a high wage.

Thayer's picture of the absurdities of the competitive market process and price theory in general is, in my view at least, essentially valid, though he overdraws it to an extent that it loses some of its persuasiveness and engenders emotional counterattack. The solution that he proposes to the problem he describes is the source of most of the countercriticisms of his position. What Thayer proposes is that the economy be operated as an *oligopoly* that is regulated through a universal participative process. His prescription for the management of institutions and organizations in general follows the same line — a participative process based in groups of five that are linked together in the fashion suggested decades ago by Rensis Likert in his linking-pin model of participative organization.[14]

It has always struck me as odd that Thayer's critique has itself drawn so much counterattack in that it is not only valid but many of his themes have been echoed by others in one form or another. The discipline of economics contains a rather substantial community of theoretical critics who make their case in terms almost as graphic as does Thayer.[15] The same can be said of the field of organization theory. Indeed, it has now become conventional wisdom in the field that the traditional hierarchical forms of organization are not the most conducive to effectiveness and productivity. Given this, one wonders why Thayer's work has engendered the resentment it has — which is not to say that he is without allies and fond admirers.

My surmise about this matter is that Thayer's work is generally misunderstood because his argument has been pressed into the traditional liberal/conservative theoretical dichotomy and, when viewed in this context, it contains central elements that draw attack from both sides, making his viewpoint seem totally off base or wrong in a fundamental way. To repeat, his attack on the principle of hierarchy of course puts off those of the conservative persuasion, who feel that authoritative institutions are an essential remedy to the defects inherent in human nature. His critique of market capitalism would seem to gain him support from the liberal side of the house — at least from welfare liberals — but they are put off by his acceptance of institutionalized oligopolistic power. For liberals of all persuasions, Thayer trusts participation too far. He sees it as the essence of a *process* of cooperation, whereas liberals can see it as no more than the basis for an adversarial checking and balancing of institutional power. In a word, Thayer's critique violates the categories of the conventional debate over social and political principles, and as a result he is labeled oftentimes as a spokesman for the radical fringe. Usually, he seems to be seen as some version or another of anarchist, and anarchism, because it falls outside the conventional frame of theoretic debate, is a position that is often simply dismissed after a summary rebuttal.

Thayer is not an anarchist, however, at least not in the sense that anarchism bespeaks a commitment to radical individualism. Indeed, he is anything but one. Although he is critical of the hierarchical and competitive nature of dialogue within academe, for example, even seeing hierarchy at the bottom of the dominant epistemological commitment in organization theory, he dismisses the anarchist philosopher of science, Feyerabend, as not offering a "real alternative," in that what Feyerabend advocates is a sort of pluralist politics in the struggle of scientists to get their theories accepted as truth.[16] This point reveals the usually unseen or unacknowledged core of Thayer's position: namely, that the true solution or alternative to hierarchy and its corollary, competition, is *for human beings to achieve a certain quality of relationship to each other as they manage their affairs.*

Hence, it is not simply the openness of process — as opposed to the closedness of hierarchy — that is important about participation. Rather it is that participatory processes provide the context or opportunity within which a certain *texture of relation* between people can be achieved and allowed to operate. Thayer's problem — if I might be allowed to put it that way — is that he leaves this part of his position almost completely implicit and undeveloped. The closest I see him coming to addressing the matter is in his prescriptions for participatory groups of five persons (which he draws from group-dynamics research) and statements to the effect that the nature of the relationship he is talking about is probably something like what goes on in a sensitivity group — an illustration that ill serves his argument, given the poor general reputation of such groups. Thayer's rejoinder to this line of critique of his work is that as long as hierarchy pervades the organizational world, it is impossible to envision completely the practicalities of an alternative. Hierarchy dominates the creative capacities of human consciousness. (Though it does not dominate — at least Thayer's — capacity for critical insight.)

His emphasis on macrolevel analysis and issues of economic organization causes him to slight this key part of his analysis. There is not opportunity to consider such matters when one works only at the macrolevel. This leaves him in the rather passive posture of arguing that we must recognize that ecological, economic, or international relations disasters are inevitable unless we reject the current hierarchy-competition paradigm. As such, he becomes not only an anarchist, but a Jeremiah, and is therefore all the easier to dismiss.

I want to make it clear that in this depiction of Thayer I see the problem in the misapprehension of his work as residing more in the institutions and processes by which academic debate is carried out than I do in Thayer himself. His part, to me, is that he sometimes presses his position too stridently and persistently. (I have described some of what I see to be the sources of distorted academic debate elsewhere.)[17] However, my purpose here is to reveal the main area of confusion in the traditional debate about authority and participation. I hope it is becoming clear at this point that I see the source of this confusion to be the fact that the traditional liberal/conservative frame for the debate has directed attention so heavily toward the question of what human nature *allows* in the way of social and political organization that it has been virtually impossible to discuss the matter of what *possibilities* or *potentials* might be found in the area of social process.

I might mention that my own prior work on this question has been frequently misperceived for this very reason. I first developed an interest in (as well as the beginnings of a perspective on) the question of social process in the mid-1960s, the point at which I began to read the works of Carl Jung and at the same time entered a collaboration with the sociologist Gideon Sjoberg.[18] The paper I read at the notorious Minnowbrook conference was a rather straightforward statement of interest in how we might, through managing the process of interaction, convert destructive conflict situations into constructive *confrontations*, as I called them then.[19] This, as well as my subsequent work, I think, largely has been interpreted as grounded in something of an antihierarchical, proparticipation commitment that drew its inspiration from modern-day humanistic psychology's image of human nature as cooperative, loving, and trustworthy. Many colleagues in departments where I have taught have constructed my work in this way, even after having read the explicit critiques of, for example, Maslowian psychology that I have issued in some of my writings.[20]

Although I do not wish to dwell overlong on this point, it bears note that an analogue to the conservatism-liberalism dichotomy "trap" at the level of epistemology is the normative-theory versus empirical-theory dichotomy. This dichotomy also has come to stereotype and frame thought about the nature of theory to such an extent that it seems virtually impossible to find an audience open to hearing an explanation of the epistemology of the process perspective (which underpins the viewpoint to be state subsequently here) because it falls into the category of neither empirical theory nor normative theory. I have frequently been no less than astounded at the certainty with which I have been told (for example, at panel sessions where I have merely mentioned this point) flatly that it is "impossible" to hold a viewpoint that is neither empirical nor normative. Most interesting to me was the reaction received by my attempt to state in writing the epistemological grounding of the process perspective — a conference paper titled "Moving Beyond the Empirical Theory-Normative Theory Double Bind." The paper was received with interest at the conference where I presented it and was subsequently published in its *Proceedings*.[21] Also, one of the conference organizers solicited it for publication in a book based on the conference papers. In working with him and the publishing house editor, however, it became clear to me that they saw the piece as a normative argument for participation and the revisions they suggested were in the direction of making this fact clearer. We finally all agreed to abandon the revision: I became frustrated at attempting to explain myself, and they became confused as to what position I was taking.

My project here has been to illustrate the analytical misapprehensions created by the traditional frame of debate. I believe that it is critical to approach further discussion and clarification of the authority-participation issue with this problem in mind. Much of the reaction that I personally have received to the Blacksburg Manifesto has reminded me of past experiences on this point. This time, however, reactions were more hard-hitting and vivid. Many colleagues and friends of mine in the field were surprised and dismayed that I had "signed on" to such a statement of faith in governmental authority. I was seen by some as having broken faith with my allies on the side of participation. Due to this, I have welcomed the opportunity to attempt to state again how the issue of authority and participation might be regarded from a process perspective, and by so doing remove the issue from the emotional and conceptual tangles in which the traditional frame has enmeshed it. The strategy I shall follow this time is to avoid critique — which I believe restimulates and evokes the liberal-conservative debate — in favor of a descriptive and positive account first of social process and then of individual human development. Finally, I will use these ideal type statements as the basis for a summary reexamination of the authority-participation issue.

An Ideal Type Model of Participation

What I wish to do here is describe what I take to be a conceptualization of participation as it could occur under the best possible conditions, as we know these conditions from experience with and research into the psychology and social psychology of interpersonal relations. I will take human nature, for the moment, to be a neutral variable — a "given." I will return to this topic in the next section of the chapter. As will be specified along the way, this model draws eclectically on a variety of conceptual and research sources. It would require a booklength work to give it full elaboration — in this chapter I can only sketch and overview it.

Assumptions About Human Nature

I begin by positing the axiom that human beings are in essence entities that develop and that possess agentry — meaning that their activities cannot be completely predicted. Human energy moves continuously through the individual into action. Human beings are, therefore, always "in motion" in the sense of developing. Further, they *act* rather than *behave*, in that their developmental agenda transcends and overrides the impingements of external stimuli, pressures, or "social vectors" that might cause them merely to respond. The world view of economics and behaviorism have so influenced the contemporary view of human nature that this assertion may seem especially implausible. Ministers and therapists have long experience with the fact that development issues in people often force them to ignore "practical" external realities. Managers also can give much testimony on this point. Happily, research on adult development and the popularization of modern psychological theories and therapies such as Gestalt psychology are raising general awareness about this matter. More will be said on this later, for now I need only specify the elements of this energy transfer.

The source of all human energy is psychological and it begins, we can posit, at the juncture of the psyche or mind and the carbon atoms of which the body is composed. The *unconscious* is the source of this energy. The idea of the unconscious, though it remains somewhat mysterious to the Western empirically oriented mind, has been widely accepted as a working concept since Freud and can be said to hold the same epistemological status as such ideas as "subatom particle" in physics and "role" in sociology. That is, it is a concept that is used to refer to and account for systematically occurring, at least secondarily observable, events in individual and social life. There are patterns in dreams and myths, for example, that transcend historical period and cultural variation.[22] These are the *collective* patterns of the unconscious. There are likewise characteristic patterns in the dream life of individuals that represent the *personal* unconscious. The unconscious accounts for such patterns, as well as other events, actions, attitudes, and so forth, which occur in individual and social life, and which appear, from the point of view of consciousness, to be irrational and inconsistent with preferred aims, values, and wishes.

Human energy moves from its psychological sources in the collective and personal unconscious through the consciousness or mind, if you will, of the individual, on through the muscles of the body, into *activity*. Activity, derived on this way, constitutes social life. The question or issue that confronts this process is how to achieve a *balanced* or *mediated* flow of unconscious energy into action. I hope it is clear at this point that the model of human nature I am drawing posits human beings to be neither good *nor* bad. The potential for both lies in the process of energy flow through them. Further, the factors affecting this energy flow are not completely individual but are indeed primarily *social*— that is, the flow depends upon the degree of evocation and the channels provided by the artifacts of society. Nonetheless, the individual must be responsible for the use of this energy. As I will describe later, this is a central paradox of the human condition.

The key element conditioning the flow of energy through the individual is the *symbolic analogue*.[23] Analogues are physical representations that "stand for," indicate, or refer to patterned configurations, that is, the *archetypes*, of unconscious energy. Analogues are the *channels* that direct energy into action. Analogues can act on unconscious energy in two ways. They can, by being inappropriate to the unconscious patterns, *block* energy, that is, provide insufficient vent for it. In this case the blocked energy pattern or archetype will regress and gain strength until it can burst through into action all at once. At the level of the individual this dynamic can be seen, for example, in the individual who can find no appropriate outlet for rage or anger. Depression or lowered capacity to act is followed oftentimes by a destructive outburst. At the level of society, the rise of Naziism in Germany is the most often-cited example.[24]

On the other hand, analogues can provide *too easy access* for unconscious energy to the outside, in which case it will pour forth into social life unmediated, usually with destructive consequences. What is generally referred to as evil, wrong, bad, or in general socially pathological, is produced by either blocked energy or by "flooding" energy. The question then becomes: how can analogues be shaped so as to prevent eruption and achieve a balanced flow of energy into activity? In answering this, we must note that analogues can be literally *anything* outside the individual — words, pictures, things, and so on. Second, to speak of consciously shaping analogues is to attempt something like pulling oneself up by one's bootstraps, in that consciousness must reflex or interact with itself and know its own reaction to an analogue without becoming overwhelmed by it. Analogues vary in the extent to which this is possible. It is rather easy consciously to arrange and decorate a room, for example, so as to evoke a certain mood. It is quite another think to know just when to stop in creating moods through the use of psychotropic chemicals. The more intimate, that is, the closer the analogue is involved in the direct expression of energy, the more difficult it becomes to deal with it consciously and thereby mediate the energy it evokes. An instructive illustration of how analogues work, and how they can sometimes be consciously revised to make them more appropriate to the development of consciousness, is the case of personal journals. Ira Progoff, in his researches into the process of journal writing, discovered that peoples' personal journals tended to return again and again to the same developmental issues, with little or no growth or movement over time. Spontaneous journal writing is an analogue that apparently allows energy to flow so easily for some that they have difficulty reflexing with what they have written. In response to this problem, Progoff designed an explicit format or pattern into which journal material could be entered. This format — his newly created analogue — enables the writer to see more clearly the issues implicit in the material and thereby to be able to reflex with it, work through it, and thereby resolve the issues it represents. By using this analogue as a channel for journal writing, the writer avoids recycling through issues or going around in circles in the journal. Progoff's journal method is an example of developing an appropriate analogue, one that leads to development and change.[25]

One point of reference for the evaluation of analogues is what I call the *law of structural congruence*. This law states that for an analogue to evoke and regulate the flow of human energy effectively, the analogue must be structurally congruent to the human form. An example of how this law operates can be found in food. We consider *food* to be those benign elements in our environment that the body, given its structure and the processes this structure entails, can safely and effectively convert into fuel and maintenance elements. Substances can be incongruent in two ways. On the one hand, they may contain an unacceptable ratio of roughage, or *excess*, to nutritional elements, in which case ingestion constitutes a waste of time and energy. An example, perhaps, is hay. On the other hand, a substance may have too high a ratio of nutritional value to roughage or excess. Foods that are the condensed *essences* of substances fall into this category — for example, butter, ice cream, liquor, and so forth. Essences are more directly dangerous to the equilibrium of the psyche (and body), but both types of problems are equally serious in the long run.

A complicating factor in this matter is that the forms that structure the unconscious are not fixed but evolve through the vehicle of individual development. As individuals gain consciousness through the integration of unconscious material, the patterns of the unconscious are altered. Hence, human nature is not fixed but mutable and amenable to development as well. The implication of this is that structural congruences of analogues to the consciousness of an individual can be used only as a *timebound* point of reference for the assessment of analogues. As consciousness, and the unconscious, evolve, patterns of congruence change. What the law of structural congruence tells us, however, is that (1) the more analogues involve essences, the more individual consciousness is required for dealing with them, and (2) the more crude or artificial analogues become, the more they will tend to retard consciousness and induce an unconscious state that will eventually lead to a problematic eruption of unconscious energy. That is, one can eat hay only so long before one lashes out in an attempt to obtain better food. The same is true of religious practices that fail to nourish the soul sufficiently.

Assumptions About Action

Since all action is at bottom an expression of individual energy, to understand the process of action and how it can be effective we must turn attention to the level of the individual. At this level the most fundamental and important truth we can know is that *individuals differ*. The main implication of this truth is the rule that individual differences must be understood nonnormatively. This idea is in profound disagreement with the conventional adjustment model currently used for thinking about individual differences. According to the adjustment model there is a right or good way for individuals to be — a way that represents effective adjustment or accommodation to the social system and that is expressed in statistically normative patterns. Hence, individual differences come to be viewed in primarily clinical terms that indicate the degree to which a given individual approximates this hypothetical model. This perspective tends to place, therefore, a negative loading on differences, and the result is that individuals come to seek to be "like everyone else," or " normal." The implicit assumption of the adjustment model is that the bulk of people are approximately the same, such that meaningful norms exist. Hence, many differences between individuals are indications of the extent to which someone may vary from the norm and not be normal.

Beginning from the assumption that people are different in basic ways from each other leads to a view that sees differences not as abnormalities but *complementarities*. There are few measurement devices available for describing individual differences in nonnormative terms. The Myers Briggs Types Inventory (MBTI) is perhaps the best currently used such device.[26] The Myers Briggs typology describes variations of preferred emphasis in individuals on four dimensions of mind: thinking, feeling, intuiting, and sensing. These mind functions represent ways of assimilating and using information. The MBTI yields sixteen specific types, and these provide the basis for identifying four major behavior pattern categories (or *temperaments*) that are easily observable as differences in information-processing styles among individuals.[27]

It bears mention that some rather striking congruences are appearing between the MBTI-types descriptions and the modern research into the physiology of the brain and the relation of brain to mind.[28] One might speculate that this brain research will eventually yield a systematic method of understanding how differences in brain physiology (for example, differing patterns of emphasis in use of functions centered in various brain lobes) result in differences in individual information-procession styles. The congruence of the MBTI to brain research even at this point makes it clear, however, that to adopt normative judgments that value one information-processing style over another is like rejecting parts of one's brain. The more sensible attitude would seem to be that one needs all of one's brain in order to be optimally effective. Likewise, it would appear that it is best to value all types of individual information-processing styles as part of an effective action process.

Indeed there is some research available using the MBTI that indicates that task teams varying in types makeup are more effective than "types homogeneous" teams.[29] At any rate I posit it as axiomatic that maximally effective action must be based on or arise from a process that is characterized by a balanced emphasis or use of the various functions of mind that the MBTI describes. Since all individuals' types represent a hierarchical ordering of these functions, it seems clear that, in general, a group process, where the group represents a balanced mix of the psychic functions (thought, feeling, intuition, and sensing) would offer greater possibility for effective action in the long run. It would likewise seem to be a valid generalization that such groups would be more effective when they employed a structured process that ensured that each major mind function would be employed in a full and systematic fashion. Such a process, in my view, has been described well by Kolb and Rubin in their Four Step Problem Solving-Learning Cycle, each step of which calls for the employment of a different mind function.[30]

Assumptions About Relationship

Mixing groups by MBTI type and having them follow a structured process that allows full utilization of the mixed capacities is by no means sufficient to ensure that effective action will result. The crux of the process approach, the element that creates the *synergy* that makes group process worth more then the cost, is *relationship*. The group members must achieve a *certain quality or texture* in their relations in order for this synergy to occur. It is difficult if not impossible to specify exactly what this quality is in interpersonal relationships. Perhaps the best we can do is describe what we know at this point as the prerequisite conditions for it and simply stipulate that what results when these conditions are met is what we mean.

First, I wish to address what might be called *strategic* considerations. Effective group relations must be based on a certain type of *relation to oneself.* Individuals must be in contact with themselves and be highly aware of their own identities, their own personal process. Some language from Gestalt psychology which describes this condition is "being grounded and bounded," meaning to be solidly aware of one's own body and one's "process" of "figure" or "want" formation.[31] One must be aware of what is going on internally each moment and be ready and willing to acknowledge or own that project. Part of achieving this condition may have to do with managing the physical processes of the body. Perhaps the ingestion of alcohol—or even sugar and other seemingly benign substances—effectively can blur this necessary base of self-awareness.

The group process must allow for and facilitate the expression of this awareness. It is my view, for example, based on my experience in working with teams as a consultant, that it is helpful if not essential to begin each work session with a statement from each person describing how he or she feels about being at the meeting and about the task or situation being faced. The next desired step is to have the group members discuss what they *want* to do—irrespective of the facts—about the matter they face. Standard procedure for groups is to do the reverse of what I have just described: namely, (1) to hide how they feel about being there on the team and instead present a "responsible" attitude, and (2) to seek to discover what the objective realities or facts of the situation indicate that they *must* do about it. It is precisely this way of operating that makes many groups and teams as ineffective as they frequently are.[32]

A second strategic factor has to do with the concreteness and immediacy of the situation or action question that the team faces. This is the matter of the timing and scale of action issues. In order for people to be able to act most effectively toward a situation, the questions they face must entail elements and require actions that are of a size and of an immediacy that is congruent with the experiential capacity of the human individual.[33] This means simply that people, if they are to act rationally, must be able *to apprehend personally* what they are to act toward. Again, effective action must employ all human capacities—thinking, feeling, the senses, the intuition. Budget numbers in the trillions are of a degree of abstraction that can outstrip the ability of thought to grasp implications; devastation can reach a scale that overwhelms the ability to distill the feeling-reality or moral dimension of the weapons that create it; the technical capacity to create, store, and manipulate information can render the actual facts a matter mysterious; complexity can boggle and stump intuition's ability to gain insight into new lines of action. I think it can be said safely that much of the irrationality of modern society is owed to the fact that the questions modern society presents (or the ways in which we are framing these questions) simply *outsize* human discretion.[34]

(3) A third strategic factor is the *stance* that the participants take toward the process. This is a complex topic, and one fraught with subtlety. A brief way of describing it would be to say that the participants must engage the process through a condition of *surrender* to it. The biblical myth of Job is perhaps a helpful image to invoke on this point. In many ways the story of Job provides a role model for the posture humankind must take toward the fate of life. We tend to remember this story now as a paradigm of misery and depression and overlook the lesson contained in the fact that through Job's surrender the story moves to a happy ending. This is a point of fundamental importance, and I feel I must explore it at the philosophical level, if only briefly.[35]

At one point (in the early 1970s) in the course of my studies toward developing the point of view I am sketching here, I explored the literature of collective behavior or crowdism. I was struck at the time at how little work, relatively speaking, had been done on the matter, and I was especially disappointed at the lack of broad-scale theoretical conceptualization in the area— until I came across the work of Elias Canetti. Canetti, though known mostly as a linguist and novelist (he won the Nobel prize for literature in 1983) is a social theorist of the most profound sort. His particular interest is the etiology of social pathology. Since I am being somewhat autobiographical here, I would note that Canetti's ideas, though obscure and esoteric, have had a tremendous impact on me. His book, *Crowds and Power*, has influenced my point of view more than any other single work I have encountered.[36] I will attempt to present at least a schema of his thought here.

At the surface level, Canetti's interest is in the irrationalities entailed by domination. He sees social pathology (perhaps through viewing the social-political history of Europe) as a dynamic that derives from elites dominating masses, who in turn react to overthrow elites. The period between actual violence and disruption is simply the time required for the conditions to ripen and for the participants to plan and prepare. Where there is domination there can be no security and stability.

What is most profound in Canetti's analysis is the way he understands the motive for domination and how domination creates social pathology. In his view, those who seek to dominate, who want to occupy the upper reaches of hierarchies, do so as a way of symbolically finding a permanent means of survival, that is, immortality. Dominators, then, are *survivors*, those who wish to avoid death.

In order symbolically to accomplish this, the dominators must establish social relations among those around them that have the effect of *stopping their human process*. This means to stop the changes, the development, that occur in people as they move through life participating in the network of human relationships that create and express their evolving identity. The extreme form of this, of course, is for the dominator to order the death of others, in that to exercise such power yields a sense of invincibility. From this extreme, the means dominators use vary in type and degree of severity. They all, however, involve the enforced *masking* of subordinates, so that spontaneous development of activity or expression is prevented. (In the contemporary jargon of social science, masks are called "roles.") The enforcement of masks depends on the use of certain *language formats*, and it is these language formats — such as commands, evaluations and judgments, secrets, and the like — that are the generic cause of the problem of social pathology. What such language does is compromise the sacredness of the person by creating circumstances that make them, de facto, members of a collective. The many become as one — as in the case of crowds and mobs.

Canetti's analysis of pathology reveals a rather specific, though implicit, picture of his model of health in social process. At the surface level of social dynamics, people must act from a sense of themselves as *persons*. A sense of personhood requires a certain amount of social space between people. This space allows the distinctively human element ("spirit," "mind," "soul," etc., are various names by which it is called) to operate and be expressed through spontaneous — which really means situation specific — action. Interpersonal space evokes soul, the collapsing of this space creates a ouija board effect, where everyone has a hand in the action, but everyone believes that someone else is in control and they are just "going along." Under such conditions evil can be evoked, when the unseen hand spells out disastrous instructions. Life in many modern organizations is very much like a ouija board session. Jerry Harvey has given this last version of this phenomenon the colorful name "Abilene Paradox."[37]

Canetti is definitely not positing an ontology of individualism, however, in making interpersonal space a key ingredient of social health. Indeed, the reverse is true, though to see this one must understand the paradox of relationship. That is, relationship, or effective and valid interpersonal process, exists where there is a strong sense of individuality on the part of participants. Indeed, we may say that the only true possibility for individuality is in relationship. The model for individuality that we most often currently accept — the autonomous actor — obscures the fact that people who are strongly individualistic in this way are, through their emphasis on individual autonomy as the vehicle for relating to others, locking themselves into a crowd relation with others and thereby compromising their individuality. The king, the boss or commander, the judge, are all chained, psychologically, to those on whom they wish to work their will.[38] In modern society we have difficulty seeing this because the irrational crowd dynamics that are set off by such figures are played out in such complex, subtle ways. It seems virtually absurd to see a street mob and a modern "rational" organization as similar. At the structural level, however, they are exactly the same because, as Canetti notes, the language formats and the pervasively judgmental nature of the relationships that are characteristic of formal organizations are precisely the devices that create conditions of collective behavior.

The same subtle dynamic occurs when one's sense of individualism is expressed in the modern concept of contract. When two parties enter a contract or any agreement they in effect put a boundary around themselves. They become directly connected through the words of the contract. The contract rather than their discretion instructs their actions. Contract, as government, collapses interpersonal space and locks together the agreeing parties in much the same way that master and slave are connected. Only in this case both parties play both the roles of master and of slave. The dynamics of organizational and contractual relationship play out more slowly than those of the mob, and hence their intrinsic irrationality is more difficult to see.

Let us now complete the circle and return to the starting place. Tracing Canetti's analysis backwards, we can see that social pathology is a result of the compression of people into crowds, where their individuality — and with it the possibility for relationship, interaction, and the rational exercise of discretion it entails — is lost. The creation of crowds occurs through the use of language formats, like commands, that have the effect of imposing masks on people and stopping their human process. Finally, at the source, those who seek to impose masks on others do so as a way of symbolically stopping the processes of change that lead, ultimately, to death. Hence, at the bottom of the problem of social pathology, in Canetti's view, is the refusal to accept death, to submit to fate.

This message, although it may seem esoteric and abstract, is in my view directly pertinent to the pathology of present societies, and perhaps especially our own. Killilea, a political theorist, argues that both Hobbes and Locke in their theories of the state accomplish the conceptual trick of making it seem that a rightly ordered political system will ensure against death either through protection of actual life or of property.[39] In Killilea's view, partly because of the centrality of Hobbes's and Locke's work to the political theory of American government, our political culture is oriented toward the avoidance of death or certainly toward a lack of acceptance of death as a natural part of life. He sees rather serious implications in this and believes that a cultural move toward acceptance of death would have major sociopolitical consequences of a positive type.

I shall explore later the question of how relevant is Canetti's exotic analysis of social pathology to our present situation. At this point I refer to it so as to evoke a metaphorical understanding of perhaps the most important strategic aspect of effective social process. That is, the acceptance of death is a metaphor for a special type of psychological surrender without which social process cannot be achieved and proceed. Our awareness of this truth, I believe, is really rather general and is followed intuitively in much of our social relations — accounting for the happy fact that our society has not been ravaged further than it has been by crowd pathologies. To my belief, I can invoke a variety of source images.

At the higher, more venerable level, is the image of scientific community. The essence of the classical image of the process of science is the idea that the relationship among scientists is one of mutual acceptance and mutual submission. I, as a scientist, have the responsibility to listen in an open, unbiased, and interested manner to your claims. You in turn must put forth your claims *in suspense*, with an attachment of doubt as well as conviction, and submit yourself to my response — meaning that you will attend to it in the same way I attended to you. I must put forth my response tentatively and with doubt. Doubt, as the primary stigmata of submission, is the essence of the process of science. Science never proves anything. It only can develop "working truth" or "truth for the time being." To make the claim of truth is to deny and stop the process. Science indeed is an end in itself, an essentially esthetic process, the main product of which is the fructification of scientists and their fellow human beings.

Today there is little attention paid to this classical image of science, and, I would venture to assert, very little science being done these days. What has replaced it is technical work directed at specific problems. Much of this work is motivated by grant money and prizes, and scientists have become adversaries. Indeed, the adversarial process seems to be the most widely held idea as to how truth is uncovered. We therefore have little sensitivity to the role of submission in the process of truth discovery.

As a second image I would mention Ghandi's idea of passive resistance or *satyagraha*. Though it is not widely recognized, passive resistance is not a method of social disruption so as to force authority to concede to demands. Rather, it was Ghandi's belief that putting oneself passively in the way of one's adversary would result in creating the psychological conditions necessary for an effective dialogue and peaceful resolution. He saw satyagraha as a way of getting at the truth, a scientific method of social analysis.[40] Closely related to this image is the Socratic method. Although the popular stereotype is that Socrates was a manipulator who coaxed his pupils into saying what he knew all along to be the truth, in fact Socrates meant it when he said he knew nothing. Socrates saw himself as submitting to a process of dialogue with his pupils. The dialogue is what led to the truth; it was a method of discovery.[41]

The contemporary research on conflict resolution is beginning to reflect awareness of the principle of submission. The Harvard Negotiations Project research, as one example, emphasizes the importance of moving, in negotiations, from the level of position to the level of "vital interests" or generic human need.[42] In order to make such a shift, the parties must cease strategizing and attempting to get "one up" on the other. They must open themselves and acknowledge what they really want to gain from the negotiations. To do so they must share feelings and concerns and reveal truly how they see themselves in the situation. Typically this is called in the literature of negotiation "trusting the process" or "trusting the other side." This language indicates rather clearly the role that submission plays in creating the conditions for a creative or synergistic negotiation process.

It bears mention also that this idea has precedent in the work of Mary Parker Follett and her idea of the "law of the situation."[43] The essence of this notion is that the generic examination of questions, the structural issues, faced in a situation will yield the most appropriate response to it. Harmon and Mayer's description of Follett shows clearly the affinities of her position and the one I am setting out here:

> Follett is perhaps the first "process" theorist of stature in American management thought. She stands clearly apart from the rationalist tradition in boldly asserting that purposes *emerge from social experience*, as do the "facts" of social activity that bear on those purposes. Moreover, there is a distinctly moral tenor evident in Follett's notion of emergent purpose, since the same social processes that give rise to it are also the formative stuff of the individual's development. "Responsibility," mentioned in each of the two preceding quotations, is possible only by active and reflexive participation in the social processes through which collective purposes unfold. Responsibility, here, does not mean adherence to an objective standard of truth arrived at through abstract intellectual thought nor obligation to a superordinate source of authority. Rather, in the personal sense that Follett intends, it refers to the self-understanding and self-realization that individuals experience when they invest their emotional energies in collaborative endeavors.[44]

To accomplish such examination, the parties involved must cease attempting to influence or persuade others to their point of view, their analysis, and their solution. The idea is that in a properly related and functioning group, the *process itself* will produce the best line of action. By truly listening to each other, the objective situation could speak to the group and identify the law governing it.

Perhaps the most graphic illustration of the principle of submission can be found in the cybernetic theories of Gregory Bateson.[45] In his theory of cybernetics, the governance of a system, indeed its "mind," resides in the *system itself* rather than at any single point or individual within the system. All cause-effect relationships are mutual, hence any attempt at assertion of control produces a countervailing effect in the opposite direction. Therefore, only the overall, the *system itself*, can produce change in a given direction.[46] To illustrate this idea Bateson uses the example of Alcoholics Anonymous. He notes that as long as any party attempts to impose controls on the alcoholic, or the alcoholic attempts to assert personal will over the addiction, the problem continues. It is only when the alcoholic *submits*, by saying "I am an alcoholic," "I am not able to control alcohol," that the regulating processes of the AA group itself begin to bring the drinking behavior under control. (The AA method continues to be the most effective treatment model for addictions.) Carlos Casteneda has reported a lesson from the wise man Don Juan which is based on this principle: "Self-importance makes you weak."[47] This is the point, at bottom, of all of Don Juan's teachings. To the extent that ego, self-importance, or individualism moved past, so that the person can participate in the power of process, strong and effective action can be accomplished.

As a last illustration, I would mention the common-law tradition of justice — though it is a teacher whom we as a society have fundamentally misinterpreted. That is, it is probably the image of the courtroom adversarial process that has shaped most heavily our culture image of how the truth of a situation is reached and how participants are to behave. What is not depicted sufficiently in most versions of this image — indeed it is intentionally obscured so as to highlight the role of the attorney's (as the client's champion) dramatic power of confrontation and argument — is the fact that the key to the power of the process is that the participants submit themselves to its spirit and its structure. The common law is, above all, modest and practical. It asserts itself only so far as to settle disputes at hand, and by respecting precedent it shows willingness to subordinate opinion to the decisions of others and let tradition set a "working definition" of justice.[48] Judges take a special posture toward the law wherein they let the law speak through them. They represent the judicial process itself. The text of the law, especially in the case of a constitution, is not interpreted in the usual sense of active construction of meaning. Rather the judge seeks to *let the text speak.* That is, the judge must become subordinate to the text.[49] In my view it is this subordinated posture people generally sense judges taking toward the law that is the basis for the deference accorded the legal process. This is true especially in the United States with its institution of judicial review, which of course many commentators have held to be flatly inconsistent with the basic tenets of democratic process.

To recapitulate, the third strategic aspect of effective social process that I am describing here entails a posture of surrender or submission. At the surface level this must hold in relations to others as a realization or actualization of submission to process. This means taking a stance outside of the ego and such in turn depends on an acceptance of the inevitable reality of death. The paradox of life followed by death epitomizes the paradox of valid relationship and effective process. In order to accept death we must accept the total aloneness (at least aloneness from the point of view of the ego) that goes with it. When we can accept our ultimate aloneness, it becomes possible to establish valid, contactful relationship to others. It is such relationship that is the essence of effective human process.

Although strategic considerations such as I have been making may seem highly philosophical and removed from the concrete realities of participation, the *tactical principles of participation* are in fact closely tied to such considerations. The tactics of effective participation that I wish to describe are, essentially, the principles of effective communication, and I know of no way to make sense of them theoretically except in terms of the considerations I have just been discussing above. After I became involved in teaching communication (as part of organization development) I found myself unsatisfied with the standard practical rationale for communication techniques — namely, that they work. It was in the midst of my search for a deeper frame within which to put them that I became interested in social pathology and came across Canetti's work. His book had a significant impact on me because it provided such a framework. Given the scope, contest, and format of this essay, and the general awareness that has now developed about most of the principles of effective communication, I will only mention and briefly describe the most widely known ones, and give more attention to those of which there is less general awareness. The theme on which I want to begin (and that I want throughout to emphasize) in this discussion is that effective communication is essentially an exercise in the management of *language formats,* that is, the specific structural displays by which meaning is put into sentences. In this, every tiniest detail counts. Language formats constitute one of the most basic and intimate levels of symbolic analogue. For this reason it is extremely difficult for a given individual to maintain a steady enough consciousness to reflex with the language formats and thereby apprehend the meaning of one's action with them. The classic fly-back toy, with paddle, rubber string, a rubber ball, is a metaphor for this point. With most symbolic analogues, the rubber string is long and it is easy to follow the ball and reflex with it. With spoken language the string is extremely short and strong, and the ball is quite likely to speed right past the paddle. This is why so much language training, even for clinicians, is acquired on a rote basis (as in the cliche, "What I hear you saying is . . . "). For most, it is simply too difficult to do on a more spontaneous basis.

The basic building blocks of the type of communication that makes for effective participation are appropriate self-disclosure, skilled listening, and adequate feedback.[50] Performing each of these skills involves simply speaking according to prescribed patterns. In the case of feedback, the pattern is quite specific: the feedback given is to describe the *event* in question, the *subsequent events,* and *one's own* feeling reaction to the events. In listening, the main prescription is to repeat back to the speaker words that are as close to the ones the speaker is using as possible, and to avoid declarations of advice, sympathy, evaluation, and so on. The emphasis is on specific, concretely descriptive language patterns, so that generalization, summary, and judgment are avoided.

In learning these skills many people exhibit rather strong resistive reactions. They feel the language is insipid, vacuous, phony, unhelpful, and uninteresting. Such resistances indicate, in my view, the degree to which crowdistic, intensely melodramatic relationships have become our cultural model of what is interesting and meaningful in human transactions. There might also be a certain sense of aloneness that is created by the language and that produces a fear reaction. (This indeed may be the *main* fuel to resistive reactions.) The sense of separation from the other, or the creation of interpersonal space, is precisely what these language formats are intended to create — so that a change process within the individuals involve can be given the room to occur. In turn, the individual movement that is gained creates the dynamic that gives energy and life to interpersonal or group *process*.

The specifics of movement within the individual and the importance of such movement to collective process is nowhere made clearer than in the Gestalt psychology of Fritz Perls.[51] The power of creating such movement, of putting people in touch with the personal dynamic that sets the "figures" or wants that each person's development is constantly presenting to him or her was demonstrated many times in the rather astounding "miracle cures" that Perls was able to achieve through encounter with certain neurotic individuals. Also, the specific language patterns that block authentic contact and that therefore stop process — for example, deflection, introjection, retroflection — are specified quite well in Gestalt theory and have been validated in both therapeutic and organization practice.

Transactional analysis, the psychology of Eric Berne and others, mirrors the Gestalt emphasis on the importance of changing language patterns so as to disentangle people from wasteful and irrational interpersonal games.[52] The idea of game as Berne uses it illustrates rather vividly the connection between Canetti's theory of social pathology, modern humanistic psychology, and organization development. In a crowd, people are not related but rather locked together in a common project that no one is truly directing; it has an autonomous dynamic with its own prescribed outcome. Nonetheless, crowd members feel they are asserting themselves, that they are related to others in the crowd — even intimately — and that the crowd project is personally meaningful. This is precisely the sort of condition that holds in an interpersonal game, even when only two people are involved. That is, virtually all games involve three stereotypical roles: victim, persecutor, and rescuer. As the game proceeds, the three parties ritually "dance" around the issue that the victim presents. Although victims play helpless, they in fact do not want help. Rather, they simply want to involve the others in a pseudo problem-solving discussion of their issues. In so far as melodrama is interesting, the point of games is that they constitute an interesting way to pass time in the company of others while avoiding true contact or intimacy with them. This is the bottom line payoff of games: the avoidance of intimacy while simultaneously maintaining involvements with others. Intimacy is strange and scary to most people because it is open and unpredictable. In general we are much more accustomed to the stronger and closer ties of games. We are more accustomed to living with each other in crowd conditions. The way out of games is to be able to gain awareness on a continuing basis of the effects of the language that we use in relating to others — when, in other words, the way we are talking places us in the comfortably predictable role of victim, persecutor, or rescuer.

One of the more recent and in some ways sophisticated theories for understanding how language impacts process is the linguistic "metamodel" of Neuro-Linguistic Programming (NLP).[53] Developed through the collaboration of a

Gestalt psychologist and a linguist (Richard Bandler and John Grinder), NLP's theory falls into two separate but complementary "halves." One of these is based on a documentation of the hypnotic techniques developed by the psychiatrist Milton Erikson.

The other half is based on linguistic analysis — using Chomsky's transformational linguistics and particularly his concept of deep structure — of the language used by therapy clients (and therapists) in discussing the life problems that brought them to therapy. The basic concept of the NLP metamodel is that people do not respond to reality directly but rather construct linguistic maps of it — that is, the descriptions they give therapists as accounts of the situations they are in. Problems occur — people become neurotically blocked and unable to act — when the map they are using shows no avenue open for action. Linguistic maps are aways amenable to redrawing, however, in that the *distortions, deletions,* and *generalizations* of which they are constituted make them only approximate pictures of the situation and its action possibilities. By challenging the patient to revise the specific language formats (which are too numerous to detail here) that create distortions, deletions, and generalizations, the therapist enables the patient to redraw the map and create a pathway out of the situation he or she is in. The utility of NLP is by no means confined to the personal problems of the therapy setting, as it is generally acknowledged as a useful new technology in the field of organization development.[54]

There is one aspect of the development of NLP that in my view has not been accorded sufficient attention. This has to do with the other half of NLP theory: hypnotic techniques. Basically, the idea here, as formulated through practice by Erikson, is to gain access to the unconscious mind — which is referred to frequently in NLP theory as the "right brain deep structure" capability of the mind — and linguistically implant metaphors that entail a happy resolution of a problem situation. These metaphors, once implanted, work their way into reality (in just the way that in the great Greek tragedy Medea's companions warned her that "thoughts" do) *implicitly,* without conscious action on the part of the subject. Erikson's ability to do this "implantion" in the context of ordinary conversation or even a formal address before a large audience, was legendary. The specific discovery to which I wish to point has to do with the language formats that Erickson used in his hypnotic techniques. What Bandler and Grinder discovered was that *these formats were precisely the ones that appear in the metamodel as the linguistic patterns that constitute problem situations as described by patients in therapy.* For example, one of the linguistic malformations that constitute the metamodel is the "Cause-Effect Statement." Such statements attribute causal power where none actually exists (e.g., "You make me angry") and in this sense are a malformed representation of reality. As such, though, they exert great — indeed, hypnotic — power over people, leading the hearer of such statements to believe they are true and to respond accordingly. The dynamics of this process can be seen in a striking research study done by social psychologist Ellen Langer and her co-workers. Langer's study involved compliance with requests to break in line at a library copy machine, as follows: "Excuse me, I have five pages. May I use the Xerox machine because I'm in a rush?" The effectiveness of this request-plus-reason was nearly total: 94 percent of those asked let her skip ahead of them in line. Compare this success rate to the results when she made the request worded only: "Excuse me, I have five pages. May I use the Xerox machine?" Under those circumstances only 60 percent of those asked complied. At first glance, it appears that the crucial difference between the two requests was the additional information provided by the words *because I'm in a rush*. However, a third type of request tried by Langer showed that this was not the case. It seems that it was not the whole series of words, but the first one, *because*, that made the difference. Instead of including a real reason for compliance, Langer's third type of request used the word *because* and then, adding nothing new, merely restated the obvious: "Excuse me, I have five pages. May I use the Xerox machine because I have to make some copies?" The result was that *once again nearly all (93 percent) agreed*, even though no real reason, no new information, was added to justify their compliance.[55] We can interpret Langer's finding as an example of how a linguistically malformed causal statement (i.e., the nonreason) can evoke unconscious compliance behavior. The implications of this strike me as potentially profound and call for further exploration. What seems indicated is that linguistically malformed statements have the power of opening access to the unconscious and structuring unconscious energy. These unconscious patterns can either be, from the point of view of conscious intentionality, good or bad, that is, productive or problematic. From the perspective of our concern here with effective process, it seems to mean that *dialogue, when unintentionally misconstructed linguistically, has the power to unintentionally induce microtrance states that produce problematic lines of behavior or that obscure the possibility for action.* Since a trance state is simply a state of concentration ("deep trances" differ from "reflection" only in degree) it could very well be that intense discussion could induce rather powerful unconscious images and metaphors inadvertently. An illustration of this phenomenon at the simplest level is the way negative commands are being used by some sports instructors to improve athletic performance. For example, in skiing, students are helped to overcome fear of steep slopes by the instructor's commanding them, at the top of a steep slope they are about to ski down: "Don't relax." Analyzed in NLP terms, what this linguistic structure does is send a surface-level message that seems sensible to the left brain, but that in fact requires a deep-structure (right-brain) interpretation. This means that in order for the injunction to be followed, a specific image of what is to be avoided must be created. Hence, the student unconsciously *images* a relaxed state of skiing — that is, what they are *not* supposed to do. This right-brain, unconscious image, tends to "work its way into reality" and govern the behavior of the student as the steep slope is skied. One wonders then, given this example, how often people in their daily lives unintentionally program themselves or others (their children, for example) into lines of action or emotional states that are, as in the skiing example, the *reverse* of what they desire and intend. Further, how often does this occur in the free-form arena of participative process as it is usually practiced?

A Summary of the Model

The ideal model of effective participation sketched here posits a view of the human individual as the focus point of an energy flow that is structured dialectically between the poles of the unconscious as source and consciousness as action point. For this flow to proceed effectively — which means, in essence, under conscious discretion — differences in personal temperament must be acknowledged, analogues must be kept appropriate, and a proper grounded relation to the self must be maintained by individuals. A state of ego submission to the process, as symbolized in relations to others, must be present, and action questions must be concrete and immediate enough to be apprehended by human capacity. The tactics of process hinge critically on the conscious awareness of and, to the extent possible, "management" of the language formats by which the dialogue of the process is carried forward.

I should note, as part of this summary, that this model by no means (at least by my surmise) exhausts what research and theory have to say about the structure and dynamics of effective participation. This model represents my own orientations and preferences as a social theorist and practitioner of organization development and group dynamics facilitation. No doubt, much could be added to what I have listed here, even within this frame. Also, others are interested in this same theoretic question from other perspectives. Jurgen Habermas is one of these, especially in that part of his work wherein he focuses on "ideal speech conditions."[56] I believe it is accurate to say that my project in setting out the model above has been to state the "ideal speech conditions" that I see as underpinning a rational participation process. Doubtlessly, there are many other ways one could approach this matter.

Hence, I do not pretend by any means to a claim of truth or comprehensiveness for this model. I only hope that the outline I have set out is plausible enough to make clear that participation is much more complex, and difficult to bring off, than we generally consider it to be. However, with enough conscious application of what we already know, it *can* work. I can give direct personal testimony to the fact that rather good approximations of the model of effective participation set out here can be created in organization development programs and in the use of mediation in negotiational conflicts. The model of participation set our here is practicable. It is not an illusory ideal that I offer only for purposes of discussion. I hope also that it is clear that what I have described here as participation has little or nothing to do with the participation of the "pluralist model." The essence of pluralism is the contending of interests through power tactics. The essence of participation is a special texture or quality of relationship that power immediately corrodes away.

Reframing the "Participation Issue"

Using the ideal type model just sketched as a backdrop, we can now turn attention more directly to the matter of the participation *issue*. The way this issue is typically framed in political-theory discussion highlights the broad question of how desirable it is to have policy matters decided by a restrictive elite versus having policy set by a more inclusive (or at the societal level, *mass*) participatory process. As noted earlier, positive and negative characterizations of both sides, all well reasoned, comprehensive, and graphic, have been put forth in abundance through the history of this debate. It is still, of course, not settled, except in a tentative de facto manner in specific settings. This ambivalence or stalemate is, however, quite natural and to be expected when one views the question from the perspective of the social ontology outlined earlier in this essay. That is, what this ontology enables one to see is that the image of the "reasonable, wise elite" is actually a coded way of referring to *consciousness*, and the image of the "impulsive, turbulent, but ultimately correct and certainly fearsomely powerful masses" is a metaphor for the collective *unconscious*. Hence the societal dialectic that is expressed through politics is a direct analogue to the psychological dialectic between consciousness and the unconscious that takes place at the level of the individual. The same tensions are evident. From the point of view of consciousness (or a rational elite), the goings-on in the unconscious (i.e., the doings of mass society) always seem unevolved, contradictory, and needing improvement. The mass man is seen as irrational. Yet consciousness continues to be beset by the wise, prudent intuition that it is dangerous to take anything but a cautionary, somewhat deferential posture toward the unconscious — just as the theorists of democracy deem it best to confer citizenship on the mass man and woman and let the count of his and her votes hold sway in public affairs.

The debate surrounding the issue of political participation, therefore, has at the psychological level been a contention over the question of how far, on the one hand, human society should attempt to assert the conscious attitude in its affairs as opposed to, on the other hand, giving vent to expressions from the unconscious. The reason that this debate has proceeded no further than it has is that it has focused on the static questions of what is the nature of elites (consciousness) and the nature of mass man (the collective unconscious) and what macrolevel structural accommodation ought to be established between the two. The dynamics of the matter, through which we can treat the question of how to ensure a continuing reflexive relationship between them, have been left unexamined. Perhaps consciousness has not until now reached a point sufficiently distant from its own involvement with unconscious processes to allow dealing with the question of these dynamics. The dialogue seems to have been carried far enough to have demonstrated that the manipulation of macrolevel variables can only be a preliminary and partial approach to the question of how to achieve effective social participation. At bottom, the issue of democratic organization has been reduced to a question of how many people should be let in on deciding public affairs. The question of *how* they are to be let in has been treated, in essence, as ancillary to this primary question. This is because the primary question has mostly been argued in terms of images of human nature, specifically whether all people, or only a few, possess the capacity for wise action. Framing the issue of democracy as a question of human nature does seem to provide a way of getting an answer about what political process should be like. This promise is an illusion, however, as agreement as to what the answer is becomes well-nigh impossible when parties are asserting basic principles and beliefs about human nature against each other. In such a case, the dialogue becomes a mutual rhetorical harangue, with one side saying, "People are sensible and trustworthy; let them all participate!" and the other saying, "People are impulsive and unreliable; they must be ruled by only a few of their betters!" When we see human nature in "either-or"/"nothing but" terms, the question of how feasible is participation as a form of governance is distorted into a dichotomy of mass democracy versus elite rule.

I hope it is becoming clear that, within the frame I am setting forth here, the question of how to achieve wisdom in public action is more one of creating *effective* participation than it is of finding the proper scope of *access* for people to participate. What is crucial is the dynamic of *how people relate* as they address issues of public action. Effective process dynamics are the essence of rational action. In my view a clear intuition as to the truth of this axiom exists generally among people. It has been my observation that in organizational life (which is the only place I have had the opportunity to observe it) when organization members sense that effective process or even an approximation of effective process exists, notwithstanding that only a small elite of leadership makes most decisions, they do not complain about a lack of participation or access to power. Indeed, they probably are happy not to bother with sharing in the chores of running the system. Demands for inclusion in the process, for the most part, are mounted, and mounted justifiably, when the interactions of the elite diverge from the essence or spirit of effective process that I hope was evoked in the model sketched earlier in this essay. It is perhaps interesting on this point to refer to the ancient Chinese theory of democratic decision making. To the ancient Chinese, discussion and voting were for the purpose of seeing which alternative procured the most harmonious number or the number of higher quality. For example, in a vote of 15-4 the option that received the 4 would be chosen, since it received a more harmonious number. Good choices were seen as being gained through process, not the exercise of power.[57]

The result of our lack of attention to process variables or the dynamics of process is that our democratic processes have been able to serve us — indeed preserve us — in only the crudest way. Because we have had structural democracy rather than democracy characterized by effective process, our politics has tended to be more reactive and curative than proactive or preventive. It has also been more heroic than developmental in its projects. That is, our democratic structures facilitate the venting or amelioration of the social problems and pathologies—the crowdism, to use Canetti's terms—that develop as a result from (among other things) the deficiencies in social process. Hence, distortions and imbalance in process that become manifest in public policies and institutions produce a corrective political response that brings the social system back into balance. (I will say more of this later.)

Nevertheless, we must keep in mind that the essence of rational action is effective participation, the essential texture of which I hope I have identified. The rather general complaint about the costs of participation and the acknowledged personal burdens it places on people reflect this axiom. My surmise is that people mostly care about the quality of the process by which policies are made and institutions are managed. They care less about being included or care not at all about inclusion when they trust that the process is valid. However, the paradox of effective participation is that because it is less burdensome—and indeed can be rewarding and personally developmental for participants—it is probably true that the more effective the process is the more people will want to (and will) participate even though the need, so to speak, is lessened.

The Authority Problem in a Different Light

It seems natural to wonder given the amount of attention we have paid to it, why we have not through our experience with participation moved its practice closer to the ideal. My guess is that the reason the world continues to hold together is that there are everywhere people in positions of authority who possess an intuitive sense of what effective participation is and are able to implement it approximately in the decision arenas over which they have purview. I have myself witnessed many such people. However, there is a major structural limitation to and constraint on the achievement of an effective process among human beings. This constraint is the fact that human beings are born immature and undergo a lifelong maturation process. The underlying factor or the precondition to the strategic and tactical variables sketched out in the ideal model presented earlier is just this: the maturity of the people involved in the process. Maturity is the prerequisite capacity that conditions the possibilities that one can execute the strategies and tactics of participation. The reality is, of course, that virtually all people are struggling with issues of immaturity. Further, the struggle is a process; gains can be made, but serious regressions or regressive episodes also occur. We can now begin to see the other half of the picture and in doing so the generic paradox of participation is revealed to us: *the precondition of effective participation is maturity and the precondition of maturity is participation's opposite—authority.* That is, it is necessary to have stable, effectively functioning authority in order to contain, structure, and move forward the process of human maturation. Hence the basic condition of a "healthy" social order is a *dialectical* condition, the two poles of which are (1) effective participative process, and (2) effective authoritative process. So, let us now turn attention to this other half of the picture.

The Role of Authority in Human Maturation

In order to sketch adequately the picture I wish to put forth here, I must set down a broadbrush backdrop that describes the structural pattern of human maturation. In doing this, I shall employ the theoretic frame and the jargon of Jungian psychology.[58] However, I should note that in my view the pattern of maturation depicted in Jungian psychology is not specific or peculiar to a specific psychological viewpoint. That is, I believe that the pattern Jung identified can be found at the core of the conventional wisdom, or folk knowledge, that is practiced in all Western cultures, at least. I say this here in order to make clear that I wish to claim a broad authority for this model of human development. I do not see its credibility as deriving from Jung's work so much as I see the credibility of Jung's work as deriving from the fact that one can see the patterns he described in the natural or intuitively based practices of human beings in family and social life. Whether this viewpoint deserves this broader legitimacy is a question readers can settle for themselves on the basis of their own observations of everyday life as children, adults, or, possibly, parents.

A Model of the Process of Human Maturation

In Jungian theory, the central issue of maturation is the integration of unconscious material so as to strengthen individual consciousness. The foundation concept of this theory is the idea of the unconscious. Since I discussed this idea earlier, I shall only note or emphasize here that the unconscious is seen to possess a dual ontological status. That is, there is a personal aspect, composed of the repressed and suppressed elements that are created in the course of a given individual's personal life, namely, the things about individuals or their life experience that they for one reason or another put out of consciousness. The broader and more important dimension of the idea of the unconscious is the *collective unconscious*. The collective unconscious is the *zeitgeist*, the world spirit, the universal and uniquely human element that connects all of humankind and that contains all of human experience. The unconscious is unknowable in the direct manner that we are accustomed to apprehending things consciously. It is a kind of life force that emanates "from the other side." Perhaps it is warranted, because this idea is so esoteric and abstract, to set out here some of Jung's own words on the matter:

> Theoretically, no limits can be set to the field of consciousness, since it is capable of indefinite extension. Empirically, however, it always finds its limit when it comes up against the unknown. This consists of everything we do not know, which, therefore, is not related to the ego as the centre of the field of consciousness. The unknown falls into two groups of objects: those which are outside and

can be experienced by the senses, and those which are inside and are experienced immediately. The first group comprises the unknown in the outer world; the second the unknown in the inner world. We call this latter territory the unconscious.

... everything of which I know, but of which I am not at the moment thinking; everything of which I was once conscious but have now forgotten; everything perceived by my senses, but not noted by my conscious mind; everything which, involuntarily and without paying attention to it, I feel, think, remember, want, and do; all the future things that are taking shape in me and will sometime come to consciousness: all this is the content of the unconscious.

Besides these we must include all more or less intentional repressions of painful thoughts and feelings. I call the sum of all these contents the "personal unconscious." But, over and above that, we also find in the unconscious qualities that are not individually acquired but are inherited, e.g., instincts as impulses to carry out actions from necessity, without conscious motivation. In this "deeper" stratum we also find the ... archetypes .... The instincts and archetypes together form the "collective unconcious." I call it "collective" because, unlike the personal unconscious, it is not made up of individual and more or less unique contents but of those which are universal and of regular occurrence.

The first group comprises contents which are integral components of the individual personality and therefore could just as well be conscious; the second group forms, as it were, an omnipresent, unchanging, and everywhere identical quality or substrate of the psyche per se.

The deeper "layers" of the psyche lose their individual uniqueness as they retreat farther and farther into darkness. "Lower down," that is to say as they approach the autonomous functional systems, they become increasingly collective until they are universalized and extinguished in the body's materiality, i.e., in chemical substances. The body's carbon is simply carbon. Hence "at bottom" the psyche is simply "world".[59]

At another point, Jung comments interestingly on the relation of the collective unconscious to the material world:

Synchronicity is no more baffling or mysterious than the discontinuities of physics. It is only the ingrained belief of the sovereign power of causality that creates intellectual difficulties and makes it appear unthinkable that causeless events exist or could ever occur. ... Meaningful coincidences are thinkable as pure chance. But the more they multiply and the greater and more exact the correspondence is, the more their probability sinks and their unthinkability increases, until they can no longer be regarded as pure chance but, for lack of a causal explanation, have to be thought of as meaningful arrangements .... Their "inexplicability" is not due to the fact that the cause is unknown, but to the fact that a cause is not even thinkable in intellectual terms.[60]

This statement is noteworthy given the indirect and metaphorical manner in which modern physics approaches the deeper levels of physical reality. The constructs of modern physics have become less and less comprehensible in the terms of ordinary consciousness as it has proceeded more and more deeply into the structure of matter. Einstein's space-time dimension and the idea of curved space are not readily imaginable except in mathematical terms.[61] By the same token, we know of the unconscious indirectly or metaphorically, through its symbolic manifestations. At the symbolic level, the primary manifestation of the collective unconscious is the idea, or sense, of the Godhead. In Jung's more secular jargon, its central symbol is the *Self*.

The project of maturation, or "individuation," as Jung called it, is the integration of unconscious material — from the personal and then the collective — into the purview of consciousness. The ultimate meaning of this process is that it yields the development or evolvement of the Godhead or the Transpersonal Self. The Transpersonal Self requires the maturation of human beings for its own "maturation," and thereby human existence is invested with a divine purpose. Hence the Jungian myth of human development is what has been called the myth of the "finite God," that is, a myth that depicts God as less than perfect or incomplete and requiring human development as a vehicle to its perfection.[62] Actually, this is only partly accurate in that in the Jungian myth human beings must always *regard* God as perfect even as one discusses the Godhead in other terms. This way of seeing the human situation is odd to modern secular consciousness, but it is a familiar line of discussion in both philosophy and, as a subtheme, throughout the history of religion.

The primary task of individual development is the establishment of valid and fructifying *relationship* to the self. Since the self is superordinate, it can never be *incorporated* into consciousness; rather a kind of conscious *dialogue* is the most that is possible. In Hegelian philosophy, the *zeitgeist* was to be developed and history moved forward through the intellect exercised as *philosophy*. In the Christian humanist tradition, God is to be found and *related to* in other human beings. For Marx, *activity* was the medium of discourse and human development. The common theme, however, is how the human person, as individual, can establish and maintain continuing and appropriate symbolic contact with the divine or the transpersonal and transcendent, and further its divinity.

In Jungian theory, this contact or relationship must be established between the individual ego and the self along the *ego-self axis*. The dynamics of this relationship span the period from birth to death and can be outlined very simply. The initial stage is where the requisite *ego or individual identity* must be developed by the individual. The person must have a standpoint, a coherence, or integrity in order to relate to the self. When all goes well in an individual's upbringing, this task is helped along by the socialization process. That is, people early in life begin to adopt value positions and out of these fashion an identity. This is a process basically of taking on selective identifications with the collective unconscious, usually as it is being represented through the institutions and culture of the society within which one is raised. Such identification entails alternate selection and rejection of aspects of the unconscious. One may choose, for example, to "be honest and to tell the truth," and by so doing one rejects "dishonesty and lying." The young person's identity is constituted of a list of such positive commitments and rejections. The person thereby gains the ego strength required to negotiate his or her way through the paths of life. However, by definition, the collective *contains all, contains everything.* From the point of view of the unconscious, all the value choices made through the conscious attitude are arbitrary. The unconscious contains in potential both positive and negative energy—or what the conscious attitude calls "good" and "evil." Any value system is in principle as good as any other because under the proper relation of ego to self *it is not the value commitments of an individual that shape his or her actions.* Rather actions derive from and are conditioned by the *relation* of the individual to the self. To refer back to the earlier discussion of analogues, what counts—in terms of good and evil or destructive or constructive—is how energy is mediated as it moves from its source in the unconscious into action. Evil occurs when it either erupts or becomes blocked (which is simply prelude to eruption).

Because the unconscious is value transcendant in this way, the ego identity one develops in the first half of life must be seen as only a starting place. As one relates to the self through the ego identity and proceeds through life, one sees again and again how, in attempting to be constructive and good by applying pristine values or ideals, destructiveness or the "not good" actually results.[63] Then at midlife it is frequently the case that the life project of the individual, be it a career, family, or other ambition, is either attained and is followed by a sense that it was not so meaningful after all, or is not attained and is seen as impossible. By this ego is broken and a crisis of meaning ensues. The values and commitments of youth are gone. This crisis is the context out of which a new relation of the ego and self can form, a relation where the self is at the center of the personality and the ego ancillary to it. An "older but wiser," "humbled but stronger" personality is the result, a personality that is fit to face the ensuing reality of death.

Although I have drawn this picture mostly as backdrop to the subsequent discussion of other more specific aspects of individuation and how they bear on participation, I do want to make one comment here on the relation of the maturation cycle to the possibilities for effective social process. It is rather obvious, I think, from the Jungian perspective sketched here, that in any collection of people seeking to participate in a process together, one would find a varied distribution of developmental stages. Further, the pattern found would relate only loosely to chronological age—or any other readily observable indicator, for that matter. Although it would no doubt help ensure that effective process could be achieved if we could limit participation to mature people, in a practical sense this is not possible, except in the most approximate way. All people are always undergoing maturation, are always to some extent immature, and even can find themselves in a maturational crisis at advanced age. There seems to be no way to arrange a perfect starting place for participatory process; any group of people will present a mixture of the required capacities.

Individuation and Reflexivity

The project of maturation is one of integrating unconscious material into consciousness; how does this occur, specifically? To make this as clear as possible in the space available here, I shall sketch out a series of closely related ideas. However, I should note at the outset that the resulting picture will be partial.

The central process of personal development is *reflexibility,* a simple but difficult idea. What it means basically is that persons retroflectively consider unconscious material as it appears in their actions and otherwise in their lives generally. The unconscious, being superordinate and autonomous, shows itself typically in spontaneous and synchronous events in our lives. This can happen anytime or anywhere. Slips of the tongue and pen are simple illustrations. If these are taken seriously and reflected upon, a kind of dialogue can be established with the aspect of the unconscious that produced the behavior. If the dialogue is based in a disinterested curiosity, which in itself indicates a certain acceptance of the unconscious manifestation, the energy that created the manifestation becomes available to help out the projects of consciousness. However, consciousness cannot ever *control* this energy. Only a kind of friendly collaboration with it — or mutual regulation, as in a dance — is possible, where the unconscious joins to assist consciousness as a result of the friendly relationship consciousness has established to it. The best metaphor for representing the person who has well integrated a large amount of unconscious material is that of a group of friends who carry on a friendly conversation as they go about their business together. No one person or *ego* is in control, which means that the superordinate *self* is directing the enterprise.

The spontaneous or synchronous manifestations of the unconscious are always in a sense *intentional* in that they are specifically compensatory to the positions adopted in the conscious attitude.

The persons who assert a set of lifestyle values that center around spontaneity and fun will find that they repeatedly put themselves in situations that teach the value of rational planning and serious reflection — and vice versa. The unconscious presses consciousness toward balance and wholeness. When consciousness ignores, denies, or critically evaluates the messages of the unconscious, the contents in those messages become more energized and emerge in more and more graphic forms. The fundamental mistake that consciousness makes, typically, is to assert "shoulds" and "oughts" against the teachings of the unconscious. Instead of reflecting on the meaning of a mistake, for example, we typically issue a criticism of ourselves ("How stupid of me") followed by an injunction against repeating the behavior that led to it. We are likely, then, either to repeat the mistake or find the message that it contains confronting us more directly in the form of another kind of error or other unconscious event.

Perhaps the two major modes of reflexivity are in (1) reflecting on relationships, and (2) reflections on life structure or pattern. Two major configurations of unconscious energy typically show themselves in relationships — so typically that one might call the task of coming to terms with them a universal developmental issue for human beings. These two figures are the shadow and the contrasexual figure, the anima/animus. The shadow represents the opposite of what we like to think of ourselves as being. It is a sort of antiego. The contrasexual figure represents the idealizations we hold of the opposite sex. So as to establish the opportunity for reflexing with these major aspects of the unconscious, we project them onto love (the anima/animus) and hate (the shadow) relationships. The task of psychological development that such projections present is to separate the projection from the actual person on whom we have put it. This is done through reflexive relationship, characterized by "speaking one's heart" and "listening with one's heart" (i.e., sincerely). As the process proceeds, the energy in the projection moves back to its source point in the projecting person — thereby enhancing him or her — and a valid person to person rather than person to (projected) object relationship is established. When a love-relationship projection resolves (through successful long-term marriage, for example) each partner comes to see the other as a unique person, living their own distinctive life, rather than as someone who is there to be what the other partner wants them to be or to meet the other partner's needs. As each partner works through their projected idealizations, they find themselves having fewer "needs" that must be met by the other, and they become more independent and self-sufficient, having now the strength to be content with their partner's being simply "who they are." So too, does this occur with shadow projections, in that as one realizes that one's shadow figure is not all bad, one can begin being a little bit like the shadow and gain important new skills, behaviors, and strengths as a result. For example, if the shadow "projectee" is seen as rigid and uncooperative — unlike the flexible, generous "projector" — the projector will find being a little rigid and jealous of one's time may enhance his or her productivity and yield a new capacity for time management. I chose to discuss projection through these archetypal illustrations as a foundation for making this point plausible: projection of some sort is a universal baseline of human relationship; the relationship where it does not exist is rare if it exists at all.

The second major mode of reflexivity, with the life structure or pattern, is also universal in the human condition. In Jungian theory the idea of a life structure or pattern has a mythic quality to it. Jung's view was that all coherent and stable human collectivities, from societies down to families, possess an unconscious pattern — still part of the collective unconscious but distinctive to the given collectivity in the way that each person's body is both unique yet part of the universal human form. Members of these collectivities, he felt, inherit the unconscious pattern of the group and must struggle with the developmental issues it contains. These larger issues, indeed, form the context within which the distinctive developmental issues of the individual are met. Hence, I must in my development become more whole among other things as an American, as an organizational member where I work, as a member of my family, and as an individual. If the idea of an inherited mythic life structure is overly mystical and esoteric to some, the same phenomenon of development can be thought of in somewhat more concrete terms as a direct analogue to the widely accepted idea, from Transactional Analysis (TA) psychology of *life script*.[63] The script in TA theory is an unconsciously formed commitment to live out the entire pattern of one's life in a specific way — as often illustrated, for example, in fairy tale stories that people hold as their favorite or most memorable. The task of development is to make this implicit life structure conscious, and, by doing so, become free of its determinism and control. To become free of its control means, specifically, to transform the energy that is rigidly or determinately configured in the mythic life structure so that this energy becomes available to one's conscious discretion. In the researches of Transactional Analysis, for example, many "hamartic" or "tragic" lifescript patterns have been documented almost to the level of act, scene, and specific lines, as in an actual dramatic script. When one is enacting such a script, enormous energy is called forth, just as when actors play out a heavily tragic drama. In theatre, this energy is structured according to the stage directions and lines of the play and, hence, the "play's the thing" in the sense that it is using the actor's energy as a vehicle for speaking to the audience. Real-life actors — ones in everyday settings — perform in this same way the scripts they have been given by their families, to name one source. When the structures of these scripts are made conscious, actors no longer have to follows stage directions and speak preformed lines. They can participate in writing their own play and freely deploy their energy within it.

Anytime a group of people come together to participate in something, they form a stage setting within which each will attempt to perform a scene from his or her particular script. The more unconsciously these script patterns are held in the individuals involved, the more autonomous they will be and hence the more chaotic and irrational will be the participative collaboration in which they engage. Anyone who has been involved in many group participation efforts has experienced the differences among groups on this score. Some groups are able to focus on the task at hand and effectively work toward it. These are the ones, perhaps, whose members are not greatly dominated by unconscious life patterns. Other groups, ones where such patterns are operating autonomously and powerfully, veer off onto tangent directions that represent the vector sum of the directions indicated by the life scripts of their individual members.

Coming to terms with the mythic structure of one's life is a major, long-term matter that has, in many instances, literally life-and-death consequences for individuals. (For example, Eric Berne, the founder of Transactional Analysis, is believed by some of his followers to have died at the moment called for in his own life script.)[65]

Another dynamic involved in the process of individuation which is also important but which takes place in a shorter — indeed daily — timeframe pattern is the *ego inflation cycle*. This process has been described well by Edinger in technical terms, but it is familiar to all human beings as the basic structure of learning from experience.[66] In general, the ego inflation cycle describes the process by which "pride goeth before the fall" and as a result the formerly prideful become "older and wiser." The dynamic can be illustrated easily with the case of a young child, though no less so than with an adult professional person: the process is set in motion when the person (as ego) comes into close contact with the affirming power of a symbol of the self, as when a young boy's mother praises him for being "such a big boy" or when one's boss lays unqualified praise on one who has just had a successful performance. Such contact always tends to *inflate* the ego, as the ego experiences symbolic contact with the self as an influx of pure energy. This inflated condition often leads the person to a heroic act (e.g., crossing the street alone like the big boys) which frequently leads to a failure experience (not seeing the light change, cars screeching brakes, mother running to the rescue). The appropriate next phase is enforced exile from the self, that is, a punishment such as being sent to one's room, whereby an ego deflation is induced. This deflation period facilitates reflection and matured integration of the experience, such that one learns one's lesson and eventually is reunited with the self symbol on a new basis (when the mother instructs the boy to come out and have milk and cookies). This process is then repeated until an "adult" level of maturity is reached whereby the person is able to sense the initial inflation, foresee and thereby forewarn oneself against the heroic act and its ensuing painful exile, and hence avoid actually living through the cycle again. That is, in principle the mature adult can carry out the cycle within his or her head and hence learn to integrate the self energy consciously, in a continuing psychological process.

It seems rather obvious that this cycle of ego inflation can afflict groups and affect the process of participative collaboration. This is particularly clear in cases where the group is involved with a confrontation or conflict situation. In such instances, success experiences especially will set up tendencies toward inflation, as victory is frequently seen as a dispensation from the dieties. This sense of being favored by the gods often induces further heroic actions. History is rife with examples of success leading to excess — especially when actions are being decided upon through a participatory process — on the part of popular movements.

Individuation at the Social Level

At the level of social process, all of the dynamics of individual development that we have been discussing here — value idealism and ego development, reflexivity with unconscious figures such as the shadow and with life-course structures, and the ego inflation cycle — reduce to an issue of finding symbolic analogues that are appropriate to the developmental dynamics of the groups that comprise society and of the society itself. That is, to recall the earlier explanation of what analogues are and how they come into play in psychological development, the forms allowed for legitimate social interaction must be balanced and must conform to the pattern of psychological energy that characterizes the participants in a group. This is due to the reality that the basic *psychological* fact of *social* life is the projection of unconscious material onto the people and artifacts of the social world. For example, the individuals in any group setting, from a club meeting or a team meeting, to society itself, will project onto — that is, tend to see in — others images of psychic figures of their own with which they are in the process of coming to terms in their individual development. A man at work might well see his shadow figure sitting across the table at a staff meeting, or a woman her ideal lover or animus figure — and vice versa. Or a person might also see in collective events opportunities for expression his or her own mythic life patterns.

As was noted earlier, the strength of the tendency to project a given content of the unconscious (such as the anima) is directly related to the extent to which a given individual has reflexively encountered that content and made it conscious. Speaking loosely, we can say therefore that the more unconscious the members of a given group are, the more they will tend to project in their relations with one another, and the more capricious and difficult their social process will be. The potential represented by their interpersonal process for their mutual development also will be diminished unless precisely appropriate analogues can be found for structuring and facilitating their interaction — analogues that are appropriate in the sense discussed earlier. Every professional group facilitator is familiar with this issue. Indeed, the central focus of professional facilitation practice is the question of how to design processes that are optimal for the accomplishment of specific tasks for specific groups. At bottom, this question amounts to how to create the conditions for a stable, steady flow of energy into activity.[67] (These, in turn, are the optimal conditions for individual development; hence accomplishment of objective tasks is not just dependent upon creating conditions conducive to individual development; rather, task accomplishment and personal development are *one and the same issue*.)

What the professional group facilitator does — or is supposed to do — is carry out an accurate reading of the level of consciousness of a given group, as an index of the typical content and strength of their projections. This assessment constitutes the basis for choosing or creating structures of interaction that will both fit the pattern of projections (i.e., not disturb participants too much) and at the same time establish conditions that will challenge group members to work through, reduce, or withdraw their projections. In all except the rarest case, this is extremely difficult to do, since very little psychological information is typically available about participants in a group. Hence, rough indicators, for the most part of the degree of heterogeneity in a group, must be relied on. In general, the more homogeneous a group, the more it will share a common set of projections, and these projections will emerge more vividly in setting the culture of the group. Greater heterogeneity induces greater holding back of projections, creating a pattern of polarization of psychological energy in the group. (As an example, a group of racists can express racial prejudice among themselves but would tend to refrain from racial remarks when members of other races are present.) In turn, the more polarized the energy, the more an open field of tension is created within which the group facilitator can work in establishing analogues. The more homogeneous the group, the more limited the possibilities in that the group will create pressure for the facilitator to buy into their projections.

The general issue of projection in social process raises a paradox: under conditions where analogues for participation can be consciously fitted to a group's consciousness, the more heterogeneous the group, the more the possibility exists for an open, participative process to be productive. In fact, in homogeneous groups, it is best, usually, to restrain participation somewhat in that more open processes simply allow the group's common projections to be reified and acted out. Little or no personal development will occur in such circumstances, and pursuit of the projections will subvert task accomplishment. Interestingly, however, restraint in the form of hierarchical structure not only prevents this from happening but can also serve as the basis for a dialectical confrontation, around the issue of authority, within the group. Such confrontation can serve as a vehicle for reflexivity and consequent work on projected unconscious material — the phenomenon of southern whites and blacks becoming friends in the military service is one example of how this happens. In groups where participants are varied, a more open process, when structured appropriately, produces withdrawal of projections, subsequent individual development, and task accomplishment. All this assumes, of course, that homogeneity-heterogeneity are in fact in a given instance an accurate indication of the group's level or pattern of consciousness.

Summary

Let us summarize now what has been said about how individual development occurs as seen in this model. The general and overall pattern of the maturation cycle is that the first half of life is spent developing idealistic value commitments as the basis for the construction of an ego. The ego provides the standing point from which the other aspects of the self can be encountered and integrated through the second half of life. This integration entails, in effect, the breaking or death of the ego as a precondition to the reconstitution of the personality on a new transcendent footing solid enough to support facing one's death.

The more specific dynamics of the process involve reflexing with one's unconscious in the form of major personality figures such as the anima/animus and the shadow, and with the mythic life structure that sets the distinctive pattern of issues that is faced by each individual given his or her place in history. Reflexivity, in turn, hinges on what could be termed a learning process by which the ego undergoes a cycle of inflation, heroic action, and deflation. Also central to reflexivity is the resolution of projections of unconscious material onto the social world. How effectively this process proceeds depends critically on the symbolic analogues that the social system makes available for interpersonal interaction. These analogues must fit the pattern of consciousness of participants and, at the same time, establish enough tension within this pattern for reflexivity to occur, as in the example of the Progoff Intensive Journal mentioned earlier.

The Matter of "Consciousness"

So far in setting out this model of individual development the key term — the term that defines the direction of development — has been left unspecified. This term, of course, is *consciousness*. The aim of one's development is to *attain consciousness* or, alternatively put, to *become conscious*. Looked at in large, mythic terms this project is carried forward at the level of the individual, the group, and society itself. That is, as I develop myself, my cohorts in the primary groups to which I belong have their development furthered, and the society of which we are all a part is furthered in the development of its consciousness.

What, though, does this mean, to develop *consciousness*? In answering this central question it is necessary to be, as physicists have been about the nature of matter (i.e., in seeing it as wave *and* particle), somewhat paradoxical. On the one hand, we can on the basis of what has already been described here assert that in one sense consciousness is a *state*. That is, the mature adult attains a condition that is qualitatively different from the condition of the immature child. This condition can easily be described in the terms set out here: the adult has undergone many episodes of ego inflation and deflation and is better able to avoid heroic action; the adult has struggled with his or her shadow and contrasexual figure, has begun to integrate these into the conscious personality, and has thereby rendered the psychic energy they represent more amenable to conscious discretion. In sum, the personality of the adult is more settled and integrated; there are fewer projections and there is more energy available to the conscious side of the personality. This is, mainly, the sense in which consciousness can be seen as a condition. As I deal with the personal unconscious material that surrounds my anima (as a male) I can render it conscious such that my relationships with all women are improved. As my team at my job works through its shadow projections onto another team in the organization and withdraws this negativity, the team and the organization attain a new level of effectiveness. As a society undertakes, for another sort of example, heroic programs and suffers disillusionment with these, the people who constitute the society itself can be said to reach a new *level* of maturity.

However, there is no ultimate goal or plateau that individuals, groups, or societies can reach within any given timeframe like a lifetime or a regime. The process is endless and only stops or is interrupted by death. Hence mature adults "are also as children." They continue to face developmental issues to the ends of their lives. Further, resting on one's laurels is not allowed; to pause and gaze with self-satisfaction at one's attained level of consciousness is simply a mark of heroic ego inflation, and the fall occasioned by pride surely will soon follow. Hence, consciousness cannot be seen entirely as an attained state. It must also be regarded as a *process* or, more accurately, as a special sort of *relationship*. The essential quality of this relationship has been specified by Edward Edinger as a simultaneous *knowing and being known*.[68] That is, consciousness arises from and continues to be evoked in a context wherein the parties to a relationship are open to each other—in the sense that both or all are working to *know together*. His words on this point are worth quoting:

> We can proceed further by examining the unconscious side of the term consciousness, namely its etymology. Conscious derives from con or cum, meaning "with" or "together," and scire, "to know" or "to see." It has the same derivation as conscience. Thus the root meaning of both consciousness and conscience is "knowing with" or "seeing with" an "other." In contrast, the word science, which also derives from scire, means simple knowing, i.e., knowing without "withness." So etymology indicates that the phenomena of consciousness and conscience are somehow related and that the experience of consciousness is made up of two factors— "knowing" and "withness." In other words, consciousness is the experience of knowing together with an other, that is, in a setting of twoness.[69]

In such a relationship the major project is the resolution of projection and, hence, increasing knowledge of the other yields or is synonomous to self-knowledge. However, the main implication is that no attainment of any level of consciousness can serve as certain insurance against unconscious action. Since perfection of consciousness is attainable only in principle, not fact, the only guarantees available against unconscious action reside in maintaining participation in a conscious, which is to say an *openly knowing, relationship*. At bottom, then, individual human development is truly a *process, something that occurs between people* and within oneself, and not something that one *attains*.

The Role of Authority in Individual Development

The idea that authority can play any positive role at all in personal development may perhaps appear rather odd. The history of the humanistic psychology movement, especially as it burgeoned in the 1960s, developed in such a way that probably the most widely understood meaning of this movement was that it was above all antiauthoritarian. Personal growth came through in the development of humanistic psychology as centrally involving a casting off of restrictions— the chains of institutional roles, the strictures of parents and bosses— and moving into joyous, free, and loving relationships. On this point, modern humanistic thinking about personal growth made a drastic break with the traditions of ancient wisdom, which almost uniformly speak of personal growth as centrally involving submission, suffering, and subordination to various forms of learning disciplines and rituals.

The viewpoint of the model being stated here draws more from these earlier traditions than from satisfaction-oriented modern psychologies. This model starts in its understanding of the role of authority from the perspective that one must deal with the generic *issue* of the human condition rather than realize the inherently available *potential* of the human condition. Human development, in other words, is not seen here as inevitable to the human situation — except at the broad sociopolitical level, a matter that will be discussed subsequently. Development will occur only when people responsibly pursue consciousness.

This generic issue can be easily described using the perspective already set out. It was shown above that consciousness is only secondarily a state and is primarily a process that is set in motion through a specific type of relationship. The essence of this relationship is a struggle to carry out an *open encounter* that yields a "knowing with," a mutual, simultaneous knowing that reveals one to oneself as the other is revealed in the relationship.[70] As one reveals oneself to another, one in fact comes in contact with the unconscious. The other represents the unconscious. Progoff says in fact, that society, as the "generalized other," *is* the unconscious. Social rules must be established because consciousness is limited and cannot cope with, on its own, the stranger relations which for the most part make up society. The precondition for reflexive relationship is a well-formed ego, an ego strong enough to confront openly its own projections. An ongoing condition on which this process depends is that the available analogues for social interaction allow for coming to terms with ego issues, that is, moments when egos are in blind conflict and/or when egos are inflated and acting heroically.

Authority, in the sense of unilaterally asserted, legitimate power-based action, is essential to these conditions and hence to the process of creating and maintaining consciousness. For example, in order for ego development to proceed effectively in children, there must be an authoritative representation of a set of socially legitimate value deals to the child. That is, society must have an ego, and a typical persona, if the socialization process on which ego development depends is to occur. Legitimacy, of course, entails authority. The values that characterize a particular society must be embodied in institutions, and it is in the nature of institutions that they are invested with authority.

Multiple institutional contexts — that is, authorized political, economic, religious, educational, family, and other, settings — are essential to personal development in other ways. The core process of development, as explained earlier, is reflexivity, or the continual process of struggling to assess and define the meaning of what one is doing. Reflexivity necessitates, in turn, that an alternative viewpoint be present, there must be something to "come up against."[71] The creation of *subjective* meanings depends on the existence of *objective* meanings from which the person can initiate the process of "reflexion." In this sense one can only define oneself against society or in tension with the values its institutions represent. This is a *dialectical* tension, meaning that there must be partial congruence and partial incongruence between the individual and society.

Where there is total conformity or total nonconformity something is not being considered adequately.

This reality produces the basic paradox of human development: institutional rules must exist if we are to develop, and hence we all have a stake in establishing, maintaining, and enforcing them. Yet such rules are useful only as points of reference for how we are to live. In other words, the rules are essential, but they are not to be taken with ultimate seriousness. In a given instance breaking the rule of fidelity in marriage may be demanded for the development of the two people involved. Nonetheless, the meaning of the experience can only be constructed against a consideration of the prohibition against adultery. Each of us is in the position of invoking the rules of society on our neighbors while at the same time we may, for our development, be called upon to break the same rules to which we hold them accountable. Some Jungians believe that attacks on and critiques of authority mainly derive from the fact that most published intellectuals have been male, and male response to the paradox described above is to become critical of the rules. To Jungians, this truth is captured in a Swiss saying: "Women with a secret love ignore morality; men with a secret love argue with morality." It is essential for both, however, that both the *choice* to ignore and the *choice* to argue are presented in the context of the love relationship. Only authoritative institutions can afford such choice.

Institutions play a more obvious role in the dynamics of the ego inflation cycle, which is of course another key dimension of development. Heroic action can best be confronted within an institutional context. Outside such a context, heroic programs usually result in violence—all too often, unfortunately, violence on the scale of war. Those in positions of authority within institutions have as one of their main responsibilities the identification and confrontation of ego inflation and heroic action. The case of Oliver North and others involved in the notorious Iran-Contra affair provides a vivid contemporary example of how inflation can create dangerous heroic actions. The positive effects of such confrontation are most easily seen in the case of parents raising children through the maturational process. Coequal to the responsibility of confronting ego inflation is the authority holder's task of reintegrating the exiled, deflated heroic actor. Maturation is not furthered unless a reuniting with the authoritative symbol of the self occurs. Hence authority holders must provide reacceptance and support to the chastised actor; this is the key part of the process for strengthening the ego of the maturing person, as it gives a quality of self-acceptance to the ego-self relationship. Indeed, it is difficult to imagine making it through childhood successfully without parents (or someone) to bring us up short authoritatively on appropriate occasions and to provide the corollary reacceptance and support. What we have not realized sufficiently—though the modern literature of adult development has begun to make this clear—is that the episodes of heroic action that characterize childhood continue (in some cases only mildly abated) throughout adulthood. Having authority figures to "come up against" and to provide support is therefore as important for adults as it is for children.

As to the individuation process generally, authority is also critical to the process of resolving projections. Especially in the case of shadow projections and other projected unconscious material that can lead to interpersonal conflict, the self — the symbol of integration and unification — must be represented in the form of authoritative figures in the situation. The traditional army anecdote of the master sergeant handling personal animosities between two of his troops illustrates this point well. When he found two men who were fighting he first assigned them to the task of filling sandbags — a task requiring, of course, that one hold the bag open while the other shoveled. If they continued to fight, he then assigned them to wash a large number of windows together — with one inside, the other outside — without leaving any unwashed spots on either side. If this did not work, he then required each to draw a picture of the other, producing as exact a likeness as humanly possible. As the story goes, his techniques never failed to settle the hostility. The psychological principle at work here is the one under discussion: resolving distorted, hateful images of the other through continued contact and revised, more accurate, perception of the other. When conflicted parties are in the grip of negative feelings toward each other, it is helpful if they are under the purview of an authority who can impose the task of resolving the projections on them. Even then, of course, the projections may persist and have to be acted out through open conflict; however, the effective use of authority can often prevent such conflict.

Authority and Management

It is perhaps clear, or at least suggested, from this sketch how authority can play a positive role for human development, and insight that runs profoundly opposite to the traditional folk wisdom about how management authority can be used effectively. The prevailing images, it seems safe to say, of what management authority is for, and how it is to be used, are that the manager is given authority for the purpose of putting pressure on employees to perform better and produce more. It is rather amazing that this belief continues to prevail so widely in the world of formal organizations, given that research into the question of how close and punitive supervision affects performance and productivity has long shown that it yields only (at best) short-run improvements that are in the long run outweighed by the costs of its other, negative effects like employee turnover, absenteeism, sabotage, and so forth.[72] Perhaps the explanation lies in the fact that managers, through dealing with people on the intimate day-to-day basis that characterizes organizational life, come to hold a strong, and valid, belief that people need authority even though they are unsure as to what this means.

The confused and incorrect way in which this valid belief comes to be acted out in practice seems to derive from a failure in both the folklore of management and the formal theory that has developed around it to distinguish sufficiently between *performance* issues and *behavior* and *attitude* problems—that is, between the employee as producer and the employee as person. Behavior problems are such matters as, at the less significant level, tardiness, unjustified absenteeism, fomenting discord among colleagues, and so on, to, at the genuinely serious level, drug addiction, alcoholism, threatening or actually violent behavior, and the like. A great deal is known about how to improve the quality of performance of people at work. It seems fair to say that both research and practice have established the effectiveness of a number of strategies and tactics for performance improvement. An inventory of these would certainly include: (1) Analyzing the work flow through a systems analysis—this answers such objective questions as whether materials and tools are of sufficient quality and the work process organized optimally. (2) Technical information and advice—this is usually delivered through training. (3) Feedback—the employee may not be realizing how and what he or she is doing. Lack of such surface information is perhaps the commonest type of human behavior issue. What is required therefore is that the person be given information about such matters in the form of *feedback*. The distinctive characteristic of feedback is that it is a specific, technically designed format for presenting information about a person's behavior to him or her. The principles on which it is based are impersonality and objectivity, in the sense that it is specific and descriptive rather than general and judgmental. The popular image of feedback is that it is any sort of frank, authoritative communication. Employees are heard to say, "I got some feedback from the Boss today: Shape up or ship out." This image could not be further from the principle on which feedback is based. If it is to work in changing the person's behavior, it must not be threatening in this overt sense. (4) Managerial counseling—this tactic is appropriate where the performance issue is embedded so deeply in the work situation that only the employee, as the person most immediately involved, can know the answer. This intensive firsthand involvement, however, often clouds the vision. Hence, what the employee needs is an opportunity to step back, listen to himself or herself reflect about the situation, and thereby sort out the best line of action for improving performance. The manager plays the role of the counselor, the person who creates the psychological space and provides the reflective listening that the employee needs in order to clarify his or her sense of the situation. When such counseling is used effectively it allows the subordinate to create solutions for tough problems in blocked situations. (5) Appropriate placement actions—the person must be moved to a position that better suits his or her capacities, skills, or proclivities. In the circumstance where none of the preceding tactics work, it is probably the case that the person is in the wrong place and what is called for is an *appropriate placement* action. Assuming that the other improvement measures have been used, this would not be seen even by the subject employee as a firing or a punishment, in that the true intent of the move is to make both the employee and the organization better off.

In sum, what must be emphasized here is that *none of the measures just reviewed involve the use of authority* in its conventional, connotative sense. Rather, they are more accurately described as collaborative efforts to problem-solve. Further, these actions represent the best of what is currently known about how to improve performance most effectively at least cost. (Why bother to fire the cook and find and hire another one when a bit of feedback that the soup is under salted will bring about the needed improvement?) The use of authority as conventionally conceived has little or nothing to do with improving, for the long run, performance.

Paradoxically, however, although improving performance is widely claimed to be the primary issue managers face, the fact is that it occupies less of their time and energy than responding to top management and employee behavior problems. However, managers do not like to see themselves as involved with their employees' behavior and attitude problems. The truth of this is reflected in the research literature on management where, until very recently, one can find virtually no discussion of these matters. The recent rather widespread establishment of employee assistance programs in both public- and private-sector organizations is evidence that the scope of the management relationship to employees is in a process of redefinition. Managers and academic theorists alike have preferred to define the manager role in rationalistic terms, as having to do only with the technical questions of performance and productivity. "I didn't hire my employees to raise them," managers like to say, indicating that they want nothing to do with a parent like role toward their employees. such a role seems inappropriately intimate, and managers feel awkward and unprepared to play it. To academic theorists, such a role comes too close to putting the manager in the posture of being a therapist or clinician for the employee, and hence violates the boundaries of disciplines and the canon that professionals stay within defined boundaries of expertise.

In fact, though, practicing managers, and academics with broad contact with the working world of organization and management, generally acknowledge, however reluctantly, that management *necessarily* demands that managers deal with subordinates at the level of personal behavior and that, indeed, the managerial relationship is unavoidably intimate — even approaching that of parent and child. Still, *general practice is to define behavior issues in performance terms and then use the authoritative position of the manager to put general pressure on the subordinate to change.* Such pressure does not improve performance; what is does do is seriously confuse the situation and work to give managerial authority a bad name.

What would help this situation is for managers to learn to separate clearly a performance problem and a behavior problem, face each squarely on its own terms, and apply appropriate techniques to the two different situations. This change is indeed happening at present, as a conceptual literature dealing with "difficult employees" is developing and this is providing the basis for management training about the problem.[73] However, there is truth to the point that managers ought not try to be parents or therapists to their subordinates. That is, the managers' actions in such situations must be limited or bounded by both considerations of expertise and the structure of the manager-subordinate relationship—that is, the relationship is at bottom an instrumental contract, not kinship or friendship. Hence, what is helpful and appropriate for managers to do regarding the behavior issues of subordinates?

This can best be described, perhaps, by discussing first the typical mistake that managers make in these situations: namely, that they all too often do indeed behave like bad parents. They become personally involved with the employee's behavior, let themselves be angered by it, express or act on the anger toward the subordinate, thereby becoming embroiled in a conflict situation. Alternatively, they just as frequently avoid facing the situation entirely, perhaps to the point of ignoring it or even covering it up. This results in an escalation of the problem to a point where it explodes into the open and must then be dealt with on a disaster-control basis. The more effective strategy is for the manager to create a confrontation while preventing the eruption of a conflict. The difference is basically this: in a confrontation, subordinates are put up against themselves — it is a *self-facing* episode.[74] In conflict, the manager himself or herself comes up against the subordinate — it is an *interpersonal dispute* episode, complete with agitation and aggression. Great changes can result from self-facing confrontation; no change and great pain are the almost certain outcome of conflict.

The key to creating effective confrontation is above all to show genuine concern and reserve hostile feelings. The texture of confrontation must be emotional flatness and objectivity contained in a context of concern for the subordinate as a person. The manager must be genuine, authentic, and must make interpersonal contact with the subordinate. Then, an objective rendering of the facts of the situation as seen by or available to the manager must be made, followed by a hearing of the facts as seen by the subordinate. That is, the situation must be mutually, not unilaterally, defined. Feelings about the subordinates' behavior, and the consequences of it for others and for the organization, can be described. Most importantly, authority must be exercised; a line must be drawn that, if overstepped by the subordinate, will set in motion certain clearly and definitely specified consequences. The manager, then, must ensure that the consequences are made real in exactly the terms specified at the confrontation.

In general terms this is an adumbration of how authority can be used effectively in dealing with behavior issues. It does not place the manager in an inappropriate role posture or call for clinical expertise, but such confrontation has been shown by experience to be helpful to people suffering from problematic psychological condition — even serious conditions like alcoholism. The confrontation may invoke the deeper strengths of the person to avoid the authoritatively specified consequences. Confrontational authority thus has a definite and positive role to play in the resolution of such issues.

The entire question of the use of authority in confrontations around behavior problems, however, must be viewed in a broader perspective. From this viewpoint one can see that the personal stakes involved in these episodes *run both ways*, which is to say that the potential for personal gain and loss inhere in both the manager's as well as the subordinate's position. Looked at from a Jungian perspective behavior problems are simply indicators that a personal developmental episode — a maturation crisis — is underway in the individual exhibiting the problematic behavior. However, as is well known in the clinical arena, whenever such problems occur the personal development, if not the mental hygiene, of those associated closely with the "presenting patient" (as the person who is defined as having a problem is termed) is called into the balance. [75] Just as it is not an accident that we fall in love with a given person (our anima or animus figure) or come to despise another given person (our shadow figure), it is likewise no accident that one is the manager to a specific person who begins to exhibit a particular behavior problem. Indeed, managers, since they have hiring, promotion, and other authority, frequently arrange unconsciously to come in contact with persons who will present them with the specific issues that they need to face in their own personal development. It is true to lesser and greater degrees that subordinates present managers with issues the managers need to face in their own development, but it is almost always true to some extent. This means that managers should not be seen as people of superior maturity (or knowledge, or anything else) who are unilaterally deciding for or judging others. Managers have as much, psychologically speaking, hanging in the balance as subordinates. Projection is a part of every human relationship, and managerial relationships are typically fraught with it. Even managers who have no explicit knowledge of projection or who abhor psychologizing about things frequently exhibit an intuitive awareness of it when they are about to exercise authority. For example, very few managers are willing quickly and summarily to fire employees from their jobs, even in cases where the employees's attitude or performance seems clearly to merit this. Managers are prone to worry, even when they speak otherwise, about whether they are misperceiving the situation and acting arbitrarily. The prototype case illustrating this point perhaps, is that common instance in which a workaholic manager hires a subordinate who follows a personal health maintenance program. To the manager, jogging at lunchtime, rather than "working through at your desk with a sandwich," amounts to laziness if not irresponsibility. In cases like this, it is likely that the subordinate is a shadow figure for the manager and represents the manager's own underdeveloped capacity to be lazy, that is, relax. If the manager ignores this possibility (which almost inevitably will be presented to him or her by intuition) and acts unilaterally and decisively — for example, by summarily firing the "lazy" subordinate, the potential for redeeming his or her own capacity to manage work stress is lost. Through struggling to work out a relationship with the subordinate, both could have come to appreciate the other's qualities more and been enhanced as they each brought out the part of themselves that was like the other. The manager might thereby avoid an impending heart attack, and the employee might gain a greater appreciation of the self-esteem that can be won through committed work performance.

As we reconceptualize authority, therefore, and see its positive contributions to human development, we must also see that authority used positively is authority used dialectically, in a two-way, back-and-forth process where all concerned can contribute to the construction of the factual picture of the situation in question. There is a special burden carried by those in positions of authority, however. This is the burden of final action. There are never final guarantees that a chosen line of action is correct, that it is not based on a misconstruction of the situation. Yet choices must be made and actions taken. This is the double bind that gives the idea of responsibility its distinctive quality. Authority holders are usually not subject to the material consequences of authoritative action—that is, they decide that others lose their jobs—on the other hand, they are always subjects to the psychological consequences of their actions.

Antiauthority ideologues often use the misbehavior of actual authority holders as an argument against authority itself. This is to make the same error as those who argue against participation on the grounds that it has in fact gone wrong so frequently as people have attempted to use it as a decision process. It is a curious sort of ad hominum argument, weak because it fails to consider that most behavior is carried out in ignorance of principle, yet it seeks to hold principle responsible. In the instance of authority, though, a case can be made from practical experience, if we broadly consider the family- and primary-group associations, as well as formal organizational contexts, as arenas in which the exercise of authority in the sense described here is carried out. Few among us do not appreciate at least some of the authoritative actions of even bad parents, and we have even more appreciation of the times that friends have acted authoritatively toward us—as illustrated by the contemporary bumpersticker, "Friends don't let friends drive drunk." One may quite justifiably believe that anarchy is desirable and feasible at some point in the evolution of the human psyche when we have all become angels, but the plain facts of everyday life seem to indicate that, for now, authority can and does play a necessary and positive role in human affairs.

Participation and Authority in the Public Administration

The central purpose of this chapter is to redeem both participation *and* authority for the world of public administrative action. The argument has been that participation, as effective social process, depends critically on certain preconditions that in turn depend upon a given level of human maturation or development. Maturation and development, in turn, depend upon the existence of stable and effective authoritative institutions and the *proper* exercise of authority within and from them. The proper exercise of authority, in turn, depends upon the achievement of a kind of openness with subordinates that is characteristic of *participation. Effective participation requires authority; effective authority requires participation.* Each is the dialectical complementarity of the other, and both form the dialectic that is at the center of the whole, *ultimately important, project of human development* — the project, in my view, that is the source of meaning in individual, social, and political life.

One of the things about The Public Administration that makes it truly distinctive institutionally — and has not been realized sufficiently — is that we as a society expect public administrative organizations to express the best of our ideals as regards human relationship, human development, and social life. This can be seen clearly in the legislated personnel policies of public agencies, such as affirmative action. Fortunately, the pressure to embody these particular ideals has now spread outside the public sector, but there will and should be other "ideals" for which the public sector should be given the task of standard bearer. Perhaps the societal attack on drug abuse will be the next of these. In any event, the public sector must remain the core, the source of the influence we wish to give such ideals. It is, then, no less than off the point to apply the calculus of instrumental rationality to public-sector agencies. They must be efficient and effective, but as efficient and effective *as they can be while giving expression to our higher ideals of human development.* Society exists for the people who make it up, not for itself. Hence when surveillance, for example, or any other government action becomes so broadly and efficiently carried out that it compromises the quality of life, it must be curtailed. In this sense it can be said that although public administration is about the attainment of social goals, these goals must find their reference point in the individual development of citizens. Hence public administration is, at bottom, about the resolving of the human psyche.

As such, we can see a number of characteristics of The Public Administration as an institution that make it distinctively conducive to the carrying out of the dialectic of participation and authority. As such, The Public Administration is a natural place from which society can carry forward the project of human development. Indeed, it may be the only place remaining for this projects, and it may be that developments in politics and society are compromising this potential.

Public Administration and Effective Social Process.

In principle the Public Administrator is placed in a position within The Public Administration that is favorable for the creation of effective process. First, the *groundedness* discussed earlier as an essential ingredient of process is helped greatly by the Public Administrator's orientation to the public interest. As a transcendent point of reference, the symbol of the public interest provides the administrator with a foundation for a sense of *vocation* as well as *career.* The career orientation is one that typically denies a sense of groundedness, since career success must be judged in relative, market terms. To judge how one is doing in one's career, one looks at how well others are doing in their careers.

This creates a sort of "exchange value" rather than a "use value" sensibility. The hallmark of the sense of vocation is that it symbolically connects one's individual activities directly to something transcendent or larger than oneself and thereby imbues the individual's life work with a sense of *intrinsic* meaning. The idea of the public administrator as *citizen*, as contributing member of the larger body politic, adds to this sense of groundedness.

Second, the administrator lives, perforce, in a subordinate posture — owing to the constitutional position of administration in our structure of government.[76] The administrator has no ultimately unilateral power. All administrative actions are hedged on all sides — by the executive, by the courts, by the legislature and, indeed, by the interested parties toward whom the actions are to be taken. Hence, the posture of the true scientist is called for: the administrator must seek to be heard and must hear. Through this process a temporary consensus can be built that will support administrative action. Subordination tends to enforce the openness that social process requires.

Third, at least relatively, the issues dealt with in the administrative process are *concrete* and *immediate*. This is perhaps the clearest hallmark of the agency perspective. The source point of the information system in administration is the actual, a specific case of the welfare mother and abused children, the toxic waste threat, the drug-smuggling operation, and so on. The physical and moral dimensions of social choices are therefore quite clear to the public administrators who deal directly with them. The physical and moral dimensions of selling more automobiles, if any, are less readily apparent to managers for General Motors. Even the abstractions of budget numbers can and should carry specific human meaning to the Public Administrator.

Fourth, The Public Administration, as a formal institutional context, provides an excellent arena for experimenting in the revision of language patterns such that the collective irrationalities of the organization are reduced. More so than with the other traits under discussion, private-sector organizations also hold this potential. They can be interested in it, however, only so far as such revisions lead to the attainment of their instrumental market purposes. The more transcendent purposes of public-sector organizations allow for a broader and deeper interest. Most of what constitutes management training should be teaching people in organizations how to talk and listen to one another differently than they are now doing. These revised communications procedures do work, and they work primarily because they create the proper space between the required communicating parties. Perhaps at this point the most visible attempts to explicitly structure language and communication processes in the administrative arena occurred in experiments in participative planning. Public agencies can legitimately seek to implement linguistic techniques that improve social process.[77]

Public Administration as a Source of Authority for Human Development

Just as The Public Administration presents those who enter it (and interact with it) especially advantageous conditions for furthering human development through the attainment of effective participative processes, so is it similarly conducive to the use of authority to this effect. Most vivid on this point is the role that administrative agencies play in presenting the official, core values that define American society. Having such a value set, as explained above, is basic to the process of ego development in children and to creating the sense of community needed to contain adult relationships. The school system, of course, is probably most influential in this role, but the basic project is carried out at all levels of government. The widely known story of the Wizard of Oz provides a descriptive, mythic image of the way The Public Administration fulfills this function. The Wizard and the City of Oz are of course symbols of ultimate authority and the source of positive transformations and benefits. What the story reveals, though, is that the Wizard's power is symbolic in the truest sense. He only provides the analogues (i.e., the Tin Woodsman's clock heart, the Scarecrow's degree, etc.) for the actual personal transformations that must occur within each of the characters and be wrought through their own actions. This is the role that government administrators play: they represent positive values and provide the analogues through which individual and social development can occur — as the people who compose society accomplish it.

The discussion of authority earlier indicated something of how authoritative public administrative institutions facilitate the processes of resolving projection and ego inflation. Government personnel policy and management processes are or should be models for organizational relationships in society generally. Changes in government policy in these areas carry direct implications for social change generally. This is why opposition to the comparable worth-pay movement has been so vehement. Its opponents recognize that the administrative change it seeks entails a drastic revision in the currently prevailing market method for pricing wages. It is also why some presidential administrations have sought to give expression to their political viewpoints through revision of administrative policies and practices. The Reagan Administration's actions in this regard are especially instructive. Its attack was not aimed at government itself as much as it was aimed at the government employee. "Fire the bureaucrats and hire contractors to do the work," seemed to be the idea. Hence, most of what has happened has been an effort to carry out a symbolic shift from valuing the public servant to valuing the entrepreneur. Affirmative action, special employees development, and other such programs are examples in the other direction. How management authority is deployed and used in government administration is a critically important expression of the identity of a society.

Also, the effort to implement national policy through our federal system has fomented an enormous amount of dialogue about our social values as our varying localistic value system have come into confrontation with the national viewpoint. The extent to which we have hammered out an identity as a national community through this process has been too much overlooked.[78] Yet the challenge to continue this project remains or is even heightened by the increasing heterogeneity of the population. Such dialogue, contained within the framework of the authoritative implementation of public policy, is probably the best vehicle available to us, as a society, for creating conscious relationship.

As a footnote to these comments about the compatibility of The Public Administration with the dialectical relation of participation and authority, I would note that the growing use, over the past decade or so, of the matrix form of organization serves as one affirmation of these assertions.[79] Matrix organization, which embodies both hierarchical structure and a system of participative, flexible teams may well fit the action implications for organization design that flow from the perspective being set out here. The same may be said of the Deming management system (which the Japanese have used with such excellent success) that has been installed in some technical-production type matrix organizations.[80] The recent apparent disaffection, under the Reagan Administration, with the matrix form of organization is one other sign among many that important intrinsic capacities are being devalued in favor of making overhead political control as complete as possible.

What About Politics?

The broad claims I have just stated about the salutary effects of The Public Administration in society raise the question of what role politics plays in social life in the reframed way of looking at things that is being presented here. In answering this question, I must begin by noting that politics as a social process must be accorded ultimate respect; the political process is the means by which society heals its collective problems, the problems caused by the limits of the consciousness of its citizens. As noted earlier, consciousness in human beings in never perfect. Every individual is subject to the autonomous activity of the unresolved unconscious material that inevitably resides in his or her psyche. Societies can be identified by the unconscious patterns that characterize the individuals who constitute them. These patterns are made manifest in collective projections (as between the United States and the Soviet Union) and in unbalanced or distorted institutional structures and role relationships (as with racism, sexism, etc.). The intrinsic tendency of the psyche, however, is always to seek wholeness and balance. This might occur through unconscious compensations. For example, in societies where men put themselves in dominant power positions, they do so by constructing authority systems like large-scale formal organizations that strongly embody the feminine principle. Such organizations tend to dominate them psychologically through the mother complex.[81] The great-mother bureaucracy provides security but on the other hand devours the creativity of the people who staff it. Such compensations, though, work only for the time being in that ultimately the underlying imbalances — which actually reflect projections that have become institutionalized — must be resolved through the individual development of a sufficient number of persons such that the institutional patterns are changed. The dialectic of generations — the struggle to resolve projections through parent-child relationships—is a powerful source of this type of change.

One function of politics is to confirm or validate developments that have been accomplished in this manner. (The case of the U.S. Supreme Court's action in *Gideon* v. *Wainwright*, where it affirmed a change that seemed far reaching but the basis for which had in fact already been laid in society, is something of an illustration of this.[82] (This is a strategy the Court has followed often in its history.) This is the happy and easy side of politics, and it is unfortunate that so little of what goes on in the political arena is of this nature.

When change at the individual level does not proceed rapidly enough, however, or when collective projections are the basis for launching heroic societal endeavors, social development must occur. Society, rather than having its development carried forward by individuals, must attempt to heal itself. Politics is this healing process. Politics, then, is above all the process by which societies come to terms with eruptions of unconscious energy, eruptions that occur because the symbolic analogues of the society have become inappropriate to its pattern of development. These eruptions may be minor and indicate mere adjustment, or they may be major and require large-scale restructuring of institutional patterns.

Politics in this light is a form of curative disease and, as such, we should not expect it to reflect consistently the characteristics of effective social process or participation as those have been described here. Politics is a power game, a game based on the pulling and hauling of interested parties' attempts to dominate. Hence, it, by its very nature, cannot be rational in the way that participation can be in principle. Socrates's speech explaining why he was going to drink the hemlock is an eloquent statement of this paradoxical nature of politics and political obligation. Politics is society struggling to settle itself through structured disruption. Politics is a collective process, a process that deals in the irrational.

Absolutely no disrespect is implied by this characterization. The collective, the irrational, are alternative names for the unconscious. Politics is the process by which a society relates to its unconscious. Politics has therefore a certain transcendent quality of its own that is unique to it. It is the process through which a society lives out its collective destiny. It is through politics that society launches heroic actions, and suffers out and learns from the failure of these. It is through politics that the dramas of societal character flaws are brought to denouement. Politics is the process of individuation writ at the scale of the collective.

Hence, we must accord politics our ultimate respect as an institutional process. At the same time, we must realize that the prevalence and predominance of politics in a society is a sign of ill health at the level of the individual psyche. Political movements are symptoms of insufficiency in the pace and quality of transformation at the individual level. This fact provides insight into the nature of political involvement. Involvement or participation in politics is something like catching the flu. Those who are vulnerable to the infection of political movements are the ones who possess issues of personal development that are congruent with the broader developmental issues of the society they are in, the issues that are reflected in problematic policies. As an illustration, we can take the United States in the 1960s and 1970s. During this period U.S. society experienced much reaction to the policy and institutional imbalances manifest in such issues as racism, sexism, the Vietnam War, poverty, the meaninglessness of middle-class materialism, and so forth. Given individuals were drawn into particular combinations of the movements that developed around these issues based on the congruence of their personal issues with the social issues. The Vietnam War, it seems fair to say, reflected an overassertion, an imbalanced use, of executive authority and national power. Those who mainly fueled the reaction to it were young people, who typically face in their own development the issue of reacting to authority. The authority problem of youth erupted with particular vividness in the 1960s probably because the baby boom generation reached adolescence and young adulthood at a time when institutional analogues of the 1950s seemed to be so naively rigid. Politics as we typically know it, therefore, is as much a symptom of the problem as it is an answer to it — or, as mentioned above, a curative disease.

Again, to say this is not to denigrate politics. As far as I can understand the matter so far, the ideal of effective social process must be approximated to many degrees. While the closer one comes to the ideal the better, important, more positive, effects can be gained from even the crudest gestures in the direction of it. Our democratic structures are far more than gestures toward the ideal, and no doubt they have saved us from disaster even as they have worked only approximately and imperfectly. Further, we must remember that ideals and perfections are just that; they are not conditions of the actual world. It is perhaps inevitable that cure and amelioration are part of the function of democratic politics.

There is, then, at least this sense in which the "politics-administration dichotomy" is true and real. Each provides a qualitatively (though at some deep and generic level they are related) different mode of moving forward the project of human development. Just as constitution writing is birth, so then is politics youth, and administration maturity, in the developmental cycle of societies. Dealing with the suffering and struggle of life is less costly and less wearing when we can contain these within the processes of administration. This does not make administration a higher form of social process than politics, however; rather it shows it simply to be a more settled aspect. Administration represents maturity, but where would we be without youth? In short, there is no better or worse of it as regards politics and administration; we need, and if we are fortunate will always have, both.

Conclusion: The Fatal Third Alternative of Technocratic Domination

There is, however, a villain in this piece, and in discussing this I will reveal this underlying motive of my attempt here to reframe the way we see the issue of authority and participation. The distortion that has emanated from the confused debate about authority and participation, especially the distortion of seeing one as good and the other as bad, has been one major factor in obscuring perception of the true danger that resides in the *specter of technicism*. What we must truly fear is that technical decision will become our dominant social process.[83]

Positive social process, from the perspective used here, is dialectical. Social process must draw its vital energy from the continuous polarization and resolution of opposites. As such, social process can never be rational in the usual sense of the term as "efficiently instrumental." However, the debate pitting authority against participation has tended to put the question in terms of which works better, that is, which is more efficiently instrumental, given the realities of human nature. This conceptual aberration had the effect of helping to move instrumental rationality into position as a superordinate value. In short, our confusion about the relation of authority and participation to social life has helped provide legitimation for the very value foundation needed to support the ascendancy of the technological imperative.

What though, is the so-called technological imperative? In the context of this essay, we can see its shape quite vividly in the sense of human life that it entails. To the technicist's viewpoint, the purpose of human life is truncated to meeting survival requirements and reducing physical drives through gratification. As Manfred Stanley puts it, "Technicism reduces the humanly possible to the technologically available."[84] Life is about "staying alive until you die and getting your kicks along the way." Absent is the notion that life draws its meaning from the project of enhancing the human psyche, the human soul. (Technicists ask, "*What* is the soul?")

When life is reduced in this way, choice and action become reified as rational calculation and efficiency. Action is evaluated by the apparent efficacy of its more *immediate* and *easily discernible effects*. Hence, technicism must pursue, can only pursue, a morality of system. Its point of reference for judging acceptability of anything is the effect it will have on the system — which means the institutions and processes that provide only necessities and gratification. Any activity is acceptable as long as it can be organized into the system and its deleterious effects neutralized. Technicism amounts to nothing less that a specter — a specter that portends the diminishment and possible loss of the human principle itself. Such strong language is appropriate because not only is this threat serious, it is insidious. Its primary trap is the powerfully appealing symbol of rational mastery, which holds out the chimeric promise that all human suffering can be eliminated through the exercise of thought and will.

The alternative view offered here is that suffering is an inescapable part of the human condition. Participation entails "suffering," and authority must be "suffered." To suffer as I am using the term here means to be involved as a whole person rather than as a role player, to be involved, in other words, at the level of genuine feeling. At the same time suffering is compensated for by progress made in human development. To the dialectical view each aspect of life is like this, entailing both suffering and reward, negative and positive.

Perhaps ultimate domination by technicism can be avoided through politics, through a groundswell reaction that creates a large-scale reorientation of our institutions. The Populist Movement in the United States appears to have been something like this to the extent that it was energized by a revulsion against large-scale corporate organizations, the new logic of economic efficiency they entailed, and the diminishment of a communitarion sense of government. The danger exists, though, that politics itself can be overwhelmed by the appeal of the technicist promise of heaven on earth. The curative disease can in some instances be fatal. I, for one, see all too many signs of this happening.

The Public Administration offers one line of response to the threat of technicism. It offers a counter-model of efficiency that stands as a true alternative to technicist efficiency. We might call this counter-model *social efficiency*, an efficiency that balances technical and political considerations for the common good and the best ideals of society. This is the efficiency of the public interest. The very ineffability of the public interest is the best indicator of its power and supremacy as a moral symbol for government. Further, we can see that action toward the public interest is conscious action. The *public interest is public consciousness*. The ideas of public interest and consciousness are in all dimensions congruent. Each can be seen as a state, as embodied in a specific action or policy, and as embodied in goals toward which we can strive. Yet both are at a more generic level *processes* that are set in motion by the attainment of a special sort of relationship. The public interest, like consciousness, can only exist as people *live it out with each other*. In seeking the public interest in this way we can achieve *isonomy*, the highest form of government: *rule by all in relationship.*

It is because the public interest, like consciousness, entails the principle of human development that it is undefinable in concrete terms. Like human development, the public interest is a process that is not amenable to easy calculation. We must reassert and cling to this symbol. Some readers of the Blacksburg Manifesto see in it a naive shortsightedness that overlooks the dangerous tendency for organizations holding to an agency perspective to become autonomous systems operating for their own sake. This danger is real, though, only when we lose sight of the symbol of the public interest. The public interest is a definitive barrier against technicism because it is embodied in the relationships of the agency to the citizens. It asks not only what is good for society in the long run — this question taken alone is a technicist vision of the public interest. It also asks at the same time, "How are actual, specific people being dealt with, treated, and related to *now*?"

What this chapter calls for in the final analysis is that we sort out our thinking about the issue of authority and participation so that we can refocus our attention on the primary symbol held in the tradition of the field: the public interest. It is a call for a return to roots. Any such reexamination must start with a study of the intellectual integrity of the field itself. Public administration has always been intellectually catholic and has derived great vigor from this openness. However, overfascination with measurement, methodological technique, the positive models of economics, and the like, has opened a door through which the perspective of technicism had invaded the field. All such devices have tremendous potential as working techniques, and I value this power as much as most, but they all were intended for application in practice within a living moral framework. When they are used without such a framework they begin to implement the implicit morality — or nonmorality — of technicism. Again, it is of critical importance that we reassert the central identity of the field as a moral enterprise.

As I read them, current sociological conditions in the field are not highly favorable to this renaissance of identity. What I have written here, for example, if it were translated into the jargon of those years, would have been readily understood and accepted in the field in the late 1950s, when I was working on an M.P.A. degree. In the time since then I have seen the field move in new intellectual directions and even diversify, but its central tendency has been to become more and more narrow and restricted at the core. These days, the orthodoxy in the field seems to hold that Aristotelian logic is the only logic, empiricism the only method, and statistical text the only rule of truth. The influence of this core perspective is such that even those who do not subscribe to and work from such an identity have become influenced by it, and discount or shun dialectical discourse, where terms are approximately specified, where evidence is seen as illustrative, and where the rule of truth is interest and plausibility.[85] Further, there seems also in this core identity a wish to avoid the psychological level of analysis.

In this context, this essay is highly vulnerable to discount or even dismissal. My best hope is that it will have two sorts of appeal: (1) at the unconscious level, where it might strike a responsive note in the perhaps implicitly developing but pervasive concern that people generally seem to have about the direction life is taking in technologically advanced societies; and (2) at the conscious level, where perhaps at least some will agree with me that we must not only *not* drop but should vigorously reassert moral dialogue around the public interest as the central identity of the field, and that when we engage in this project, it is appropriate and necessary to be both psychological and dialectical.[86] Nothing less than society itself and ultimately even the human principle is at stake in the matters discussed here. Ours is an organizational society, and The Public

Administration contains our only official organizations. How we shape and operate these organizations sets the course of our future.

Notes

1. Edmund Burke, *Reflections on the Revolution in France* (New York: Liberal Arts Press, 1955).

2. Thomas Hobbes, *Leviathan* (New York: The Liberal Arts Press, 1958); and John Locke, *Second Treatise on Government* (New York: The Liberal Arts Press, 1952).

3. A. Sigler, ed., *The Conservative Tradition in American Thought* (New York: Capricorn Books, 1964); Walter E. Volkomer, ed., *The Liberal Tradition in American Thought* (New York: Capricorn Books, 1969); and Kenneth M. Dolbeare and Patricia Dolbeare, *American Ideologies* (Chicago: Rand McNally, Collins Publishing Co., 1976).

4. Dwight Waldo, *The Enterprise of Public Administration* (Novato, Calif: Chandler and Sharp, 1981).

5. H. Gerth and C. Wright Mills, eds., *From Max Weber: Essays on Sociology* (New York: Oxford University Press, 1946).

6. Roscoe Pound, "The New Feudalism," *American Bar Association Journal* 16 (September 1930): 355-358.

7. Allyn A. Morrow and Frederick C. Thayer, "Materialism and Humanism: Organization Theory's Odd Couple," *Administration and Society* 10 (May 1978): 86-106.

8. Alvin Gouldner and Richard A. Peterson, *Notes on Technology and the Moral Order* (Indianapolis: Bobbs-Merrill, 1962); Richard Sennett, *Fall of Public Man* (New York: Knopf, 1977); and Peter Berger, Brigitte Berger, and Hansfried Kellner, *The Homeless Mind* (New York: Vintage, 1974).

9. William A. Schambra, "The Roots of the American Public Philosophy," *Public Interest* 67 (Spring 1982): 36-48.

10. Robert C. Tucker, ed., *The Marx-Engels Reader* (New York: W. Norton, 1972).

11. Frederick C. Thayer, *End to Hierarchy and Competition Administration in the Post-Affluent World* (New York: New Viewpoints, 1981).

12. Frederick C. Thayer, "Award-Winning Research: A Critique," *The Journal of Applied Behavioral Science* 18, 1 (1982); Administrative Reform as of 1980: A Critical View," *Politics, Administration and Change* 6, 1 (Jan.-June 1980), Bangladesh); "Organization Theory as Epistemology: Transcending Hierarchy and Objectivity," in Carl Bellone, ed., *Organization Theory and the New Public Administration* (Boston: Allyn and Bacon, 1980); "Values, Truth, and Administration: God or Mammon?" *Public Administration Review* (Jan./Feb. 1980); The President's Management Reforms: Theory X Triumphant," *Public Administration Review* (July/August 1978); Collaborative Work Settings: New Titles and Old Contradictions," *Journal of Applied Behavioral Science* (with Allyn Morrow) (September 1977); "And Now the Deregulators: When Will They Learn?" *Journal of Air Law and Commerce* 4 (1977) (published 1978); "the NASPAA Threat," *Public Administration Review* (Jan./Feb. 1976); and "On Man, Work, Society, Income, Property and Theft," *The Bureaucrat* (Spring 1974).

13. Frederick C. Thayer, *Rebuilding America: The Case for Economic Regulation* (New York: Praeger, 1984).

14. Rensis Libert, *New Patterns of Management* (New York: McGraw-Hill, 1961).

15. Benjamin Ward, *What's Wrong with Economics* (New York: Basic Books, 1972); Oskar Morgenstern, "Thirteen Critical Points in Contemporary Economics Theory: An Interpretation," *Journal of Economic Literature* 10 (December 1972): 1163-1189; Michael Baram, "Cost-Benefit Analysis: An Inadequate Basis for Health, Safety, and Environmental Regulatory Decisionmaking," *Ecology Law Quarterly* 8 (1980): 473-531; G.L.S. Shackle, *Epistemics and Economics* (Cambridge University Press, 1972); *Time in Economics* (Amsterdam: North Holland, 1958); and John V.

Krutilla, "Reflections of an Applied Welfare Economist," *Journal of Environmental Economics and Management* 8 (1981): 1-10.

16. Paul K. Feyerabend, *Against Method: Outline of an Anarchistic Theory of Knowledge* (New York: Schocken 1978).

17. Orion F. White, Jr., "Communication Induced Distortion in Scholarly Research—The Case of Action Theory in American Public Administration," *International Journal of Public Administration* 5 (1983): 119-150.

18. Gideon Sjoberg, *A Methodology for Social Research* (New York: Harper & Row, 1968); Orion F. White, Jr., and Gideon Sjoberg, The Emerging New Politics in America," in *Politics in the Post-Welfare State*, eds., M. Donald Hancock and Gideon Sjoberg (New York: Columbia University Press, 1972); and Gideon Sjogerg, M. Donald Hancock, and Orion F. White, Jr., *Politics in the Post-Welfare State: A Comparison of the United States and Sweden* (Bloomington, Ind.: The Carnegie Seminar, Department of Government, Indiana University, 1967).

19. Orion F. White, Jr., "Organization Change and Administrative Adaptation," in *Toward a New Public Administration*, ed. Frank Marini (Scranton: Chandler, 1971).

20. Orion F. White, Jr., *Psychic Energy and Organizational Change* (Beverly Hills: Sage, 1973).

21. Orion F. White, Jr., "Beyond the Empirical Theory-Normative Theory Double Bind," in *Experiential Learning and Professional Education*, eds., Eugene Burne and Douglas Wolf (Dallas: Edwin L. Cox School of Business, Southern Methodist University, 1979).

22. C. G. Jung, *Man and His Symbols* (Garden City, N.Y.: Doubleday, 1964).

23. Ira Progoff, *Jung's Psychology and Its Social Meaning* (Garden City, N.Y.: Anchor, 1973).

24. Walter Odajnyk, *Jung and Politics* (New York: New York University Press, 1976).

25. Ira Progoff, *At a Journal Workshop: The Basic Text and Guide or Using the Intensive Journal Process* (New York: Dialogue House Library, 1977).

26. Gordon Lawrence, *People Types and Tiger Stripes* (Gainesville, Fla.: Center for Applications of Psychological Types, 1982); and Isabel Briggs Myers and Peter B. Myers, *Gifts Differing* (Palo Alto, Calif.: Consulting Psychologist Press, 1980).

27. David Keirsey and Marilyn Bates, *Please Understand Me* (Del Mar, Calif.: Prometheus Nemesis Books, 1978).

28. Sally P. Springer and George Deutsch, *Left Brain, Right Brain* (New York: W. H. Freeman, 1981); Thomas R. Blakeslee, *Right Brain* (New York: Berkley Books, 1980); Richard M. Restak, *The Brain* (New York: One Books, 1979); Michael Gazzaniga, *The Social Brain* (New York: Basic Books, 1985); and Marilyn Ferguson (exec. ed.), *The Brain-Mind Bulletin* (Los Angeles: Interface Press, 1988), passim.

29. Mary H. McCaulley, "How Individual Differences Affect Health Care Teams," *Health Team News* (April 1975); and Robert Doering, "Enlarging Scientific Task Team Creativity," *Personnel* (March-April 1972): 43-52.

30. David A. Kolb, Irwin M. Rubin, and James M. McIntyre, *Organizational Psychology: An Experiential Approach to Organizational Behavior*, 4th ed. (Englewood Cliffs: Prentice-Hall, 1984); and Edgar H. Schein, *Process Consultation: Its Role in Organization Development* (Reading, Mass.: Addison-Wesley, 1969).

31. Frederick Perls, Ralph F. Hefferline, and Paul Goodman, *Gestalt Therapy* (New York: Delta Books, 1951); Joen Fagas and Irma L. Shepherd, eds., *Gestalt Therapy Now* (New York: Harper & Row, 1971); Chris Hatcher and Phillip Himelstein, eds., *The Handbook of Gestalt Therapy* (New York: Jason Aronson, 1976); Edward W. L. Smith, ed., *The Growing Edge of Gestalt Therapy* (Secaucus, N.J.: Citadel Press, 1977); and Stanley M. Herman and Michael Korenich, *Authentic Management: Gestalt Orientation to Organizations and Their Development* (Reading, Mass.: Addison-Wesley, 1977).

32. Bobby R. Patton and Kim Giffin, *Problem-Solving Group Interaction* (New York: Harper & Row, 1973).

33. Cynthia McSwain, "Personal Development and Decentralization—An Alternative to Humanist Liberalism," paper presented at American Society for Public Administration Annual Conference, Honolulu, Hawaii, 1982.

34. Ivan D. Illich, *Tools for Conviviality* (New York: Harper & Row, 1973); *Deschooling Society* (New York: Harper & Row, 1971); and *Medical Nemesis: The Expropriation of Health* (Monrovia, Calif.: National Health Federation, 1976); and Ernst Friedrich Schumacher, *Small is Beautiful: A Study of Economics as if People Matter* (New York: Harper & Row, 1975).

35. C. G. Jung, *Answer to Job* (Cleveland and New York: World Publishing, 1970).

36. Elias Canetti, *Crowds and Power* (New York: Viking, 1963).

37. Jerry B. Harvey, "The Abilene Paradox: The Management of Agreement," *Organizational Dynamics* 3 (Summer 1974): 63-80.

38. G.W.F. Hegel, "The Phenomenology of Mind (New York: Macmillan, 1910).

39. Alfred G. Killilea, "Some Political Origins of the Denial of Death," *Omega* 8 (Fall 1977): 205-214; "Death Consciousness and Social Consciousness," *Omega* 11 (Fall 1980): 185-200; and Death and Democratic Theory: The Political Benefits of Vulnerability," *Midwest Quarterly* 25 (Spring 1984): 283-297.

40. Joan Valerie Bondurant, *Conquest of Violence: The Ghandian Philosophy of Conflict* (Berkeley: University of California Press, 1969).

41. Leonard Grob, "Leadership: The Socratic Model," in *Leadership: Multidisciplinary Perspectives*, ed. Barbara Kellerman (Englewood Cliffs, N.J.: Prentice-Hall, 1984), p. 263-280.

42. Roger Fisher and William Ury, *Getting to Yes* (Boston: Houghton Mifflin, 1981); and I. William Zortman and Maureen R. Berman, *The Practical Negotiator* (New Haven: Yale University Press, 1982).

43. Mary Parker Follett, *Creative Experience* (New York: Longmans, 1924); and *The New State* (New York: Longmans, 1926).

44. Michael M. Harmon and Richard Mayer, *Organization Theory for Public Administration* (Boston: Little, Brown, 1986), p. 43.

45. Gregory Bateson, *Steps to an Ecology of Mind* (New York: Ballantine, 1972).

46. Gareth Morgan, "Cybernetics and Organization Theory: Epistemology or Technique?" *Human Relations* 35 (July 1982): 521-536; and "Rethinking Corporate Strategy—A Cybernetic Perspective," *Human Relations* 36 (April 1983): 345-360.

47. Carlos Castaneda, *The Fire from Within* (New York: Simon & Schuster, 1984).

48. Herbert J. Spiro, *Government by Constitution: The Political Systems of Democracy* (New York: Random House, 1959).

49. E. Corwin, *The "Higher Law" of American Constitutional Law* (Ithaca, N.Y.: Great Seal Books, 1928).

50. Stanford Weinberg, ed., *Messages* (New York: Random House, 1974); Richard V. Farac, Peter R. Monge, and Hamish M. Russell, *Communicating and Organizing* (Reading, Mass.: Addison-Wesley, 1977); and John E. Jones and J. William Pfeiffer, eds., *The Annual Handbook for Group Facilitators* (La Jolla, Calif.: University Associates, Inc.).

51. Frederick Perls, Raloh F. Hefferline, and Paul Goodman, *Gestalt Therapy*; Joen Fagan and Irma L. Shepard, *Gestalt Therapy Now*; Chris Hatcher and Philip Himelstein, *The Handbook of Gestalt Therapy*; Edward W. L. Smith, *The Growing Edge of Gestalt Therapy*; and Ann Herman and I. Korenich, *Authentic Management: A Gestalt Orientation to Organizations and Their Development*.

52. Eric Berne, *Games People Play: The Psychology of Human Relationships* (New York: Grove Press, 1970); *Beyond Games and Scripts* (New York: Grove Press, 1976); and *What Do You Say After You Say Hello* (New York: Grove Press, 1972).

53. Richard Bandler and John Grinder, *The Structure of Magic*, vols. 1 and 2 (Palo Alto, Calif.: Science and Behavior Books, 1975); *Patterns of the Hypnotic Techniques of Milton H. Erickson, M.D.* (Cupertino, Calif.: Meta Publications, 1975); and *Frogs into Princesses* (Moab, Utah: Real People Press, 1979); Leslie Cameron and Richard Bandler, *They Live Happily Ever After* (Cuper-

tino, Calif.: Meta Publications, 1978); and Robert Dilts et al., *Neuro-Linguistic Programming*, vol. 1 (Cupertino, Calif.: Meta Publications, 1980).

54. Erich Neilsen, *Becoming an O.D. Practitioner* (Englewood Cliffs: Prentice-Hall, 1984).

55. Robert Cialdini, *Influence, Science and Practice*, 2nd ed. (Boston: Scott Foresman/Little, Brown, College Division, 1988), p. 4-5.

56. Jurgen Habermas, *Toward a Rational Society* (Boston: Little, Brown, 1973); and *Communication and the Evolution of Society* (Boston: Beacon Press, 1979).

57. Herman Borenzweig, *Jung and Social Work* (New York: University Press of America, 1984).

58. Edward C. Whitmont, *The Symbolic Quest* (Princeton, N.J.: University Press, 1969); and C. G. Jung, *Collected Works*, vols. 1-20 (Princeton: Princeton University Press, 1957).

59. C. G. Jung, *Memories, Dreams, Reflections* (New York: Random House, 1965), p. 401-402.

60. Ibid., p. 401.

61. Roger S. Jones, *Physics as Metaphor* (New York: New American Library, 1982).

62. Jung, *Answer to Job*.

63. Cynthia J. McSwain and Orion F. White Jr., "The Case for Lying, Cheating and Stealing— Personal Development as Ethical Guidance for Managers," *Administration and Society*, 18 (4 February 1987) 411-433; and Erich Neumann, *Depth Psychology and a New Ethic* (New York: Harper & Row, 1969).

64. Claude M. Steiner, *Scripts People Live* (New York: Grove Press, 1974).

65. Ibid.

66. Edward F. Edinger, *Ego and Archetype: Individuation and the Religious Function* (Baltimore: Penguin, 1972).

67. Anthony G. Banet, "A Theory of Group Development Based on the I Ching," in *Creative Psychotherapy*, ed. Anthony G. Banet (La Jolla, Calif.: University Associates Press, 1976).

68. Edward Edinger, *The Creation of Consciousness* (Toronto: InterCity Books, 1984).

69. Ibid., p. 36.

70. Cynthia J. McSwain and Orion F. White, Jr., "The Issue of Authority and the Learning Process: Founding Theory in Myths," *Southern Review of Public Administration* (December 1979): 309-322.

71. Edinger, *Ego and Archetype*.

72. Likert, *New Patterns*.

73. Jane Meredith Adams, "The Problem Employee," *New England Business* 4, 7 (April 19, 1982): 62-63, 65; Charles W. Bolyard, "Rescuing the Troubled Employee," *Management World* 12, 9 (October 1983): 15-16, 25; Christine Filipowicz, "The Troubled Employee: Whose Responsibility?" *Personnel Administrator* 24, 6 (June 1979): 17-22, 33; Randolph W. Flynn and William E. Stratton, "Managing Problem Employees," *Human Resource Management* 20, 2 (Summer, 1981): 28-32; Joseph Follman, *Helping the Troubled Employee* (New York: AMACOM, 1978); Robert J. Hilker, *Behavior Problems in Industry* (Chicago: Illinois Bell Telephone Co., 1976); William Hoffer, "How to Help a Troubled Employee," *Association Management* 35, (March 1983): 67-73; Robert Hollman, "Managing Troubled Employees: Meeting the Challenge," *Journal of Contemporary Business* 8, 4 (October 1979): 43-57; Donald Phillips and Harry J. Older, "A Model for Counseling Troubled Supervisors," *Alcohol, Health and Research World* (Fall, 1977); Eugene Pressler, "Counseling the Problem Employee," *Management World* 10, 3 (March 1981): 41-42; Robert F. Reardon, "Tackling the Problem of Troubled Employees," *New Englander* 22, 8 (December 1975): 50-52; Philip V. Schneider, "There is a Better Way to Help Troubled Employees," *Office* 89, 5 (May 1979): 46, 50, 146; and Ron Zemke, "Should Supervisors Be Counselors?" *Training* 20, 3 (March 1983): 44-53.

74. McSwain and White, "Issue of Authority."

75. M. Scott Peck, *The Road Less Traveled* (New York: Simon & Schuster, 1978).

76. John A. Rohr, *To Run a Constitution: The Legitimacy of the Administrative State* (Lawrence: Universtiy Press of Kansas, 1986).

77. John Friedman, *Retracking America: A Theory of Transactive Planning* (Garden City, N.Y.: Anchor Press/Doubleday, 1973); *Good Society: A Personal Account of its Struggle with the World of Social Planning & Dialectical Inquiry into the Roots of Radical Practice* (Cambridge, Mass.: MIT Press, 1979); and David Godschalk, *Participation, Planning and Exchange in Old and New Communities* (Chapel Hill, N.C., Center for Urban & Regional Studies, 1972).

78. Schambra, "American Public Philosophy.".

79. Walter F. Baber, *Organizing the Future: Matrix Models for the Post-Industrial Policy* (University, Ala.: University of Alabama Press, 1983).

80. W. Deming, *Quality, Productivity, and Competitive Position* (Cambridge, Mass.: MIT Center for Advanced Engineering Study, 1982).

81. Jerome Bernstein, *The Decline of Rites of Passage: The Impact on Masculine Individuation* (New York: C. G. Jung Institute, 1980).

82. Anthony Lewis, *Gideon's Trumpet* (New York: Random House, 1964).

83. Manfred Stanley, ed., *Social Development* (New York: Basic Books, 1972); Siegfried Gideon, *Mechanization Takes Command* (New York: W. W. Norton, 1948); Jacques Ellul, *The Technological Society* (New York: Knopf, 1964); and Langdon Winner, *Autonomous Technology: Technics-out-of-Control as a Theme in Political Thought* (Cambridge: MIT Press, 1972).

84. Stanley, *Social Development.*

85. Orion F. White, Jr., and Cynthia McSwain, "Transformational Theory and Organizational Analysis," in *Beyond Method*, ed. Gareth Morgan (Beverly Hills: Sage, 1983).

86. Robert N. Bellah, et al., *Habits of the Heart* (Berkeley: University of California Press, 1985); and Daniel Yankelovich, *New Rules* (New York: Random House, 1981).

7. Active Citizenship and Public Administration

CAMILLA M. STIVERS

With mere instruction in command
So that people understand
Less than they know, woe is the land;
But happy the land that is ordered so
That they understand more than they know.

— Laotsu

The last two decades have not been kind to the public service. The Great Society's demise; Watergate; the cold dawning of the age of scarcity; two successive presidents elected on antigovernment platforms — all have combined to cast a deepening shadow on the administrative state. Once widely regarded, if not with favor, at least with tolerance, it now occupies the status of necessary evil and — generally excepting provisions for the common defense — has been placed on a strict reducing diet. And although many public servants may be truly heroes to their clients,[1] as a group, bureaucrats have fallen on hard times. Theorists of public administration are much occupied these days with a quest for new bases of legitimacy.

The Blacksburg Manifesto has expanded this theoretical quest beyond tacit boundaries long maintained by positivist social science. The positivist frame of reference shaped a value-free, data-based search for general laws that has largely governed the modern understanding of public administration theory, at least since the days of Herbert Simon's *Administrative Behavior* and Glendon Schubert's *The Public Interest*. Together with standards of administrative neutrality and scientific management set by founding theorists such as Wilson, Goodnow, Gulick, Urwick, and Taylor, this positivist perspective put the field at odds with the ancient notion that theory aims at both truth and goodness. Subsequently, despite Dwight Waldo's critique and a glimpse of Camelot afforded by the "New P. A." movement, public administration theory took the post-World War II demise of the politics-administration dichotomy not as an opportunity to assert or reflect upon value dimensions of administrative theory, but as a mandate either to document the terms of interest group-dominated policy making and bureaucratic politics, or to attempt to scientize management and policy. For public administration, the term *normative theory* remains essentially an oxymoron.

Given this historical context, the tack taken by the Blacksburg Manifesto is new: it argues that the legitimacy problems of modern public administration are not those of effective management, simply, but of governance, that is, of administration in support of a polity. Moreover, present legitimation difficulties of American public administration stem from contextual tensions inherent in our particular political system, a constitutional representative democracy committed both to individual freedom and justice and to national prosperity and stability, attempting to find its way through a complex postindustrial age.

These contextual tensions, which are essentially value conflicts, are poorly addressed by administrative theory that conceives of itself as a set of positivist covering laws. From the Manifesto's perspective, public administration theory is a theory of governance, of a particular state with a unique constitution and history, reflecting potentially conflicting aims, being conducted within the context of a certain political economy. An important corollary of the Manifesto, then, given the intellectual history of the field, is that American public administration can only chart its course successfully by rethinking the nature of theory itself, that is, by rejoining truth and goodness.

The perspective of this essay is that the quest for such a normative theory of American public administration must include an examination of the nature of the relationship between administrative practice and the ultimate source of values in a democratic polity, that is, the people. I want to argue that active citizens are a necessary ingredient in the normative justification sought by the Manifesto. *Administrative legitimacy requires active accountability to citizens, from whom the ends of government derive. Accountability, in turn, requires a shared framework for the interpretation of basic values, one that must be developed jointly by bureaucrats and citizens in real-world situations, rather than assumed. The legitimate administrative state, in other words, is one inhabited by active citizens.*

There are several conceptual and practical barriers to the development of active citizenship, which are a function of American political history and of our reigning theoretical assumptions. This essay will reflect on those that appear especially relevant to a theory of the administrative state.

Ideas of Citizenship

The citizenship question has already attracted fresh interest in the field. "Citizen participation," injected during the 1960s and 1970s into government at all levels, has survived the demise of the activism that gave it birth. Public administration literature reflects a continuing sense that various relationships between bureaucrats and citizens are instrumental to the effective formation and implementation of public policy.[2] Citizens as consumers, as sources of needed information and support for particular programs, as the putative ground of basic values underlying public decisions, and as cooperators in the production of public services ("coproducers") — all are roles well established in bureaucratic thinking. Citizen participation is still, however, more typically treated as a cost both to citizen and bureaucrat than as a benefit,[3] and one finds little evidence in the literature of substantive decision making by citizens.

It is clear, however, that the institutionalized relationships that do exist have not been sufficient unto the public administration's need for legitimacy. Contributors to a 1984 special issue of *Public Administration Review* remarked on the current apathy of citizens and their lack of understanding of the policy process. The dialogue dwelt at length on the need to "revitalize citizenship by means of the craft of public administration,"[4] and reflected on the disparity between the weak view of citizenship held by the framers of the Constitution and a residue of "high citizenship" that nevertheless persists in our civic culture.[5] Uniting the contributors was a sense that bureaucrats *need* citizens in a way, and of a kind, that is new. But there is growing suspicion that the kind of citizens needed, and the way in which they are needed, may be fundamentally at odds with current arrangements, which are deeply rooted in the history of our polity.

Citizenship at the Founding

The system's original intent, embodied in the Constitution, was to leave citizens free to pursue their private interests, having entrusted the public good to a structure that filtered and refined citizen views to produce government both "adequate to the exigencies" that would ensue and protective of individual liberty. As James Kettner's history of American citizenship has pointed out, the founding notion of "citizen" deviated very little with respect to rights and duties from the English common-law idea of "subject." Both subjects and citizens had rights to property, liberty of person or conscience, and access to the courts.[6] The chief distinction lay in the source of the link between the individual and the state. Subjectship was a bond of personal allegiance inherent in one's place in the order of things. Just as the monarch's right to rule was divinely ordained, so were the subject's obligations of fealty. English liberal contract theory replaced this understanding with the idea of the citizen who *chooses* to commit himself to a relationship to the state. In return for his allegiance to republican principles, adherence to the Constitution, and responsible behavior, the citizen was assured civil and political rights. Thus, liberal citizenship depended, at least in theory, not on birth or station in life but on belief and consent; but the idea remained free of any notion of active involvement in governance, either as privilege or obligation.

The framers of the American Constitution reflected this understanding in their view of popular sovereignty as a catalyst. Through an act of will, the people cause the system to spring to life, much as the clockwork universe is set in motion by deism's subsequently remote Creator; thereafter, they serve as a theoretically required but practically blunted source of legitimacy, a collective ghost in the machine of governance. Moreover, the framers' view of human motivation as almost exclusively a matter of self-interest reinforced the barrier against any idea of active citizenship, a vital assumption of which, as we shall see, is the possibility of action in the public, as distinguishable from individual selfish, interest.

A number of the framers, however, notably the Anti-Federalists, feared that excluding citizens from active participation would have a negative effect on their understanding of and confidence in government, and thus, ultimately, on the quality of government itself. Their argument was that if the polity isolates citizens from the governance process, it is very likely to produce people who only know how to act selfishly and thus ensure a self-fulfilling prophecy. The Anti-Federalists, as John Rohr points out, "lost" the founding argument.[7] But Herbert Storing has observed that even those of the framers who were the least sanguine about human nature had to have assumed, in grounding their government in the ultimate sovereignty of the people, some basis for confidence in popular wisdom.[8] All could not be "degrees of depravity." Yet, as the resulting compromise demonstrates, when it came to the dynamics of the *novus ordo saeclorum*, the framers were a risk-averse group. They placed their bets on a system that both fostered and depended upon the civic virtue of a small group of leaders, rather than on the practical genius of the people as a whole.

The beneficial effects of this calculus are apparent in the present-day stability, prosperity, capacity for incremental change, and relative freedom of our system, which is, indeed, as Hamilton wanted it to be, "the envy of the world." But the ongoing price that is paid, one somewhat obscured by these very benefits, is reflected in growing unease over the quality of citizenship, a concern that may have arisen out of a need to legitimate the public service but has wider implications.

Active Citizenship: The Tradition and Its Critics

Since I have said that ideas of active citizenship appear to be at odds with our traditions and current arrangements, a brief sketch of this concept is in order. The notion originates in Aristotle's idea that the citizen is a member of the state. Although the characteristics of membership vary with the nature of the state, the mark of this form of citizenship is "participation in giving judgment and in holding office."[9] The citizen takes his [sic] turn ruling and being ruled.[10]

Distinctive to the act of ruling is *phronesis*, or the exercise of practical wisdom, an essential ingredient of citizen virtue. Thus, the polity that enables citizens to practice *phronesis* for the good of all is the best form of government. Aristotle held that "man is a political animal,"[11] that is, the capacity for political activity is a defining feature of human nature. In his view we become fully human only in the exercise of citizenship; the contemporary notion of the "private citizen" would have been, for Aristotle, a contradiction in terms.

From its Aristotelian roots, then, active citizenship derives the following dimensions: membership in the polity, which involves both ruling and being ruled in turn; the exercise of practical wisdom or judgment; and capability of action in the public interest, which implies not self-sacrifice but action on a different plane from the one where private interests apply.

This ideal, although it has persisted in the ensuing history of Western political thought, has been dogged by criticism of what appear to be fairly serious practical defects, particularly the apparent implausibility of its implementation in any society of a scale and complexity beyond that of the Greek city-state. Rousseau, an ardent proponent, himself believed that active citizenship could only be realized in a society small and economically homogeneous enough to keep the clash of individual interests within bounds and thus allow democratic sentiments to flourish, nurtured by the experience of participation in governance.[12]

Another difficulty was raised by liberalism's assertion of individual rights, which, although originally formulated as an attack on the divine right of kings, had the additional effect of casting the shadow of tyranny upon any other interpretation of the general good than the sum total of individual interests. The good of all came to be seen as inherently threatening to individual freedom, or at least as implying individual self-sacrifice as the price of its attainment. Also problematic for active citizenship is the liberal view of human nature as essentially self-interested, which supports the individual's right to commit himself to the polity by means of a contract but casts doubt on his ability to act dispassionately thereafter. Our own founding dialogue treated human nature as a danger to be controlled by means of the structure of the state, so that "interest would do the work of virtue." For liberalism, then, active citizenship was inimical to freedom and inconsistent with human nature.

Thus, we are faced with significant theoretical barriers to the development of a modern form of active citizenship. Such a project must justify the manner in which citizens may exercise decisive judgment for the general good within a massive, complex post industrial state. And it must address the formulation of some definition of the public interest consistent with our ideas of individual freedom and human nature.

Contemporary Contextual Barriers

Moreover, the political economy of the administrative state appears to leave little room for a more active, less instrumental view of citizenship than we now have. The advantage pluralism imparts to the organized and the well equipped makes it difficult to envision a policy-substantial role for ordinary citizens, one that goes beyond the advisory committee or coproduction. Oligarchy is ubiquitous, and cooptation appears inevitable. Public administrators, no matter how sincerely interested in active citizenship, find it hard to think of something both helpful and possible to do in support of it.

The Manifesto reflects this aspect of the dilemma in pointing to the tension in our political economy between individual liberty and justice, on the one hand, and on the other, societal stability and prosperity. Posed thus, the issue of governance embodies the liberal conflict between individual and group needs, in which societal goals are won at the inevitable cost of at least some of the freedom of most individuals, and perhaps most of the freedom of some. Framing the problem in this way implies that, in practice, bureaucrats who want to deal humanely with clients find their intentions blocked by seemingly impervious structures and processes, such as "regulations" or "partisan mutual adjustment"; while those who aim simply to apply comprehensive criteria end up running roughshod over individual citizens. Praxis appears to require a Hobson's choice.

Another difficulty lies in the professional image of the public administrator, which has been dearly won but — as presently constituted — is deeply at odds with active citizenship. Professionalism in public service implies not only the ideal of neutral competence that dates back to Wilson and Goodnow, but also a unique ethic of commitment to the public interest. Acknowledging the political dimensions of public administrative practice, this ethic is worked out in the exercise of administrative discretion and in an assertion of special competency (as well as obligation) to identify community needs, weigh competing demands, and aim for, although never surely reach, the public interest. But absent any other view of the public interest than as a bargain among competing claims, this obligation in practice assumes typical guises, either a search for technically correct solutions (the only defensible "right" answers) or the hammering out of zero-sum trade-offs. The public servant is either a neutral analyst or a referee, but in either case, as a professional, claims unique qualification for governance. Active citizenship appears to present a fundamental challenge to this claim, for it suggests that the exercise of judgment in the public interest, the crucial capability for the practice of governance, is a skill not only within the capacity of ordinary citizens but necessary to their full human development. If this is true, then the question of what is special about the practice of public administration is in need of reexamination.

Terry Cooper is surely right that public servants are "citizen-administrators . . . employed *as* one of us to work *for* us" and bearing the responsibility for encouraging participation by other citizens.[13] By implication, then, the terms of the relationship between citizens and the state depend a great deal on the content of administrative practice, especially upon the exercise of discretion. But the argument thus far suggests that existing structural arrangements and the terms of the professional persona may require us to expand our understanding of public service in order to develop a praxis that nurtures active citizenship. What modes of participative action are possible for citizens given the political economic contexts of public organizational life? Is there an expanded form of professionalism that takes pride in facilitating citizens' practical wisdom rather than claiming exclusive right to the art of judgment?

The Public Administration's Need for Active Citizens

The public administration appears to be hard up against the reality that the administrative state cannot be legitimated by apathetic, ignorant, or misled citizens. The previously cited dialogue in *Public Administration Review* reflects a consensus that, although there are many knowledgeable, concerned citizens, as a group they appear ill-equipped to validate, let alone take part in public policy formation and implementation. The Anti-Federalist prophecy seems to have been fulfilled.

A normative theory of the administrative state requires a people whose capabilities extend beyond breathing life into the state at the moment of its birth. The founding dialogue of the meaning and purpose of governance must be thought of as a conversation that continues throughout the life of the state, one requiring the involvement of both bureaucrats and other citizens so that they share an understanding of its meaning. Shared meaning is what makes true accountability possible. The polity *is* what its members say and do about it. One who has no part in this saying and doing can hardly be a member, nor can he or she be the source of values to ground administrative practice, in any sense compelling enough to ensure that administration remains truly responsive to the popular will.

Hannah Arendt has observed that the framers' creation of a new body politic was only half successful because the structure of the government they devised closed off forever to most of the populace the world-building public speech that was the framers' own happiness and the primary means to preserve the spirit that generated the act of foundation. The Revolution,

> while it had given freedom to the people, had failed to provide a space where this freedom could be exercised. Only the representatives of the people . . . had an opportunity to engage in those activities of "expressing, discussing and deciding" which in a positive sense are the activities of freedom.[14]

For Arendt, public expression, discussion, and decision bring into being the public space, indeed political life itself. From this perspective, freedom is more than the liberal absence of government interference in private decisions. It also implies active capacity to shape the public decision-making process itself.

Arendt's argument suggests that if The Public Administration wants citizens to acknowledge its legitimacy, it must develop modes of practice through which a public space can be created, one in which there is membership for both bureaucrats and citizens. It is not enough for public administrators to have decided among themselves in what senses the public service is legitimate. Validating the administrative state must be accomplished in and by a community made up of bureaucrats and active lay citizens alike. Thus "refocusing the American dialogue" about public administration entails not only a shift in what we discuss; we must also widen the dialogue. We cannot simply talk about governance; we must talk with citizens.

The modern American administrative state cannot be guided by an abstract will of the people, which set the clock ticking in 1789 and need only wind it at election times. Given the state's size and complexity; given the domination of the policy process by interest groups; given mass-media tendencies to over-simplification, symbolic politics, and ideology, the views of the people have come to pass through so fine a filter that even Madison would no longer recognize them. More direct links are required between administrative practice and the popular will.

The legitimacy of the administrative state depends on consistency not only with the terms of the Constitution, but also with that which is more basic than the Constitution. If the modern state has evolved to a point at which its members no longer have fundamental confidence that it aims at the public good, then it may be time to resurrect Chief Justice Taney's insight in the famous *Charles River Bridge* case: government may not legitimately do something that will "diminish its power of accomplishing the end for which it was created," that is, "to promote the happiness and prosperity of the community by which it was established."[15] If the public service is debased in the eyes of citizens and presidents alike, if the notion of the public interest is empty of any content save compromise, if citizens and bureaucrats no longer trust one another — in short, if our ways of governance have diminished our power to strive towards the ends for which the state was created, perhaps these are reasons enough to "refocus the American dialogue," so that citizens are included in the conversation.

A Theory of Active Citizenship

I want now to address some conceptual dimensions of active citizenship that are implied by the general terms outlined earlier, that is, ruling and being ruled in turn; exercise of practical wisdom; and capability of action in pursuit of general interests. This effort must take full account of the contextual difficulties I spoke of: the historical development of the polity, the existing political economy of the administrative state, and the terms of professional public administration.

Membership: Commitment and Community

The root problem of modern American citizenship is the question of citizen consciousness of common membership in a polity of general interests. Our political heritage has preserved the idea that citizenship is a matter of conscious choice, of commitment; but the terms of the contract — the exchange of individual civil and legal rights in return for personal allegiance and lawful behavior — simply bind each citizen to an abstract state rather than to a community of other real beings.

Paul Ricoeur has observed that the contents of an ideal state — for example, equality before the law, the evenhanded exercise of power — cannot be achieved in actual political practice, either in terms of the distribution of resources or of the imposition of constraints. For Ricoeur, this built-in tension between the ideal of law and the real of administration (what the framers called a government of laws versus a government of men) amounts to a form of alienation that is the essence of the political and, indeed, the human condition.[16] The significance of this point is not as a way of rationalizing about the justice of current societal resource distribution. Rather it reminds us that human action never fully exhausts the meaning implicit in the terms we use to refer to it; therefore the extent to which practice corresponds to expressed ideals is inherently a matter of judgment. Thus the significance of commitment to political life is problematic, for it implies entrance into a permanent state of interpretive tension, an ongoing balancing act.

Moreover, the contract itself is not the result of a conscious choice, at least for the vast majority of Americans who are born into their citizenship and never have occasion to examine its terms. The contract that animates American governance took shape in a single, decisive act. Therefore, as Ricouer points out, it must be discovered in individual reflection to become operative; and the terms of citizenship are currently so limited that there are few situations in which the average citizen would be likely to engage in action that would encourage such reflection.

The type of membership in the polity necessary to active citizenship depends on consciousness of commitment to a set of ideals. It also requires transformation of one ideal, the equality of individuals, into the basis of a real bond *among* individuals. But this transformation only grows from acceptance of the inevitable gap between the ideal and the real, of which Ricoeur speaks. Unless we understand that our intentions — the ends for which the state was formed — are ultimately out of reach, we will be unable to practice the trust in one another that enables us to accept the inevitable imperfections of actual policies.[17] Bringing the contract into the realm of governance, into politics, involves a leap from abstract equality and authority to real — therefore flawed — practices that bind us together as we act and reflect upon our actions. The normative significance of the contract must be mediated in the world, in concrete situations and relationships.

In fact, equality before the law is not all we have in common: there are also needs we share, which Michael Ignatieff argues could form the basis for a bond among us, if only the modern age had a language adequate to their expression.[18] But liberalism's assertion of individual rights took aim at the shared sense that each person had a preordained place in the order of things, an awareness that had justified need-based obligations that were public yet not civil. The loss of the sense of belonging that followed upon liberalism's victory has become emblematic of modernity,[19] and we no longer know how to talk about shared needs and obligations in a language that poses no threat to the individual. The word *community* evokes either nostalgia for something the postindustrial age can never reclaim, or fear that one's rights are about to be trampled upon.

Besides, we are told, our society is too complex and its institutions too massive for us to conceive of a public space to which we all belong, such as the one of which Arendt speaks. Sheldon Wolin has suggested that the loss of an operative political community took place as long ago as the shift from the civic intimacy of the Greek city-state to the abstract symbols of authority upon which the Roman Empire depended to bind its citizens together, symbols that would evoke the state's power despite its members' physical dispersion.[20] In any case, current reliance upon abstractions and symbols of governance is near total. What is there about "the needs of strangers"[21] that could bind us to them? What are the terms of the postindustrial community? Is there a "city" where a praxis of active citizenship can be conducted?

Community: Need for an Ontological Ground

Finding the answers to these questions depends partly upon resolution of a basic issue that has long divided social theorists, that is, the relationship between structure and action. This is an important concern for active citizenship, because the sense of efficacy necessary to praxis has been dissipated by widespread agreement among practitioners and theorists that the contextual structural barriers I have described are generally beyond the control of actors. Praxis requires a new understanding of these structures, one that gives reason for hope that societal members can assert some measure of control over them.

The ontological primacy of societal structures over the perceptions and activities of social actors has been defended by theorists as diverse as structural functionalists and Marxists; while interpretivists, for their part, have claimed that structures are nothing *but* the intersubjective constructions of actors. The terms of this dispute have been detailed exhaustively in the literature;[22] thus there is no need to repeat the arguments here. Although structuralists of various persuasions have generally dominated social science, the claims of interpretive sociology have won increasing numbers of adherents. Each camp has posed questions that the other has found difficult to answer. For example, interpretivists have not provided — despite reification theories — a completely convincing account of pervasive inequities in the distribution of material resources and frequently have appeared to accept injustice as the price of stability in a fragile social reality. Structuralists, on the other hand, have had difficulty explaining social action in terms that leave room for the distinctive intentionality of human subjects; their perspective has failed to account for human actions, which are not fully determinable based on knowledge of their structured properties. Despite its pervasiveness, the possible relevance of this theoretical question to the issue of active citizenship has not yet been explored.

Critics assume that structural barriers such as the existing political economy and the complexity of public bureaucracy restrict possibilities for the practice of active citizenship, regardless of its consistency with constitutional and other norms. In order to show how citizens can exercise decisive judgment about real-world public problems, a convincing argument must demonstrate that citizens can function definitely: not just within the interstices of existing regularities but in relation to altering them over time. Belief in this possibility would be aided by understanding that bureaucratic and other structures are constituted by the practices of societal members. Without underestimating the difficulty of such an aim, if the source of these barriers can be shown to be human action itself, then perhaps we have the capacity to reshape them.

Such an accomplishment could serve as a catalyst for the kinds of real practices and conscious commitment that unite citizens through a sense of efficacy and shared meaning instead of pitting them against one another. At present, "the system," "bureaucracy," and "politics" are seen as enveloping presences that overwhelm and smother the intentional and autonomous actions of people before they can have any impact. Praxis must be freed from its present perceptual trap, in which those who have an interest in action in the world see structures as having a life of their own and are thus rendered helpless before them.

The realm of praxis is day-to-day, mundane activity, where there is neither time nor inclination for speculation about the nature of social reality. These necessary theoretical roots, however, must in principle be deemed available to anyone willing to reach for them: "In a process of enlightenment there can be only participants."[23]

Structuration: Potential Paradigm for Citizenship

The structuration theory of Anthony Giddens offers a potential frame of reference for active citizenship, for it expressly aims to end the characteristic social science dualism of structure and action that reinforces actors' perceived lack of control over societal structures. Giddens argues that human social practices ordered across space and time both reproduce the existing systems within which they take place and are in turn reproduced by them. "In and through their activities agents reproduce the conditions that make activities possible."[24] According to Giddens, social systems are patterned activities situated within a particular spatial and historical context; their properties, or "structures," consist of rules and resources that act in a manner analogous to the syntax of a sentence, both enabling and constraining action. By "resources," Giddens refers not only to institutional symbols and normative sanctions but also to "transformative capacity . . . over objects, goods or material phenomena" as well as over persons. Use of rules and resources both maintains them and makes further use of them possible.[25]

Crucially for applying his theory to active citizenship, Giddens insists on the knowledgeability of human actors as the source of the patterns that constitute structures: it is actors' shared consciousness and ongoing reflexivity that form the basis for the continuity of practices. Giddens argues that "to be a human being is to be a purposive agent, who both has reasons for his or her activities and is able, if asked, to elaborate discursively upon those reasons."[26] The outlines of structuration theory give full weight to the contextual dimensions of action, so that actors are seen as constrained significantly by situated practices that have preceded and now surround them. But humans, as agents, have the capability "to intervene in the world . . . to make a 'difference.' "[27] Thus, for Giddens, power is neither simply a matter of individual will or capacity, nor is it a property of systems: it is a relationship—a dialectic of control:

> Power within social systems . . . presumes regularized relations of autonomy and dependence between actors or collectivities in contexts of social interaction. But all forms of dependence offer some resources whereby those who are subordinate can influence the activities of their superiors.[28]

The knowledgeability of actors is bounded, it is true, on one side by the unconscious and on the other (the locus of misunderstanding and ideology) by unacknowledged conditions and unintended consequences of action. But Giddens insists that there is no insight social analysis can uncover that lay actors cannot "get to know about and actively incorporate into what they do."[29] And these conditions and consequences, in turn, cannot be understood fully—by professional analysts, for example—without checking the results of analysis against the knowledgeability of actors.[30] Therefore the "revelatory model" of the natural sciences, in which experimental findings correct commonsense beliefs, is inappropriate to social science, where the subjects of research are able themselves to reflect, assess, and act upon findings.[31] The uncovering of conditions and consequences of action has the potential to increase the capability of actors to change things: humans are not inert objects but agents able to apply the results of analysis, and regarding them as such is a political stance.[32]

In essence, Giddens's argument is that all actors *as* actors have some element of control over the reproduction of societal structures and, further, that they can learn and apply knowledge about the unacknowledged conditions and unintended consequences of action in order to produce change.

The Knowledge Community

This line of thought suggests that the potential for a praxis of active citizenship depends on restoring the active sense of such capacities through the development of a practical framework, that is, a community of knowledge, wherein members could come, in pursuit of shared reflexive understanding of the conditions and consequences of social action, to expand their knowledge and capacity to "make a difference." In such a community, all members possess inherent knowledgeability and membership is open to anyone who desires it. Conceiving of citizenship as in part membership in an open community of knowledge is consistent with the idea that all individual parties to the founding contract are equal. Such a community would enable members to form the bonds of trust that, I have argued, develop from the sharing of real-world practices guided by ideal aims.

The notion of a knowledge community is an extension of the view that knowledge has its genesis in restricted intersubjective agreements about meaning, argued in Thomas Kuhn's theory of paradigms.[33] Such agreements define criteria by which the adequacy of explanations is judged. This has been recognized at least tacitly in the field of public administration by a number of policy theorists who argue that decisions about what counts as evidence are inherently based on agreement within a discipline about how data are to be assessed. Criteria are, in other words, intersubjective products grounded in shared commitments that must themselves be taken as given. For example, Goodin and Wilenski have suggested that standards of efficiency in policy research derive their power from a shared desire to maximize our ability to satisfy people's wants, and that this desire, in turn, is grounded in an agreement about basic respect for people.[34] Charles Anderson argues that the justification of standards of judgment must be considered a part of policy rationality; in his view, authority, justice, and efficiency — because of a prior agreement about their significance — can logically be considered necessary considerations in any rationally defensible policy argument.[35] Central to such claims about the nature of validity criteria is their origin in a process of intersubjective agreement. It is when we turn to the question of whose agreement counts in a particular validation process that we come up against the political implications of theories of knowledge, which are the source of my insistence that membership in a knowledge community of active citizenship must be open on principle.

Because knowledge criteria are a product of agreement, the membership characteristics of the relevant knowledge community partly determine, in any specific instance, what comes to be known. What counts as knowledge will be a function of communal interests and aims, since, as Habermas has said, validity criteria in any system of knowledge cannot be derived decisively from the terms of the system itself but must be selected based on the informed judgment of community members.[36] A particular community, however, must be prepared to submit the content of its consensus to the scrutiny of a larger community of nonspecialists, who must be able to deem it rational, according to metastandards that cut across paradigmatic lines. Thus, as Alvin Gouldner argues, there is a culture of discourse shared by all educated persons that enables them to make reasoned judgments about aspects of specialized work; in this way, members of a particular discipline are not a law unto themselves. Legitimation of the criteria of any group involves reference to a larger group. "Like any consensus of persons," Gouldner observes, "those processes held to produce 'truths' also have an inescapable political dimension."[37] Thus reference of criteria to the judgment of a broader community of nonspecialists is implicit in standards of basic respect, authority, and justice to which policy research, as well as other modes of knowledge acquisition for governance, is held. No community of knowledge can be autonomous that does not embrace the whole society.

The only type of knowledge community available to us up to now has depended on terms that limit membership. The political significance of the terms of membership in communities of knowledge suggests that we need to broaden our definition of the politics of administration beyond the weighing of claims and the strategies of policy negotiation to include administrators' shared understanding of what constitutes knowledge. Thus, when bureaucrats decide how to decide an issue and only then turn to citizens for "input," they have made a political choice. A judgment that the selection of decision criteria lies outside citizen competence is not a neutral conclusion. It is a choice about community membership. Active citizens belong to a polity that is in part a knowledge community. The right to say what is real or true, and how we know it, is a political one.

Clearly, this recognition is at odds with the professional stance of public administration, for the very essence of professionalism as we now understand it is to claim the right to limit to members the process of deciding how to decide. The suggestion that active citizenship implies participation in the constitution of knowledge undercuts a fundamental tenet of professionalism, but this perspective is essential as the starting point for development of modes of administrative practice that are accountable to citizens because they include rather than isolate them from direct knowledgeability about governance.

A political understanding of deciding how to decide implies a process that can be consistent with the shared values of an open knowledge community. Deciding how to acquire the knowledge we need in order to govern implies a prior decision about the ends of government; therefore, practice must have conscious reference back to the ideal of the polity. For example, Hobbes understood that if the primary purpose of government is the maintenance of order, a neutral, scientific discourse is required for practice, because words do more than refer, they also reflect the interests of speakers:

> For though the nature of that we conceive be the same; yet the diversity of our reception of it, in respect of different constitutions of body, and prejudices of opinion, gives everything a tincture of our different passions. And therefore in reasoning, a man must take heed of words; which besides the signification of what we imagine of their nature, have a significance also of the nature, disposition, and interest of the speaker . . . for one man calleth *Wisdome*, what another calleth *feare*; and one *cruelty*, what another *justice* . . .[38]

Those who have the power to name names — in Hobbes's world, the sovereign — can silence others in the interest of maintaining order. Citizens accept this, Hobbes concludes, out of a similar interest, that is, in order to protect themselves from each other. The tie between interests and language implies that a key task for modern American governance, then, must be developing a knowledge practice — a language of politics — consistent with the full range of our shared political interests: not only order, but equality, freedom, and justice as well. It is easy to grasp the relationship between an interest in order and public discourse that is witnessed by a silent citizenry. But our polity has broader purposes; they call for a new discourse.

Practical Wisdom and the Agency Perspective

I have said that active citizenship begins with membership in an open community of knowledge, and that this community derives its potentiality from an awareness that actors' knowledge and activities, as the means by which societal structures are reproduced, imply their inherent capacity to understand their situations and to make a difference. I have also argued that the sense of trust necessary to unite such a community has its source in an appreciation of the essential tension between the ideal and the real that is of the nature of the political and a definitive aspect of the human condition.

The Nature of Practical Wisdom

Another required dimension of active citizenship is the exercise of *phronesis*, or practical wisdom. As Habermas observes, Aristotle held that political knowledge could not be considered equivalent to scientific knowledge because its subject matter "lacks ontological constancy as well as logical necessity."[39] Politics is only capable of a prudent understanding of the situation, that is, phronesis, a mode of knowledge inherently contingent and variable. The foundations of this understanding of political knowledge, consistent with a view of politics as the doctrine of the good life, were challenged by Hobbes's aim to make political knowledge scientific, in the sense that we now understand that term, that is, susceptible to prediction or control.[40] The move from practical wisdom to science, as we have seen, launched a quest for lawlike generalizations that separated governance from the ends — other than the maintenance of order — that animated it and transmuted it to a mode of action akin to mastery of a technique. The restoration of an understanding of governance as the exercise of practical wisdom, then, involves moving away from the idea that most administrative decision making can be made definitive and comprehensive, toward greater reliance on tentative strategies that self-correct through frequent feedback of information about their effects. Practical wisdom implies, as well, the exercise of judgment within the context of a process that renders it accountable to citizens, as I have already suggested.

Lukacs has observed that "the organization is the form of the mediation between theory and praxis."[41] There is a tendency among critics of post-industrial bureaucracy to see it as oppressive and impervious, to the exclusion of its enabling qualities. As the Blacksburg Manifesto points out, however, big public organizations do many necessary and worthwhile things. But beyond that, the "agency perspective" identified by the Manifesto can be seen as a mediation between theory and practice, embodying the organizational exercise of practical wisdom and thus constituting a felicitous frame of reference for active citizenship.

The Agency Perspective and Citizenship

As Gary Wamsley's chapter in this volume argues, the agency is more than organizational standard-operating procedures and bureaucratic politics. It is a normative and contextual framework for the practice of public administration, both in terms of history and of the political-economic structures within which it is embedded: one that blends specialized expertise with shared awareness of value dimensions such as the agency mission, constitutional and legislative mandates, and organizational culture.[42]

Using the agency as a level of focus supports several elements necessary to ground a theory of active citizenship. First, Ricoeur's notion of the political as a tension between the ideal of law and the real of administration, thus the locus of practical wisdom, is similar to Wamsley's view of administrative action as both contextual and grounded in values of the polity. In addition, Giddens's stress on the knowledgeability of actors suggests that the agency perspective *is* precisely the knowledge and capability of agency members about structural and historical context, normative order, and specialized practice. Seen in this way, Wamsley's argument provides powerful support for the view that agency members, who are in fact *agents*, have some measure of control over their agencies, for these structures both make action possible and are reproduced, maintained, and changed by it. Action within the context of the agency, because it blends the ideal of the polity and the real of administration, consists of the prudent approach to dealing with particular situations that is practical wisdom, wisdom that can make a difference.

The agency perspective is thus consistent, as far as it goes, with the conceptual requirements of an administrative praxis for active citizenship. The key missing ingredient is active accountability to citizens, mediated in dialogue and joint action, which sows seeds of trust that are required in order that administrative discretion can be exercised. Bureaucrats must find opportunities and develop frameworks for working with citizens so that citizens will trust them to choose rightly when circumstances preclude citizens' active participation. The agency is enriched by conversations and action with citizens, which provide a dimension of reality — both benefits and costs — that breathe life (i.e., accountability) into codes of professional ethics, constitutional and legislative provisions, and technical expertise.

The vision of the agency enriched by citizens' practical wisdom is consistent with the field's oldest tradition. Early writers were genuinely concerned to make the practice of public administration responsive to popular control. Frank Goodnow's classic *Politics and Administration* makes a strong case that politics must control administrative action in order that the expression of the public will be realized in its execution.[43] This recommendation reflects an interest in accountability to the true meaning of the popular will: not simply winning the support of citizens ("legitimation"), but administrative practice consistent with the public's understanding of underlying values. Later writing about the politics of administration declined steadily away from this commitment to grounding practice in the will of the people, toward the pluralism that made a virtue of necessity by defining the public interest to be whatever emerged from contention among organized groups.

But early municipal reformers stressed the need for bureaucrats to tap the capabilities of citizens: their idea of "efficient citizenship" was firmly based on faith in citizen capacity to develop a deeper understanding and efficacy with respect to the governance process given access to information necessary to the development of sound judgments. According to William H. Allen's *Efficient Democracy*:

> Without these facts upon which to base judgment, the public cannot intelligently direct and control the administration of township, county, city, state, or nation. Without intelligent control by the public, no efficient, progressive, triumphant democracy is possible.[44]

Henri Bruere saw government as an instrument of effective community cooperation requiring a "new social sense" and observed that "inadequate or wasteful methods, and citizen ignorance of civic business are . . . the principal obstructions to progressive government."[45] Frederick A. Cleveland observed that "true government [is] the rational product of social experience. This experience can come from the people only."[46] These early writers recognized the importance of a polity that unites bureaucrats and citizens in common aims and activities, rather than consigning them to separate realms of existence.

The advent of scientific management appears to have reinforced existing political and economic factors militating against popular control, or "efficient citizenship" as the reformers saw it. There was a shift from the understanding of factual knowledge as a necessary ingredient for public learning, to factual knowledge as a tool of efficient management. Nevertheless, the seeds of real trust in the public's capacity to acquire knowledge and practical skills that would support governance were there in the field's earliest days. Therefore the suggestion that we reassess decision making and implementation to make them more consistent with an expanded knowledge community of citizenship is radical in the sense of returning to our roots but not in the sense of tearing them out. What I am advocating is a restoration of balance.

A strategy of balance would accord respect to the historical heritage, while recognizing that there are changes to be made which are not incremental adjustments to existing arrangements, nor can they be fully planned for. What can be planned is a process that accommodates such change because it is grounded in a commitment to *societal learning*.[47] This approach to change views knowledge as an ongoing process constituted by members of a community, and it accords to members the status of ultimate end rather than instrument to some other goal. Thus it is an appropriate conceptual basis upon which to construct an administrative praxis for active citizenship.

Societal Learning: An Approach to Discretion

Societal learning assumes that humans can make genuine improvement in their individual and societal ability to cope with the issues that confront them. It thus presents a contrast to the classic liberal view of human nature, since it implies that, whatever our other innate characteristics, they are less significant than the built-in ability to learn, and therefore to develop. If we do come into the world with a strong bent toward self-interested behavior, we can nonetheless learn to behave otherwise, including to practice phronesis for the good of all. Societal learning aims at individual and social judgment capacity, the fostering of mutual respect, and the recognition of mutual interdependence. This is in contrast to maintenance learning, or ongoing fixed repertoires that are closed, rule-based, authoritative, and focused on problem-solving through analysis. Maintenance learning is consistent with a view of human nature as essentially given and in need of stringent limits. Societal learning, which is open-ended, contextual, participative, and focused on understanding and synthesis, views humanity as, whatever its current status, capable of development.

The societal learning perspective is crucial to our ability to deal with the challenges of postindustrial society, which are too complex and uncertain to be susceptible to maintenance learning strategies. We have tended to place so much faith in science that we assume that societal problems can be solved once and for all. The American ideology of progress aims at perfectability, and the existence of essentially uncontrollable factors is a reality we tend to ignore. We pretend to be incrementalists, but in our heart of hearts we believe that small adjustments are something we must settle for because of the messiness of politics, rather than their being all we are capable of. The public does not see the inherent limits of "progress" either—particularly since we oversell programs in order to get them funded—and so, when results fall short, the public perceives government as ineffective. Yehezkel Dror sees policy making as a process of "fuzzy gambling," in which ascertainable probabilities do not add up to 1.0, thus risk is not fully predictable and uncertainty cannot be eliminated. Thus, he argues, the public needs to be educated to the essential riskiness of public policy.[48]

From the perspective of active citizenship, Dror's point supports the notion of an essential gap between the ideals of the polity and the reality of governance, one that can only be closed by the public's trust in government officials to do the right thing. As I have argued, this trust must be established in real-world relationships and conversations between bureaucrats and citizens, relationships in which citizens have a substantive role, that is, an opportunity to rule. The societal learning perspective offers guidelines for the development of these kinds of relationships. In large measure, it is the bureaucrat's faith in technical expertise and in the possibility of comprehensive solutions that make him or her hesitant to turn to the citizen. But the societal learning perspective argues that, as David Korten puts it, if bureaucratic structures are to evolve, organizational process must shift from

> the isolation of variables or the control of bureaucratic deviations from centrally defined blueprints . . . [to] effectively engaging the necessary participation of [societal] system members in contributing to the collective knowledge of the system and in generating policy choices out of . . . a social interaction process.[49]

This argument implies that administrative practice need not face a Hobson's choice. Active citizenship is not fundamentally at odds with managerial efficiency; on the contrary, through the exercise of discretion within an agency framework, one newly accountable to real human beings as well as to abstract ideals, citizens can be seen as the most crucial ingredient of administrative effectiveness. Democratic decision making need not be thought of as something purchased at the sacrifice of efficiency, if one realizes that the complexity and uncertainty of modern-day governance demand tentative strategies, social interaction, frequent feedback and adjustment, in order that administrators minimize their vulnerability to forces no one can understand or control fully. From this perspective, postindustrial complexity and massive bureaucracy are not only *not* inconsistent with active citizenship, they positively require it.

The agency perspective thus acts as a "city" within which to practice active citizenship, as administrative discretion grounded in the accountability that develops out of face-to-face interaction and dialogue, and situated by agency memory and contextual insight, expands the public space to include those the Founders left out so long ago.

Active Citizenship and the Public Interest

The discussion turns now to reflection on the question of the meaning of "shared values" or "the public interest," as both the ground and aim of administrative practice and active citizenship. I have argued that legitimate bureaucratic discretion implies a form of accountability to citizens that is more tangible than (not a replacement for) professional codes of ethics or constitutional and legislative provisions. Although individual conscience and consultation with agency colleagues obviously are important normative mediators in administrative practice, they must be anchored in the larger world—in the public space—by dialogue and joint action with citizens, so that citizens play a real part in *constructing* the shared interpretation of values: values that then continue to apply in administrative situations where citizen participation is not practical. Citizen views must be accorded real weight: if advice, they must be truly "advice which cannot safely be ignored."

A substantive public decision-making role for citizens is important as a mechanism for constructing a shared understanding of the public interest. In this way, it becomes possible for administrators to check the content of their own consensus discursively against the wider understanding of a larger community of nonspecialists, so that the agency perspective does not act as an interpretation unto itself. Justification of agency actions, or legitimation, then becomes tied to a practice of accountability, as administrators fulfill the obligation to give good reasons and take citizens' expressed views seriously.

In his reflection on "the needs of strangers," Ignatieff points to Saint Augustine's distinction between the freedom to choose and the freedom of knowing one has chosen rightly. Unredeemed reason, which is all that liberal heritage and modernity appear to allow us, can never be certain that its choices are right.[50] But though our intellectual traditions leave us little confidence in the transcendent, administrators can still find a basis for knowing they have chosen rightly, when they have not simply conducted thought experiments but have also consulted citizens who are fellow members in a wider community of knowledge.

The process view of the public interest argued by the Manifesto and developed in Charles Goodsell's essay in this book,[51] reflects the understanding that not being able to quantify the public interest or to reach full agreement about the correct translation of values into action are not the same as having nothing basic to which administrative discretion must hold itself accountable. One may never have full confidence that the choice itself is right, but one may approximate such confidence in the knowledge that one's claims have been checked against the interpretations offered by citizens. Again, we aim at the ideal knowing that its tension with the real is never to be resolved. When bureaucrats and citizens understand this together, the basis for trust is established.

A substantive role for citizens is also important if we are to nurture the sort of citizen whose participation we need not fear. Human nature may be self-interested and passionate to a considerable extent, but, as we have seen, the societal learning perspective offers a framework within which to conduct an administrative praxis that assumes that, however we find them, citizens are capable of learning and developing, becoming more knowledgeable and understanding.

Enlightenment, however, works in both directions. As Peter Berger has argued in *Pyramids of Sacrifice*, the paths society takes cannot be decided by experts, because there are no experts on the desirable goals of human life. No one is "more conscious" than anyone else: it is simply that our different interests and experiences make us attentive to differing sets of information. When people become expert in one area, they neglect other data. Convincing someone that your approach is better, therefore, is a transaction among equals; thus the administrator's turn to citizens must be grounded in *cognitive* as well as political respect. Legitimation of the administrative state requires that citizen and bureaucrat move toward each other, not that one come to the other, in order that citizens and bureaucrats may begin the task of constructing agreements of meaning.

From this perspective, the public interest is not something administrators alone are qualified to define. Yet there is something unique about the administrative role, for the public interest connotes government action as an agent for all societal members. Such action is generally understood to take account of the full range of its effects, not just the interests of vocal claimants. Also, it is binding action, which will be enforced against all societal members.[53] Governmental, therefore binding, action for the good of all is the essence of what we mean — bureaucrats and citizens alike — when we use the term *public interest*. Its meaning in any particular situation inevitably occupies the space between the ideal and the real, of which I have spoken.

The uniqueness of the administrator's role thus has centrally to do with the power that he or she is able to exercise: the power to give binding answers to public questions. This makes the administrator's practical wisdom, that is, administrative discretion, more potent than that practiced by other citizens. We have seen that it reaches to the very core of what constitutes knowledge and who is empowered to say so. Therefore, administrative discretion presents unique opportunities for expanding membership in the knowledge community, for fostering societal learning, and for creating mechanisms for dialogue and joint action. In Giddens's terms, the exercise of administrative discretion is the mode in which the bureaucrat reflects the status of *agent*, or one who has the knowledge and capability to make a difference, no matter how constraining the circumstances.

This understanding of administrative discretion opens the way to a new interpretation of the politics of administration. Cynthia McSwain has argued that the liberal heritage gave us the understanding that the only sort of interests administrators could serve would be selfish ones, either their won biases or the claims of interest groups. If so, the only alternative — the only "democratic" practice — was neutral competence. McSwain observes that the concept of administrators as neutral implementors of policy decided by the outcome of contention among interests long ago lost its hold on the field.[54] But, as John Rohr points out, the ideal of administrative subservience to the legislature comes not from the Constitution but was Wilson's and Goodnow's claim: that faithful adherence to the popular will required not separation of powers but separation of functions. The framers, however, were willing to blend legislative, executive, and judicial functions in one branch of government; they did so in their idea of the Senate. Thus, the exercise of legislative and judicial functions by public administrators is not at odds with the intent of the Constitution.[55] The idea that there is no conceptual legitimacy to the interconnectedness of politics and administration thus only holds if we have no viable notion of general interests. It is only if all interests are private and selfish that politics, or the weighing of claims, must be seen as inherently pernicious.

In my view, the notion of the public interest is alive and well. We all have a commonsense understanding that the demands of interest groups do not add up in some mysterious way to the general good, because we commonly check their claims against the public interest *even if*, when pressed further to specify it in the situation at hand, we are unable to do so precisely. And we need not feel that the *public interest* is therefore a nonsense term or a cry of emotion, as positivism would have us conclude. On the contrary, the continued currency of the term reflects widespread understanding that disinterested behavior is possible. The process view of the public interest put forward by the Manifesto and argued more fully by Goodsell suggests that administrative discretion can be legitimated by self-conscious devotion to the idea of the public interest. My only addition to this argument is that administrators not take their own perceptions of the public interest at face value without checking them discursively against the views of citizens. The effort to develop structures and processes for empowering citizens, for giving them opportunities to rule, reflects devotion to the public interest and accountability back to the source of all that happens in the public space. Thus will bureaucrats address the alienation that Ricoeur says lies at the heart of all politics, which is that power can never be exercised with full equality of effect. Thus will they evoke the trust that enables them to give a binding answer that people will view as legitimate.

Administrative Practice for Active Citizenship

The kind of interactive administrative governance envisioned in this paper, joining citizens with public administrators in shared practice and understanding, is more than a pipe dream. Although particular agencies vary in the political-economic context within which they are situated, as well as in mandates and other rules and resources, nevertheless much can be done within the existing circumstances of most agencies.

Establishing Frameworks for Interaction

Relationships between public administrators and citizens that constitute a community of citizenship can be fostered by laws, regulations, policies, procedures, and ongoing actions that share responsibility with citizens in conduction agency affairs. Within given legislated mandates, administrators can use their discretion to approach rule-making and the design of agency processes so that not just clients and interests groups but members of the general public participate as fully as possible in policy making and in implementation. Such arrangements do not entail "privatization," or the divestiture of public responsibilities, but rather substantive cooperation between citizens and administrators in which citizens are seen as co-governors and co-decision makers, not simply as consumers or providers of services.

An example of this kind of relationship is the federal Community Health Center program in the Department of Health and Human Services. Groups of grassroots citizens hold authority for expending federal grant funds to organize and deliver a complex array of health services in deprived areas, in accordance with applicable laws and regulations. In essence, this program gives citizens the authority to make judgments about what constitutes the public interest in particular situations, by translating broad guidelines into the specific needs of local communities with which they are familiar. Although public administrators monitor citizens, the latter have considerable authority within their sphere. In addition, through regular substantive interaction with administrators, citizens participate in shaping what amounts to a shared interpretation of relevant rules. Public administrators do not simply tell citizens how things are; instead, together citizens and officials work out agreements of meaning and action that bind them both. The agency perspective is shaped by citizens and administrators alike.[56] A similar arrangement is reflected in the transfer to public-housing tenants of the authority for managing their own complexes, as in the District of Columbia, where residents of Kenilworth-Parkside Gardens have contracted with the U.S. Department of Housing and Urban Development to oversee their apartment development.[57]

Beyond the delivery of specific services, there are workable arrangements that will foster open communities of knowledge that admit citizens to membership in the process of interpreting the public interest. Here, administrators interact with citizens in order to determine the possible range of policy choice and the type and content of knowledge relevant to particular decisions. Together, administrators and citizens develop an agenda of possibilities — a substantive vision specific to the perspective and mandate of particular agencies.

An example is the process followed by the Berger Inquiry in Canada, which evaluated the proposed natural-gas pipeline from Prudhoe Bay through the Mackenzie Valley. All parties to the inquiry were required to submit a list of pertinent documents in their possession and to share this information on request. Funding was provided to native groups, environmentalists, municipalities, and small businesses to improve their ability to participate on an equal footing with the pipeline companies. Community hearings were held throughout the affected area, in which all participants could speak in their own languages.

As a result of the process, a range of views was heard that broadened the usual definition of costs and benefits beyond the context of industrialization, modernization, business and employment expansion, to take in renewable resources, the cultural identity of native peoples, and cooperative endeavor. The inquiry was one factor in the decision of the Canadian Cabinet to reject the Mackenzie Vally proposal, though vigorously promoted by petroleum corporations, in favor of another pipeline project.[58]

Professionalism and Citizenship

There are certain ways of going about daily administrative life that will support the stance I have advocated, that will constitute, in effect, revisions to the code of professional behavior.

The first is personal reflexivity: an accounting to self, a deliberate process of becoming conscious of one's memberships in relevant subcommunities of knowledge, including professional, socio-economic, gender-based, and racial. Sex, race, income level, and occupation are not just neutral characteristics, but also imply agreements to which one has subscribed, tacitly or explicitly, agreements with political implications. Reflexivity also includes an awareness of limits on the rationality of action, as well as on its efficacy: subjectively, action is constrained by the unconscious; objectively, by unacknowledged conditions and unintended consequences. Ultimately, reflexivity is a turning back out of self to others, in recognition of the intersubjective nature of knowledge itself and one's participation in its construction. This turn is both the epistemological and the normative ground of an administrative practice that is consistent with active citizenship.

A second practice is the development of a critical approach to the context of administration. As I have said, all knowledge is interested. The critical approach, which is grounded in an interest in human freedom,[59] seeks to reexamine institutional practices in light of new knowledge about the political and economic dimensions of administration. Such a reexamination would explore how the unacknowledged political-economic conditions surrounding administrative practice shape and sometimes determine the level of citizen knowledgeability and capability to deal with policy issues. Such a critical approach is part of one's consciousness of being an agent, that is, one who can make a difference.

A third element of practice is a commitment to the giving of reasons, which is the essence of public decision making, not something added onto an otherwise factual-neutral process of policy formation.[60] The giving of reasons is an old American tradition, dating back at least to the *Federalist Papers*, which aimed to convince citizens by appeals both to rationality and the sensibilities. Although, as Gordon Wood has shown, the framers' knowledge community was an elite one,[61] their approach demonstrates the assumption that understanding is both a matter of intellectual grasp of issues and of affiliative feeling. Citizen trust in the public administrator's commitment to the giving of reasons — a trust developed in concrete situations — is the basis for confidence in government even in the absence of opportunity to engage in dialogue on a given question. This confidence stems from the conviction that, if confronted, administrators could give good reasons for what they do, that is, they could convince citizens that they were acting in the public interest. Such a commitment also reflects a societal learning perspective, one that hold that citizen can learn from the reasons they receive, and can give reasons in return.

Thus, the public administrator's role is unique in its centrality, not in its elevation. For one thing, public administrators have greater access than do other citizens to relevant information. This information forms the basis for their own judgments about issues as well as the basis for improving citizens' practical wisdom, much as the early reformers viewed facts as the ground of efficient citizenship. Perhaps the reformers were too sanguine in their belief that knowledge would lead to supportive understanding, and they certainly gave little emphasis to the political-economic context of administration and its impact on decision making. Nevertheless, facts are important, and administrators are well placed not only to facilitate citizen access to them but also to aid in contextual interpretation. Administrators are in better position than citizens to perceive the ideological dimensions of policy making, if their own information-seeking is supported by personal reflexivity. They have the knowledgeability and capability to make available to citizens information that will uncover unacknowledged conditions and unintended consequences; thus can do much, if they will, to facilitate change.

I have already argued that much of the uniqueness of the administrative role lies in the power to exercise discretion in the public interest. But there is also the matter that more of the public servant's life is involved in the public space than is true for other citizens. This does not make public administrators better, but it does make them special. They are due respect for their willingness to carry a vital societal obligation. The public administrator's commitment gives him or her a sense of the whole that others might well view as a burden. This same sense, of course, supports recognition that the limits of communities of knowledge and action are expandable, on principle. These aspects of the administrative role facilitate the development of models for the practice of active citizenship: "imagined alternatives," as Graeme Duncan has called them, grounded in the sense that much more is possible even within given political-economic conditions.[62] Duncan argues that citizens' knowledge and understanding may be limited at present by preexisting rules and resources; they may appear apathetic, self-interested, or deceived. Yet, when and if they change, it must be because *they* want to, and through a process consistent with our political values. Echoing Habermas once more, in a process of enlightenment there can be only participants.

From this perspective, the public administrator as agent of active citizenship aims to develop, from his or her knowledge and experience, frameworks and situations around which citizen knowledgeability and capability can crystallize. Out of a sense of the whole unique to the administrative role grows a new form of understanding that has the potential to build bridges among the different frames of reference found among citizens, and to clarify, little by little, the acknowledged conditions and unintended consequences of life in the American administrative state.

This form of understanding takes in but exceeds both factual and interpretative modes, both propositional knowledge and empathy. It is critical understanding, which builds upon facts and grounds itself normatively in sympathetic connection with the givens of people's existences, but refuses to rest in these. Such a *praxis* requires critique: of self, of the contexts of practice, of the constitution of knowledge. And it understands that change, indeed governance itself, is never to be fully within the control either of citizens or bureaucrats, who are alike in being part of a tension that is never to be resolved, an unfolding that is by its nature beyond our full comprehension.

Notes

1. For an argument in this vein, see Charles Goodsell, *The Case for Bureaucracy,* 2nd ed. (Chatham, N.J.: Chatham House, 1985).

2. Camilla Stivers, *Active Citizenship in the Administrative State,* unpublished Ph.D. dissertation, Virginia Polytechnic Institute and State University, Blacksburg, Virginia, 1988, p. 76-77.

3. Lawrence A. Scaff, "Citizenship in America," in Joyotpaul Chauduri, ed., *The Non-Lockean Roots of American Democratic Thought* (Tucson, Ariz.: University of Arizona Press, 1977), p. 44-62.

4. Louis C. Gawthrop, "Civis, Civitas, and Civilitas: A New Focus for the Year 2000," *Public Administration Review* 44, Special Issue (March 1984): 103.

5. See John A. Rohr, "Civil Servants and Second Class Citizens," *Public Administration Review,* op. cit., 135-140.

6. James H. Kettner, *The Development of American Citizenship, 1608-1870* (Chapel Hill, N.C.: University of North Carolina Press, 1978), p. 323.

7. John A. Rohr, "The Administrative State and Constitutional Principle," Center for Public Administration and Policy, Virginia Polytechnic Institute (mimeo), prepared for delivery at the Annual Meeting of the American Political Science Association (September 1983), p. 11.

8. Herbert A. Storing, *What the Anti-Federalists Were For,* (Chicago: University of Chicago Press, 1981), p. 73.

9. Aristotle, *The Politics,* III,i (New York: Penguin, 1981), p. 169.

10. Ibid., III,iv, p. 182. Aristotle's theory of the state is notably deficient as a model for the present day because of his view that women were by nature unqualified for membership.

11. Ibid., III,vi, p. 187.

12. See the summary of Rousseau's argument in Carole Pateman, *Participation and Democratic Theory* (Cambridge: Cambridge University Press, 1970), p. 22-27.

13. Terry Cooper, "Citizenship and Professionalism in Public Administration," *Public Administration Review,* op. cit., p. 143-149.

14. Hannah Arendt, *On Revolution* (New York: Pelican, 1963), p. 126 ff.

15. Quoted in Arthur M. Schlesinger, Jr., *The Age of Jackson* (Boston: Little, Brown, 1953), p. 325.

16. Paul Ricoeur, "The Political Paradox," in William Connolly, ed., *Legitimacy and the State* (New York: New York University Press, 1984), p. 250-272.

17. Sheldon Wolin, *Politics and Vision* (Boston: Little, Brown, 1960), p. 62.

18. See Michael Ignatieff, *The Needs of Strangers* (New York: Viking, 1984).

19. See, for example, Peter Berger, Brigitte Berger, and Hansfried Kellner, *The Homeless Mind* (New York: Vintage, 1974).

20. Wolin, op. cit. p. 72-76.

21. Ignatieff, op. cit.

22. See, for example, Gibson Burrell and Gareth Morgan, *Sociological Paradigms and Organizational Analysis* (London: Heinemann, 1979).

23. Jurgen Habermans, *Theory and Practice* (Boston: Beacon Press, 1973), p. 40.

24. Anthony Giddens, *The Constitution of Society* (Berkeley, Calif.: University of California Press, 1984), p. 2.

25. Ibid., p. 33.

26. Ibid., p. 3.

27. Ibid., p. 14.

28. Ibid., p. 16.

29. Anthony Giddens, *Central Problems in Social Theory* (Berkeley: University of California Press, 1979), p. 248.

30. *The Constitution of Society,* p. 285.

31. Ibid., p. 335.

32. Anthony Giddens, *Profiles and Critiques in Social Theory* (Berkeley: University of California Press, 1982), p. 16.

33. Thomas S. Kuhm, *The Structure of Scientific Revolutions,* 2nd ed. (Chicago: University of Chicago Press, 1970).

34. Robert E. Goodin and Peter Wilenski, "Beyond Efficiency: The Logical Underpinnings of Administrative Principle," *Public Administration Review* 46, 6 (November-December 1984): 513.

35. Charles W. Anderson, "The Place of Principles in Policy Analysis," *American Political Science Review* 73, 3 (September 1979): 711-723.

36. Jurgen Habermas, *Knowledge and Human Interests* (Boston: Beacon Press, 1971), p. 304 ff.

37. Alvin Gouldner, *The Dialectic of Ideology and Technology* (New York: Oxford University Press, 1976), p. 21.

38. Thomas Hobbes, *Leviathan* (Penguin, 1982), p. 109.

39. Habermas, *Theory and Practice,* op. cit., p. 42.

40. Ibid., p. 43.

41. Georg Lukacs, *History and Class Consciousness* (Cambridge, Mass.: MIT Press, 1971), p. 299.

42. Gary Wamsley, "The Agency Perspective: Crucial Focal Point for the Public Administrator," unpublished manuscript, Center for Public Administration and Policy, Virginia Polytechnic Institute and State University, Blacksburg, Va., 1985.

43. Frank J. Goodnow, *Politics and Administration* (New York: Macmillan, 1914).

44. William H. Allen, *Efficient Democracy* (New York: Dodd, Mead, 1907), p. ix.

45. Henri Bruere, *The New City Government* (New York: D. Appleton, 1912), p. xii.

46. Frederick A. Cleveland, *The Growth of Democracy in the United States* (Chicago: Quadrangle Press, 1898), p. 159.

47. James W. Botkin, Mahdi Elmandjra, and Mircea Malitza, *No Limits to Learning* (Oxford: Pergamon Press, 1979).

48. Yehezkel Dror, "Policy Gambling: A Preliminary Exploration," *Policy Studies Journal* 12, 1 (September 1983): 9-13.

49. David Korten, "The Management of Social Transformation," *Public Administration Review* 41, 6 (November-December 1981): 613.

50. Ignatieff, op. cit., p. 62.

51. Charles Goodsell, "Public Administration and the Public Interest."

52. Peter Berger, *Pyramids of Sacrifice* (New York: Anchor, 1976), p. 127 ff.

53. Richard Flathman, *The Public Interest* (New York: Wiley, 1966), p. 3-6.

54. Cynthia McSwain, "Administrators and Citizenship: The Liberalist Legacy of the Constitution," *Administration and Society* 17, 2 (August 1985): 131-148.

55. Rohr, "The Administrative State and Constitutional Principle," op. cit. See also Rohr's essay in this volume.

56. A more detailed discussion of the Community Health Center Program can be found in Stivers, *Active Citizenship in the Administrative State,* op. cit.

57. *Washington Post,* May 20, 1985.

58. Douglas Torgerson, "Between Knowledge and Politics: Three Faces of Policy Analysis," *Policy Sciences* 19 (1986), p. 33-59.

59. Habermas, *Knowledge and Human Interests,* p. 310-311.

60. See William Dunn, "Reforms as Arguments," *Evaluation Studies Review Annual* (Beverly Hills: Sage, 1983).

61. Gordon S. Wood, "The Democratization of Mind in the American Revolution," in *Moral Foundations of the American Republic,* ed. Robert H. Horwitz, 2nd. ed. (Charlottesville, Va.: University Press of Virginia, 1979), p. 102-128.

62. Graeme Duncan, "Human Nature and Radical Democratic Theory," in *Democratic Theory and Practice,* ed. Graeme Duncan (Cambridge: Cambridge University Press, 1983), p. 187-203.

8. Public Administration and the Defense Department: Examination of a Prototype

PHILIP S. KRONENBERG

Needed: An Institutional Prototype

The Blacksburg Manifesto[1] represents a vigorous call both to reexamine the premises upon which American public administration rest and to reorient practice in the public sector itself. Thus, there are both conceptual and operational challenges to conventional wisdom that are embodied in the Manifesto.

Those who have responded affirmatively to the Manifesto, as well as some of its critics, seem to feel that the positive appeal of its intention to upgrade the role of public administration is constrained by a degree of naivete. One attribute of this alleged naivete is the implausibility of actually implementing some of the more essential features of its prescriptions. Like most proposals for radical change, its critics allege that it exceeds the "art of the possible."

One approach to evaluating the quality of the Manifesto's argument is to seek out a set of institutional arrangements that approximate the circumstances that would obtain if the Manifesto were actually implemented in the contemporary United States. This would help us flesh out some of the abstractions that are found in the Manifesto and put the public administration community in a better position to assess the strengths and weaknesses of its prescriptions.

One institutional test case that is available to us is the Department of Defense. This agency offers us an empirical context that approximates many of the expectations that the Manifesto authors hold out for general public administration if their prescriptions were to be implemented.

The Blacksburg Manifesto offers itself as a basis for a useful national dialogue about the proper contribution of public administration to the quest for effective governance of our republic. I intend to contribute to that dialogue in this chapter by examining the Department of Defense as a test case of the prescriptions that are set forth in the Manifesto.

To accomplish my purpose, I will (1) examine the features of the Department of Defense which make it appropriate as a test case of the Manifesto for public agencies in the operational world, and (2) assess the implications of this test case for the Manifesto as a theoretical guide to rethinking governance in contemporary America.

Defense Department as Test Case

Any attempt to find an institutional test case with which to examine the Manifesto's "real-world" characteristics must provide an example that is plausibly representative of general public administration *and* offers some essential implementation of the prescriptions found in the Manifesto. My intention in this section is to profile the ways in which the institutional characteristics of the Department of Defense are representative of general public administration and to examine the ways in which the department reflects central prescriptions of the Manifesto.

As Representative of General Public Administration

The Department of Defense (DoD) provides an important example of a large public agency which can serve as a test case for the kind of public agency that is called for in the prescriptions of the Blacksburg Manifesto. The extent to which DoD is substantially representative of general public administration is manifest in six dimensions.

First, it is a large agency in terms of its funding. DoD budgets have been substantial over the years, often ranking first among federal agencies during the periods of the Korean and Vietnam wars. Although total spending for welfare, social security, and health has been more than double the defense budget in the late 1970s and early 1980s,[2] DoD continues to be a major claimant on federal resources.

Second, and another attribute of its scale, is its status as an employer of a very large workforce. DoD looms large in this respect with 300,000 officers and over 1.8 million people in the enlisted ranks of the active-duty armed forces (these figures do not include almost 1 million civilians who are part-time members of military-reserve and national-guard organizations throughout the United States).[3] What is perhaps more noteworthy in terms of DoD's representativeness of other large public agencies is the fact that there are 1 million civilian employees of the department who constitute almost 40 percent of the total federal *civilian* workforce.[4] Thus, DoD is the largest civilian employer in the federal government. Its closest competitors in the federal workforce are Veterans Administration (220,600), Health and Human Services (134,000), Treasury (126,000), and Agriculture (106,900).[5]

A third feature of DoD is its task complexity. It employs cooks, physicians, social scientists, biologists, attorneys, engine mechanics, musicians, and historians, among a host of other functional and disciplinary specialists in both its uniformed and civilian positions. A relatively small percentage of people in DoD are engaged in the tasks that directly involve military combats skills.

Structural complexity parallels the task complexity found in DoD. There is a relatively small (about 2,500 people) Office of the Secretary of Defense, an Organization of the Joint Chiefs of Staff with less than 2,000 people, the Departments of the Army, Navy (which includes the Marine Corps), and Air Force of about 1 million civilian and military people each, and over a dozen "defense agencies" (e.g., Defense Logistics Agency, Defense Mapping Agency, Defense Intelligence Agency, Defense Contract Audit Agency) which report to the secretary of defense outside of the military service departments. This level of structural complexity is further increased by virtue of the fact that the three military departments within DoD do not "own" or command the military forces that they help organize, train, and equip. Although the U.S. Army, U.S. Navy, U.S. Marine Corps, and U.S. Air Force (and in wartime, the U.S. Coast Guard) certainly *influence* the fighting doctrine and professional careers of people in these armed services, their formal assignment and control as combat units is given to yet another set of structures known as the six Unified Commands (e.g., U.S. Pacific Command) and three Specified Commands (e.g., Strategic Air Command). The senior generals and admirals in charge of these commands are formally responsible to the secretary of defense and the president, not to the senior military and civilian leaders of the military service departments (although their informal linkages to their "home" military services are substantial).

A fifth element of representativeness is found in the geographic distribution of DoD personnel. Taking uniformed U.S. Air Force people as one indicator of this, one finds that one-fifth are stationed in foreign countries. These troops are frequently supported by large numbers of civilian employees; the 61,500 uniformed USAF personnel assigned in 1984 to the United States Air Forces in Europe were associated with almost 10,000 civilian employees of the Department of the Air Force. Of course, the military and civilian personnel of DoD are distributed throughout the United States; there are over 100 major Air Force bases in the United States and over 2,000 minor installations across this country.[6]

Finally, one should note that the personnel of DoD are as likely to be representative of the general population of the United States as any department of the federal government. The military took the lead among the agencies of government after World War II in racial desegregation efforts, and DoD has generally been an exemplar in its concern with this difficult area of social policy.[7]

As Representative of the Manifesto

Even if DoD reflects many of the key attributes of other general public administration agencies, there is still the issue of how well it serves to demonstrate the prescriptions found in the Manifesto. Does its institutional culture reflect central themes found in the advocacy of the Manifesto? I think it does in the four areas that are at the heart of the Manifesto's argument.

Public Administrators as Self-Conscious Trustees of the Public Interest

One theme of the Manifesto is that the career staffs — the public administrators — should be trustees of the public interest with a unique sense of commitment to serve the public interest relevant to a particular societal function in a fashion that transcends limited instrumental or pragmatic goals and seeks the long-term welfare of the society and its democratic constitutional processes. This theme is reflected in the uniformed officer corps of the military which serves — in a manner paralleling similar qualities found in the foreign service officer corps and the U.S. Forest Service, among others — as a career establishment endowed with a commitment to the public service.

Officer Corps as Model Public Administration Cadre The career officer is a professional operating in a bureaucratic context with its division of labor around specialized skills and its commitment to career development around achievement norms. The culture of the officer corps places a very high priority on a commitment to duty to one's organization and one's country within an operational ethic that places an imperative on honest dealing with "brother" officers; all of this in a context that gives a very visible commitment to the physical defense of one's country and to the values that it represents.

A Bureaucratic Profession The military is a "bureaucratic" profession as distinct from the "associational" professions like medicine and the law in which the professional practitioner tends to function independently and to operate in a direct personal relationship with the client.[8] Bureaucratic professions like the military possess a high level of specialization of the labor *and* responsibilities within the profession, and the profession as a collective entity renders a service to society at large.

Duty, Honor, Country The importance of public service that is embedded in the traditions of the officer corps as a bureaucratic profession has evolved an obligation to service based on achievement that has increasingly displaced the ascriptive roots of the feudal military establishment. This transformation can be attributed to the growing skill structure of the military profession that has undermined the effectiveness of an ascribed basis of authority.

The operational ideal of the military profession in the United States is captured by the word "Duty Honor Country" that appear on the coat of arms of the U.S. Military Academy at West Point. John Lovell's study of the institutional evolution of the military service academies points to the central mission of those institutions as "professional socialization":

> The socialization process involves the transmission not only of skills and information, but also of organizational values and traditions. If socialization is successful, the academy graduate will have received not only the "tools of his trade," but also the motivation and feeling of identification that links him to earlier generations of military professionals and to the society which he serves.[10]

Lovell goes on to argue that this professional socialization not only instills a sense of obligation to serve and defend one's country but reinforces the notion of loyalty in more personal terms. The routines of Naval Academy training, for example, not only reinforced belief in "maintaining the watch faithfully at sea," in order to protect one's country, but also because the lives of one's shipmates might be in danger. "That is why loyalty was so closely tied to duty and honor."[11]

This commitment to public service resembles a "calling" to a religious vocation. Morris Janowitz has observed that military officers frequently equate their profession and the ministry; he quotes a letter by a retired naval captain who wrote his son about this linkage:

> The naval profession is much like the ministry. You dedicate your life to a purpose. You wear the garb of an organized profession. Your life is governed by rules laid down by the organization. You renounce your pursuit of wealth. In a large measure you surrender your citizenship; renounce politics; and work for the highest good of the organization. In the final analysis your aims and objects are quite as moral as any minister's because you are not seeking your own good, but the ultimate good of your country.[12]

General "Hap" Arnold, the great commander who built and led the U.S. Army Air Force during World War II, tells a parallel story about himself that reinforces this sense of calling and moral commitment to a concept of public service — if in a less solemn tone. Arnold had been told by his father to go to college at Bucknell College and then enter the ministry. His brother was directed by his father to seek admission to West Point. As it turned out, Arnold took the West Point entrance examination instead of his brother and entered the academy:

> I have never understood why my friends laugh when I tell them this. As my career did work out, it came to require as much sheer faith as any preacher's. Or perhaps I should say, as any other preacher's, since it actually took as much evangelism, and maybe more years, to sell the idea of Air Power as it would ever have taken me to sell the Wages of Sin.[13]

A Career of Praxis — A Synthesis of Theory and Action The career of the typical military officer involves rotation through assignments with operational forces, in staff assignments, and in training or educational programs. The logic behind this is to prepare an officer for increasing responsibility while not minimizing the officer's grasp of operations at the tactical level. The extent to which time in one's career is allocated among these three areas varies greatly among the services and has been different among those who retire as a lieutenant colonel or colonel in contrast to those who become general or flag officers.[14]

This orientation toward reconciling or integrating theory and action is very much grounded in experience and pragmatism. One manifestation of this is the great attention given to the development of explicit doctrine that is then to be implemented by operational leaders. It is taken very seriously and, while the linkage between "prescription" and operational behavior is never perfect, it is more self-conscious and more professionally significant than is generally true of the normative regimes found in formal organizations. Another facet of this orientation is the attention to history — especially military history — in the professional literature of the military and the sifting of insights from the "lessons learned," both from wars and campaigns, and from efforts to cull tactical and strategic wisdom from the lives of "the great commanders."

Agency Perspective as a Repository of Unique Capacity

The Manifesto argues that public agencies are repositories of a unique capacity to serve the public interest relevant to a particular societal function and that proper pursuit of the public interest requires the "agency perspective."

What one finds at the core of the Department of Defense as a public agency that fosters this agency perspective is the military officer corps: a large and sophisticated bureaucratic profession, existing within multifaceted complex organizational arrangements, with a rich tradition of service to country and to organizational missions. A career in the military involves the officer in a learning environment filled with demands to test theory and doctrine in operational, practical settings.

It is perhaps more accurate to think in terms of agency perspectives in the plural rather than the singular when one refers to the Department of Defense. The historical roots of the institutional forms and values that characterize the modern Department of Defense spring from somewhat distinctive orientations rooted in the eighteenth-century American army and navy that have evolved into the modern U.S. Army, U.S. Navy, U.S. Marine Corps, and U.S. Air Force. Indeed, "agency perspective" in the sense that it is defined in the Manifesto would have to reflect sensitivity as well, to the distinctive qualities associated with central components *within* each of these military services, such as found in the unique doctrinal and operational traditions of infantry, artillery, and cavalry — armor forces — among others — within the U.S. Army (and the civilian establishments affiliated with each of these three "combat arms") or in the "surface navy," "naval aviators," and "submariners" within the U.S. Navy. The fact that agency perspective is identified in a somewhat unique way within each of these major components of the Department of Defense is consistent with the positions taken in the Manifesto and is a quality shared by most large public agencies, such as the Department of Health and Human Services with its several health and social service components.

This institutional home of the uniformed officer corps is shared with a substantial body of career civilian employees who inject an impressive array of technical and managerial skills and experience into the organic capacity of DoD to serve the public interest. They participate in the core perspectives of the uniformed members in each DoD component that their work roles characteristically support. The large civilian component of DoD's human resources brings a varied and talented pool of education, skills, and experience to the agency. The sharing of agency perspectives within this civilian workforce of DoD is encouraged both by the socialization of these civil servants to the organizational missions of the major DoD components and by the fact that many defense agency employees are former members of the armed forces or are members of the military reserves.

This set of circumstances, characteristic of the officer corps and its civilian employee associates, places the Department of Defense squarely in an ethos that clearly represents the agency perspective in government service. The military officers with their civilian colleagues are visibly surrounded by symbols of duty and service and are engaged in a distinct bureaucratic profession operating in the public interest and pursuing missions of grave national importance. This is the fullest expression of the agency perspective.

Public Administration as a Legitimate Participant in a Constitutional Order

The Constitution of the United States provides for the establishment and direction of armed forces in several clauses, beginning with the reference in the Preamble to the need of "We the people . . . " to "provide for the common defense." The principal clauses of the Constitution relevant to defense and the functions of a legitimate, institutionalized military establishment are:

Designate a commander-in-chief. Article II, Section 2, specifies that "The President shall be Commander in Chief of the Army and Navy of the United States, and of the Militia of the several States, when called into the actual Service of the United States . . . "

Declare war. This is reserved to the Congress under Article I, Section 8.

Finance a military establishment. Article I, Section 8, empowers Congress to raise revenues to ". . . provide for the common defense . . . " and to "raise and support Armies" and "provide and maintain a Navy . . . "

Incorporation of state-based military reserves into the national military establishment. The "militia clauses" are Article I, Section 8, which empowers the Congress to organize, arm, and discipline the militia, to call up the militia to federal service, and to govern militia which may be called to federal service, and Article II, Section 2, which empowers the president to act as commander-in-chief of the militia, when militia units are called to federal service.

Organize the military establishment. Congress is empowered in Article I, Section 8, to "make Rules for the Government and Regulation of the land and naval Forces . . . "

Appoint military officers and other defense officials. Article II, Section 2, of the Constitution provides that the president has the power, "by and with the

Advice and Consent of the Senate," to appoint all officers of the government (Congress may by law vest appointment of "inferior Officers" in the president alone).

The Constitution, then, offers a basis to view the national military establishment as a legitimate player in the process of governance. But how far does that legitimate role extend? The normative strategy of the Blacksburg Manifesto calls for the maintenance of a constitutional order in which The Public Administration as a corporate entity is a key, legitimate participant which must not " . . . cower before a sovereign legislative assembly or a sovereign elected executive." Presumably, the institutional embodiment of The Public Administration in the Defense Department resides in the career officer corps.

Much attention has been given in the literature to the concept of "civilian control of the military" as a central theme that is grounded in the Constitution. The roots of that notion rest in rather explicit terms on the role of the president as commander-in-chief and on the role of the Congress in creating, funding, and laying out the rules for organizing the armed forces and the policy-making bodies that attend to national security matters. Must the corporate bureaucracy of the armed forces "cower" before a sovereign Congress or sovereign president or (politically appointed) secretary of defense in the name of "civilian control of the military"? The Manifesto, presumably, would answer *no*. Though the Manifesto is silent on the role of The Public Administration-in-Uniform, one would expect that consistency would compel the authors of the Manifesto to grant to the military service establishment the same treatment as it gives to the civil service establishment. The Public Administration, in or out of uniform, has a unique constitutional legitimacy in the view of the Manifesto.

This position of the Manifesto would appear to parallel a controversial statement by Douglas MacArthur. The general protested Harry Truman's decision to sack him for what MacArthur judged to be a bankrupt and dangerous policy by denouncing

> . . . a new and heretofore unknown and dangerous concept that the members of our armed forces owe primary allegiance or loyalty to those who temporarily exercise the authority of the Executive Branch of the Government rather than to the country and its Constitution which they are sworn to defend. No proposition could be more dangerous.[15]

MacArthur's statement seems congenial to the position of the Manifesto in that the Manifesto encourages a perspective on policies and programs that transcends the political preferences of elected politicians and opts for fidelity to larger constitutional priorities. MacArthur seems to be doing just that as a senior representative of the officer corps who articulates what the Manifesto would call "agency perspective" in defense of the constitutional order.

To paraphrase the Manifesto: The Constitution to some extent explicitly and to a greater extent implicitly and through historic practice has assigned a more demanding and significant role to The Public Administration-in-Uniform as well as The Public Administration-in-Civilian Garb.

The Authority of The Public Administration Rests on a Process-Oriented Discovery of the Public Interest

A fourth central theme of the Manifesto is that the legitimacy of the career public service as a major participant in American governance must rest on its contribution — through the "agency perspective" — to discovering and then defining the public interest. This theme rejects a search for "correct" content or substance in defining the public interest. Instead, the Manifesto asserts the problematic nature of the public interest and compels a role for career agency personnel that involves a process orientation to contain, if not resolve, the conflict among competing interests in the society.

The preceding section of this chapter pointed to the constitutional pluralism that divides authority among Congress, president, and national and state governments in the conduct of the government, including military affairs. This constitutional pluralism combines with America's pluralist political reality and our socioeconomic pluralism and bureaucratic pluralism[16] to provide the infrastructure on which the process-oriented pursuit of the public interest occurs in the sphere of defense administration. And it is here that the Defense Department again serves as a useful test case of the Manifesto.

The Manifesto's notion of "discovering and defining" the public interest resembles in many respects the concept of strategic management that has emerged in the policy systems management literature over the past twenty years. The term *strategic management* has become associated with the policy level of decision making in complex organizations.[17]

Management at this level involves decisions oriented toward the future of the organization regarding its environmental niche; key resources, markets, and clientele; characteristic technologies, goods, and services; and its unique organizational climate. In a public agency like the Department of Defense, strategic management also involves processes that define the public interest in terms of that agency.

The strategic management system that produces these definitions of the public interest in the national security arena rests on a process involving many organizations both in and out of government. They are subject, especially in the three military departments within the Department of Defense, to the interactive and often conflictive forces of leadership, personal incentives, and interorganizational processes that shape the agency perspectives within the department. And, of course, they are all embedded in the larger structure of constitutional pluralism discussed above.

Most key choices in military affairs are made in the context of institutionalized decision processes both

— within the Defense Department (which involve the three military departments, the Organization of the Joint Chiefs of Staff, and the Office of the Secretary of Defense) and

— among the Defense Department and other agencies and organizations of the executive branch (including the Office of Management and Budget, the State Department, the CIA, and the National Security Council staff among others), the Congress (especially national-security-related authorization and appropriation subcommittees), and the private sector (especially aerospace firms).

Among some of the more prominent institutionalized decision processes are the National Security Council system (concerned with coordination of interagency policy initiatives and crisis response), the DoD Planning-Programming-Budgeting System (PPBS) together with the Program Objectives Memorandum (POM) prepared by each military service that builds the defense budget, the Joint Strategic Planning System, the weapons system acquisition process, and the congressional authorization and appropriation processes. The formal details of each of these and other institutionalized systems are constantly changing; There is a vast literature that addresses these formal decision-making systems.[18] Although specific examination of these systems is outside of the scope of this chapter, their role must be noted because they form the setting that *defines* the public interest in the context of the Defense Department.

Each of these institutionalized decision processes and their related informal processes involves different clusters of individuals, groups, and organizations that operate with different concepts of time, different sets of goals, rely on different information sources, engage differently sized staffs with different personal and work experiences, and apply different criteria to evaluate performance, producing different kinds of outputs.

This weblike network is huge, if one includes the subtle — often informal — interactions that reach across U.S. society, indeed across the globe. An illustration of this was the sale by General Dynamics of 348 F-16 fighter planes to Denmark, Norway, Belgium, and the Netherlands in 1975. The web in this single case involved high politics in seven capitals and four major corporations, rough international competition among General Dynamics, Northrop, France's Dassault, and Sweden's Saab, as well as byzantine intrigues in the U.S. Air Force and the U.S. Navy.[19]

The point here is that the process of strategic management that defines the public interest from the agency perspective of the Department of Defense is a web that includes but often transcends the formal institutionalized processes. As a result, the outcomes of national policy decisions are not entirely under the control of a president or a secretary of defense in any clear sense. Instead, they are shaped largely by an adversary process among "quasi-sovereignties," to use Desmond Ball's term.[20]

The most publicly visible of these quasi-sovereignties within the Department of Defense is the Office of the Secretary of Defense, the putative "central management" agency of the department. The collection of institutional forums and multiple decision centers that give tone and shape to the agency perspectives that contend within the Defense Department are imperfectly tied together in this small agency. OSD is the principal place in the department where a — typically diffuse — concept of the public interest in the arena of national security policy becomes enunciated. It is here that the major conflicts over defining missions and resource priorities and central strategic concepts are resolved, or at least adjusted, to allow a satisfactory modus vivendi among the contending military services and other organizational players. And it is here that one finds an effort to reconcile the competing expressions of agency perspective that accommodate rather than obliterate the distinctive richness of orientation of the four armed services as concepts of the public interest are developed and operationalized in the swirl of American politics.

Implications of the Test Case

The Strong Culture of a Bureaucratic Profession

We have seen in this brief examination of the Department of Defense that there is found in the case of DoD substantial support for the central themes of the Manifesto.

First, the bureaucratic profession of arms reinforces a sense of its unique role as trustee in pursuit of the public interest in the context of national security and defense of the Constitution.

Second, DoD in general — and each of the military services more particularly — support a robust sense of themselves as repositories of strategic knowledge, their historical tradition of honorable success in combat, and their mastery of warriors' skills. This élan about their capacity to act and confidence in their sense of purpose is quite consistent with the Manifesto's notion that Agency Perspective taps into a unique repository of resources to serve the public interest.

Third, the sustained commitment of the American officer corps to the supremacy of civilian authority under a constitutional rule together with the practice — very evident since World War II — of being an aggressive participant in the legislative and executive politics that shape national security policy combine to reflect the Manifesto's advocacy of the career public service as a legitimate participant in governance.

Finally, this examination of the interorganizational decision making in the strategic management of DoD demonstrates the commitment to a process-oriented development of public interest goals that conform to the Manifesto's prescriptions in this area.

Worrisome Aspects of DoD Case

Some stocktaking is needed here. Since this chapter is meant to examine defense administration and DoD as a powerful example of the Manifesto's promise and not be a paean to the Manifesto, it is necessary to take a look at this example with the warts on (warts, I would suggest, that are more a product of deficiencies in our system of politics and governance than in the Blacksburg Manifesto). Only in that way can we continue to build on the very constructive momentum that has been imparted by the Manifesto to our dialogue about American governance.

Viewed in the round, this collection of attributes in DoD is quite positive in terms of consistency with a modern democratic system of governance and offers evidence — to the extent that Defense Department administration reflects the prescriptions of the Manifesto — that would support the prescriptions found in the Manifesto concerning the career public service.

But other images emerge from the Defense Department case that are not wholly supportive of the Manifesto when we explore more closely[21] the traits of DoD's professional ethos, agency perspective, concepts of the public interest, and constitutional attributes. What we find are features of defense administration that depart from our positive expectations based on the Manifesto. These must be examined as the first step in a two-part assessment of the implications of defense administration as a test-bed for exploring the Manifesto. The second step will be to take these findings and use them as a basis to try to extend some of the concepts of the Blacksburg Manifesto.

Trustees of the Public Interest

A key theme of the Manifesto argues that public administrators should be trustees of the public interest with a unique sense of commitment to serving the public interest in the functional sphere of their agency. This is problematic in the Department of Defense, especially with respect to the nature of professionalism that has evolved in the officer corps.

The professionalism of the officer corps defines the context in which the public interest is pursued in the arena of military affairs. If this professionalism is clouded by competing or uncertain norms, then the officer corps as a corporate establishment grows uncertain about what is held in "trust" as it pursues the public interest. During and subsequent to the Vietnam War, the character of professionalism of the officer corps has been ambivalent in its sense of the public interest.

The heart of this uncertain professionalism — and the turbulence thereby imparted to the collective "vision" of the officer corps as a trustee of the public interest — seems to derive in large part from the tensions that have developed between the military's combat mission and its warrior ethos, on the one hand, and, on the other hand, the huge resource management task associated with the defense establishment of the United States as a superpower.

Despite the growth in importance of technical and managerial competencies within the military, the need for the warrior persists due to the requirements of combat and, therefore, sets a limit to "civilizing" managerial tendencies.[22] But this persistent warrior orientation does not easily accommodate itself to the modern, complex Department of Defense operating in an equally complex pluralist polity.

It is, then, a true dilemma in which the requirements for managing the complex resource acquisition, inventory, and distribution problems that demand the attention of the technical and resource management elements are to a degree at odds — in terms of operating culture and purposes — with those whose primary concern is with the planning and employment of military force. This produces tensions within the goal-setting processes of the national security establishment which muddy the development of viable notions of the public interest. This problem was illustrated during the Vietnam War by the frequent rotation of officers to and among combat commands. Although this rotation practice had advantages for the career management of officers (by giving a combat "experience" to many officers which served them well at promotion time), it has been widely deplored[23] as undermining the combat effectiveness of U.S. fighting units.

The issue here goes beyond a "warrior-manager" dilemma. An additional distinction merits mention: an all-volunteer armed force that is "accessed" (not "recruited") by largely material and occupational incentives — rather than in terms of an obligation to the state and political community and an opportunity for public service — creates a different texture of institutional values, concept of purpose, and level of personal commitment to undertake demanding and potentially dangerous duties.

The issues here about a public interest trusteeship by DoD concern the proper role of military force in the conduct of American policy and how U.S. objectives relate to the instruments of politico-military action. Public discussions of this trusteeship responsibility were on hold for many years due to the isolationism that followed U.S. withdrawal from Vietnam. They began to reappear rather timidly only after the Carter Administration failed in its use of military forces to extract American hostages from Iran and did not really become asserted in our national dialogue until the Reagan Administration employed military force in Lebanon, Libya, Grenada, and — in its most vigorous application — in naval escort duty in the Iran-Iraq "tanker war."

But while the morale of military professionals has been enhanced by these largely successful operations, the clarity of vision among these professionals about the nature of the public interest and their roles as "trustees" is still uncertain. The only element of certainty concerning its institutional role is that the career military professionals are committed to avoiding another failure like Vietnam. But avoidance of political and institutional failure is not necessarily the same as a concept of the public interest.

This matter raises an unsettling question about the prospects behind the optimism of the Blacksburg Manifesto: if the professional military establishment cannot clearly define its normative grounding as a trustee of the public interest, given the rich traditions and national symbols that are mobilized by terms like "national security" and "military requirements," what hope is there for cadres of the career public service associated with missions that are less central to national survival and popular consensus?

Unique Agency Capacity

A second major theme of the Manifesto argues that public agencies embody unique capabilities that are available to serve the public interest in their areas of societal function. What is the experience in the Department of Defense in the matter of agency perspective?

The "agency capacity" available in the Department of Defense has produced mixed results in terms of security requirements for the efficient use of national resources in the pursuit of America's international policies and strategic interests — the public interest set in global terms.

Three sources of this problem, which raise questions about the "agency capacity" of DoD, are (1) conflict between ultimate military missions and bureaucratic priorities, (2) the resource bias, and (3) the instability of funding for DoD programs.

Priority of Mission v. Bureaucratic Politics

The warrior-manager dilemma mentioned in the previous section also has implications for the unique capacity of a public agency to pursue the public interest. That dilemma shapes the way the principal component agencies of DoD mobilize organizational resources in order to produce the ends to which those resources are directed. Thus, it shapes the way they interpret the public interest. At the heart of this matter is the question of where the primary loyalties of the senior leaders in DoD lie: success in armed combat or success in bureaucratic conflict?

The essence of agency capacity for military organizations is the ability to mobilize and employ military forces on behalf of missions to deter adversaries or successfully engage them in combat. General Bruce Palmer, a senior troop commander in the Vietnam War and a West Point classmate of General William Westmoreland (the top commander of U.S. ground forces during much of the U.S. war in Vietnam), argued in his recent book about the Vietnam War that while the civilians who ordered our Army were foolish and did not understand the uses and limits of military force or even the political constraints they faced at home, the top military leaders were also to blame for trying to protect the parochial institutional interests of the four individual services; the joint chiefs each wanted a piece of the action for their own service and acquiesced to the government's war policies without voicing the doubts they maintained about its effectiveness.[24]

What Palmer and others have illuminated is that the pursuit of one's "agency perspective" may indeed become a quest for parochial interests that undermine a concept of a larger public interest. It is noteworthy that there were only a handful of critics[25] of our Vietnam policies within the officer corps during most of that war *until* it became clear that the United States had lost the war.

Resource Bias

The key, strategic choices that are mentioned again and again by DoD insiders focus on budgets, on getting sufficient resources — in time — to operate current programs at adequate levels and to avoid denying resources to promising areas of investment. The oscillation of support for defense programs causes some to say that the heart of strategic management is a resource problem: figuring out how to manage the decremental process of reducing the pool of proposed programs. Many judge that strategic choices in this decremental process are seldom aided by substantive goals. Organizational growth and survival — more the latter — are seen as dominant. Policy is seen as having less and less a role in this system. Some insiders feel that by its organizational logic, the Department of Defense is designed primarily to buy systems, not to make and implement strategy and policy.

Instability of Resource Commitments

The history of defense spending is replete with fluctuations. One can audit the pattern subsequent to World War II and discover major investments in research and development, facilities, and force structure which are reversed or interminably protracted due to shifting winds of support on the Hill, turnover of advocates in the senior ranks of the contending bureaucracies — thus affecting the configuration of advocacy — and of course, a change in the resident at the White House who seeks to differentiate his policies from those of his predecessor. This contributes to the dynamics that undermine long-term planning and efforts to resist reactivity at the policy level, a problem that is discussed below.

The Dark Side of Constitutional Pluralism

The Manifesto rests on a central theme that its normative order is based on the Constitution. This linkage to the Constitution makes legitimate, according to the Manifesto, a major role for the career public service in national governance. The normative order rests on separation of powers. But certain consequences of that constitutional arrangement in the Department of Defense have some clear disadvantages that give reason to question this theme of the Manifesto.

Huntington's "Subjective Control" Thesis

The most compelling interpretation of the evolved constitutional position of defense administration in DoD is provided by Samuel Huntington in *The Soldier and the State*.[26] His basic thesis is that the U.S. Constitution precludes "objective" civilian control of the military.

Huntington rejects the widely held belief that the Constitution provides for civilian control. That belief would endow the Constitution with the ability to restrict the military by means of "objective civilian control" that would be compatible with a high level of military professionalism. Such a form of "objective" civilian control would be based on making a clear distinction between responsibilities that are political and those that are military. This form of control also would provide for the institutional subordination of the military to civilian authorities.

Huntington asserts that these elements of civilian control are "conspicuously absent" in the Constitution. Instead, he sees a constitutional mixing of political and military functions, which injects politics into military affairs and military affairs into politics. The provisions of the Constitution that are reputed to establish civilian control are, for Huntington, those which actually inhibit control: militia clause, separation of powers, and the commander-in-chief clause. These constitutional clauses, he argues, divide control over (1) the militia between the national government and the state governments, (2) the national military forces between Congress and the president, and (3) the military departments between the president and the departmental secretaries (of Army, Navy, and Air Force).

The upshot, for Huntington, is that we have "subjective" civilian control based on this constitutional pluralism in which the military is *both* shaped *and* limited by the consequence of the struggles over the distribution of power within the federal system, between Congress and the president, and within the executive branch — rather than being directly influenced as a subordinate entity in a formal authority relationship. The emergence of an independent military professionalism is similarly constrained by a process that draws the officer corps of each service and its several components into the strife among the multiple centers of power in American politics.

This suggests that there is a dark side to the strengths associated with a vigorous agency perspective. Strong agencies like the military departments not only can manipulate the constitutionally ordained division between executive and Congress but are encouraged to do so. This has led military policy and the military establishment in directions that often have not, in the historical experience of the post-WWII era, produced results that reasonable men and women would label "the public interest." The scope and duration of our failed involvement in the Vietnam War, the growth of reliance on nuclear forces in our strategic standoff with the Soviets, our failure to extract from our NATO allies a equitable sharing of the burdens of defending Western Europe, and the persistent inability of our political executive to rationalize and clean up the inefficiency and sleaziness in our weapons acquisition programs all illustrate in major ways the negative consequences of agency perspective. The perverse side of the agency perspective is even reflected in the relatively less damaging but dramatically tragic incident known as "Desert One," the abortive attempt in April 1980 to rescue American embassy hostages in Iran.[27]

Impacts on Stable Policy Development

One of the more distressing features of the postwar era in American foreign policy has been our national incapacity to develop stable policy commitments and then "stay the course."[28] This has become a serious issue both in

— its impact on our nation's role in a competitive, often dangerous world (in terms of economic and military competition) where we reject long-term concerns on behalf of short-term payoffs (e.g., competition with Japan, ozone layer deterioration), and

— in the way that we make choices: by assuming that we must look at issues primarily in terms of the short haul, we focus on short-term rewards *and* on cutting our short-term costs if the world changes in unpredictable ways or if our judgment proves faulty (e.g., approving new, unproved weapons development programs that pump up budgets far beyond our capacity to sustain political support or fiscal responsibility in the light of our economic strength and competing national priorities).

In many respects, it is the constitutional pluralism that the Manifesto endorses and strengthens by its advocacy of an agency perspective that seems to drive out a view of and commitment to the long-term interests of the United States. For example, the great sensitivity of the Congress to the shifting preferences of the American people to support long-term, stable defense programs has resulted in a series of starts and stops of many weapon systems which have wasted tremendous amounts of resources as we stretch out and then accelerate spending for various systems. The result is that the unit cost of each weapon we buy increases tremendously and — unless the world suddenly becomes a less threatening place — we get the combined effect of acquiring fewer weapons than we need and paying a premium for being less well defended.[29]

In retrospect, we have wasted hundreds of billions of tax dollars by this practice of letting short-term popular mood shifts cause national priorities to oscillate in the political competition between Congress and the executive. This pattern of whipsaw policy making does two unhappy things:

First, it wastes our national treasure (and creates severe opportunity costs for important domestic spending requirements) and forces our politics to pretend that there is a "fair-share" distribution between the money we need for defense and the money we need for social programs. The reality is that the requirements of the defense sector are driven by very different realities than those of the social services sector.

Second, we also create policy disarray in our relations with other countries who find our policy commitments unreliable.

Perhaps Woodrow Wilson said best what can be seen as one of the consequences of the constitutional pluralism endorsed by the Manifesto when he described the character of our policy process.

> Nobody stands sponsor for the policy of the government. A dozen men originate it; a dozen compromises twist it and alter it; a dozen offices whose names are scarcely known outside of Washington put it into execution.[30]

Impacts on Professionalism

Huntington, when writing *The Soldier and the State* in the mid-1950s, concluded that the continuing high level of post-World War II defense activities required by the Cold War intensified the impact of the separation of powers on civil-military relations in three ways. First, it enhanced the role of Congress with respect to both military policy and military administration. Second, it shifted the focus of congressional-military relations from the supply units of the military departments to the professional heads of the services and thereby heightened the tension between the separation of powers and military professionalism. Finally, it tended to produce a pluralistic or balanced national military strategy. These are all linked to the professionalism issue.

In the historical view of Huntington, it was the separation of powers that restrained the development of military professionalism in this country. The continuing high level of defense activity associated with the Cold War increased the tension, in his judgment, between military professionalism and the separation of powers. This tension takes the form of placing a senior representative of the military in a dilemma where he may *either* have to criticize publicly the commander-in-chief if he gives his professional opinions to Congress (assuming they depart from presidential or secretary-of-defense policies) *or* he may deny to Congress the advice to which it is constitutionally entitled when he subordinates his professional judgment in order to act as a political defender of the administration policy. This poses a difficult set of circumstances for the military professional:

> Military professionalism and objective civilian control become impossible if the administration punishes officers for presenting their professional opinions to Congress, if congressmen insist upon using the soldiers to embarrass the administration, or if the soldiers stray beyond their field of expertise into those of politics and diplomacy.[31]

It is not a situation that encourages the orientation to the public interest that the Manifesto supports. Unfortunately, this form of tension and its constitutional source is a serious part of the reality of all members of the career public service.

Process Dynamics: Convoluted Web of Strategic Management

The fourth theme of the Manifesto that was addressed earlier — the notion that the problematic nature of defining the public interest requires a process-oriented role for the career public service — leads one to further examination of the strategic management process in the Department of Defense.

It was argued in an earlier section of this chapter that the Office of the Secretary of Defense is a key place at which contending concepts of the public interest as agency perspectives and the policy preferences of various players interact. This catalyst image is certainly congenial to the Manifesto's idea of process dynamics as the birthing room of the public interest.

But there is strong evidence indicating that the public interest is not always well served by this process. Again and again in post-WWII history we find examples of an agency perspective at work that clouds a larger view of the public interest, such as:

— service parochialism in the Vietnam War that inhibited development of an integrated strategic rationale on the part of the United States and masked the truth about the quicksand that the United States was slipping into.
— service parochialism that compelled involvement by representatives of all our military services so that we fielded a poorly integrated combat force that failed to rescue the U.S. embassy hostages in Teheran in 1979.
— the insistence by the individual military services that they develop and field separate weapons systems when other services may have requirements for similar weapons — often at great cost to the taxpayers and of questionable value to the military services

Even the Iran-Contra affair could be viewed as partially the product of the perverse consequences of an agency perspective (maintained by elements of the NSC staff leadership) pursuing policy initiatives that departed from the policy orientations of two other large agencies (Departments of Defense and State) that also had major stakes in national security policy and different concepts of how the public interest was best to be served. The Defense Department and the State Department were certainly at odds with Robert McFarlane, John Poindexter, and Oliver North about the significance of supporting Operation Staunch, the declared policy of arms embargo against Iran.

And this problem not only attaches itself to the formulation of policies but to their implementation, as well. Archie Barrett, in a searching critique of Defense Department management and organization during the Carter Administration, concluded that the key to improving the Department lies in the secretary's appreciation of his interest in administration and his success in imposing this interest as a policy commitment throughout the Department of Defense. Barrett makes the point that " . . . the substance of an adequate national security posture, the ultimate concern of a secretary of defense, is directly related to, and can be little better than, the organization responsible for designing it."[32] Unfortunately, the organization "responsible for designing it" is an interorganizational structure in which the semiautonomous military departments operate largely outside of firm direction from the secretary and the Office of the Secretary of Defense.

The institutionalized strategic management processes and their less formal dimensions constitute what properly can be called the "convoluted web of strategic management"[33] in the national security arena. The characteristics of this web can be attributed to three factors that bear on the manner in which agency perspective becomes transformed into a concept of the public interest.

"Fair-Share" Syndrome

The rich network of competing, interservice advocacy for resources within the Defense Department is faced with an interesting dilemma. At any point in time, many of these advocates have equally compelling program proposals but the resource constraints prevent all of them from successfully prosecuting their advocacy. Therefore, certain decision rules have evolved in DoD to discriminate among these "equally attractive" proposals. A key rule seems to be that decision makers should minimize the extent to which proposals are to be viewed as competing *alternatives*. Rather, the process of advocacy defines, in categorical terms, their *relevance* to the political context in which they are embedded. One interesting example of this that I observed when I was working in the Office of the Secretary of Defense[34] was the effort on the part of some Army, Navy, and Air Force leaders to associate certain of their space-based warning and defense systems that had been under development under the auspices of their individual military services as consistent with the new commitment announced by President Reagan to develop a "strategic defense initiative" to counter the threat of attack by Soviet ballistic missiles. But they saw their continued development as being maintained under individual control by their separate military departments. What they seemed to say was, "We have been doing 'Star Wars' already and we should get our 'fair share' of the new money."

The Futility of Planning

Morris Janowitz has argued that "trend thinking" and the inability to be imaginative in contemplating revolutionary developments have inhibited the military in its ability to develop new programs and policies and to engage in planning beyond a kind of linear extrapolation of things that are tried and true.[35] John Collins has similarly argued that defense planning renders a weak performance based on traditional strengths in our culture of decision making. Collins argues that our genius for muddling through and relying on "quick fixes" is inadequate to the long-term challenges of a complex and threatening world.[36]

An interpretation of why the defense community does not strategically manage and plan better — at least for the long term — is that such planning is discouraged by the incentives system. Planning is thought to be an exercise in futility. A rational, career-minded officer or defense bureaucrat would view placing much stock in long-term planning as counterintuitive.

Part of the problem derives from the fact that long-range planning is, obviously, based on forecasts of the future. Our lack of confidence in these forecasts due to politico-military and technological uncertainties places all long-term planning efforts in a skeptical light.

But there is another source of this vulnerability or implausibility of long-term planning. It is because long-term planning requires DoD decisionmakers to risk resources or political support for alternatives that represent departures from currently accepted definitions of the situation or from currently workable programs. These "definitions of the situations" and "programs" tend to be cast in terms that are one-dimensional: air warfare threats, maritime warfare threats, and land warfare threats.

This narrow orientation prevents the development of long-term thinking that is multi-dimensional. A threat from Soviet tanks, for example, produces Army plans that use counter-weapons that are consistent with Army doctrine and traditions and forces. The problem is not that U.S. Army tanks or helicopters may not be an appropriate response to the long-term threat coming from Soviet armor formations, but that a more responsive long-term solution might be to develop new airborne weapons for deep battlefield interdiction of Soviet tanks that are more a part of the war-fighting doctrines and traditions of the U.S. Air Force. But the U.S. Army is not likely to foster support of programs that will enhance U.S. Air Force budgets.

Programmed Reactivity at the Policy Level

Francis Rourke makes this point:

> . . . it is questionable if the concentration of power over foreign affairs in the White House does anything to solve the major problem associated with decision-making by bureaucratic organizations — the failure to open up and explore all alternatives before making decisions. In broadening the authority of the special assistant over foreign policy, Nixon and Kissinger had the ostensible objective of widening the options of the president on the issues that came before him. Their fear was that the national security organizations in the executive branch would negotiate and compromise differences on issues and present the president with a united front in support or opposition to a projected course of action. In such situations, the president would be reduced to the role of ratifying not initiating foreign policy decisions.[37]

Here, Rourke is identifying a key problem that Nixon wanted to avoid: being confronted with the type of bureaucratically staffed consensus that leaves the president with no options other than acceptance or rejection. President Eisenhower had been criticized for letting his staff system operate in this fashion[38] and President Nixon (and certainly Henry Kissinger, both as the president's national security advisor and as secretary of state) was sensitive to keeping his staffs "on tap but not on top." At issue here is the tendency toward *programmed reactivity* on the part of public agencies.

An important point to be made here is that public bureaucratic agencies, quite properly, are more capable at *reacting* to policy cues than they are to *initiating* policy. They are also more likely to react to political direction and to other sources of influence in their environments in *programmed* ways. These are bureaucratic institutions that offer the citizens, as part of their agency capacity, reliable performance of some — but not all — of the great tasks that are part of the governmental process. Public agencies are not "general-purpose" institutions. Each agency is a relatively specialized institution. That is at the core of the unique agency capacity that the Blacksburg Manifesto so correctly highlights. Even the Department of Defense develops a certain narrowness of style, sensitivity, and capability, in spite of its tremendous institutional resources. We seldom ask the Defense Department to perform as if it were the Department of Health and Human Services or the Environmental Protection Agency. It has extraordinary capacity as an agency, but it also has certain "trained incapacity," to use a very old concept coined by Robert Merton.[39]

Therefore, the programmed, reactive limits of its advocacy represent both a strength and a source of narrowness for the public agency and its ability to contribute to the "discovery" of a consensus on public policy. I will not deny the value to the public dialogue of the informed contribution of an agency to the public interest debate. But my concern is that the enthusiasm of the Manifesto ignores the special "incapacity," to use Merton's term, that agencies bring to the debate.

Because of their highly patterned nature, programs in bureaucratic agencies, once started, become very hard to shut off from within. For this reason, the linkages with resource priorities of this reaction-prone incapacity to develop and sustain a political dialogue around priorities and commitments in defining the public interest are striking. This is illustrated by the difference between defense policy and budget debates under President Eisenhower and those that emerged under President Kennedy.

Eisenhower as president could define the size and capabilities of our military forces and propose defense budgets to prepare for "the long haul" and, thereby, justify discouragement of new naval and ground forces proposals on the grounds that they were largely irrelevant to our central national purposes. Thus, Eisenhower kept a cap on Army and Navy ambitions by his definition of the national security requirements of the United States in terms that relied heavily on the Air Force and strategic nuclear deterrence.[40] This shaped the context in which advocacy occurred on behalf of or in opposition to various defense programs and mediated the incentive structure within the three services and the Defense Department and the political milieu in which they existed. When the new president, John Kennedy, announced the United States would "pay any price, bear any burden . . . in the name of freedom around the world . . . ," there were programmatic implications for the three military services which, effectively, removed the restraints on their proposal of new programs ad policies and encouraged a new definition of public interest that inevitably led to greater activism in world affairs, including our military adventures in Southeast Asia.

By taking the lid off of the restraints on agency perspective that Eisenhower had imposed, President Kennedy evoked and rewarded the restive impulses for growth and program expansion in all the military services. These were legitimated by talk of bold and noble new "missions" by the Kennedy Administration and were associated, of course, with a clear sense that the world was more threatening than had been understood by Eisenhower.

It is notable to those who wish to argue that these (ultimately rejected) initiatives came from the elected politicians that one hunts in vain for evidence that senior career officials of the military services became advocates for restraint during this period of expansion. It is equally clear that the defense agency experiences at the juncture of the Eisenhower-Kennedy administrations were not in the least unique. The same phenomenon accompanied the transition from the administration of President Carter to that of President Reagan.

Part of the Reagan electoral mandate was to rebuild the nation's defenses that had begun to deteriorate during the first Nixon Administration. Reagan and Secretary of Defense Weinberger established a clear mandate for program and mission expansion of all the military services as they undertook both to modernize and rebuild the armed forces. Agency initiatives from all four services went off the scale, even exceeding at the "wish list" level the generous increases in obligation authority that characterized the first Reagan Administration. Once again, one is hard pressed to find evidence of any cautionary impulses coming out of the uniformed career leaders of the four military services about the possibility that the groundswell of support for defense spending that the American people gave Reagan in 1980 would peter out. It is plain to see that few uniformed voices, committed to the public interest from an agency perspective, were raised to admonish that front-loading of defense budgets early in the 1980s might contribute to devastating fiscal deficits that would undercut in a few years the texture of a revitalized defense posture.

These three elements of the "web of strategic management" in the Defense Department represent in a crucial way the structural dynamics that are endorsed by the Manifesto. The encouragement of vigorous processes "to search for the public interest," as the Manifesto puts it, amount to encouragement of more vigorous bureaucratic politics among agencies in pursuit of budgetary and programmatic self-interest. It also reflects an orientation in the Manifesto that seeks to affirm the role of public agencies as political players and rejects the view that officials who are "politically responsible" (in the special meaning of that term which is associated with those who must stand for election) should have an exclusive role in setting policy. Rather, the Manifesto seems to embrace the belief that a meritocratic career bureaucracy is equally responsible politically when compared with elected officials and should have an equal degree of influence in making public policy and interpreting the public interest.

Beyond The Blacksburg Manifesto

The preceding section of this chapter has attempted to clarify some of the implications of the views in the Blacksburg Manifesto that come from lessons derived from the experience of the Department of Defense. In the case of each of the four central themes of the Manifesto, this examination has produced cause to recommend caution in one's optimism about the expectations that one should have about implementation of the Manifesto's prescriptions. Given this, what steps might be taken to refine and augment the insights of the Manifesto?

An important function served by the Blacksburg Manifesto, intended by its authors, was to stimulate an enhanced dialogue about the nature of the career public service and future directions that should inform that dialogue and the world of public action that is its referent. The academic community has responded with an outpouring — usually thoughtful — of analysis and prescription that bears on the issues raised by the Manifesto.

My examination in this chapter of defense administration and the military institution was part of that community of response. The following comments are intended to contribute to the dialogue started by the Manifesto authors and, it is hoped, extend it.

It is my sense that the prescriptions of the Manifesto remain underdeveloped in the area where agency perspective may be called into question as an apology for self-serving parochialism produced within the coalitional dynamics of large organizations that affect the public interest. It may well be that the agency perspective can, for example, transcend the parochialism of the individual military services that one finds in the Department of Defense because of the coequal commitment of the Manifesto to the larger public interest.

This merits exploration in our continuing dialogue. The remarks that follow seek to focus on areas that may strengthen the penetration of the root problems of American governance by the basic concepts of the Manifesto.

Anatomy of Strategic Choice

The factors that were discussed above as contributing to the large-scale complexity within DoD should be viewed as the more visible elements of a much larger pattern of relationships that extend well beyond the formal boundaries of the Department of Defense. They include other departments and institutions of government at all levels and in many other countries. They include nongovernmental institutions, as well, prominently in the industries that propose, design, manufacture, and market weapons and other defense material.

It is useful to visualize the field of defense as comprised of several major interorganizational coalitions that cut across these governmental and nongovernmental organizations and are associated with key areas of strategic choice. The most obvious of these coalitions shape weapons acquisition and the substance of foreign policy. But there are others that are at least as significant in influencing defense matters, such as the coalitions built around key domestic social programs in the Congress, which—in effect—constrain the level of residual fiscal resources that will be available for defense programs.

Most of the time, interaction among these coalitions on substantive matters is ritualistic and trivial. Generally, the people I interviewed in my 1981-82 research felt that these coalitions operate with high levels of mutual exclusivity. Several people suggested that a prime example of this pattern was the annual ritual of the Defense Guidance. The Defense Guidance is issued by the secretary of defense to the military services and other DoD agencies and is supposed to be an authoritative statement of DoD priorities for the five years ahead in the arena of policy, strategy, and force structure. The view is held by many that the interaction among representatives of the service, policy, and weapons coalitions during the formulation of the Defense Guidance is largely ritualistic because there is little in this document that is binding on any of these coalitions.

The relative autonomy and mutual exclusivity of these coalitions may mean that they have, in political terms, a "life of their own" that may make policy control over them very difficult for any central decision makers. This also may mean that these coalitions are both motivated and able to resist major policy shifts by strategic decision makers.

The vigor of these coalitions may account for the great difficulty one may observe in those who try to garner support for a new policy initiative or defense program. The working of these loosely connected coalitions may mean that the problem of consensus development is less a matter of their resistance or sabotage than it is that such departures from the current arrangements are viewed by many coalitional actors as irrelevant. In concrete terms, this resistance to new initiatives is reflected in the continuing influence of the service departments over strategic decisions in the resources area. This influence should be viewed as counterproductive if our interest is building an effective military force that the country can afford in a context of other legitimate priorities for public resources. For example, in the course of my interviews in the early 1980s I discovered that a surprising number of Air Force officers held the view that service parochialism got in the way of an effective defense against an increasingly capable, threatening Soviet Union.

Many defense professionals hold the view that there is poor coordination among the decision processes that affect the Department of Defense. The point is made repeatedly that staffs do not coordinate with each other and that plans of the separate military services are not sufficiently interdependent. The "objective" force plans (plans that spell out the military forces we would need *if* we seriously intend to pursue all of our declared national objectives — it is never expected that these levels of forces will *actually* be funded), the specific war plans for various actual contingencies, the Program Objectives Memorandum from each service, the Five Year Defense Program, the Defense Guidance, the budget — none were thought to be well articulated with the others.

Few thoughtful observers can propose solutions to the structural bias that seems to favor service parochialism and some of the other attributes of coalitional dynamics in the advocacy structure. Some view reform of the formal structure that is supposed to interface and coordinate the four armed services for joint planning and military advice (the so-called JCS system) as a step in the right direction. But there remains cause for pessimism that structural reforms that have been produced by DoD and in Congress in recent years would make much of a difference.

Many Pentagon insiders seem to be impressed with the great difficulty of finding *any* structural formula for dealing with these problems of interest-group parochialism driving programs and the failure to connect key plans, priorities, and resources. Coalitional dynamics are too hard to fix with structural reform, in their judgment. In this context, it is not clear that enhanced reliance on an agency perspective will be productive for the public interest. It may instead be critical that advocates who share the philosophical commitments of the Blacksburg Manifesto may undertake more productive efforts by deemphasizing the agency perspective and accentuating their concern with the public service ethos of the public administrator who is committed to the public interest.

Determining the "Public Interest": Content v. Process

Is there such a thing as "good" public policy? As I read the Manifesto, the answer depends on our ability to fragment or compartmentalize public policy into its appropriate "agency perspective" zones for evaluation. That would seem to me to be the upshot of relying on a process orientation within an agency perspective. The experience of the Defense Department would suggest that a process orientation leads to a distribution of resources to insure that all agencies — especially the three major services — get their fair shares. If this is not a "process" orientation, what is it? Unfortunately, it does not inspire confidence that the public interest is better served.

An alternative thrust that might have value is to acknowledge the process character of the discovery of the "public interest" constrained by a regime of constitutional values and a respect for the spirit of the law, recognizing that elected legislators and elected executives have a very central and legitimate role in lawmaking. From that launching pad the Blacksburg perspective might usefully move to explore quite openly the special virtues that come to public service given the unique characteristics of bureaucratic rationality. This discussion of bureaucratic institutions could examine the contributions that are special to the meritocratic norms and professionalism of career bureaucracies and use that as a point of transition to examine critically the substance or "content" of values that should be considered in our attempts to define the public interest.

Encouraging Suboptimization and Political Naiveté in a Bureaucratic Profession

The contemporary experience in DoD of national security decision making is such that a persistent deconcentration of priority setting devolves influence from OSD to the agency level, which in this case is the military services. This produces an Air Force that focuses on fighting other air forces but fails to support land forces, and a Navy that resists development of strategic sealift capabilities to take heavy ground forces into a potential combat theater. It also encourages a career incentive system that fosters refinement and elaboration of the interests of the component agency without concern for the legitimate goals of the other components in a system that should presume coordination of a division of labor.

The only form of interdependence that regularly emerges in DoD is that of the political accommodation among the services in which trade-offs are made in order to sustain support for each other's higher-priority programs. This suggests that the Manifesto is politically naive because the Manifesto seems to assume that a bureaucratic profession can rise above such horse-trading. If that is *not* the implicit assumption, then it would be useful to spell out how the corporate character of what must be considered a "bureaucratic profession" would deal with organizations in networks that must set and adjust their priorities interactively. For example, how does the Manifesto's image of the career public service resist the impulses that caused the joint chiefs of the armed forces to bargain over how they would insure that each service got a "piece of the action" in Vietnam or Desert One or Grenada?

Need to Clarify the Proper Role of Conflict within the Political Culture

Although there is abundant sensitivity in the Manifesto to conflict between the career public bureaucracy and other institutions—principally political institutions—it is less clear what the view of the Manifesto is on the matter of conflict borne of different agency perspectives and resource scarcities (which are always with us). It is very clear in the experience of DoD that competition over resources is a crucial and persistent part of the reality of the Department of Defense intramurally and in its interactions with nondefense agencies of government. The Manifesto needs to provide a more complete development of the role played by conflict in its analysis of the career public service.

Also, it would be helpful if there were some clearer sense about the contribution of conflict to "the public interest." As realists, the authors of the Manifesto are acutely aware of the presence of conflict in public life. Yet I come away from the Manifesto with the sense that conflict is viewed as something negative, a part of the terrain of the politics but not having any positive quality in its own right. In the military, of course, the culture thrives on competition and conflict. Can the Manifesto accept the notion that conflict has positive functions? I think it needs to do so.

Seductions of Consensus Theory

These comments about the lack of a clear posture in the Manifesto about the social consequences and roles of conflict reflect my sense that the Manifesto has a fundamental commitment to consensus as the desired state of relationships in mega-institutions like our large governments. The experience of the Department of Defense is rooted in learning to build and coordinate large and complex organizations in turbulent and uncertain environments that are filled with hostility and often lack consensus about how to do things and what things are to be done — and in what order.

The concepts in the Manifesto seem to be more congenial to orientations that suggest notions of harmony and cooperation rooted in theories of small-group dynamics — with homogeneous groups. These concepts also seem to be premised, drawing again on small-group dynamics, on views that assume public organizations are relatively simple and unitary rather than complex and multi-organizational.

Finally, the treatment in the Manifesto seems to be uncomfortable with the reality that this country's political culture is rooted in competitive — if modified — free-enterprise economics and individualism. The point I am making is not that every facet of our facet of our political culture is to be endorsed as optimal, but that a normative theory for the career public service needs to be congruent with those realities. It is not clear that this is the case.

Quest for Analogues to "The Private Administration"

To help The Public Administration better accommodate the central features of a political culture and a political economy that are essentially capitalistic, individualistic, and global-metropolitan in character — and to help challenge those sections of the Manifesto that are insensitive to the distinct characteristics of our national culture — one might explore some parallels in the subculture of "The Private Administration" to gather useful insights into how one might proceed to refine the concept of The Public Administration:

Political Marketing. Washington, D.C., is awash in people and organizations engaged in marketing of ideas, priorities, programs, and personalities. It does not just happen at the Pentagon. It is all over the government, and the concept of marketing — endemic in our political economy — might illuminate some dark corners of The Public Administration.

Competitive Spirit. Our national culture reflects a zest for competition that resides quite comfortably with cooperative behavior in a variety of settings. An institutional competitive spirit is part of our business culture and is reflected in the cultural competition within our liberal tradition of positive government. Competition is not necessarily destructive of community goals nor does it necessarily produce zero-sum relationships among the participants. Our emerging concept of The Public Administration could profit from a better understanding of the positive attributes of competition.

302 PUBLIC ADMINISTRATION AND THE DEFENSE DEPARTMENT

Antiauthoritarianism. Antiauthoritarianism and resistance to militarism seem to be built into the business and popular culture in this country, notwithstanding the "iron triangle" of the military-industrial complex of which one leg is the government in several institutional forms. But they are part of our larger culture, as well, and they condition popular attitudes about the role and style of the state — civil and military — and therefore have important implications for understanding the possibilities of The Public Administration.

Conglomerates. We probably have much to learn about the proper role and the sources of perversity in the spheres of policy and management by looking at business entities composed of heterogeneous elements from unrelated industries. Is not government a grand policy conglomerate?

The Public Administration of a Superpower

Colonel Harry Summers brooded in *On Strategy* about the bases for our failure in Vietnam and its contrasts with the Korean war. He pointed to our decision in Vietnam to go beyond trying to repel the externally supported aggression by committing ourselves to nation-building. In South Korea we left internal problems to the Republic of Korea government.

> Why didn't we do the same thing in South Vietnam? There are several reasons for our overinvolvement. One has to do with the climate of the times. Observers have faulted our intervention in Vietnam as evidence of American arrogance of power — attempts by the United States to be the World's Policeman. But there is another dimension to American arrogance, the international version of our domestic Great Society programs where we presumed that we knew what was best for the world in terms of social, political, and economic development and saw it as our duty to force the world into the American mold — to act not so much the World's Policeman as the World's Nanny. It is difficult today to recall the depth of our arrogance. In March 1962, discussing the degree to which American military advisors become political — "directing, influencing, or even managing the local government's policies and operations," the editors of *Army* wrote "although the official U.S. policy is to refrain from injecting Americans into foreign governments *under our tutelage and support*, the pragmatic approach is to guide the *inexperienced and shaky* governments of the emerging nations by *persuasion and coaxing* if possible, and by *hard selling and pressure* if the soft methods don't work."[41]

Should we be, as Summers put it, the "World's Nanny"? That is a question that should be capable of being addressed in the context of the career public service. The United States is a global, metropolitan state, a superpower. We have considerable power in economic, military, political, and cultural terms. Whether we use it well or poorly is a central issue affecting our sense of the public interest. The resolution to that issue requires a sustained and penetrating national dialogue about what we are about in the world and the linkages between internal and external policy commitments within a broad context in which "the public interest" comprehends priorities beyond our shores. That the career public service should make a significant contribution to that dialogue would seem to be in the spirit of the Manifesto. Yet it is not clear from the Manifesto how that contribution would be made. Nor is it clear what incentives are at work for career people in The Public Administration that would help them relate to such a dialogue. Where should one turn for guidance in building The Public Administration?

The Evocative Role of the Manifesto

The authors of the Manifesto acknowledge that there are "inherent problems and pathologies that we deny or ignore at our peril." I hope that the problems that I have described as "worrisome" in this test drive of the Manifesto through the Defense Department are appropriate grist for the constructively critical dialogue that has been launched so successfully by the authors of the Manifesto.

The United States as a democratic nation-state and the vision of civil society which it represents have lost a bit of their luster around the world when compared with both the pre-WWI luxury of isolation and the post-WWII exertions of Pax Atomica. Our earlier relative moral and material dominance globally is challenged in various ways by the strong-weak Soviet Union, the economic powerhouse of Japan and the Asian Tigers, a unifying superconfederation in Europe, and the unruly power of states like China and Brazil, among others.

It is essential, then, that we are renewed by a search for normative grounding in our concepts of good governance and virtue in public service. The authors of the Manifesto offer us valued leadership in addressing that need.

The power of their thesis and the momentum that their initiative has imparted illuminate important issues and generate a compelling sense of direction. The Blacksburg Manifesto is a lodestar for the Public Administrator and The Public Administration.

NOTES

1. Gary L. Wamsley, Charles T. Goodsell, John A. Rohr, Orion F. White, and James F. Wolf, "The Public Administration and the Governance Process: Refocusing the American Dialogue," *A Centennial History of the American Administrative State*, R. C. Chandler, ed., (NY: The Free Press).

2. Thomas R. Dye, *Understanding Public Policy*, 5th ed. (Englewood Cliffs, N. J.: Prentice-Hall, 1984), p. 239.

3. U.S. Office of Management and Budget, *Budget of the United States Government Fiscal Year 1984*, appendix, p. I-G1, I-G3.

4. Claire E. Freeman, "Civilian Personnel and the Readiness Equation," *The Bureaucrat* (Fall, 1985).

5. These figures on civilian employment in the executive branch are 1985 estimates. U.S. Office of Management and Budget, *Budget of the United States Government Fiscal Year 1984*, "Special Analyses," p. I-2.

6. "An Air Force Almanac," *Air Force Magazine* (May 1985): 190, 191, 195.

7. Conscription was traditionally considered to be one important basis for insuring that the American armed forces mirrored the general population. For a thoughtful assessment of the post conscription environment, see: Claudia Mills, "The All-Volunteer Force: Second Thoughts After the First Decade," *The Bureaucrat* (Spring, 1984).

8. Samuel P. Huntington, *The Soldier and the State: The Theory of Civil-Military Relations* (Cambridge, Mass.: Harvard University Press, 1967), p. 10

9. Morris Janowitz, *The Professional Soldier: A Social and Political Portrait* (Glencoe, Ill.: Free Press, 1960), p. 60

10. John P. Lovell, *Neither Athens Nor Sparta? The American Service Academies in Transition* (Bloomington and London: Indiana University Press, 1979), p. 245.

11. Ibid., p. 246.

12. Quoted in Janowitz, op. cit., p. 115.

13. Henry H. Arnold, *Global Mission* (New York: Harper, 1949), p. 6.

14. Janowitz, op. cit., p. 168-171.

15. Huntington, op. cit. (1967), p. 353.

16. Samuel P. Huntington, *The Common Defense: Strategic Programs in National Politics* (New York: Columbia University Press, 1961), p. 168.

17. An important contributor to the study of decision making at this level has been H. Igor Ansoff. See his *Corporate Strategy* (New York: McGraw-Hill, 1965) and *Strategic Management* (New York: Wiley, 1979).

18. A good general description of these institutionalized decision processes is found in: Amos A. Jordan, William J. Taylor, Jr., and associates, *American National Security: Policy and Process* (Baltimore: Johns Hopkins University Press, 1981). A more detailed treatment of this subject is: *Joint Staff Officers Guide*, AFSC Publication No. 1 (Norfolk V.: Armed Forces Staff College, 1 January 1982).

19. Ingemar Dorfer, *Arms Deal: The Selling of the F-16* (New York: Praeger, 1982).

20. Desmond Ball, *Politics and Force Levels: The Strategic Missile Program of the Kennedy Administration* (Berkeley, Calif.: University of California Press, 1978), p. 268.

21. Much of my interpretive analysis of DoD and military institutions in this section of the chapter is based on research conducted during 1981-1982 when I was on leave from Virginia Tech and serving as a research professor at the U.S. Air War College. During that period, I interacted regularly with a number of key people in the services, the JCS, and Headquarters U.S. Air Force, and I interviewed about 120 experienced senior people from DoD, the military services, other government agencies, and the aerospace industry.

22. Janowitz, op. cit., p. 33.

23. For different perspectives on this issue see: Edward N. Luttwak, "On the Need to Reform American Strategy," in Philip S. Kronenberg (ed) *Planning U.S. Security: Defense Policy in the Eighties* (New York: Pergamon, 1981), chap. 2; and Lewis Sorley, "Turbulence at the Top: Our Peripatetic Generals," *Army* (March 1981): 14-24.

24. Book review by John G. Kester of Bruce Palmer, Jr., *The 25-Year War: America's Military Role in Vietnam*, in *The Washingtonian* (January 1985): 68-75, passim. Kester, now a Washington attorney, was a deputy assistant secretary of the Army (1969-1972) and a special assistant to Secretary of Defense Harold Brown (1977-1978). As a historical (and perspective-seeking) aside, one should note that Halberstam points out that General Bruce Palmer—who was on the short list of candidates for COMUSMACV (Commander, U.S. Military Assistance Command, Vietnam) from which General William Westmoreland was selected (Palmer was the youngest officer on the list and then considered the brightest general in the Army; p. 678)—was sanguine in 1967 about the outcome in Vietnam before the Tet offensive of 1968 and he so advised Ambassador Ellsworth Bunker. The following vignette from the Halberstam book makes this point and also illustrates another attribute of what I call reactivity in the convoluted web of strategic management that flows from agency perspective:

But not everyone had gone dovish on the President [when he fired McNamara to the World Bank in November 1967], neither General Westmoreland nor another important member of the team in Saigon, Ambassador Ellsworth Bunker. When this kindly, gentle New England patriarch with perhaps the most enviable and least assailable reputation in American government — everyone spoke well of Ellsworth bunker — arrived there in 1967, the doves had all felt a surge of optimism. Bunker's record for sensitivity and integrity were impeccable; at State a certain excitement had been kindled by Bunker's appointment. But Bunker, who had been so open-minded in the Dominican crisis, was very different in Saigon; the American flag was planted now, American boys were dying, and though he was freed of the mistakes of the past, he felt the need to justify the past American investment. So he bought all the military estimates and assumptions; he was the bane of some of the younger men on his staff who worked desperately to bring him together with doubters, to tell him that the whole thing was hopeless and that we were stalemated. But Bunker was confident, and in the next five years he became one of the two or three most important and resilient players, in particular standing behind Thieu and Ky at the time of Tet, when most people were ready to write them off. So in 1967 if the military were optimistic, Bunker was optimistic. When members of his staff and journalists brought him unfavorable estimates, he turned away. He could not understand why they were so pessimistic, he said, when generals as able as Bruce Palmer were optimistic. Why, Bruce Palmer was one of the finest and most intelligent officers in the U.S. Army, they had worked together in the Dominican crisis, and General Palmer had assured him that things were going well in Vietnam. (David Halberstam, *The Best and the Brightest* Random House, 1972, p. 784-785

25. One of the foremost among these few critics was Lieutenant Colonel Bill Corson who published, on the day of his retirement from the U.S. Marine Corps, a broad critique of the way in which U.S. military and political leaders changed our policy and strategy from one of nation-building and the development of South Vietnam's indigenous political, economic, and military institutions to one involving the large-scale investment of U.S. ground, air, and naval forces. See William R. Corson, *The Betrayal* (New York: Norton, 1968).

26. Samuel Huntington, *The Soldier and the State* (Cambridge: Harvard University Press, 1957).

27. Colonel Charlie Beckwith, head in 1980 of the Army's antiterrorist Delta Force unit and ground commander of the doomed hostage raid into Iran, characterized the perverse fruits of an agency perspective that breeds service parochialism when he commented in a Senate hearing on the training and structure of the rescue forces assembled for the mission. In response to a question from Senator Sam Nunn about ". . . what we can do to preclude this kind of thing happening in the future?," Beckwith replied:

Sir, let me answer you this way . . . . If Coach Bear Bryant at the University of Alabama put his quarterback in Virginia, his backfield in North Carolina, his offensive line in Georgia, and his defense in Texas, and then got Delta Airlines to pick them up and fly them to Birmingham on game day, he wouldn't have his winning record. Coach Bryant's teams, the best he can recruit, practice together, live together, eat together, and play together. He has a team.

What Colonel Beckwith chose not to do — as a team-oriented warrior who would not impugn the bravery or professional skill of his brother officers in the other services or the national military command structure — was to extend his metaphor more completely to reflect the fact that there were multiple nodes and levels of planning, training, and operational control which insured that each service and every major player in the political and military decision-making structure had a piece of the "action." If he had, his backfield would have been *from* the University of North Carolina, his defense *from* the University of Texas, etc., all operating on different radio channels with a committee of coaches. Not a bad arrangement for a media event like an All-Star Game but a poor basis to field a team for a serious contest.

See Col. Charlie A. Beckwith, USA (Ret.) and Donald Knox, *Delta Force* (New York: Harcourt Brace Jovanovich, 1983), p. 294-295.

28. For an analysis of this issue in terms of the full sweep of American history, see Brewester C. Denny, *Seeing American Foreign Policy Whole* (Urbana and Chicago: University of Illinois Press, 1985).

29. For a powerful analysis of this phenomenon, which examines all of the major U.S. weapons systems in considerable detail, see: Franklin C. Spinney, edited and with commentary by James Clay Thompson, *Defense Facts of Life: The Plans/Reality Mismatch* (Boulder and London: Westview Press, 1985.

30. Woodrow Wilson, *Congressional Government* (Boston, 1885), p. 318.

31. Huntington, *The Soldier and the State*, op. cit. p. 418.

32. Archie D. Barrett, *Reappraising Defense Organization: An Analysis Based on the Defense Organization Study of 1977-1980* (Washington, D.C.: National Defense University Press, 1983), p. 285.

33. There have been efforts since 1985 to use reorganization of the Joint Chiefs of Staff and of the relationships among the JCS, the unified and specified commands, and the military services, together with management and weapons acquisition reforms within the service departments and the Office of the Secretary of Defense, to reduce this "convoluted web of strategic management." The principal initiatives here were the Packard Commission (President's Blue-Ribbon Commission on Defense Management) recommendations and the Goldwater-Nichols DoD Reorganization Act of 1986, as well as a series of reforms (primarily in the acquisition and procurement management areas) initiated by the Congress beginning in 1981. It is not at all clear that these reform efforts have reduced the service parochialism of the "convoluted web," given the continuing evidence of abuse and inefficiency with the weapons acquisition process. The lack of clarity is also due to the dramatic changes that have affected the Department of Defense since 1986, including the reorganization efforts themselves, strategic changes in East-West relations, several intelligence and political scandals involving the national security community, a series of budget reductions, and changes in the White House and the senior leadership of the NSC, the department, and the services.

34. During 1982-1983 I was on a leave of absence from my university working in the Pentagon bureaucracy as Special Assistant to the Director of European Forces Theater Assessments and Planning in the Office of the Secretary of Defense.

35. Janowitz, op. cit., p. 28.

36. John M. Collins, *U.S. Defense Planning: A Critique* (Boulder, Colo.: Westview Press, 1982).

37. Francis E. Rourke, *Bureaucracy and Foreign Policy* (Baltimore: Johns Hopkins University Press, 1972), p. 73.

38. Paul Y. Hammond, "The National Security Council as a Device for Interdepartmental Coordination: An Interpretation and Appraisal," *American Political Science Review* (December 1960): 899-910. Cf. Graham T. Allison, *Essence of Decision*; Roger Hilsman, "Congressional-Executive Relations and the Foreign Policy Consensus," *American Political Science Review* (September 1958); and Morton Halperin, "The Gaither Committee and the Policy Process," *World Politics* (April 1961).

39. Robert K. Merton, "Bureaucratic Structure and Personality." *Social Forces* 18 (1940): 564.

40. Arnold Kanter, *Defense Politics: A Budgetary Perspective* (Chicago: University of Chicago Press, 1979), p. 82.

41. Summers, op. cit., p. 104-105. The quotation in *Army* magazine if by Norman and Spore, "Big Push in Guerrilla War," p. 34 emphasis added by Summers. Colonel Summers had the unique experience of being chief of the negotiations division of the U.S. Delegation to the Four-Party Joint Military Team in Hanoi in 1975.

Appendix. Selected responses to the Blacksburg Manifesto

JOSEPH H. SHERICK., Department of Defense Inspector General, December 1984:

Many of the points raised in the essay ("The Public Administration and the Governance Process: Refocusing the American Dialogue") coincide with my experience during 40 years of Government service. In particular, your assertion is well taken that ". . . agencies are repositories, and their staffs are trustees of, specialized knowledge, historical experience, time-tested wisdom, and most importantly, some degree of consensus as to the public interest relevant to a particular societal function."

The challenge to the public administrator is to provide his "sound analysis and feasible options" without being perceived as an obstruction by elected officials, their political appointees, the public, Congress, or any of a number of special-interest groups.

Hopefully, increased dialogue directed at the conflicting forces which prevail in the public administration arena will go a long way toward making the administrator an accepted partner in the decision-making process. Your essay is certainly a step in this direction.

HOWELL BAUM, Associate Professor, University of Maryland at Baltimore, School of Social Work and Community Planning, January 1984:

I have been interviewing public administrators, and I have been examining the transcripts for common themes. I am struck by the isolation of public administrators—isolation from clients or constituents, often isolation from organizational superordinates, and considerable isolation from opportunities to make the types of moral choices which the paper formulates.

DEAN RUSK, Professor, University of Georgia School of Law, April 13, 1987:

I am a bit skeptical about the implications at some points in your paper that what you call "the public administration" should have some sort of autonomy of its own. It seems to me to be fundamental in our constitutional system that administrators must be subject to the direction of those elected by the people to give them direction—subject to the laws and the constitution. To me, there is a fundamental difference between the role of the professional services before and after a decision is made by duly constituted authority. Prior to the decision, during the discussion period, our leadership is entitled to the widest range of discussion and controversy about the issues involved. If that kind of dialogue does not come naturally, the top officers must probe and see that it comes forward, else they themselves will be blinded. After a decision is made, it is incumbent upon the administrators to give effect to it, despite their personal reactions, else the democratic process would be frustrated.

PHILIP SCHORR, Professor, Long Island University, June 7, 1983:

While I agree with your desire to refocus the public administration debate; to move the agenda from a discussion about ends ("whether") to questions of means ("how and what form?"), I would like to believe that our "ends" have already been agreed upon so as to be able to permit us to shift the focus of the dialogue. But, have we as a nation, firmly accepted the regime values expressed in our founding documents? If so then it is probably appropriate to focus on the means for enhancing freedom and justice.

BAYARD L. CATRON, Professor, The George Washington University, School of Government and Business Administration, March 1987:

Some people will be uncomfortable with the "religious" tone of the document. Academics and professionals often resist proselytizing and attempts to convert them to a civil religion. But the essay *is* religious in a certain sense, and necessarily so: It is religious in the sense that credos always are, and also in the sense that it is calling attention to aspirations and ideas that represent the "highest and best" in human social life. But you should be as clear as possible, in my judgment, that the essay is neither theological nor doctrinaire — not theological because it is in no sense theist (the "religion" might be best termed transcendental humanism), and not doctrinaire because the essay is intended to enliven and revitalize the dialogue about the public interest rather than substantively defining it is an article of faith.

MARSHALL DIMOCK, Professor of Public Administration, March 1987:

I liked the thrust of the paper and I like it now. The tone and writing remind me very much of some of the *Federalist Papers,* and of course, there could be no better format. Also, the topic is timely — certainly one of a half-dozen topics which may control the future well-being of the country.

RALPH HUMMEL, Professor Institute of Applied Phenomenology, Spruce Head Island, Maine, February 1987:

Unless we redefine the built-in imperatives of both politics and bureaucracy, we can't become clear on what the tensions between the two cultures are and what needs to be done to resolve them. The nature and role of public administration does take place within the wider context of the political culture, and the weight of one has to be measured against the clout of the other. So doesn't the question become: "What form *can* the role of public administration take?"

LAURENCE O'TOOLE, Professor, Auburn University, May 17, 1983:

You might want to consider whether you want to clarify and delineate your "Agency Perspective" more carefully. For instance: (a.) Does the Agency Perspective contribute to the "parochialism" of the public interest, the fragmentation and erosion of public purpose and the centrifugal pressures which have franchised pieces of public authority to policy subsystems? (b.) Is there come circularity in the argument regarding The Public Administration's derivation of its ethical compass from "the long-term public interest as the agency sees it"? How is the Agency Perspective established and changed?

DONALD K. PRICE, Professor of Public Management, Harvard University, John F. Kennedy School of Government, March 3, 1987:

I am heartily in accord with your views that the old rigid distinctions between policy and analysis, or between facts and values, have been detrimental and that a new conception of the career service needs to be developed that recognizes its role as a part of the constitutional system, dedicated to a defense of the broad public interest against technical specialties.

LINDA WOLF, Associate Executive Director, American Public Welfare Association, April 20, 1987:

To me, the public administration is best served by the posture that the meaning of public interest is forever a problematic notion. In reading the literature surrounding Watergate, one of the themes that comes through is the absolute certainty in the Nixon White House that the public interest resided and was embodied in the President. Seeing the public interest as always problematic creates immense dilemmas for the practitioner but, to my mind, these issues are far less troublesome to him/her or the society than is certainty. The practical consequence of such a "mind set" is more likely to be (1) tentative action steps rather than a headlong rush to "solution," (2) a consistent curiosity about ends which makes "creating learning institutions or systems" an artificial expression, (3) humility about "grand designs" and a greater awareness of the unique contribution and responsibility of each individual to a national debate about purposes, (4) an attentiveness to the words of public discourse and its world-opening quality. These consequences aid administrative action and support the necessity of admitting and the purposes of "doubt" in a way that I find thrilling.

Regardless of the "holes" you or others may see in your work, its significance shines through. I heard Luther Gullick's words, but I was also watching his face during the paper presentation. There was genuine emotion on that face—chords seemed to be struck for him creating beautiful and poignant music. Your music and orchestration must be heard by others.

Do you know the story of the rabbi and the divinity student regarding true and false prophets? The student wanted to know how you tell the difference between the true and false prophet. The rabbi told him there was no way to "tell" the difference—no gauge to slip over their heads and if there were there would be no human dilemma and life would have no meaning. Then, returning to his stern Old Testament stance he said, ". . . But its terribly important that we *know* the difference."

DAVID R. BRADLEY, M.A., Civil Servant and Guardian Fellow at Nuffield College, Oxford, London, England, April 1987:

The issues which appear to be addressed in the paper seem to be relevant to contemporary British policy interests.

GENE LEWIS, Professor, New College of the University of South Florida, March 11, 1987:

I would very much like to see the next draft if one is to be produced. I do think that it should continue for I can think of no more worthy project for the discipline and for the country as well
. . . .

The problem of governance lies precisely in the "gap between its need and the capacity of our elected officials to provide it." The point, of course, is that what is to be governed is inchoate. The last, most significant American revolution is, in my view, the diffusion of modern life in all its richness, complexity, injustice and absurdity to the state. Despite the dumb assertions of bureaucrat-baiting pols, the plain fact is that we the people and our elected pols want that state in virtually everything that concerns us. Business wants markets manipulated to reduce uncertainty and constituents want to keep their jobs. This is hardly news. What is news is that the state year after year has dealt with these sorts of desires positively. It always and everywhere gets the blame for the inevitable negative externalities because it is the easiest target and never really strikes back.

Speaking to the unsatisfactory resolution of the problem of Representation — Here we go directly to the Constitution and begin a critique which I believe to be fundamental . . . . I agree that the Constitution was flawed in this regard as a result of probably reasonable compromise over serious problems of power. Today, I think that the problem has gone far beyond those resulting from the original document. Do appointed officials serving in administrative roles indeed represent citizens? I certainly think so. What form does such representation of persons take? In the "organic" relationship of public administration to the Constitution and tradition encompassed by the representational relations of say the peanut-butter sector of the agricultural community?

D. O. COOKE, Deputy Assistant Secretary of Defense, Office of the Assistant Secretary of Defense, April 1985:

I read it with great interest and have since distributed it to members of my staff.

You and your colleagues deserve credit for having made an original and refreshing contribution to the analysis of public administration and the role of the public administrator. Your paper provides an important convergence point for what has heretofore been described as a disjointed body of theory on this important subject. The paper deserves broad dissemination to both practitioners and teachers of the public policy process.

DR. PHILIP J. COOPER, Professor, SUNY, Albany, 1984:

Let us consider the charges appropriately leveled at the Blacksburg document. In general, they are that the document: (1) is self-contradictory; (2) asserts as facts highly disputed contentions, e.g., the validity of neutral competence, the representativeness of the bureaucracy, the constitutional legitimacy of the existing administrative state, and the existence and interpretation of the public interest; (3) stoops to ad hominem argument; (4) overargues points having some legitimate basis (and only some basis one might add); (5) vastly overstates the claim to legitimacy of existing bureaucratic roles and the intentions of the framers concerning administrators as against elected officials; and (6) taken to its logical conclusion, the argument is destructive of the structural foundations of the Republic. Before summarizing the evidence in support of these more general charges, let us consider specific problems within the document.

That theme of special place and distinctively worthy performance occurs in another context in a different part of the paper. The argument runs as follows. Not only has bureaucracy been less evil than its critics charge, but its long-run performance at high standards confers upon the public administration special status.

Over the sweep of our history our Agencies have for the most part been staffed by persons who have taken seriously the task of faithfully executing the will of the state and the public interest as best they could determine these . . . . It follows that in such a noble enterprise only the hopelessly stupid or obdurately insensitive could have failed to develop some special competence and moral authority.

In the first instance, the claim of satisfactory performance is not one to be accepted without question. For just as anyone holding great power can do great good, so can they wreak havoc upon those whom they presumably ought to serve. The history of the Immigration and Naturalization Service, the Interstate Commerce Commission, the Federal Bureau of Investigation, the Bureau of Indian Affairs, the General Services Administration, and the Internal Revenue Service place the claim of overall satisfactory performance in some jeopardy. But, for the moment, grant that agencies have operated reasonably well and benevolently; it does not necessarily "follow" that one gains "special competence" except in the narrowest meaning of the term or, worse, that one is thereby vested with "moral authority." And even if the bureaucracy could make such a claim, what governmental institution or official would be denied the same claim? Further, if all could make such a claim, why should those who must face the electorate not assert their preeminent role and claim to authority establishing a clearly and continuously subordinate role for the bureaucracy?

The Blacksburg paper goes on to assert that the special claim comes about as a result of something called "the Agency perspective" which is a combination of subject matter expertise, experience, and commitment to the public interest. That concept is used in a variety of ways in the remainder of the paper, but an examination of one such application suggests a number of difficulties with this approach to discussions of governance. The paper warns that administrators as well as those who evaluate administrators should not take a "program perspective" focusing on "outputs" and evaluating performance on "bottom line" measures. But if one accepts the "special competence" claim to legitimate authority advanced in the first few pages of the paper, then a policy or program perspective is closely tied to the "Agency perspective" and the agency perspective is special precisely because of its focus. The authors cannot both claim legitimacy by virtue of expertise and experience and simultaneously assert a superior capacity for broad spectrum integrative understanding of the public interest. And to the degree that the agency perspective is a crucial element in understanding public administration, it necessarily entails a kind of agency pluralism, the governmental analog of interest-group liberalism.

Recognizing this relationship between substantive policies and agency identity is not necessarily the same as saying that a program or policy perspective is or should be oriented toward or evaluated purely by quantitative output measures such as those described in the paper. The more important problem of the agency perspective is why one finds interagency conflicts between, say, the Departments of Agriculture and Interior or between HUD and HHS. Why are these agencies' perspectives so often in conflict? And given that conflict, how can we evaluate their work? Moreover, what is wrong with rigorous efforts to compel agencies to demonstrate performance? The notion that all output measures are mindless and simplistic is unworthy of further comment. No one has argued that simplistic measures are satisfactory proxies for an adequate understanding of efficiency.

The paper argues that "the distinctive agency perspective is one that deserves greater legitimacy than it is accorded by our political culture." Among the weaknesses inherent in that assertion is the fact that a number of agencies are plagued internally by conflicting roles. Examples include the FAA obligation to maintain safe and efficient air transport while promoting the aviation industry and the Department of Agriculture's operation of consumer programs in an agency dedicated primarily to agribusiness producers.

Finally, this assertion of fundamental legitimacy insists on a textual support from the Constitution itself. So be it. Let us check their reading of the document. The Blacksburg paper states: "Executive Departments, Post Offices, postal roads, an Army, a Navy, tax collection, the regulation of commerce, the militia — all these are specifically mentioned in the Constitution." These terms arise in the Constitution in two contexts. All of these terms but executive departments are taken from Article I, Section 8. But Article I begins by asserting that "All Legislative Powers herein granted shall be vested in a Congress of the United States, which shall consist of a Senate and House of Representatives." In Section 8, known as the provision on enumerated powers of the legislature, the language is permissive but not mandatory. It reads:

The Congress shall have Power To lay and collect Taxes . . . To regulate commerce . . . To Establish Post Offices and Post Roads . . . To raise and support Armies . . . To provide and maintain a Navy . . . To make Rules for the Government and Regulation of the land and naval forces; To provide for calling forth the Militia to execute the Laws of the Union . . .

The legislature may choose to exercise these powers or it may refuse to do so.

The other reference to these constitutional terms comes from Article II, Section 2 in which the President is granted power to "require the Opinion, in writing, of the principal Officer in each of the Executive Departments, upon any Subject relating to the Duties of their respective Offices . . . " and to "appoint Ambassadors, other public Ministers and Consuls, Judges of the Supreme Court, and all other Officers of the United States . . . " But that article nowhere states that the President shall have a power, comparable to the necessary and proper clause of Article I, Section 8, which would permit the chief executive to "create all offices necessary and proper for carrying into effect the aforementioned executive powers." Therefore, the basis for administrative legitimacy is a matter of statute arising not from the Constitution itself, but from a discretionary exercise of the legislature.

The more important problems with discussion of politics/administration questions are the remaining two. First, the Blacksburg paper marches forthrightly up to the politics/administration problem, then turns on its heel and marches smartly away again. Specifically, it defines away the problem on the one hand and ignores it on the other. It says: "at the highest level . . . . there is no dichotomy." It then holds that at the "level of behavior and action, there is and always has been, if not a dichotomy, at least a considerable distinction." This, we are informed, stems from an implicit understanding of role differentiation, not defined but nevertheless present. "Finally, . . . prescriptively and theoretically . . . we should acknowledge, elucidate and extend the distinction (undefined in the paper) between governing and ruling." One is at a loss from this to understand whether there is or ought to be such a thing as the politics/administration dichotomy and, if so, what the concept means.

A final point on this aspect of the paper concerns the attempt to meld this discussion back into the claim to legitimacy by recounting the development of the judicial role and its similarities to the rise of the administrative state. Three things should be said. The first is that volumes questioning judicial claims to power are legion. The second concerns "their reputation for fairness" in England. That is only partly true when one recalls the need for the creation of the office of the Chancellor in Equity. Third, the argument ends noting the establishment of judicial authority under *Marbury v. Madison.* Marbury still has its critics. The more appropriate assertion would have been that Article III specifically recognizes an independent judicial power even if the individual courts are created by the legislature; a constitutional stature to which public administration does not rise.

There are other problematic points in the remainder of the paper. It asserts that public administration is "no monolith" yet the entire paper focuses upon an institution carefully referred to as "The Public Administration." Either there is such an institution or there is not. The authors argue against responsiveness to majority pressures not consonant with the public interest. Yet the paper elsewhere asserts that "The Public Administrator 'represents' (not simply reflects) the American people, as well as, if not better than elected officials." The claim appears to be that administrators provide virtual representation and that it is equivalent to that provided by elected officials. Without more, such claims contain substantial inconsistencies.

The paper argues that public administrators should be neither philosopher-kings nor mandarins, but trustees. When one asserts a trustee role, one raises a problem for, as well as a defense of, public administration. The trustee role requires a duty to a principal in which the trustee is obliged at all costs to avoid conflicting interests. That is not possible in public administration unless the trusteeship is so broadly defined as to be meaningless.

The paper ends its substantive argument with a troublesome assertion. It holds that the public administrator should "Play to the judicious few, rather than the vociferous many or the powerful few." One would be quite accurate in asserting that one of the reasons such an argument as the Blacksburg Statement was felt necessary is precisely because public administration has played to the judicious few — and the injudicious few. Group speak, in-group identification, "old-hand" credentials, and power games more accurately reflect the tools perceived by many in the field as more useful than the fanciful agency perspective described by the Blacksburg group.

Taken to its logical conclusion, the argument advanced in the Blacksburg Statement is destructive of the Republic. That argument runs as follows. Since bureaucrats have equivalent legitimacy, are as representative as (and in some ways more representative than) elected officials, are less subject to whims of momentary political pressure, and have the support of expert knowledge, skills in effective execution of policy, and managerial efficiency coupled with an agency perspective on "transcendent purpose," why bother to have elected officials or the institutional trappings of a republic at all? Why not simply surrender and declare for bureaucracy over democracy? Not yet gentlemen, not yet.

DR. HERBERT KAUFMAN, Professor Emeritus, Yale University, September 1987:

If you believe, as I do, that there can be no political democracy unless top government officials (1) are chosen and can be unseated through free, competitive elections, and (2) are able collectively to effectuate their will by directing and controlling the behavior of the administrative officers and employees who perform the administrative tasks of government, you will be disturbed, as I am, by the Blacksburg Manifesto. Its basic thrust is incompatible with the second of these requisites of democracy and it therefore cannot be reconciled with the logic of democratic government that flows from these (among other) premises. Elections don't mean much if the career officers and employees of governments feel no moral obligation to conscientiously obey elected officials acting through constitutionally prescribed procedures.

The Manifesto treats bureaucrats as members of a separate branch of government coordinate with the elected branches, as Norton Long proposed a generation ago, and holds that they are entitled to pursue their own visions of the public interest.

I'm sure the authors of the Manifesto are as committed to democratic government as I am. It is clear, however, that their criteria of democracy are different from mine. Election confers no greater "title" to govern in their system than appointment does. The sacral rituals of the democratic process, and all the substantive consequences of these practices, are reduced to mere procedural details. This outlook I cannot accept. That is the crux of the difference between them and me. What is at issue is the meaning of democracy, not merely the place of bureaucrats in our polity. The discussion therefore ought to begin with that subject.

Despite the awkwardness and the defects and the uncertainties and the occasional abuses and distortions of the electoral process that are all too familiar, for me it confers on the winners, however small the margins of their victories, a special status in the system, a unique entitlement to deference, that civil servants and other participants in politics do not enjoy. This legitimacy is a slender reed on which to hang so many hopes. Weakening it, as the Blacksburg Manifesto surely would, ill serves democracy as I understand it.

One possible response to this uneasiness is that the Manifesto only recognizes current realities. Administrative agencies already use their discretionary powers to advance or retard the policies of elected officials. One may therefore infer that we would be better off to take account of what actually goes on instead of clinging to an outmoded, unrealistic, unattainable ideal, especially since the elected branches of government, the public at large, are well-equipped to keep bureaucrats in line when they think corrective measures are necessary.

But I find this response unsatisfactory. If the will of elected officials is only partially effective now, while the principle of bureaucratic deference to elected officials is standard doctrine (and it *is* standard doctrine or there would be no need for the Manifesto to urge change), imagine how much more ineffective their leadership would be were bureaucrats trained and encouraged to depreciate it. Moreover, though administrative agencies may indeed be restrained by other participants in the governmental process, the success of these restraints rests in large measure on the acceptance by most bureaucrats of the primacy of those elected to office. If most of them reject this unique legitimacy, the restraints would dissipate in the ensuing chaos. Without voluntary compliance on the part of the great bulk of any population, the power of sanctions soon breaks down. This is as true of the population of civil servants as of taxpayers and the citizenry generally. Hence, inculcating in civil servants the belief in and practice of obedience to elected officials is an important element of any form of democracy even if this goal is only approached rather than attained. Abandoning the goal as an ideal toward which the bureaucracy should strive, as the Manifesto counsels, would not ratify existing realities; it would create a radically new reality inimical to democratic government.

I find a bit ironic the document's ardent advocacy of the obligation of administrative subordinates and the public to respect the authority of administrative leaders after the authority of elected leaders has been so dramatically downgraded in relative terms. The portrait of "the Public Administrator" strikes me as idealized; bureaucrats seem to me identified with and spokespeople for special interests more frequently than they appear as defenders of a more general "public interest," however that may be defined. Furthermore, their devotion to their programmatic objectives, which is proper and even laudable, tends to make them insensitive to other values that often complicate and impede their efforts. Indeed, the Manifesto's confident statement that they can "serve as a cooling, containing, and directing foil to the capitalist economic system" glosses over their frequent role as protectors, defenders, and advocates of capitalist interests.

These objections, however, pale beside the major problem. The central matter is the clash between the Manifesto and the requirements of electoral democracy as I define it. It is at this level that I prefer to take issue. I agree with the authors that bureaucrat-bashing is neither useful nor fair; bureaucrats are often the scapegoats for political shortcomings not of their making. But we certainly don't have to imperil democratic government to deal with that situation. Democratic government faces enough perils without needlessly adding another to the roster.

Index

About the Authors

ROBERT N. BACHER is presently employed as the Executive for Administration and Assistant to the Bishop of the Evangelical Lutheran Church in America whose national headquarters are in Chicago. Dr. Bacher holds degrees from Texas A&M University, Lutheran School of Theology at Chicago, Temple University, and a doctorate in public administration from the University of Southern California, Washington Public Affairs, in Washington, D.C. Dr. Bacher has written various publications on church administration and public administration, including an article on public careers (James F. Wolf, co-author). He currently resides in Northwest Chicago with his wife, Shirley.

CHARLES T. GOODSELL is Director and Professor, Center for Public Administration and Policy, Virginia Polytechnic Institute and State University. His research interests have been eclectic down through the years, centering on comparative public administration, international business, corporate philanthropy, Latin America, public bureaucracy, the citizen-bureaucrat encounter, regulation of business, the delivery of human services, and most recently the architecture of public spaces. His books include *The Social Meaning of Civic Space* (1988), *The Case for Bureaucracy* (1983 and 1985), *The Public Encounter* (editor, 1981), *American Corporations and Peruvian Politics* (1974), and *Administration of a Revolution* (1965). He received his education at Kalamazoo College (B.A., 1954) and Harvard University (Ph.D., 1961). In addition to Virginia Tech, he has taught at the University of Puerto Rico and Southern Illinois University. Also he has held visiting appointments at the University of Texas and Carleton University. He is active in a number of professional associations and is a member of the National Council of the American Society for Public Administration and the Executive Council of the National Association of Schools of Public Affairs and Administration.

PHILIP S. KRONENBERG, a professor in the VPI Center for Public Administration and Policy, has been an active contributor over the years to public administration and public policy inquiry. He was a participant in the 1968 Minnowbrook Conference on the New Public Administration and has served on five editorial boards in our field. His current research focuses on the conflicting national priorities among trade, advanced technology, and defense. He offers his Colloquy paper on the Defense Department as a test case that directs "friendly fire" toward certain aspects of the Manifesto. He is well qualified to do so, given his extensive scholarship in areas of national security and foreign policy (his 1981 book, *Planning U.S. Security,* involves a sweeping assessment of the constitutional, political, and institutional shape and misshape of the defense policy area) together with his practical experience in the Office of the Secretary of Defense (as Special Assistant to the director of European Forces) and as a consultant to the Navy Department, FEMA, and the Office of Management and Budget.

JOHN A. ROHR's books *To Run a Constitution* and *Ethics for Bureaucrats* are milestone works in normative theory and provide a solid foundation for dialogue about the Founding, the Constitution, and legitimacy of the Public Administration. Dr. Rohr's many scholarly works in normative theory have provided both the inspiration and the guiding rudder for much of the Blacksburg thought. Dr. Rohr is a professor at The Center for Public Administration and Policy at Virginia Polytechnic Institute and State University.

CAMILLA M. STIVERS, a graduate of the CPAP program, provides a binding link in the Blacksburg perspective, that of citizenship and citizen participation. Currently in the Department of Political Science at Evergreen State College in Washington, she also provides a feminist perspective. Her work, "Toward a Community of Knowledge: Active Citizenship in the Administrative State," will appear in the forthcoming *Return from Oz: Refounding the Public Administration* from Sage.

GARY L. WAMSLEY is the founding director of the Center for Public Administration and Policy at Virginia Polytechnic. Dr. Wamsley may best be known for his work with Mayer Zald, *The Political Economy of Public Organizations*, in addition to his contributing authorship to the Blacksburg Manifesto and his work on the agency perspective. In addition to his many other credentials, he has been editor of Administration and Society since 1979. His expertise in public management covers many fields including the selective service, national security, and budgeting.

ORION F. WHITE is a professor at the Center for Public Administration and Policy at Virginia Tech. Dr. White is widely recognized for his work in organizational development and behavior, and mediation. He serves as a consultant and change agent for numerous federal and state agencies. A respected scholar and writer, Dr. White has made enduring contributions to the literature of human development within organizations. He was a participant of the original Minnowbrook Conference and has been deeply involved in normative issues in public administration in the past twenty years.

JAMES F. WOLF is Director for the Center of Public Administration at the Northern Virginia Facility. An experienced consultant for the public service in organizational change and behavior, Dr. Wolf has been, in addition to a professor, a training coordinator for the Presidential Management Intern Educational Programs; the U.S. Department of Agriculture, the Environmental Protection Agency, among many others. He is the author of articles on professionalism in the public service.

operations — org — strategic
tactics — tactics
strategy — operations
— inst

flexible
operations — Strategy
tactics — tactics
short — operations
flexible

reverse   org   org trackina
(1)   (2)